DIVERSI'

MW00638123

Expressions of support for diversity are nearly ubiquitous among contemporary law firms and corporations. Organizations back these rhetorical commitments with dedicated diversity staff and various diversity and inclusion initiatives. Yet, the goal of proportionate representation for people of color and women remains unrealized. Members of historically underrepresented groups remain seriously disadvantaged in professional training and work environments that white, upper-class men continue to dominate. While many professional labor markets manifest patterns of demographic inequality, these patterns are particularly pronounced in the law and elite segments of many professions. *Diversity in Practice* analyzes the disconnect between expressed commitments to diversity and practical achievements, revealing the often obscure systemic causes that drive persistent professional inequalities. These original contributions build on existing literature and forge new paths in explaining enduring patterns of stratification in professional careers. These more realistic assessments provide opportunities to move beyond mere rhetoric to something approaching diversity in practice.

SPENCER HEADWORTH is Graduate Research Coordinator at the American Bar Foundation and a PhD Candidate in Northwestern University's Department of Sociology, and will begin as Assistant Professor of Sociology at Purdue University in August 2016. He studies crime, social control, law, inequality, organizations, and professions. His dissertation, "Policing Welfare," examines dedicated welfare fraud control units, a novel intersection between the worlds of public benefits and law enforcement.

ROBERT L. NELSON is the MacCrate Research Chair in the Legal Profession at the American Bar Foundation and Professor of Sociology and Law at Northwestern University. He studies law, inequality, and the legal profession. He is the author of *Legalizing Gender Inequality: Courts, Markets, and Unequal Pay for Women in America* (with William Bridges) which won the best book award from the American Sociological Association. From 2004–2015, Nelson served as Director of the American Bar Foundation.

RONIT DINOVITZER is Associate Professor of Sociology at the University of Toronto and is cross-appointed to the Institute for Management and Innovation. Her work focuses on the social structure of the legal profession and on professional ethics. Ronit is a Faculty Fellow of the American Bar Foundation where she is a co-investigator on "After the JD," the first national longitudinal study of US law graduates, and she has now completed the first national survey of Canadian law graduates.

DAVID B. WILKINS is Lester Kissel Professor of Law and Director of the Center on the Legal Profession at Harvard Law School. He is a globally recognized scholar on the legal profession, having written more than eighty articles and coauthored one of the leading casebooks in the field. Professor Wilkins is a Member of the American Academy of Arts and Sciences and a Corresponding Member of the Spanish Royal Academy of Doctors.

CAMBRIDGE STUDIES IN LAW AND SOCIETY

Cambridge Studies in Law and Society aims to publish the best scholarly work on legal discourse and practice in its social and institutional contexts, combining theoretical insights and empirical research.

The fields that it covers are: studies of law in action; the sociology of law; the anthropology of law; cultural studies of law, including the role of legal discourses in social formations; law and economics; law and politics; and studies of governance. The books consider all forms of legal discourse across societies, rather than being limited to lawyers' discourses alone.

The series editors come from a range of disciplines: academic law; socio-legal studies; sociology; and anthropology. All have been actively involved in teaching and writing about law in context.

Series editors

Chris Arup *Monash University, Victoria*
Sally Engle Merry *New York University*
Susan Silbey *Massachusetts Institute of Technology*

A list of books in the series can be found at the back of this book.

DIVERSITY IN PRACTICE
Race, Gender, and Class in
Legal and Professional Careers

Edited by

SPENCER HEADWORTH

ROBERT L. NELSON

RONIT DINOVITZER

DAVID B. WILKINS

CAMBRIDGE
UNIVERSITY PRESS

CAMBRIDGE
UNIVERSITY PRESS

University Printing House, Cambridge CB2 8BS, United Kingdom

One Liberty Plaza, 20th Floor, New York, NY 10006, USA

477 Williamstown Road, Port Melbourne, VIC 3207, Australia

4843/24, 2nd Floor, Ansari Road, Daryaganj, Delhi - 110002, India

79 Anson Road, #06-04/06, Singapore 079906

Cambridge University Press is part of the University of Cambridge.

It furthers the University's mission by disseminating knowledge in the pursuit of
education, learning and research at the highest international levels of excellence.

www.cambridge.org
Information on this title: www.cambridge.org/9781107559196

© Cambridge University Press 2016

First published 2016
First paperback edition 2017

A catalogue record for this publication is available from the British Library

Library of Congress Cataloging in Publication data
Diversity in practice : race, gender, and class in legal and professional careers /
Spencer Headworth, Robert L. Nelson, Ronit Dinovitzer, and David Wilkins, editors.
pages   cm. – (Cambridge studies in law and society)
Includes bibliographical references and index.
ISBN 978-1-107-12365-6 (Hardback : alk. paper)
1. Practice of law. 2. Law–Vocational guidance. 3. Social
perception. 4. Multiculturalism–
Law and legislation. 5. Discrimination. 6. Minorities. 7. Prejudices.
I. Headworth, Spencer, editor. II. Nelson, Robert L., 1952– editor.
III. Dinovitzer, Ronit, 1971– editor.
K120.D58 2015
331.11–dc23   2015028169

ISBN 978-1-107-12365-6 Hardback
ISBN 978-1-107-55919-6 Paperback

CONTENTS

CONTRIBUTORS

Juliet R. Aiken is the Program Director of and Clinical Assistant Professor for the Master's in Industrial Organizational Psychology at the University of Maryland, College Park. Juliet's research focuses on diversity, professional development, and statistics/measurement. Prior to her work at the University of Maryland, she was the Deputy Director of the Center of the Study of the Legal Profession, where she conducted empirical research on the legal profession and advised Georgetown Law administration, faculty, staff, and students on conducting empirical research.

Louise Ashley is a lecturer in Human Resource Management and Organizational Behaviour at Royal Holloway, University of London and a Visiting Fellow at the Centre for Professional Service Firms at Cass Business School. She specializes in researching the implementation and development of diversity and inclusion programs in large, multinational professional service firms, with a particular focus on gender and social class. Louise has published articles in leading academic journals and recently co-wrote the chapter on diversity and inclusion in the Oxford University Press *Handbook of Professional Service Firms*.

Forrest Briscoe (AB Harvard, PhD MIT) is an Associate Professor of Management at the Smeal College of Business, Penn State University, and an International Research Fellow at the Centre for Professional Service Firms, Oxford. His research interests include professional organizations, employment practices and careers, and change and diffusion processes in organizational fields. He also recently completed a fellowship from the Alfred P. Sloan Foundation supporting his investigations into the role of workplace networks in the careers of corporate lawyers. Forrest currently serves as an Associate Editor for Administrative Science Quarterly, and also for the Academy of Management Annals, and he sits on the board of the Organization & Management Theory division of the Academy of Management. Forrest enjoys teaching at all levels, and on occasion also provides consulting services to law and healthcare organizations.

Lissa L. Broome is the Wells Fargo Professor of Banking Law at the University of North Carolina School of Law. She directs the Center for Banking and Finance and serves as the Faculty Advisor to the North Carolina Banking

Institute journal. She also heads the Director Diversity Initiative (DDI), whose goal is to increase the gender, racial, and ethnic diversity on public company boards of directors. Professor Broome teaches Banking Law and Secured Transactions and writes about the regulation of financial institutions in addition to corporate board diversity.

John M. Conley is William Rand Kenan, Jr. Professor of Law at the University of North Carolina at Chapel Hill. A lawyer and anthropologist, he has written several books and numerous articles on such topics as the anthropological and linguistic study of the American legal system, the culture of business and finance (with William O'Barr), scientific evidence, and the law of intellectual property as applied to emerging technologies. Recent research projects have focused on the cultural and linguistic aspects of the corporate social responsibility movement (with Cynthia Williams), corporate boards (with Lissa Broome and Kimberly Krawiec), and the emerging discipline of genetic medicine.

Meghan Dawe is a PhD Candidate in the Department of Sociology at the University of Toronto. Her dissertation analyzes stratification in the legal profession, comparing data on lawyers from the After the JD project, the first national longitudinal study of law graduates in the United States, and the Canadian Law and Beyond Study, the first national study of law graduates in Canada. Meghan's research focuses on the sociology of work and professions and the sociology of law, crime, and punishment.

Ronit Dinovitzer is Associate Professor of Sociology at the University of Toronto, where she is cross appointed to the Institute for Management and Innovation (IMI). She is also a Faculty Fellow at the American Bar Foundation in Chicago. As a sociologist of the professions, she conducts research on the legal profession, including the social organization of lawyers, the context of labor markets, and the role of diversity in professional careers. She has pursued this work through her involvement with the After the JD project and the Law and Beyond Study.

Liz Duff is Head of Westminster Law School at the University of Westminster. She was one of the founders of the Law and Diversity program at the University of Westminster School of Law. Her principal research focus is currently law, diversity, and equality. She has been a consultant to the UKCLE on matters relating to the LLB curriculum and widening participation and she has also advised a number of universities on this area. She has carried out funded empirical research for a number of organizations including the Law Society of England and Wales and the Legal Services Board and has previously published articles in the *Journal of Law and Society*, the *Modern Law Review*, the *Journal of the Sociology of Law*, and the *Law Teacher*.

Laura Empson is Director of the Centre for Professional Service Firms, Cass Business School, London. Her research into professional service firms encompasses issues such as: leadership, governance, succession planning, organizational, cultural and identity change, professionalization of management, mergers and acquisitions, knowledge transfer, and partner evaluation and reward systems. She has published numerous articles in leading international academic journals, as well as translating her research for a practitioner audience, most notably in her 2007 book, *Managing the Modern Law Firm* (Oxford University Press) which was described by The Times as marking a "seminal moment in the development of management theory in this sector." Together with colleagues she is currently editing the *Oxford Handbook of Professional Service Firms* (Oxford University Press), to be published in late 2015. She was previously Associate Professor (Reader) at the University of Oxford. Before becoming an academic, Laura worked as an investment banker and strategy consultant. She has a PhD and MBA from London Business School and a BSc(Econ) from University College, London.

Elizabeth H. Gorman is Associate Professor of Sociology at the University of Virginia. She holds a JD from the University of Chicago and a PhD in Sociology from Harvard University. Her research on professional work, the legal profession, and inequality in professional organizations has been published in the *American Journal of Sociology*, *American Sociological Review*, *Law and Society Review*, *Work and Occupations*, and other journals.

Spencer Headworth is Graduate Research Coordinator at the American Bar Foundation and a PhD Candidate in Northwestern University's Department of Sociology, and will begin as Assistant Professor of Sociology at Purdue University in August 2016. He studies crime, social control, law, inequality, organizations, and professions. His dissertation, "Policing Welfare," examines dedicated welfare fraud control units, a novel intersection between the worlds of public benefits and law enforcement.

Fiona M. Kay is Professor of Sociology at Queen's University. She researches the sociology of law and sociology of work and occupations. Her scholarship includes investigations of inequality in the legal profession, mentorship and professional development, lawyers' pro bono service, and jurisdictional boundaries across professions of law. She is currently engaged in a longitudinal study examining career pathways of lawyers in Canada. A second study, in collaboration with Elizabeth Gorman, focuses on retention and advancement of racial minorities in corporate US law firms. These projects are funded by grants from the Social Sciences and Humanities Research Council of Canada (SSHRC) and the Law School Admission Council (LSAC).

Young-Kyu Kim is an Assistant Professor of Management at Korea University Business School. He received his PhD from the University of Chicago Booth

School of Business in 2008. From 2008 to 2010, he was with the Harvard Law School Center on the Legal Profession as a postdoctoral research fellow. His research interests include social networks, organizational status and identity, and social mobility of individuals and firms. Currently, he looks into education reform in Korea, based on his past experience on various legislative reform projects in Korean public sectors, and studies careers of Korean law school graduates.

Kimberly D. Krawiec is the Kathrine Robinson Everett Professor of Law at Duke University and teaches courses on corporate law, financial regulation, and contested or "taboo" trades. Her research on corporate boards employs an ethnographic method to analyze directors' views on the workings of the corporate boardroom and board relations with management, with a special emphasis on directors' views on race and gender diversity in the boardroom.

Daniel Muzio is Professor of Professions and Organization at the University of Newcastle, a director of the Professions Work and Organization Research Group, and a founding editor of the Journal of Professions and Organization. Previously he has held academic positions at the Universities of Manchester, Leeds, and Lancaster and he currently holds visiting positions at Manchester Business School, Cass Business School, the University of Law in London, and Said Business School at the University of Oxford. His research focuses on professions and knowledge workers, their work, management, and organization. His research has been published in leading journals, including *Organization Studies*, *Sociology*, *Human Relations*, *The Journal of Management Studies*, and *The Journal of Economic Geography*. Daniel is currently coediting the *Oxford Handbook of Professional Services Firms* to be published in 2015 by the Oxford University Press.

Robert L. Nelson is a sociologist of law who studies law, inequality, and the legal profession. His books include *Legalizing Gender Inequality: Courts, Markets, and Unequal Pay for Women in America* (with William Bridges) which won the best book award from the American Sociological Association, and *Urban Lawyers* (with John Heinz, Edward Laumann, and Rebecca Sandefur). He was Director of the American Bar Foundation from 2004–2015, is co-director of the Research Group on Legal Diversity, and is a principal investigator in the After the JD Study of Lawyer Careers.

Yung-Yi Diana Pan is Assistant Professor of Sociology at Brooklyn College – City University of New York, and earned her PhD from University of California, Irvine. She has broad research interests in race and ethnicity, processes of racialization, immigrant adaptation, identity formation, professional socialization, and law and society. Her current research challenges traditional theories of immigrant integration by underscoring the significance of race and phenotype in elite professions. She is working on her first book, which examines the professional socialization and continued racialization of Asian American and Latino law students.

Milton C. Regan, Jr. is Co-Director of the Center for the Study of the Legal Profession and McDevitt Professor of Jurisprudence at Georgetown University Law Center. His work focuses on ethics, the legal profession, corporations, and national security. He has taught at law schools in China, Spain, and Australia. Before joining Georgetown, he clerked for Judge Ruth Bader Ginsburg on the US Court of Appeals for the District of Columbia Circuit and for Justice William J. Brennan, Jr. of the Supreme Court of the United States, and worked as an associate at Davis Polk & Wardwell in Washington, DC. He is the author of numerous books, articles, and book chapters.

Christopher I. Rider is an Assistant Professor of Strategy at Georgetown University's McDonough School of Business. His research draws on organization theory to study individual outcomes like entrepreneurship and mobility; organizational behaviors like hiring and staffing; and organizational outcomes like founding, change, and survival.

Carroll Seron is a Professor in the Department of Criminology, Law and Society, with courtesy appointments in the Department of Sociology and School of Law at the University of California, Irvine. Her research focuses on the sociology of the professions, where she has conducted research on the impact of changes in the gender and racial composition of the legal profession and engineering.

Hilary Sommerlad is Professor of Law and Social Justice, University of Leeds. She is a Fellow of the Academy of Social Sciences, serves on the editorial boards of the Journal of Law and Society and the International Journal of the Legal Profession, and is Articles Editor of Legal Ethics. She practiced as a legal aid lawyer, and this experience is reflected in her research interests; these include the cultural practices of the professional workplace and diversity in the legal profession. She has published widely on these issues, including a report commissioned by the Legal Services Board and a chapter (with Louise Ashley) "Equality, Diversity and Inclusion" in the *Oxford Handbook of Professional Service Firms* (2015).

Adina D. Sterling is an Assistant Professor of Organizational Behavior at Stanford University's Graduate School of Business. Her research investigates social structure in labor and product markets, strategic HR practices, and careers. Currently much of her research investigates the impact of trial employment on labor market and intra-organizational outcomes. She earned a PhD in Organization and Management from Emory University's Goizueta Business School in 2011 and a BS degree in chemical engineering from Ohio State University in 2002.

David Tan is Assistant Professor of Management and Organization at the University of Washington's Foster School of Business. His research focuses on the institutional and legal environment of business, including work examining careers and organizations within the legal services industry.

Jennifer Tomlinson is Professor of Gender and Employment Relations and Director of the Centre for Employment Relations Innovation and Change at the University of Leeds. Her research is grounded in the discipline of sociology and engages with questions relating to how social theory can help to explain patterns of gender and inequality in employment relations, labor markets, and organizations. Her research on inequalities, gender, and diversity within the professions and professional organizations has been published in leading journals including *Human Relations*, *Work, Employment and Society*, and *Gender, Work and Organization*.

Andrew von Nordenflycht is an Associate Professor of Strategy at the Beedie School of Business at Simon Fraser University in Vancouver, British Columbia. He received a BA in History from Stanford University and his PhD in Management from the MIT Sloan School of Management. He researches the ownership and management of human capital intensive firms, with a focus on professional services and airlines. In particular, he has studied the emergence of publicly-traded corporations in professional services and their effects on industry structure, creativity, and professional ethics. His research is published in leading management journals and he is the coauthor of *Up in the Air: How Airlines Can Improve Performance by Engaging Their Employees*.

Lisa Webley is Professor of Empirical Legal Studies at the University of Westminster, Westminster Law School and Faculty Research Director for Social Sciences and Humanities. She is also Senior Fellow at the Institute of Advanced Legal Studies, University of London. As a socio-legal researcher she conducts research on equality, diversity and inclusion in the legal profession, legal ethics, access to justice, and alternative dispute resolution and the law. She is Secretary of the International Association of Legal Ethics, and a member of the Equality, Diversity and Inclusion Committee of the Law Society of England and Wales.

David B. Wilkins is a world-renowned scholar on the legal profession. He has written more than eighty articles and is the coauthor of one of the leading casebooks in the field, and has given more than forty-five endowed academic lectures around the world. His recent professional accomplishments include: Aptissimi Scholar of the Year (ESADE Law School 2014), Honorary Doctorate in Law (Stockholm University 2012), Distinguished Visiting Mentor Award (Australia National University 2012), Genest Fellowship (Osgood Hall Law School 2012), and the Scholar of the Year Award (American Bar Foundation 2010). Professor Wilkins is Member of the American Academy of Arts and Sciences, and a Corresponding Member of the Spanish Royal Academy of Doctors.

ACKNOWLEDGMENTS

The editors would like to thank the contributors, the American Bar Foundation and its supporters, and the Research Group on Legal Diversity for making this project possible. They also gratefully acknowledge the participants in the 2013 Conference of the RGLD and the generous Northwestern University partners who helped sponsor that event: the Office of the Provost, the School of Law, the Graduate School, Weinberg College of Arts and Sciences, and Kellogg Graduate School of Management.

INTRODUCTION

SPENCER HEADWORTH AND ROBERT L. NELSON

"Diversity in practice" carries dual meanings. First, it refers to the growing demographic diversity of law and other professions. One of the most profound transformations in professional fields in the last four decades has been the entry of large numbers of women and people of color. The title also refers to enduring inequalities in professional careers, despite rhetorical commitments to diversity and investments in pro-diversity initiatives. An established feature of contemporary professional associations and prestigious professional firms is their embrace of diversity as a goal, and diversity and inclusion programming is widely used. However, in practice, inequalities persist. This volume critically addresses both aspects of diversity in practice, examining the current state of inequality and identifying mechanisms that reproduce advantage and disadvantage.

The research reported here reveals dramatic gaps between rhetoric and reality in achieving diversity in law and other professions. Despite professional leaders' public pronouncements about the importance of diversity and inclusion, the chapters contained here document the persistence of inequalities of race, gender, and class in the professions. These chapters demonstrate that these inequalities are often sustained through more subtle mechanisms than the kinds of explicit discrimination that characterized earlier periods of the Anglo-American legal profession (Abel 1989; Auerbach 1976; Epstein 1981). These mechanisms include the ongoing impact of stereotypes and discrimination; forms of credentialism that prioritize elite educational pedigrees and have disproportionate effects on

1

members of historically underrepresented groups; inequalities in network ties and social capital; and structural changes in professional work that intensify intra-professional stratification, including globalization, technological advances, and blurring lines between law and business.

The weight of these collective findings was not preordained by our selection of authors and papers. As part of an ongoing effort by the Research Group on Legal Diversity of the American Bar Foundation, we issued a call for papers on "Pursuing Diverse Talent in Legal and Professional Services: Research within and across Professions, Organizations, and Societies." We chose for publication those papers that made original empirical contributions to the central theme of the conference. It is a fair reading of this research, conducted by scholars from different disciplines and with different methods, that inequalities of race, gender, and class remain a fundamental problem for law and other modern professions.

In this introduction we first provide an overview of the theoretical and empirical literature on the sources of inequality in legal and professional careers. We discuss several dimensions of professional inequality relevant to this volume's new empirical contributions. First, we document the significant underrepresentation of racial/ethnic minorities in the legal profession and introduce how characteristics of higher and professional education contribute to the problem. Next, we briefly touch on the large body of literature on the social psychology of inequality and discrimination, discussing the impact of stereotype threat and implicit bias on aspiring lawyers who are people of color or women. We then review research that demonstrates persistent gender inequality in the legal profession. This research shows that relatively modest earnings gaps between men and women early in careers grow over time; this section goes on to describe public policies and features of workplaces that drive the trend of growing inequality over the course of careers.

We then consider patterns of exclusivity in the kinds of elite contexts that are at the pinnacle of the legal, professional, and business worlds, and the focal points of many of the chapters in this volume. After briefly discussing patterns of inequality in large law firms, which have dominated the corporate sector of the legal profession since their emergence in the early twentieth century, we note recent developments that threaten to shake up the established order and consider their implications for diversity. We conclude this part of the introduction by discussing how this volume's findings fit into broader theories of inequality and noting the wide-reaching implications of inequalities in legal careers. Much more is at stake than equality of opportunity in the professions. Law cannot provide equal justice to all segments of society, nor will law be perceived as capable of equal justice, if the professionals that serve in the justice system do not resemble the diversity of society at large.

Following this introduction of background information on inequalities in the professional world, we introduce the remainder of the volume. The chapters are organized in three sections that address central features of equality and opportunity in modern professions. The chapters in the first section directly address the rhetoric of diversity in elite contexts and juxtapose that rhetoric with measures of actual progress. In the second section, chapters examine points of entry to professional careers in law, in science, and in professional services. These chapters emphasize the continuing significance of professional education for early career opportunities. Professional education shapes the identities of aspirants to professional careers and thereby shapes their prospects for success. The chapters in the third section of the book analyze the determinants of success in the careers of diverse attorneys. Working from a variety of innovative approaches, these chapters reveal both the challenges and the opportunities that diverse attorneys face in the current marketplace for professional services.

THEORETICAL AND EMPIRICAL BACKGROUND

Race and ethnicity, education, and the leaky pipeline to professional practice

We begin with simple statistics about the pipeline to professional careers in law. Overall, Black Americans make up 12.6% of the general population (Humes, Jones, and Ramirez 2011: 4) and 14.5% of high school graduates (Snyder and Dillow 2011), but their presence among college graduates declines to 9.8% (Snyder and Dillow 2011), among law school graduates to 6.9% (Snyder and Dillow 2011), and they comprise some 4.3% of lawyers (US Census Bureau 2012: 394). Latinos make up 16.3% of the general population (Humes, Jones, and Ramirez 2011: 4) and 15.1% of high school graduates (Snyder and Dillow 2011), but only 7.9% of college graduates (Snyder and Dillow 2011) and 6.5% of law school graduates (Snyder and Dillow 2011).

The 2010 Census recorded 3.4% of lawyers as Latino (US Census Bureau 2012: 394).[1]

The pipeline to professional practice is long and leaky, and the factors that produce the observed demographic inequities are numerous and complex. Focusing for the moment just on the world of higher education, relatively low rates of college graduation represent a significant source of leaks in the pipeline carrying people of color into the law and other prestigious professional occupations. Less than half of the Latino, Black, and Native American students who enroll in four-year colleges graduate in six years: among 2002 new enrollees, the rough percentages who did so were 49, 40, and 38, respectively, compared to 67% of Asian-American/Pacific Islander students and sixty percent of White students (Snyder and Dillow 2011: 485). Trends in choices of college majors also hold implications for the talent pool from which future lawyers emerge. The majority of law school graduates were social sciences or humanities majors in college, and less than 10% majored in natural science or technical fields like engineering or computer science. Holding other relevant factors constant, students from less advantaged socioeconomic backgrounds are considerably less likely than their more affluent peers to choose majors in the arts and humanities, and more likely to choose technical or vocational majors (Goyette and Mullen 2006; Ma 2009).

Minority aspirants are further hindered by the importance of undergraduate grades in the law school admission process, with Black men and women and Latino men graduating with significantly worse grade point averages than their White male counterparts (Massey and Probasco 2010). Although Black and Latino students comprise a larger portion of applicants to law school than of college graduates, they are more likely to be "shut out" in the application process – that is, accepted by no law school (Nussbaumer and Johnson 2011). Further, Black and Latino students who successfully complete the application process and matriculate into law school are more likely to drop out and less likely to graduate than their White counterparts.

Data on variation in bar passage rates are unfortunately limited; however, the results from the Law School Admission Council's (1998) National Longitudinal Bar Passage Study indicate that members

---

[1] According to the After the JD (AJD) sample, Latinos make up 4.5% of the population of US lawyers seven years after passing the bar and 3.2% twelve years after (Sandefur and Nelson 2014: 21).

of racial/ethnic minority groups who graduate from law school are less likely to eventually pass the bar (77.6% of Black graduates, 87.7% of Latino graduates, and 91.9% of Asian-American graduates, compared to 96.7% for White graduates) (Wightman 1998: 32). In terms of overall legal employment, a recent survey of law school graduates by the National Association for Law Placement found that 79.2% of non-minority 2013 graduates were employed full-time in February 2014, compared to 72.3% of minority graduates. The discrepancy is slightly more pronounced considering specifically jobs for which bar admittance is a requirement: 66.8% of non-minority graduates held those jobs, compared to 57.6% of minority graduates (NALP 2014: 59).

Overall, members of historically marginalized racial and ethnic groups remain starkly disadvantaged in gaining entry to legal careers. While an array of historical and structural causes are at work in producing this disadvantage, attention to higher education contexts reveals significant factors that impede the prospects of minority aspirants who reach that relatively late stage of the professional pipeline.

The social psychology of inequality and discrimination

Along with structural and institutional factors, social psychology can help explain disparities in educational outcomes across demographic groups. Research on educational achievement has demonstrated the impact of racial and gender stereotypes on performance. Stereotype threat effects occur when individuals from ability-stigmatized groups feel pressure when completing academic tasks on which poor performance could confirm negative group stereotypes. This pressure leads to anxiety and distraction, which in turn lead to underperformance. These reduced outcomes are observed specifically when tests are presented as measures of ability, rather than non-diagnostic exercises, demonstrating the significance of stereotypes regarding the intellectual abilities of members of different demographic groups to performance on such examinations. In a landmark study, Steele and Aronson (1995) showed that Black test-takers performed comparably to their White counterparts on a verbal assessment presented as non-diagnostic of ability, while performing relatively worse when the test was presented as an assessment of intellectual ability. Subsequent research has demonstrated similar effects for women, for instance, showing women to underperform on a math test presented as indicative of gender disparities, an effect curtailed by presenting the test as gender-neutral (Spencer, Steele, and Quinn 1999). Threat effects are, perhaps ironically, strongest among students who strongly identify with academic achievement, as these students feel the greatest pressure to avoid confirming negative group stereotypes (Steele 2010: 58).

Stereotype threat effects have been most frequently studied at the collegiate level, but researchers have also demonstrated the impact of stereotype threat on middle school (Cohen et al. 2006; Cohen et al. 2009) and high school (Reardon et al. 2009) students. These effects grow in significance under accountability-driven educational reforms such as the No Child Left Behind Act, which link school funding to performance on standardized assessments. These types of measures incentivize faculty and administrators to dedicate considerable portions of educational time and resources to increasing students' test scores, inculcating "teaching to the test" approaches that sacrifice other curricular areas. Linkages of school funding to mean proficiency scores can lead to reduced funding and shortages of highly qualified teachers for disadvantaged schools; cyclical entrenchment of test-driven curricula; and substantial incentives to displace low-scoring students (Darling-Hammond 2007; Kim and Sunderman 2005; Meier and Wood 2004; Ryan 2004).

Furthermore, individual performance on placement tests like the ACT and SAT is an essential prerequisite of higher education, and similar testing requirements obtain for admission to graduate and professional schools; stereotype threat is implicated in each of these testing situations. For aspiring law students, the Law School Admission Test (LSAT) is immediately relevant. The use of LSAT scores – and particularly minimum required scores – in law school admissions has a disproportionate negative impact on racial and ethnic minorities, especially Black and Latino aspirants (Godsil, Banner, and Kang 2012; Randall 2006). According to data from the Law School Admission Council (LSAC), the nonprofit corporation that administers the LSAT, both women and racial/ethnic minorities exhibit struggles with the LSAT. Female test-takers' average scores over recent years have been between 2.3 and 2.6 points lower than those of their male counterparts (Dalessandro, Anthony, and Reese 2012: 17).[2] With the exception of Asian Americans, whose scores are comparable to those of

---

[2] Interestingly, test-takers who chose not to report a gender have had the highest average scores of any group over recent years, with a larger advantage over male test-takers than that of men over women since the 2006–2007 testing year (Dalessandro, Anthony, and Reese 2012: 17).

White test-takers, scores for members of racial/ethnic minority groups have also been relatively low. In the 2011–2012 testing year, Black test-takers' average score was more than ten points lower than that of their White counterparts, and test-takers who self-reported as Hispanic/ Latino averaged scores more than six points lower than White test-takers (Dalessandro, Anthony, and Reese 2012: 20).

At each stage in the professional pipeline that involves evaluation based on subjective judgments, explicit prejudices among decision-makers against members of particular demographic groups clearly can have negative effects on the prospects of members of those groups. However, conscious biases (whether explicit or concealed) about the characteristics or capacities of different categories of people are not necessary for unequal outcomes from evaluation and selection processes that involve discretionary judgments. Implicit bias – the unconscious attachment of stereotypes and attitudes to members of different demographic groups – can affect decision-making processes without the implicated actors even being aware (Kang et al. 2012). The implications of implicit bias are suggested by foundational research, such as results from the Implicit Association Test (IAT) demonstrating disparities in evaluative attributions of positive and negative characteristics to members of different racial/ethnic groups (Greenwald, McGhee, and Schwartz 1998; Greenwald et al. 2009). Similarly, gender remains an important dimension of the status hierarchies that order cultural, occupational, and organizational life. Gender may also implicitly influence the assessment of skills and performance, thus contributing to the perpetuation of gender inequality in professional contexts (Ridgeway 2011).

These social psychological phenomena can help explain research findings that demonstrate the ongoing impact of employment discrimination in both professional and nonprofessional settings (see Bertrand, Chugh, and Mullainathan 2005). Audit studies measuring callbacks offered by real prospective employers to fabricated resumes for a range of jobs, from entry-level to managerial, in Chicago and Boston found that fictitious applicants with very "White-sounding" names needed to send out about ten resumes to get a callback, compared to the about fifteen resumes required for callbacks for applicants with very "African-American-sounding" names. In total, a White-sounding name provided the same callback advantage as an additional eight years of work experience. Furthermore, the positive effects of a stronger resume are diluted for ostensibly Black applicants, relative to their ostensibly

White counterparts (Bertrand and Mullainthan 2004). A similar field experiment, focused on low-paying positions in New York City, recruited real people to apply for jobs. In this research, White applicants were twice as likely as their Black counterparts to be called back or offered a job, and Latino and Black applicants whose fictitious back-stories included clean criminal records saw comparable outcomes to White applicants presented as recently released from prison (Pager, Western, and Bonikowski 2009). Related research has demonstrated that such effects are not limited to racial/ethnic minorities, showing evidence of employment discrimination against openly gay male applicants (marked by fictitious resumes listing service as the treasurer in a gay community organization, with service as treasurer in a campus "Progressive and Socialist Alliance" as the control condition) (Tilcsik 2011).

While not the primary focus of this volume's empirical contributions, these types of social psychological threats and biases represent an important dimension of the subtle mechanisms so important in driving contemporary inequality. They play a crucial role not only in shaping the population of would-be professionals who reach the career stages this volume addresses, but in a host of other important social arenas as well. Their effects on law and legal institutions demand careful consideration.

Gender, time, and workplace culture

Despite some progress, women continue to lag behind men in legal careers. In the period immediately following law school graduation, they are less likely than men to be employed (83.6% to 85.3%), employed full time (75.9% to 78.6%), and (narrowly) less likely to be employed in jobs requiring bar passage (64.2% to 64.5%) (NALP 2014: 59). Women's mean salaries in these first jobs are less than $80,000, compared to men's mean salaries of more than $84,000 (NALP 2014: 72).

These initial disparities grow as careers progress. Workplaces of all types exhibit common patterns of less favorable outcomes over the course of women's careers, as initial disparities in hiring are compounded by lower rates of promotion and higher rates of turnover, limiting opportunities to take leadership roles and fill executive positions (Milligan et al. 2014). In the legal profession, women are less likely to make partner than men, and are more likely than men to be found in non-equity partnerships twelve years after admission to the bar (Sterling, Sandefur, and Plickert 2014: 66). A 5% income gap after two to three years of work grows to 20% after twelve years (Sterling, Sandefur, and Plickert 2014: 67).

For those members of underrepresented groups who make it over the hurdles of the education and job application processes, the workplace often presents a fresh set of difficulties. These difficulties may take the form of struggles to balance work and home life. The distribution of household labor has failed to track women's expanded presence in the labor market since the mid-twentieth century, as women continue to dedicate far more time than men to household work and family caregiving. US public policy on work and family trails the rest of the developed world, exacerbating the problems of work-life balance that disproportionately affect women, contributing to the pressures that cause many to leave their careers (Williams 2010). Despite some progress in women's economic status, women's full-time earnings are still around 80% of men's (Blau and Khan 2007), although there is evidence of continued narrowing of the gender pay gap in primary labor market jobs with voluntary turnover (Kronberg 2013).

Professional employment presents a particular organization of time that holds different implications for men than for women. Professional careers tend to be "greedy" when it comes to working hours; now more than ever in the era of email and smartphones, professionals are expected to always be "on." The unbounded time demands of professional careers often translate into both men and women dedicating long hours to their work. For women, these work demands are often coupled with relatively less control over private time and a greater share of household and child-rearing tasks, to which they continue to dedicate far more time than men (Bianchi et al. 2000; Hochschild 2012 [1989]; Seron and Ferris 1995). Professional men are more likely than their female counterparts to have a significant other who stays at home to care for young children. One recent study found that among rain-makers – highly successful partners in law firms who generate business by recruiting new clients or developing relationships with established clients – men were more than ten times more likely than women to have a stay-at-home spouse (Drake and Parker-Stephen 2013: 15).

Studies of professional culture have identified characteristics in these work environments that may be inhospitable to members of historically underrepresented groups, including women. Scholars working in this vein have highlighted the significance of professional role confidence – "individuals' confidence in their ability to fulfill the expected roles, competencies, and identity features of a successful member of their

9

profession" – in explaining persistence in a professional career (Cech et al. 2011; see also Pan, this volume; Seron, this volume). In workplaces dominated by masculine culture, women find themselves pressed into conventional roles that entrench and exacerbate gender inequality, while simultaneously impeding individuals' prospects for career advancement (Williams 2010). Other research, focusing only on single people (and thus eliminating the potential impact of discrimination against married women and caregivers), has suggested that female professionals who challenge gender stereotypes – say, by possessing strong quantitative skills – may appear incongruent with expectations within the professional culture, and accordingly face penalties in promotion (Merluzzi and Phillips 2013).

The historical dominance of men and marginalization of women in the professional world has precipitated the construction of work structures and cultures that continue to advantage men. As many of this volume's contributors suggest, these sexist structures and cultures are less obvious than the blatant forms of discrimination and harassment that were more common in previous decades (although these still occur with some regularity). It is the systematic but obscured character of these mechanisms that make them so entrenched and difficult to change.

Large firms and elite exclusivity

As a professional occupation that has a monopoly on legal services and the power of self-regulation, lawyers enjoy noteworthy prosperity and prestige (Abel 1989; Larson 1977). However, these rewards are not equally distributed across all members of the profession. Scholars of the legal profession have long observed dramatic differences in the incomes and prestige of lawyers working in different fields of law and for different clients (Carlin 1962; Carlin 1966; Heinz and Laumann 1982; Heinz et al. 2005; Ladinsky 1963). Heinz and Laumann (1982) developed the highly influential concept of the two hemispheres of the legal profession: the personal client and corporate client hemispheres. Personal client lawyers often came from ethnic and religious minorities, attended lower prestige local law schools, and practiced in fields serving personal clients. Corporate client lawyers often came from traditionally elite ethnic and religious backgrounds, attended elite national law schools, and practiced in fields serving corporate clients. While corporate hemisphere lawyers enjoyed higher prestige and often higher earnings in the mid-1970s, at the time of the first Chicago Lawyers survey, these advantages grew dramatically between 1975 and 1995. In 1975, the relative portion of legal spending in Chicago between the personal and corporate client sector was roughly equal. By 1995, personal client lawyers received about one-third of legal spending in Chicago compared to two-thirds for the corporate client sector. As a result, the incomes of personal client lawyers fell after adjusting for inflation, while corporate client lawyers saw a significant gain in real income (Heinz et al. 2005).

Sitting atop the corporate client sector were the elite law firms organized on the Cravath model of highly selective recruiting from elite law schools, intensive socialization in firm work practices, and an up-or-out partnership hierarchy (Nelson 1988; Smigel 1964). Despite making up a relatively small proportion of all lawyers, these firms were very important in symbolic and real terms. They defined the nature of elite law practice. And they provided legal representation to the most powerful concentrations of corporate and governmental power (Abel 1989). Given their predominance in the corporate legal services market, the determinants of success at these firms has been a focal point of much legal profession research. Through the 1950s and 1960s many elite law firms discriminated against women and Jews (Smigel 1964). While these patterns began to break down late in the 1960s, even by the mid-1970s, Heinz and Laumann found patterns of exclusion in prestigious corporate fields. Twenty years later, corporate practice was no longer the exclusive preserve of White Anglo-Saxon men and significant numbers of women had entered elite law practice (Heinz et al. 2005). The critical issue had become whether women and minorities were achieving positions of partnership and firm leadership at the same rate as White men.

Even before the financial collapse in 2008 administered a shock to the economic health of many large law partnerships, scholars had begun to question the long run viability of the corporate law firm model. Galanter and Palay (1991) suggested that "the tournament of lawyers" on which partnerships were based could not be sustained. The competition for profits-per-partner was based on an increasingly steep pyramid of associate and non-equity partner labor. The post-2008 world revealed the financial problems that some firms faced, as significant numbers of large firms collapsed. As the shake-up in corporate law took place, there were reports that women and minorities had suffered disproportionately in firm layoffs and downsizing.

Given the relative stagnation in the movement of women and minorities up the partnership ladder in major law firms, scholars began to theorize about why this was the case. Wilkins and Gulati (1996: 541) suggested that clear patterns had emerged in how firms invested in different groups of associates. Some were directed into a "training track" and others to a "flatlining track." Wilkins and Gulati (1996: 541) drew an analogy between training in law firms and royal jelly, a nourishing supplement that provides bee larvae the opportunity to mature into queens, rather than into common worker bees; associates directed into the training track are thereby provided opportunities for advancement closed to those outside the track. In the firm environment, formal mentorship and training opportunities; desirable, high-profile work assignments; and chances for informal networking can have significant implications for career trajectories, and access to these experiences is unequally distributed among demographic categories of young lawyers (see Galanter and Palay 1991; Hull and Nelson 2000; Kay, Hagan, and Parker 2009; Nelson 1988).

Even in the current era in which there is a supposed war for talent, hiring practices at large law firms have helped perpetuate patterns of demographic inequality. This in part reflects the continuing import-ance of credentialing as a *de facto* requirement for gaining entry to the professional elite. As Randall Collins observes, "In law, as in other areas, American structure has fostered a school oriented contest mobil-ity system" (1979: 159). Elite firms continue to concentrate their recruitment and interviewing efforts at the most prestigious, expensive, and exclusive universities, thus functionally eliminating from consider-ation those who do not meet this fundamental eligibility threshold. In some cases, not only prestigious, but "super-elite" private university pedigrees are a minimum threshold for consideration for elite profes-sional service employers (Rivera 2011; Webley et al., this volume).

Various sorting processes produce the subset of the students enrolled at the select institutions from which elite organizations recruit. From an early age, less-advantaged students face barriers in gaining access to elite schools. Conversely, better-resourced students enjoy very signifi-cant advantages (see, e.g., Condron and Roscigno 2003; Kozol 1991; McNeil 2000). Even after gaining admission to a particular school, students from different backgrounds face strikingly disparate pathways through the educational process. Privileged students are able to draw on resources and connections unavailable to less-advantaged students (see Seron, this volume). Differential access to social, cultural, and financial capital precipitates vastly different results for students who embark on nominally similar educational journeys (Armstrong and Hamilton 2013; Massey and Probasco 2010).

Employers use sorting processes based on subjective judgments to further winnow the population of candidates who reach this stage of the educational pipeline. Faced with a pool of demonstrated talent, elite employers rely on associations with elite institutions at earlier stages of education (Smigel 1964) and involvement in particular types of exclusive, resource-intensive extracurricular activities (Rivera 2011). Both tendencies reproduce White, male, upper-class advantage and uphold barriers to entry for historically underrepresented groups.

At hiring events on or near campus, revenue-generating professionals – not HR specialists – carry out face-to-face interviews with potential future colleagues.[3] Tellingly, these interviews are in large part about evaluating candidates' degree of "fit" with the firm; those conducting the interviews generally feel that educational pedigree provides a good basic indicator of qualification, and focus more on trying to identify candidates who will integrate smoothly into the work environment's milieu. This results in a homophilic pattern of "cultural matching." The evaluators assess candidates based on their perceived degree of fit with firm culture and similarity to the interviewer him- or herself. These processes perpetuate firms' homogeneity (Ashley and Empson, this volume; Rivera 2012, 2015).

The legal academy represents another influential segment of the professional elite. Members of the law professoriate occupy uniquely important positions within the legal profession as a whole, as the primary agents of the organizations centrally responsible for professional education, socialization, and ultimately, (re)production; as "repositories and distributors of legal information" (Katz et al. 2011: 1); and, in some cases, as prominent public figures, relative to their counterparts in private practice and the corporate sector. While Black and Asian-American legal academics have achieved representation in the ranks of tenure-track professors commensurate with their presence in the general population, members of these groups remain underrepresented among tenured professors, and Latino and female professors are underrepresented in both tenure-track and tenured positions (American Bar Association 2013).

---

[3] Elite law schools vary from their counterparts here; while most professional service firms apply some achievement-based floors for interview eligibility (grades, extracurriculars), top-level law schools require firms to interview all applicants. Firms may suggest grade point minimums for interviewees, however (Rivera 2011: 74).

The continuing centrality of credentialism in law faculty hiring decisions helps explain these ongoing disparities. Recent data show that non-White candidates and women are significantly more likely than their White male counterparts to be provided the opportunity to give job talks, but are no more likely to receive any job offers, including job offers from elite schools. Rather, the best predictor of job offers is the status of one's degree-granting institution. Graduates of Tier I law schools – and especially graduates of the top three *US News & World Report*-ranked law schools (Yale, Harvard, and Stanford) – are significantly more likely than the graduates of other law schools to receive job offers for faculty positions. The preference for Harvard, Yale, and Stanford is especially pronounced for higher-status faculty positions (George and Yoon 2014). Thus, the array of factors that have historically contributed to the underrepresentation of women and racial/ethnic minorities at elite educational institutions continue to hamper diversity in the law professoriate, especially at elite institutions.

Despite a rhetoric of openness and change, elite professional settings continue to exhibit patterns of exclusivity along the lines of race, gender, and class. Yet as we move into the twenty-first century, changes in the market for professional services and the global economy may significantly reshape these large firms. What are the implications of those changes for diversity and inclusion?

The restructuring of elite professional firms: globalization, technology, and blurring boundaries between law and business

Coeditor and contributor David Wilkins (2014) asserts that there are three fundamental transformations taking place in elite law firms in the wake of the global financial crisis of 2008: 1) the globalization of economic activity and the shift in rates of economic growth from the global north to the global south; 2) continuing changes in information technology that are revolutionizing the provision of legal services; and 3) the blurring of the boundary between law and business, or law and other types of professional services. In Wilkins' view, and that of other leading commentators on the changing landscape of legal services (Henderson 2014; Susskind 2008, 2013), these changes threaten the old order of elite corporate law firms. They predict an accelerating number of large law firms will fall apart or be absorbed in other large entities.

The ultimate outcome of these processes for large law firms is uncertain. Also unclear is their impact on patterns of inequality in elite firms.

On the one hand, globalization mandates greater social diversity in law firms. To obtain global reach, including the kinds of local contacts critical to effective global practice (Silver, Phelan, and Rabinowitz 2009), professional service firms must incorporate lawyers from diverse locales and almost necessarily diverse social backgrounds. Indeed, evidence points to greater minority representation in law firms with more international offices (Chambliss 1997).[4]

On the other hand, as professional firms become larger and more culturally diverse, they may not become more egalitarian along the lines of race, gender, and class. In the US legal profession, women starting their careers in the year 2000 have left employment in firms of more than 100 lawyers at much faster rates than men (Sterling, Sandefur, and Plickert 2014: 65). In terms of race and ethnicity, both Black and Asian-American lawyers were disproportionately likely to leave these large firm settings, compared to their White counterparts (Latino lawyers were the racial/ethnic group least likely to leave employment in large firms) (Dinovitzer, Wilkins, and Nelson 2014: 74). While Wilkins cites research on the feminization of lawyers globally – that is, the rapid influx of large percentages of women into various national legal professions (Michelson 2012) – that will not necessarily translate into the rise of women in elite professional practice. On the contrary, in the restructured world of law practice, in which legal work is unbundled into more specialized and less remunerative tasks, we can expect that traditionally advantaged groups may remain atop the new organizational structures, while women and minorities are concentrated in less prestigious, less rewarded roles. The chapters by Webley et al. and Sommerlad in this volume strongly suggest at least the persistence, and more likely the intensification of inequality as elite law practice is restructured globally. Indeed one of the original authors of the "tournament of lawyers" suggests we have entered a new stage in the evolution of the large firm. Large law firms no longer can be characterized as an associate-to-partner competition, but must be seen as an "elastic tournament" which includes new forms of employment relationships for lawyers, nonequity partnerships, more marginal and nontraditional types of legal labor, and the emergence of specialized, non-attorney managers (Galanter and Henderson 2008).[5]

---

[4] Although firms are only supposed to count diverse lawyers of American citizenship, and not foreign nationals, it is not clear that this rule is always observed.

[5] See also Ackroyd and Muzio (2007) on the move from labor market closure to internal organizational closure in English and Welsh firms.

Professional inequalities in broader context

At one level, the lack of diversity in the legal profession reflects broader patterns of inequality in the United States and the United Kingdom. The underrepresentation of women and racial/ethnic minorities in elite law practice is not unique to law. It appears that many of the same causal elements that produce unequal outcomes in legal careers operate in other professional occupations. Some recent research indicates that among younger professionals, Black and Latino underrepresentation in law is roughly comparable to the underrepresentation we see in other prestigious professions (Nance and Madsen 2014). In a wide range of organizational contexts, not just law, there are relatively high attrition rates for racial/ethnic minorities, and these attrition rates can be difficult to improve. Data from a large financial services firm, for instance, show that higher diversity rates at the time of hire are associated with lower job turnover, and that minority employee turnover increases when same-race presence in the workplace dwindles. Turnover rates, however, do not show a corresponding decrease when minority group representation improves during the course of employment (Sorensen 2004). These types of results suggest that inquiry and interventions aimed at diversity and inclusion in the law should be seen as part of a larger agenda for advancing equal opportunity. The chapters in this volume recognize these connections to inequality at large. While they directly study the mechanisms that produce inequality in large law firms and other elite professional contexts, these can be seen as particular instances of widely operating social processes.

Yet, there are also important reasons why inequalities in the law demand special attention. Beyond the intrinsic injustice of disproportionate access to well-paying careers of substantial influence in politics, economics, and culture, the failure to build a more diverse legal profession creates other unique social costs. Law is a crucial and singularly meaningful system of social organization. Lawyers are pivotal actors in the process of moving from the abstract written rules of law to social application. They are frequently responsible for devising and executing legal activity. It is reasonable to presume that social backgrounds have some effect on the way these tasks are carried out, with implications for a host of implicated parties (Nelson 1988, 1994). Furthermore, an education and career in law often represents a launching point for other influential lines of work, notably including elected and appointed government positions. Shortages of diverse talent in law can thus translate into shortages of diverse talent for other important fields.

Diversity in the legal profession can have very concrete effects on outcomes in the criminal justice system. A striking example is found in a study of sentencing in large urban counties by King, Johnson, and McGeever (2010). They found that, compared to White defendants, Black and Latino defendants faced greater odds of incarceration overall, but that this effect was significantly mitigated for Black defendants as county-level concentrations of Black attorneys increased. Similarly, while Black and Latino defendants received longer sentences overall, the disparity in Black and White defendants' sentences decreased as Black representation among lawyers in the county increased, and greater Latino representation among local lawyers translated into reduced disparities for both Latino and Black defendants. These results suggest the importance of diversity in the legal profession to the delivery of equal justice under the law.

THE ORGANIZATION OF THE VOLUME

I Rhetoric and realities

Across employment settings, organizations and their leaders have moved toward a greater degree of uniformity in expressed commitment to diversity as a desirable goal. The chapters in this section document these rhetorical commitments, and address departures between rhetorical stances embracing diversity and thoroughgoing professional diversification.

In "Action after the Call," David Wilkins and Young-Kyu Kim open the conversation about diversity in the legal profession through their analysis of the 2004 "Call to Action." In 2004, Richard Palmore, then general counsel of Sara Lee, issued the now famous Call, which represented an attempt to increase racial/ethnic and gender diversity in the legal profession through leveraging the influence of large companies. The Call asked general counsels to sign a statement pledging to incorporate diversity performance as a factor in choosing their companies' legal representation, and to reduce or terminate their relationships with firms that do not demonstrate commitment to diversity. The Call to Action has been at least a superficial success, with more than 135 companies signing on, and has inspired new internal diversity initiatives at a number of prominent corporations. The Call has helped elevate diversity in the conversation around the purchase of legal services, with general counsels now regularly referring to diversity as an important criterion in their selection processes. Yet, there is little empirical evidence of a substantive effect of the Call on diversity within large law firms, where growth in the representation of women and people of color has been modest.

This chapter addresses this empirical lacuna, reporting on the results of a 2006–2007 study of S&P 500 general counsels. Drawing on the results of 131 completed surveys and 44 interviews with general counsels, the authors find that law is still fundamentally a relationship business. By far the most significant reported factors in legal purchasing decisions are results in similar cases, reputation, and prior relationship. In general, diversity commitment is a solidly second-order consideration to general counsels, below firm size and close to quality control systems and ethical infrastructure in a cluster of factors deemed "somewhat important." The importance placed on diversity is not uniform across companies, however: signatories of the Call to Action are more likely than non-signatories to consider diversity important or very important, and companies who have joined the Minority Corporate Counsel Association are even more likely to value diversity. There is also good evidence that the presence of general counsels and board members from historically underrepresented groups is positively related to diversity valuation, and that diversity is valued more highly by members of the Fortune 500. The chapter discusses the relationship between these and other findings and demand side diversity efforts like the Call to Action. The authors describe the implications of data-driven examinations of firm practices for the future of diversity initiatives.

Krawiec, Conley, and Broome pick up the thread of corporate board diversity from Wilkins and Kim. Their chapter highlights the extent to which a lack of diversity is not solely a problem in the legal profession, but in prestigious professions and among elites more broadly. Their research provides rare insights into the world of corporate leadership. Based on interviews with fifty-seven corporate directors and other directly relevant parties on the topic of diversity in corporate boards, they examine an influential arena in which racial/ethnic, and particularly gender, diversity lags behind even that of elite law firms. As in the legal field, corporations and their leadership have vigorously vocalized their commitments to increasing diversity; yet, substantive progress has been lacking. The authors' data and analyses address this phenomenon by asking their interlocutors to comment on the observed slowness in improving board diversity. In their responses, there is a nearly universal rhetorical commitment to diversity in the abstract. When respondents are asked to provide comments on their experiences of the positive influences of diversity on board operations, however, they struggle. Most are unable – or unwilling – to provide concrete examples of how diversity provides benefits. The authors analyze what causes this pattern. Do respondents truly lack experiences in which they felt diversity had a salutary effect on board functioning? How do the benefits of diversity they perceive in practice fit with the rhetorics of equality and inclusivity they espouse? Without a clear recognition of diversity's benefits, it is unlikely that corporate boards will pursue diversity as strongly as their rhetoric would imply.

Ashley and Empson's chapter also goes beyond law. It provides results and analysis from studies of large UK professional service firms, including three accountancy firms, two law firms, and one consultancy firm, as well as one large London-based investment bank. Ashley and Empson give center stage to class as an analytical category. Across their research sites, the authors find a uniform reliance on credentialism. With enormous and seemingly ever-growing numbers of applicants for job openings, firms feel compelled to institute decision rules for winnowing the crowd, and more often than not rely on educational pedigree as a marker of ability and promise. This approach functionally eliminates most young people from less affluent families who could not afford elite educations, regardless of aptitude or promise. In many cases, interviewees acknowledge this fact, as well as the disadvantages posed by such an approach in terms of identifying candidates with the highest likelihoods of creativity and success. Beyond offering an ostensible "shortcut" to the best and brightest candidates, elite educational credentials provide significant symbolic and social capital. Employing graduates of top schools helps firms signal their own elite status. The firms also report that they believe this practice helps lubricate functioning within a social environment largely populated with similarly credentialed individuals. The authors identify among their respondents a willingness, in the abstract, to consider candidates with different sets of qualifications. The "catch," however, is that they desire such candidates to have already demonstrated their talent elsewhere. The unifying theme between these approaches is risk aversion – firms wish to insulate themselves from risk, either by relying on universities for initial sorting or through outsourcing to another organization the first decision to take a risk on a less conventional candidate.

II   Entering professional careers: Barriers, ladders, and basement doors

The chapters in this section address the barriers to entry that limit access to professional practice and describe two different ways that access may be possible: "ladders" and "basement doors." These chapters focus on the organizations involved in professional training and hiring, where members of historically underrepresented groups continue to face significant impediments. Taken as a group, the chapters demonstrate the significance of deeply rooted features of professional environments in curtailing the accessibility of professional careers.

The first two chapters in Section II focus on the United States, and the second two chapters on the United Kingdom. Both pairs of chapters demonstrate the burdens members of underrepresented groups face when pursuing education and success in professional contexts with pronounced patterns of exclusivity. These exclusive characteristics may derive from the cultures of professional training or work environments, as the US-focused pieces describe, or they may result from exclusionary credential-based hiring practices, as the UK authors observe. In either case, access to the professional world may hinge on a ladder – additional capital to help surmount barriers – or a basement door – passage into the professional work environment as a member of a marginal sub-professional labor force.

Pan's chapter reports on data from interviews with sixty-three women law students. The majority of these interviewees are Asian-American (n=25) or Latina (n=22), and Pan focuses on these women's experiences with gendered and racialized assumptions and prejudices in law school. The study describes a male- and White-dominated environment, in which women of color face assumptions related to both their gender and their racial/ethnic identity and the interactive effects of these characteristics. The result is an experience of "typecast socialization," which entails negotiating presumptions about professional seriousness vis-a-vis family obligations, pigeonholing as "angry women of color," and particular familial pressures linked to their intersecting gender and racial/ethnic identities. The chapter adds a valuable level of analysis by comparing the experiences of women of color students at two very different law schools: one nationally ranked as a top 20 law school, and one a much less selective Tier 4 law school. Pan notes that students at the less prestigious school are more likely to bring "real world" experience with them. These students also have comparatively greater access to role models and mentors evidencing career success. These resources prove valuable in dealing with the law school environment. The author draws on her research findings to offer suggestions for how law schools can enhance support for students who are women of color.

Like Pan, Seron engages with issues of intersectionality in the experiences of women of color preparing for professional careers, focusing specifically on professional diversity in STEM fields (science, technology, engineering, and mathematics). Her chapter reports on a subset (n=9) of the author and her colleagues' ongoing longitudinal study of racial/ethnic minority women who aspire to careers in engineering (see Cech et al. 2011 for a discussion of the larger study). The chapter explores the experiences of women of color who hope to achieve careers in a professional field that is noted for a particular cultural tendency toward patriarchy and racialized patterns of thought and behavior. Women of color find themselves in a "double-bind" in their experiences within this cultural environment, owing to their combined status as both racial/ethnic and gender minorities. The interviewees for this study – four Black, four Asian-American, and one Latina – are graduates of prestigious undergraduate institutions. As a group, they represent an exception to the general trend of attrition that plagues women of color in STEM fields, as eight of the nine remain in a STEM field, and the ninth in another area of scientific research. Seron's analysis points to the importance of class in explaining these women's relative success. They enjoyed substantial advantages in life: most of their parents were professionals, and each had exceptional educational opportunities. While a small sample, the detailed life histories of these women indicate the power of capital associated with class privilege to provide a "ladder" to overcome impediments posed by gender and racial/ethnic background. This piece reminds us that, while wealth may be the most obvious source of the intergenerational reproduction of advantage, well-educated, professional parents often pass a host of other opportunities and resources on to their children that other parents may be unable to provide.

The two chapters on race/ethnicity and class in the UK legal profession complement the chapters on American women of color. First, Webley and her coauthors analyze findings from seventy-seven interviews with aspiring lawyers. Their study points to the central role of educational credentialism in perpetuating professional inequalities in England and Wales. The primary proxies that firms use as markers of prospective employees' excellence are often functionally discriminatory toward BAME (Black and Minority Ethnic) and women candidates.

Firms – especially elite firms – place major emphasis on the perceived quality of one's university training, overwhelmingly preferring candidates from Oxford and Cambridge, along with other prestigious educational credentials, extracurriculars, and unpaid work history. These experiences provide the opportunity for young people to acquire cultural and social capital, which strongly advance a candidates' case with prospective employers. Those who are already advantaged have disproportionate access to crucial qualification-enhancing environments. This pattern serves to reproduce class disadvantage for others. The authors suggest that a move away from reliance on these proxies for candidates' "quality" and toward more meaningful assessments of skills and capacities is necessary to improve equity in access to legal careers.

Sommerlad focuses on the development of a "precariat" within the English legal profession. As the professional elite, particularly in the corporate sector, continues to be controlled by a narrow segment of mostly upper class White men, a distinct sub-profession dedicated to low-prestige, low-paying "support work" has emerged. This group is a compelling instance of the type of marginal, "non-tournament" lawyers that Galanter and Henderson (2008) identify as a key characteristic of the new core-and-periphery firm model emerging in the elite legal services industry. Sommerlad's precariat exists on the periphery of the legal profession proper, working long hours with little chance of advancement and generally no job security. Interviews with young lawyers provide examples of low-level employees being exploited for a few months of unpaid work before being unceremoniously "ditched," or possibly moved into a low-paying position doing administrative work. Overwhelmingly, firms are filling these positions by drawing from relatively vulnerable segments of the legal services labor market, including racial/ethnic minority candidates and graduates of less prestigious schools. Many of these individuals, having amassed considerable debt in acquiring educational credentials, feel trapped in exploitative "factory" work environments. Sommerlad's analysis offers an interesting counterpoint to most of this volume, and work on inequality in the professions in general: rather than focusing on the processes by which members of underrepresented groups are blocked from inclusion in mainstream professions, she addresses the emergence of a sub-profession in which historically underrepresented groups are overrepresented. Thus, facing barriers to participation in the top – or even the middle – of the professional world, disadvantaged candidates may be brought into the work environment through a "basement door," serving as marginalized labor without access to the major rewards of professional careers or meaningful opportunities for advancement. Sommerlad's analysis demonstrates the importance of looking at diversity across the range of legal work settings. The legal precariat reintroduces in a new form the marginalization of certain kinds of legal work and certain kinds of legal workers – a process largely ignored in the diversity rhetoric of leaders of elite professional firms.

III   Inequality and opportunity in the careers of diverse attorneys

Section III turns to what happens in the career trajectories of diverse attorneys after they gain entry to the world of law practice. These chapters track how careers both flourish and founder, examining the organizational characteristics, work conditions, and personal networks that drive patterns of inequality, as well as the failures of employee development programs aimed at creating fair opportunity structures. This section demonstrates the uphill battle that workplace culture and business practices impose on women and people of color, and suggests what types of systemic changes may be needed for progress toward equal opportunity.

First, Kay and Gorman report results from their analyses of nearly 1,400 offices of large law firms from across the United States. They compare the representation of racial/ethnic minorities in various law firm settings, examining trends across firm size, profitability, and office distribution, as well as the impact of developmental practices and cultural values within law firms on minority representation. The authors find that minorities are underrepresented as a whole in large, corporate-centric firms – with all racial/ethnic minorities combined constituting 8.9% of lawyers and less than 5% of partners – but larger and more profitable firms tend to have higher levels of racial/ethnic diversity. Diversity is concentrated in branch offices to a greater degree than principal offices, and in offices with higher associate-to-partner ratios. The chapter's analysis of firm policies and practices provides a sobering account of the (in)effectiveness of many employee development programs. The authors address the hypothesis that racial/ethnic minority and White attorneys enter firms with roughly equivalent capacities and resources, but that greater opportunity and organizational investment provide advantages to White lawyers (see Kay, Hagan, and Parker 2009; Wilkins and Gulati 1996). In their observations of formal and informal employee development programs – focused on general programs rather than minority-centered interventions – they reach the perhaps surprising conclusion that efforts to "level the playing field" by offering equitable access to networking and training opportunities did not improve minority advancement, as measured by minorities' representation in partnership. Some interventions even had negative effects. The authors offer thoughts on how to interpret this result and make suggestions for how future research might help address how best to foster minority advancement.

Aiken and Regan's study combines the benefits of longitudinal research with the deep, rich insights made possible by closely tracking lawyers' careers. Specifically, the authors track job mobility over time in a sample of 1,618 alumni from one prominent law school, examining differences between women and men lawyers. Building on prior research showing that women face lower rates of partnership and higher rates of downward mobility and professional attrition, the authors seek to improve understanding of gender disparities in the legal profession by directly addressing the mechanisms of job turnover in law, and how those mechanisms vary between men and women lawyers. Their findings provide further evidence of the gender inequities in work-life balance. In all legal sectors, and controlling for a range of potentially relevant factors, women are more likely than men to leave a job because of family responsibilities, including accommodating a significant other. Men, on the other hand, are more likely to leave jobs for perceived opportunities to build their practices or enjoy greater financial rewards. The authors discuss their findings across practice settings and consider implications for practical interventions.

Briscoe and von Nordenflycht's research highlights the significance of network ties and interpersonal connections in the course of professional careers. The authors present the results of a quantitative case study of a large corporate law firm, addressing the key question of how partners build the body of client revenue under their control. The sizes of partners' books of business are closely related to their power and status within firms (not to mention their personal incomes) (Nelson 1988). Understanding the factors that determine the size of these client revenue streams is crucial to understanding stratification in law firm leadership and the legal profession more broadly. The authors identify two broad strategies for building client relationships: *inheritance*, in which intra-firm relationships are exploited to gain control of, and possibly expand, existing client relationships, as older partners retire or otherwise move on professionally; and *rainmaking*, in which partners utilize external social networks, as well as work on building those networks, to bring in new clientele. The authors point out that the rainmaking strategy entails more manifest risk to those partners who utilize it, as it necessitates establishing new relationships, with associated investments of time and effort, investing time in non-billable networking, and dealing with competition from other firms. Taking advantage of an unusually rich dataset of billing and personnel records from the firm in question, the authors show that, in general, both inheritance and rainmaking strategies are effective in increasing client revenues. However, for female and racial/ethnic minority partners, the story is quite different: not only is the inheritance strategy less effective, it is actually negatively associated with client billings. The rainmaking strategy, on the other hand, proved more effective for female than for male partners. The authors note the implications of a homophily effect – a tendency to connect with others similar to oneself (see McPherson, Smith-Lovin, and Cook 2001) – for explaining their findings, and discuss how their results should steer practical interventions and future research.

Like Briscoe and von Nordenflycht, Rider, Sterling, and Tan point toward the impact of network ties on career trajectories, through a creative and innovative study of career mobility in the wake of firm dissolutions. As it did other sectors of the US economy, the Great Recession hit the legal profession hard. The authors note Black lawyers' generally higher levels of attrition from the profession and lower levels of achieving partnership, the growth of interorganizational mobility in legal careers, and the importance of social networks to professional success. Their research takes advantage of the natural quasi-experiment provided by the failures of large firms in 2008 and 2009 to access a unique large sample of roughly contemporaneous interfirm transitions – more than 1,400 lawyers who lost their jobs in the wake of the economic downturn. The individuals affected by unanticipated firm dissolutions offer something close to a random sample of lawyers working in large, business-oriented firms, in contrast to lawyers who leave their firms for other, probably nonrandom, reasons (Rider 2014). Their findings provide clear evidence of racial advantages – and disadvantages – in job transitions. Compared to lawyers of other racial/ethnic backgrounds, Black lawyers were less likely to find new employment, with Black associates the least likely of any group to find a new job, and White partners the most likely. Further, the quality of new positions varied across racial/ethnic groups: White lawyers had the best chances of finding work at profitable and prestigious firms, and Black lawyers had worse chances than White lawyers and lawyers of other races. The authors' analysis implies that variation in networks of professional relationships between lawyers of different races may help explain the observed differences in career mobility outcomes.

In the last chapter in this section, Dawe and Dinovitzer report results from the After the JD Study, a nationally representative sample of US lawyers who passed the bar in 2000. Dawe and Dinovitzer examine the effect of immigrant status on lawyers' earnings. Focusing their investigation on lawyers with foreign-born parents, they find that these "immigrant offspring" earn significantly more than third-plus generation lawyers, a finding congruent with their greater representation in urban markets, longer average working hours, and higher likelihood of elite law school pedigrees. Overall, the authors observe that Asian-American lawyers are the highest paid of any racial/ethnic group in the AJD sample, controlling for a range of relevant factors. Asian-Americans are also far more likely than their counterparts of other racial/ethnic backgrounds to be immigrant offspring: more than 83% of Asian-American lawyers are the children of foreign-born parents, compared to just 47.5% of Latino lawyers, 19% of Black lawyers, and 4.1% of White lawyers. While Asian-American lawyers who are the children of immigrants see reduced earnings relative to Asian-Americans who are not the children of immigrants, they still earn more than the next most prosperous group, third-plus generation White lawyers. These findings complicate a straight-forward account of minority disadvantage; the authors discuss their results and the intersectionality of race/ethnicity and immigrant status for Asian-American lawyers in terms of theories of model minorities, stereotype promise, and ethnic capital. This finding adds complexity to our understanding of professional labor market demographics, and points to the significance of less-obvious forms of diversity such as immigrant status in shaping patterns of inequality and opportunity in professional careers.[6]

CONCLUSION

This volume advances the theoretical and empirical understanding of the evolving character of diversity and inequality in legal and

---

[6] It is worth noting that this chapter also suggests the potential value of more fine-grained demographic categorizations: the broad racial/ethnic categories used here are likely masking considerable variation between lawyers of different national origins, which could further illuminate the phenomena under investigation.

professional careers. Corporate clients, elite suppliers of professional services, and elite professional associations all publicly espouse commitment to diversity in hiring and promotion. Despite these rhetorical commitments to diversity and inclusion, upper-class White men continue to enjoy substantial advantages over their counterparts in the law and other Anglo-American professions. The research contained in this volume details the persistence of professional inequalities by race, gender, and class, with a particular focus on elite professional sectors. While direct forms of discrimination continue to operate in the professional world, as they do elsewhere in society, this volume sheds light upon more subtle mechanisms at work in reproducing professional inequality, such as credentialism and network ties. It also points toward new forms of inequality emerging in correspondence to changes in professional services organizations and labor markets.

There are some exceptions to patterns in professional stratification, as we see in the work of Seron, Dawe and Dinovitzer, and Briscoe and von Nordenflycht. It is striking that where we see such exceptions, they are not the products of diversity initiatives, but of the deployment of various forms of capital by new entrants to professional fields. We do not infer from such studies that pro-diversity programs have no effect; we simply do not have an adequate set of rigorous evaluations to judge the many diversity programs in operation today. What we can infer is that barriers to equal opportunity are endemic to the cultures of schools and workplaces, labor market structures, and practices of hiring, promotion, and work assignment. More than public commitments to diversity and workplace sensitivity trainings will be required to systematically dismantle such barriers.

Continued progress toward equality requires moving beyond these first steps on the road to diversity and inclusion and engaging with the tough, systemic issues to which these authors call our attention. Much work remains to be done, both in policy and in research. The inequalities documented in these chapters are deeply rooted in society more broadly and in the social structure of professional services markets and organizations. Effectiveness in diversity interventions requires sensitivity to both general patterns of social stratification exemplified in professional settings and mechanisms of inequality specific to professional careers. We hope the chapters contained here inspire further efforts to understand what will bring about diversity in practice, as well as programs that can make meaningful progress toward that goal.

REFERENCES

Abel, Richard L. 1989. *American Lawyers*. New York: Oxford University Press.

Ackroyd, Stephen, and Daniel Muzio. 2007. "The Reconstructed Professional Firm: Explaining Change in English Legal Practices." *Organization Studies* 28(5):729–747.

American Bar Association. 2013. "Law School Faculty & Staff by Ethnicity and Gender." Chicago, IL: Section of Legal Education and Admissions to the Bar.

Armstrong, Elizabeth A., and Laura T. Hamilton. 2013. *Paying for the Party: How College Maintains Inequality*. Cambridge, MA: Harvard University Press.

Auerbach, Jerold S. 1976. *Unequal Justice*. New York: Oxford University Press.

Bertrand, Marianne, Dolly Chugh, and Sendhil Mullainathan. 2005. "Implicit Discrimination." *American Economic Review* 95(2):94–98.

Bertrand, Marianne, and Sendhil Mullainathan. 2004. "Are Emily and Greg More Employable than Lakisha and Jamal? A Field Experiment on Labor Market Discrimination." *American Economic Review* 94(4):991-1013.

Bianchi, Suzanne M., Melissa A. Milkie, Liana C. Sayer, and John P. Robinson. 2000. "Is Anyone Doing the Housework? Trends in the Gender Division of Household Labor." *Social Forces* 79(1):191–228.

Blau, Francine D., and Lawrence M. Khan. 2007. "The Gender Pay Gap: Have Women Gone as Far as They Can?" *Academy of Management Perspectives* 21(1):7-23.

Carlin, Jerome. 1962. *Lawyers on Their Own: A Study of Individual Practitioners in Chicago*. New Brunswick, NJ: Rutgers University Press.

——— 1966. *Lawyers' Ethics: A Survey of the New York City Bar*. New York: Russell Sage Foundation.

Cech, Erin, Brian Rubineau, Susan Silbey, and Carroll Seron. 2011. "Professional Role Confidence and Gendered Persistence in Engineering." *American Sociological Review* 76(5):641–666.

Chambliss, Elizabeth. 1997. "Organizational Determinants of Law Firm Integration." *American University Law Review* 46:669–746.

Cohen, Geoffrey L., Julio Garcia, Nancy Apfel, and Allison Master. 2006. "Reducing the Racial Achievement Gap: A Social-Psychological Intervention." *Science* 313(5791):1307–1310.

Cohen, Geoffrey L., Julio Garcia, Valerie Purdie-Vaughns, Nancy Apfel, and Patricia Brzustoski. 2009. "Recursive Processes in Self-Affirmation: Intervening to Close the Minority Achievement Gap." *Science* 324 (5925):400–403.

Collins, Randall. 1979. *The Credential Society: An Historical Sociology of Education and Stratification*. New York: Academic Press.

Condron, Dennis J., and Vincent J. Roscigno. 2003. "Disparities Within: Unequal Spending and Achievement in an Urban School District." *Sociology of Education* 76(1):18–36.

Dalessandro, Susan P., Lisa C. Anthony, and Lynda M. Reese. 2012. "LSAT Performance with Regional, Gender, and Racial/Ethnic Breakdowns: 2005–2006 through 2011–2012 Testing Years." Law School Admission Council: LSAT Technical Report 12–03.

Darling-Hammond, Linda. 2007. "Race, Inequality, and Educational Accountability: The Irony of 'No Child Left Behind'." *Race, Ethnicity, and Education* 10(3):245–260.

Dinovitzer, Ronit, David B. Wilkins, and Robert L. Nelson. 2014. "Race and Ethnicity." In *After the JD III: Third Results from a National Study of Legal Careers*. Chicago, IL: American Bar Foundation and NALP Foundation for Law Career Research and Education.

Drake, Monique, and Evan Parker-Stephen. 2013. "The Rainmaking Study: How Lawyers' Personality Traits and Behaviors Drive Successful Client Development." Bloomington, IN: Lawyer Metrics.

Epstein, Cynthia Fuchs. 1981. *Women in Law*. New York: Basic Books.

Galanter, Marc, and William Henderson. 2008. "The Elastic Tournament: A Second Transformation of the Big Law Firm." *Stanford Law Review* 60(6):1867–929.

Galanter, Marc, and Thomas Palay. 1991. *Tournament of Lawyers: The Transformation of the Big Law Firm*. Chicago, IL: University of Chicago Press.

George, Tracey E., and Albert H. Yoon. 2014. "The Labor Market for New Law Professors." *Journal of Empirical Legal Studies* 11(1):1–38.

Godsil, Rachel D., Stuart Banner, and Jerry Kang. 2012. "Brief of Experimental Psychologists as Amici Curiae in Support of Respondents." In *Fisher v. Texas*: Supreme Court of the United States.

Goyette, Kimberly A. and Ann L. Mullen. 2006. "Who Studies the Arts and Sciences? Social Background and the Choice and Consequences of Undergraduate Field of Study." *Journal of Higher Education* 77(3):497–538.

Greenwald, Anthony G., Debbie E. McGhee, and Jordan L. K. Schwartz. 1998. "Measuring Individual Differences in Implicit Cognition: The Implicit Association Test." *Journal of Personality and Social Psychology* 74(6):1464–1480.

Greenwald, Anthony G., T. Andrew Poehlman, Eric Luis Uhlmann, and Mahzarin R. Banaji. 2009. "Understanding and Using the Implicit Association Test: III. Meta-analysis of Predictive Validity." *Journal of Personality and Social Psychology* 97(1):17–41.

Heinz, John P., and Edward O. Laumann. 1982. *Chicago Lawyers: The Social Structure of the Bar*. New York: Russell Sage and Basic Books.

Heinz, John P., Robert L. Nelson, Rebecca L. Sandefur, and Edward O. Laumann. 2005. *Urban Lawyers: The New Social Structure of the Bar.* Chicago, IL: University Of Chicago Press.

Henderson, William D. 2014. "From Big Law to Lean Law." *International Review of Law and Economics* 38:5–16.

Hochschild, Arlie. 2012 [1989]. *The Second Shift: Working Families and the Revolution at Home.* New York: Penguin.

Hull, Kathleen E., and Robert L. Nelson. 2000. "Assimilation, Choice, or Constraint? Testing Theories of Gender Differences in the Careers of Lawyers." *Social Forces* 79(1):229–264.

Humes, Karen R., Nicholas A. Jones, and Roberto R. Ramirez. 2011. "Overview of Race and Hispanic Origin: 2010." *2010 Census Briefs.* Washington, DC: US Census Bureau.

Kang, Jerry, Mark Bennett, Devon Carbado, Pam Casey, Nilanjana Dasgupta, David Faigman, Rachel D. Godsil, Anthony G. Greenwald, Justin Levinson, and Jennifer Mnookin. 2012. "Implicit Bias in the Courtroom." *UCLA Law Review* 59:1124–1186.

Katz, Daniel Martin, Joshua R. Gubler, Jon Zelner, Michael J. Bommarito II, Eric Provins, and Eitan Ingall. 2011. "Reproduction of Hierarchy? A Social Network Analysis of the American Law Professoriate." *Journal of Legal Education* 61(1):1–28.

Kay, Fiona M., John Hagan, and Patricia Parker. 2009. "Principals in Practice: The Importance of Mentorship in the Early Stages of Career Development." *Law & Policy* 31(1):69–110.

Kim, James S., and Gail L. Sunderman. 2005. "Measuring Academic Proficiency under the No Child Left Behind Act: Implications for Educational Equity." *Educational Researcher* 34(8):3–13.

King, Ryan D., Kecia R. Johnson, and Kelly McGeever. 2010. "Demography of the Legal Profession and Racial Disparities in Sentencing." *Law & Society Review* 44(1):1–32.

Kozol, Jonathan. 1991. *Savage Inequalities: Children in America's Schools.* New York: Random House.

Kronberg, Anne-Kathrin. 2013. "Stay or Leave? Externalization of Job Mobility and the Effect on the U.S. Gender Earnings Gap, 1979–2009." *Social Forces* 91(4):1117–1146.

Ladinsky, Jack. 1963. "Careers of Lawyers, Law Practice, and Legal Institutions." *American Sociological Review*: 47–54.

Larson, Magali Sartaggi 1977. *The Rise of Professionalism: A Sociological Analysis.* Berkeley, CA: University of California Press.

Ma, Yingyi. 2009. "Family Socioeconomic Status, Parental Involvement, and College Major Choices–Gender, Race/Ethnic, and Nativity Patterns." *Sociological Perspectives* 52(2):210–234.

Massey, Douglas, and LiErin Probasco. 2010. "Divergent Streams: Race-Gender Achievement Gaps at Selective Colleges and Universities." *DuBois Review* 7(1):219–246.

McNeil, Linda. 2000. *Contradictions of School Reform: Educational Costs of Standardized Testing*. New York: Routledge.

McPherson, Miller, Lynn Smith-Lovin, and James M. Cook. 2001. "Birds of a Feather: Homophily in Social Networks." *Annual Review of Sociology* 27:415–444.

Meier, Deborah, and George H. Wood (eds.). 2004. *Many Children Left Behind: How the No Child Left Behind Act is Damaging Our Children and Our Schools*. Boston, MA: Beacon Press.

Merluzzi, Jennifer, and Damon Phillips. 2013. "Elite MBAs and the Curse of the Smart (Single) Woman: How Marital Status and Talent in Math Affect Early Career Promotions." Paper presented at *Pursuing Diverse Talent in Legal and Professional Services: Research Within and Across Professions, Organizations, and Societies*. Chicago, IL: American Bar Foundation.

Michelson, Ethan. 2012. "Women in the Legal Profession, 1970–2010: A Study of the Global Supply of Lawyers." *Indiana Journal of Global Legal Studies* 20: 1071–1137.

Milligan, Patricia A., Brian Levine, Linda Chen, and Katie Edkins. 2014. *When Women Thrive, Businesses Thrive*. New York: Mercer North America.

NALP. 2014. *Jobs & JDs: Employment and Salaries of New Law Graduates, Class of 2013*. Washington, DC: National Association for Law Placement.

Nance, Jason P., and Paul E. Madsen. 2014. "Diversity in the Legal Profession: A Comparative Empirical Analysis." Paper presented at *Bias and Law: Third Annual Conference of the Research Group on Legal Diversity*. Chicago, IL: American Bar Foundation.

Nelson, Robert L. 1988. *Partners with Power: The Social Transformation of the Large Law Firm*. Berkeley and Los Angeles, CA: University of California Press.

——— 1994. "The Future of American Lawyers: A Demographic Profile of a Changing Profession in a Changing Society." *Case Western Reserve Law Review* 44:345–406.

Nussbaumer, John R, and E. Chris Johnson. 2011. "The Door to Law School." *University of Massachusetts Roundtable Symposium Law Journal* 6:1–35.

Pager, Devah, Bruce Western, and Bart Bonikowski. 2009. "Discrimination in a Low-Wage Labor Market: A Field Experiment." *American Sociological Review* 74:777–799.

Randall, Vernellia. 2006. "The Misuse of the LSAT: Discrimination Against Blacks and Other Minorities in Law School Admissions." *St. John's Law Review* 107:107–151.

Reardon, Sean F., Allison Atteberry, Nicole Arshan, and Michal Kurlaender. 2009. "Effects of the California High School Exit Exam on Student Persistence, Achievement, and Graduation." *Institute for Research on Education Policy & Practice Work Paper*: Stanford University.

Rider, Christopher. 2014. "Educational Credentials, Hiring, and Intra-Occupational Inequality: Evidence from Law Firm Dissolutions." *Working paper*: Georgetown University.

Ridgeway, Ceclia. 2011. *Framed by Gender: How Gender Inequality Persists in the Modern World*. New York: Oxford University Press.

Rivera, Lauren A. 2011. "Ivies, Extracurriculars, and Exclusion: Elite Employers' Use of Educational Credentials." *Research in Social Stratification and Mobility* 29:71–90.

——— 2012. "Hiring as Cultural Matching: The Case of Elite Professional Service Firms" *American Sociological Review* 77:999–1022.

——— 2015. *Pedigree: How Elite Students Get Elite Jobs*. Princeton, NJ: Princeton University Press.

Ryan, James E. 2004. "The Perverse Incentives of the No Child Left Behind Act." *NYU Law Review* 79:932–989.

Sandefur, Rebecca, and Robert Nelson. 2014. "Demographic Characteristics of AJD Lawyers—A Trend Over Time." Pp. 19–24 in *After the JD III: Third Results from a National Study of Legal Careers*. Chicago, IL: American Bar Foundation and NALP Foundation for Law Career Research and Education.

Seron, Carroll, and Kerry Ferris. 1995. "Negotiating Professionalism: The Gendered Social Capital of Flexible Time." *Work & Occupations* 22:22–48.

Silver, Carole, Nicole De Bruin Phelan, and Mikaela Rabinowitz. 2009. "Between Diffusion and Distinctiveness in Globalization: US Law Firms Go Glocal." *Georgetown Journal of Legal Ethics* 22:1431–1471.

Smigel, Erwin O. 1964. *The Wall Street Lawyer*. New York: Free Press.

Snyder, Thomas D., and Sally A. Dillow. 2011. *Digest of Education Statistics 2010*. Alexandria, VA: National Center for Education Statistics, U.S. Department of Education.

Sorensen, Jesper B. 2004. "The Organizational Demography of Racial Employment Segregation." *American Journal of Sociology* 110(3):626–671.

Spencer, Steven J., Claude M. Steele, and Diane M. Quinn. 1999. "Stereotype Threat and Women's Math Performance." *Journal of Experimental Social Psychology* 35(1):4–28.

Steele, Claude M. 2010. *Whistling Vivaldi: How Stereotypes Affect Us and What We Can Do*: New York.

Steele, Claude M., and Joshua Aronson. 1995. "Stereotype Threat and the Intellectual Test Performance of African Americans." *Journal of Personality and Social Psychology* 69(5):797–811.

Sterling, Joyce, Rebecca Sandefur, and Gabriele Plickert. 2014. "Gender." in *After the JD III: Third Results from a National Study of Legal Careers*. Chicago, IL: American Bar Foundation and NALP Foundation for Law Career Research and Education.

Susskind, Richard E. 2008. *The End of Lawyers? Rethinking the Nature of Legal Services*. New York: Oxford University Press.

    2013. *Tomorrow's Lawyers: An Introduction to Your Future*. New York: Oxford University Press.

Tilcsik, András. 2011. "Pride and Prejudice: Employment Discrimination against Openly Gay Men in the United States1." *American Journal of Sociology* 117(2):586–626.

US Census Bureau. 2012. "Statistical Abstract of the United States: 2012." Washington, DC: US Census Bureau.

Wightman, Linda F. 1998. "LSAC National Longitudinal Bar Passage Study." in *LSAC Research Report Series*. Newtown, PA: Law School Admission Council.

Wilkins, David B. 2014. "Making Global Lawyers: Legal Practice, Legal Education, and the Paradox of Professional Distinctiveness." HLS Center on the Legal Profession Research Paper No. 2014–26: Available at SSRN: http://ssrn.com/abstract=2526789.

Wilkins, David B., and G. Mitu Gulati. 1996. "Why Are There So Few Black Lawyers in Corporate Law Firms? An Institutional Analysis." *California Law Review* 84(3):493–625.

Williams, Joan C. 2010. *Reshaping the Work-Family Debate: Why Men and Class Matter*. Cambridge, MA: Harvard University Press.

1

RHETORIC AND REALITIES

THE ACTION AFTER THE CALL

What general counsels say about the value of diversity in legal purchasing decisions in the years following the "Call to Action"

DAVID B. WILKINS[1] AND YOUNG-KYU KIM[2]

I   INTRODUCTION*

In 2004, Richard Palmore, then general counsel (GC) of Sara Lee, issued his now famous "Call to Action." Working through the Association for Corporate Council, the Call was designed to get companies to use their leverage as important clients to pressure the law firms with whom they work to increase their efforts to recruit, retain, and promote women and minority lawyers by making diversity a significant factor in hiring decisions. Specifically, the Call asked GCs to sign a statement in which they pledge:

> that we will make decisions regarding which law firms represent our companies based in significant part on the diversity performance of the firms. We intend to look for opportunities for firms we regularly use which positively distinguish themselves in this area. We further intend to end or limit our relationships with firms whose performance consistently evidences a lack of meaningful interest in being diverse
>
> (Call to Action 2004).

* Thanks to participants at the Research Group on Legal Diversity and at faculty workshops at Temple and Duke for helpful comments on prior drafts.
[1] Lester Kissel, Professor of Law, Vice Dean for Global Initiatives on the Legal Profession, and Faculty Director of the Center on the Legal Profession, Harvard Law School.
[2] Assistant Professor, Korea University Business School and Affiliated Faculty Member of the Center on the Legal Profession, Harvard Law School.

Judged by the number of signatories, the Call to Action has been an impressive success. Eventually, well over 100 leading GCs signed the Call (Coyoca 2010). Moreover, Palmore's efforts have inspired other companies to adopt their own diversity initiatives. Many companies, including major purchasers of legal services such as Wal-Mart, Microsoft, and Sears have enacted supplier diversity initiatives that expressly include legal services (Institute for Inclusion in the Legal Profession 2011). Indeed, it is fair to say that in the years following the Call to Action, it has become standard practice for GCs of US companies to state that they consider diversity to be one of the most important criteria in evaluating law firms. As proof of this reality, GCs frequently point to the fact that they require firms with whom they do business to file regular reports detailing the firm's diversity statistics, including the number of women and minorities working on the company's matters (Minority Corporate Counsel Association 2014).

Notwithstanding the fact that leading GCs are nearly unanimous in claiming that diversity is one of the most important factors in law firm hiring decisions, however, there is very little empirical evidence to back up this claim. Indeed, given the relatively modest progress that most large law firms have made in improving their overall diversity statistics in the decade since the Call was issued, one might argue that what evidence there is appears to lead in the opposite direction (Minority Corporate Counsel Association 2014). Yet, as diversity advocates would undoubtedly point out, the overall diversity in law firms is at best a crude measure of the impact of programs such as the Call to Action, since these numbers say nothing about what law firm diversity would look like in the absence of these programs.

This chapter makes a modest contribution to providing an empirical assessment of the Call to Action's effectiveness. It does so by examining the results of a quantitative and qualitative study conducted in 2006–7 of what the GCs of S&P 500 companies say about the criteria they employ when hiring – and terminating – law firms in "very significant" legal matters (Coates, DeStefano, Nanda, and Wilkins 2010). In the course of this study, one of the factors that we asked these GCs to evaluate is the importance of diversity in making hiring decisions of this kind. As a result, we have direct evidence of how these important decision makers claim to evaluate diversity in the years shortly following the Call to Action in the cases that matter to large companies – and to the law firms who seek to represent these companies – the most.

In the following pages, we use these data to investigate three questions that we believe are central to evaluating the success of the Call to Action, and of corporate diversity initiatives generally: (1) How do GCs rate the importance of diversity relative to other factors in deciding whether to hire outside counsel for important legal work? (2) are there differences among companies in the relative importance they place on diversity, and if so, what factors might explain these differences? and (3) does the manner in which companies value diversity have implications for other aspects of the relationship between companies and law firms?

Although we believe that the data we present shed important light on each of these questions, we acknowledge that we cannot definitively resolve any of these issues – let alone the more general question of whether the Call to Action has been an effective tool for promoting diversity in large law firms. To answer that question, one would have to collect data about whether companies that have signed the Call actually hire more women and minority lawyers than those who do not, and for what kinds of legal work. To our knowledge, there is no systematic empirical study that provides data on these questions, although what evidence there is tends to confirm the view that even companies with express diversity policies appear only to "use diversity as one of many criteria in selecting outside counsel and rarely implement strategies to reward in-house counsel for choosing diverse outside counsel or bestow more business upon those firms that are succeeding in their diversity endeavors" (Institute for Inclusion in the Legal Profession 2011: 8). Because the survey we conducted was not designed to investigate the effectiveness of the Call to Action – or, for that matter, the issue of diversity at all – we do not address this bottom line question. Instead, consistent with our goal of understanding what GCs say about how they purchase legal services for "very important" work, we examine the impact of the Call to Action solely from the perspective of what these chief legal officers said about the importance they attached to diversity in law firm hiring decisions of this kind.

Nevertheless, four aspects of our study distinguish it from the typical reports about the "business case for diversity" published in the popular and legal press. First, as indicated earlier, the questions we asked about diversity were in the context of a broader investigation about legal purchasing decisions in which diversity was simply one of a number of possible factors that we asked GCs to consider. As a result, our research subjects were not primed to think about their commitment to diversity in a manner that might otherwise have biased their responses in favor of demonstrating a greater commitment to this criterion. Second, precisely because we collected information about a broad range of issues that might affect the legal purchasing decisions of large companies, we are able to cross-tabulate what GCs say about diversity with other factors about the substance and process of legal purchasing that arguably shed light on the role that diversity actually plays in this context. Third, our sample of companies is far bigger – and far more representative – than the ones typically used in other diversity studies, or in studies about legal purchasing generally (Coates et al. 2010). Our sample contains a broadly representative mix of S&P 500 companies, and the quantitative and qualitative data we collected come solely from GCs. This allows us to compare (and contrast) companies that are of broadly similar size, and to obtain the opinion of the person with final authority over legal purchasing decisions.[3] Finally, in addition to the data from our surveys and interviews, we have also collected additional information about the companies in our sample with respect to diversity and other issues. We are therefore able to make correlations between what GCs told us about their commitment to diversity and other actions that these companies have taken that may reflect on the credibility of these responses.

The rest of this chapter proceeds in five additional parts. Part II briefly recounts the history leading up to the Call to Action, and underscores why one should not take at face value the near-universal support for diversity GCs express. Part III then describes our study and the other data we have collected about corporate diversity. Parts IV and

---

[3] The fact that GCs have the final authority over legal purchasing decisions, however, does not mean that they are the ones who actually hire outside counsel in every case. As many GCs told us in our interviews, law firm hiring decisions are often made by deputy or assistant GCs, particularly in less important matters, and occasionally by senior business executives or even the board of directors in the most significant matters. However, in the kind of "very significant" matters that we address in this chapter, even if the GC does not make the actual hiring decision (which they frequently do), these chief legal officers play a central role in establishing the criteria which subordinates in the legal department and outside counsel are obligated to follow, and exercise final review over whether these criteria have been properly applied in particular cases. This supervision and review is likely to be particularly important with respect to diversity issues, since more junior attorneys within the legal department may be hesitant to be seen as giving this criterion more weight than what they perceive that the GC would give, especially in the kind of "very significant" cases we are addressing (Wilkins 1999).

V use these data to investigate the first two questions identified earlier—how GCs rate diversity relative to other factors when making legal purchasing decisions, and what factors about the company, its legal department or its experience with law firms, appear to influence this judgment. Finally, Part VI addresses our third research question by providing some concluding thoughts exploring the implications of what we have learned about the role of diversity in legal purchasing decisions for other aspects of the evolving relationship between large companies and their outside law firms.

II DEMAND SIDE DIVERSITY INITIATIVES

When Richard Palmore issued the Call to Action in 2004, he was following in a tradition that had begun almost two decades earlier: using the purchasing power of corporate clients to change the internal diversity practices of large law firms.[4] The tradition began in 1988 with a letter written by Harry Pearce, the GC of General Motors (GM) – at the time still the largest and most iconic American corporation – to all of the company's outside lawyers. The letter was written at the urging of Dennis Archer, the newly appointed chair of the American Bar Association (ABA) Commission on Minorities in the Profession, to dispel the popular belief, as stated in the ABA's report, that large companies did not want minorities working on their legal matters. Pearce's letter expressly disavowed this notion and urged firms to include "minority lawyers at the requisite level of experience" on all GM matters (Wilkins and Gulati 1996: 596, note 394). In conjunction with the Minority Counsel Demonstration Project, which sought to introduce corporate counsel to minority lawyers, the goal was to increase the income and status of minority lawyers by increasing demand for their services.

These efforts met with mixed success. After an initial flurry of activity, many companies did little more than send the same letter every year to their outside counsel expressing support for diversity and requesting information about their practices, but doing little else, particularly with respect to important work and work given to large law firms (Wilkins 2004). As a result, notwithstanding commitments

---

[4] Indeed, Palmore's Call has even deeper roots in President Kennedy's famous 1963 Call to Action urging the organized bar to support his civil rights initiatives. The bar responded by creating The Lawyers Committee for Civil Rights Under Law (Connell 1997; Hunter 1963).

expressed by GM and other corporate clients, lawyers working in major law firms remained overwhelmingly white and male, particularly at the partnership level (Wilkins and Gulati 1996).

In part because of the limited success of these early efforts, Charles Morgan, the GC of Bell South, wrote another letter in 1999 urging companies to use their purchasing power to pressure law firms to increase their internal diversity (Fritz 2002). This time, Morgan expressly urged his fellow GCs to demonstrate their commitment to this issue by signing on to the letter.

On one level, the response was overwhelming. Eventually, more than 350 companies signed Morgan's letter (Fritz 2002). At the level of implementation, however, the results continued to be mixed. Although many companies talked more about diversity, there was still little evidence that they were willing to actually put their money where their mouths were, particularly with respect to taking away work from firms whose diversity numbers failed to improve from year to year (Wilkins 2004).

It was against this background that Richard Palmore issued his Call to Action. Palmore's efforts differed from those that had gone before in two important respects. First, Palmore was the first person spearheading such an effort that had direct experience with the issues at hand (Levs 2004). As one of the first black partners in any major law firm in Chicago before moving in-house at Sara Lee, Palmore had experienced firsthand the difficulties of being a minority lawyer in a corporate firm – and the frustrations associated with the prior efforts outlined earlier. Second, perhaps because of this history, Palmore's initiative was the first to expressly urge companies to make diversity a significant criterion in hiring outside counsel for important matters, and to get tough with firms who failed to make progress (Levs 2004).

As indicated earlier, in terms of getting buy-in from major companies, the results appear to be impressive. Not only have more than one hundred companies signed the Call, but supplier diversity initiatives and diversity reporting requirements have become *de rigueur* in virtually every major company in America (Institute for Inclusion in the Legal Profession 2011). This emphasis by companies seems to have had an effect on law firms as well. Virtually every law firm now has a diversity initiative or committee, with many employing full-time diversity professionals (Minority Corporate Counsel Association 2009). When asked about the driving force behind these programs, both participants and observers alike most frequently respond that these initiatives are the result of "client demand" (Mahoney 2013). Indeed, the claim that clients want diversity is at the core of the "business case" that has become the accepted rationale for why large law firms should care about diversity (Mahoney 2013).

The numbers, however, do not appear to match the rhetoric. Although the percentage of women and minorities in large law firms has increased in the years since the Call to Action, the overall level of diversity in large law firms is far lower than one might have expected given all of the attention that has been focused on these issues since 2004 (Institute for Legal Inclusion 2011). Indeed, there is evidence that progress on diversity has stalled in recent years, particularly at the partner level. This is clearly true for minorities, where the percentage of black and Hispanic partners has actually declined in recent years (Triedman 2014). Although there has been more progress with respect to women, even here the overall percentage of female partners in large law firms remains stuck at just over 17%, with the percentage of those who hold important leadership roles significantly lower than even this figure (Smith 2014). Indeed, even the percentage of women making partner in the cohort of lawyers who entered the bar as late as 2000 is far below that of their male counterparts (Dinovitzer et al. 2009: 63–65).

It is against this backdrop that we hope to contribute to understanding the disjunction between the rhetoric of corporate America's commitment to diversity and the reality of what has – and has not – been achieved.

III   RESEARCH DESIGN

The current research is part of a larger study conducted in 2006–7 on the legal purchasing decisions of large companies (hereinafter "Corporate Purchasing Project" or CPP) (Coates et al. 2010). The goal of this study was to determine the factors that GCs consider when hiring, firing, and managing the work of outside counsel in "very significant" legal matters.[5] To investigate this issue, we conduct a bipartite research

---

[5] We defined "very significant" legal matters as matters with a strategic importance to the company, such as litigation with a very high risk liability exposure, high risk regulatory matters, and large mergers and acquisitions transactions – but not of such importance that they would qualify as "bet the company" work that only occurs very infrequently.

strategy consisting of (1) interviews with 44 GCs from large companies likely to be heavy users of outside legal services (primarily in the areas of investment banking, commercial banking, pharmaceuticals, and oil and gas; our interview sample consists of more than two-thirds of GCs in S&P 500 companies in these sectors) and (2) a survey sent to all of the GCs of S&P 500 companies which elicited a 28% response rate (n=139). Interviews were conducted in person or by phone for approximately one hour, and in all but five cases were recorded.[6] Questions were semi-structured and designed to elicit information about how the GC selected outside counsel for very significant matters, as well as general information about the structure and operation of the company's legal department. The survey, which consisted of twenty-eight largely closed-ended questions, was administered either by mail or over the phone. Taking account of the overlap between the interview and survey samples, we ended up with 166 unique respondents, one-third of all S&P 500 companies, and between 30 and 40% of the revenues, assets, and employees represented by the companies in this index.

Both the interview and the survey sample are broadly representative of the entire S&P 500. In order to test this proposition, we compared respondents versus non-respondents in both samples with respect to their assets, employees, and net income. In all respects both groups were roughly equivalent. To the extent that there were significant differences on other measures, survey respondents tended to have larger revenue, legal departments, and demand for legal services than non-respondents, which suggests that we captured a disproportionate share of the largest consumers of legal services in our sample. All things considered, this should make our conclusions about the value large companies place on diversity likely to be even more robust.

IV WHAT GCS SAY ABOUT THE VALUE OF DIVERSITY RELATIVE TO OTHER FACTORS

In examining the legal purchasing decisions of large companies, CPP was designed to test the accuracy of what had become the prevailing wisdom about the relationship between companies and law firms. According to this standard account, since the 1980s companies have moved aggressively to reduce their legal costs by breaking up the cozy

---

[6] In cases where the respondent declined to be recorded, the interviewer took contemporaneous notes.

long-term relationships that most of these organizations traditionally had with their primary outside law firm (Wilkins 2010). The mechanism by which clients have accomplished this goal is simple. Rather than relying on outside law firms to "diagnose" the company's legal problems and find the appropriate specialist to whom the problem should be "referred," corporations began building sophisticated and extensive in-house legal staffs to perform these functions internally (Gilson 1990). In addition to competing directly with law firms by "taking work inside," these sophisticated purchasing agents have also taken control of the process by which the legal work that continues to go to outside firms is sourced, priced, and supervised. Law firms are now made to compete for legal work through "bake offs" and "beauty contests" in which the winners are selected through some combination of price and the expertise of the specific lawyers who are going to work on the particular matter. In this brave new world, the story goes, GCs hire "lawyers, not firms," with the kind of long-term relationships that used to dominate the corporate legal market just a generation before quickly going the way of the dinosaur. Indeed, in the eyes of many observers, companies would soon be purchasing legal services the same way that they procured paper clips, in a spot market in which every new piece of work is put out for competitive bidding, with price and specific expertise as the dominant criteria for selection (Lin 2003).

By the time we began talking to GCs in 2006, this standard account had clearly become the dominant framework by which GCs, outside firms, and academic commentators viewed the legal marketplace – and for good reason. In-house legal departments were among the fastest growing segment of the U.S. legal profession, with many companies boasting law departments that were as large as some of the largest law firms (Wilkins 2010). Moreover, "requests for proposals" (RFPs) and other standard procurement tools had become ubiquitous in the legal market, with some companies like General Electric's GE Capital even moving to online auctions to choose their outside legal vendors (Lin 2003). Finally, there was plenty of evidence that GCs were placing great value on the individual lawyers who were working on their matters, often following "star" lawyers from firm to firm as these rainmakers pursued ever larger profits and platforms in the increasingly active lateral partner market (Coates et al. 2010). Notwithstanding these trends, we questioned whether the corporate legal market was really heading for a spot-contracting procurement model, particularly for important work.

1 It's the relationship, stupid!

Two additional trends occurring in parallel with those described previously suggested that the situation might be more complex than the simple story portrayed by the maxim "we hire lawyers, not firms." First, after spending most of the 1980s and 1990s breaking apart their long-term relationships with law firms, thereby multiplying their number of law firm relationships, many of these same companies had begun instituting measures explicitly designed to move in the opposite direction. Following the lead of DuPont Chemical Company, which in the early 1990s reduced the number of law firms performing legal services for the company' from 350 to 35, a growing body of companies adopted "preferred provider" programs and other measures that resulted in the overwhelming percentage of outside legal spending going to a relatively small number of law firms (Sander 2006). Second, along with this "convergence," GCs began to articulate an additional maxim just as loudly and forcefully as "we hire lawyers, not firms." "What we really want," GCs increasingly proclaimed, "are lawyers who understand our business" (Wilkins 2010). As a result, companies began looking for law firms who were willing – and able – to "partner" with in-house lawyers and business leaders to integrate legal services into the company's business practices to achieve its long term goals. Collectively, these trends seemed likely to increase, rather than decrease, the value of long-term relationships with outside counsel.

Both the qualitative and quantitative data we collected in CPP confirmed that relationships at the firm level continue to be important to GCs, particularly when hiring – and firing – lawyers for very significant work. Thus, 60% of the companies in our sample gave 80% or more of their legal work to twenty-five or fewer firms, with 39% concentrating this work in ten or fewer law firms (Coates et al. 2010). Moreover, the relationships companies have with the law firms who make their list of preferred providers are "stickier" than the spot-contracting model of "lawyers, not firms" would lead one to suspect. GCs frequently claim that they routinely dismiss law firms that fail to provide top-quality service, or refuse to conform to their policies. The GCs we interviewed often made similar claims. As one GC explained, citing a sentiment that we heard frequently explaining refusals to work with firms that failed to follow their directions: "They were very unresponsive about consulting with us and taking directions from our in-house staff.... Why would you hire a firm that thinks some of that is beneath them" (Confidential Interview). Although we have

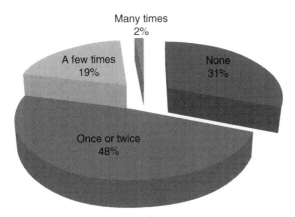

Figure 2.1 "Important" Law Firm Relationships Terminated in Previous Three Years

no doubt that instances where law firms are dismissed for providing bad service or failing to follow directions occur with far greater frequency than they did in the past, the more systematic data from our survey suggest that such dismissals are still relatively rare. Thus as Figure 2.1 indicates, when asked how many times the respondent had terminated an "important" law firm relationship in the last three years, 79% reported that they had done so less than "once or twice," with almost one-third (31%) acknowledging that they had not done so at all. Only 21% claimed that they "frequently" terminated these important relationships.

Indeed, although GCs often talk about evaluating lawyers on the basis of their expertise or performance, the overwhelming majority conceded that "relationships" were still the most important criteria in deciding whether to hire or fire law firms for very significant matters. As a crude – but compelling – indication of this importance, consider the word cloud from our qualitative interview transcripts presented in Figure 2.2. The word most commonly used by GCs to characterize their law firm purchasing decisions is "relationship." A plethora of specific quotations from the interviews confirm this importance. As one typical GC put it: "I tend not to do a beauty contest where firms come in with RFPs and proposals." Instead, this GC acknowledged, "I try to identify firms with whom we already have relationships, that on a personality basis, the way they do their business, the type of people they have, meshed up with us" (Confidential Interview).

The survey data also confirm the primary importance of relationships in hiring law firms for very significant matters, as well as the other

Figure 2.2 Interview Word Cloud
Source: Wordle.net

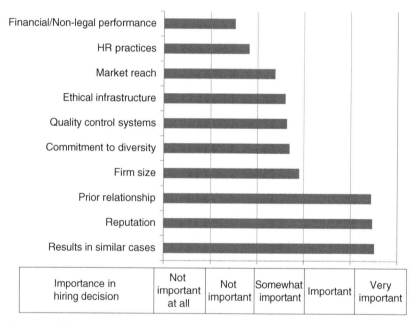

Importance in hiring decision	Not important at all	Not important	Somewhat important	Important	Very important

Figure 2.3 Hiring Factors

prominent words on our word cloud: "know[ledge]" and prior "work." The survey asked GCs to rate the importance they attached to 19 different factors about law firms when hiring counsel in very significant matters on a scale of 1 (not important at all) to 5 (very important). Figure 2.3 depicts the survey responses. (For simplicity we have reduced the 19 categories to 10 by grouping similar categories together.)

As Figure 2.3 underscores, three factors – results in similar cases, reputation, and prior relationship – dominate all other considerations. Indeed, these three are the only ones to cross the threshold of being considered "important" – let alone "very important" – by respondents. All other considerations, including a firm's commitment to diversity, are at best of secondary importance in this context. Indeed, many of the considerations to which law firms often pay the most attention, such as whether the firm has an office in a particular location ("market reach") or its profitability ("financial performance"), are not even considered "somewhat important" by the GCs in our survey sample when making important hiring decisions. Once again, notwithstanding all of the pronouncements about law firms being just like "any other vendors," whose services can be bought on a spot-contracting model, the CPP underscores that law is still – as it has always been – fundamentally a relationship business.

This result should not be surprising. To operate effectively, spot-contracting markets depend upon a high degree of commodification, or, at minimum, relatively reliable and easily observable measures of quality. As indicated earlier, the important reduction in information asymmetry between companies and outside law firms brought about by what the legal scholar Robert Rosen has accurately dubbed "the inside counsel movement" has indeed produced a great deal of commodification in the corporate legal services market over the last twenty years (Rosen 1989). When the stakes are high, however, most GCs continue to view legal services as what economists call a "credence good," where even the most sophisticated consumers have a difficult time evaluating quality outcomes *ex ante*, or measuring results *ex post* (Cheserant and Harnay 2013). In such a market, reputation and experience typically remain very important. And relationship-driven markets tend to produce homogeneity, not diversity.

2   Relationships favor established players

Given the characteristics of the market for high-end legal services, it is not surprising that diversity is at best of secondary importance. By definition, these are cases in which the stakes are high – both for the company, and for the GC making the legal purchasing decision. Even the most enthusiastic diversity advocate would concede that a law firm's commitment to diversity is a proxy for its ability to produce quality results – a proxy whose correlation with actual outcomes is likely to be even harder to demonstrate in this setting than it is in the corporate arena where the "business case" for diversity was originally formed (Wilkins 2004). Although it is important to recognize that the three factors upon which the GCs in our survey claim to rely on the most – "results in similar cases," "reputation," and "prior experience" – are proxies as well, it is entirely predictable that GCs, most of whom probably got their current jobs based on similar factors, would consider these proxies more directly related to quality than diversity, at least on average.

The fact that most companies now concentrate their legal spending in a relatively small number of providers is likely to reinforce this tendency. Although convergence is popularly portrayed as a way to reduce cost and drive discounts in so-called "commodity" work, most companies have realized that if they want their preferred providers to do their low-end work effectively, they also have to give them a reasonable chance at landing more lucrative premium assignments (Wilkins 2010). Thus, companies now give a significant portion of their work in very significant cases to law firms with which they have existing relationships – relationships that, as we have seen, are rarely terminated (Coates et al. 2010). As a result, GCs have less ability to make hiring decisions based on diversity. The fewer the number of firms that a company uses, the less room it has to give new work to another firm that may have better diversity numbers.

To test this hypothesis, we compared the importance that a GC assigned to a firm's commitment to diversity in making the company's last hiring decision in a very significant matter, with the number of preferred providers receiving 80% or more of the company's outside legal spending in the last year. As Table 2.1 indicates, we found that the greater the number of preferred providers, the more likely it was that the GC ranked commitment to diversity highly in making hiring decisions. This correlation certainly does not conclusively prove that greater convergence tends to impede diversity efforts. It is possible, for example, that companies that use a greater number of preferred providers may do so in order to engage specialty law firms in areas such as employment discrimination where diversity tends to be more highly valued (Wilkins 2004).[7] Nevertheless, this correlation does confirm minority lawyers' anecdotal but common reports of GCs saying that they would like to give them more business, but find it difficult to do so

---

[7] We return later to the implications of employment discrimination litigation on the degree to which a company is likely to value a law firm's commitment to diversity.

TABLE 2.1   Number of Preferred Providers and Commitment to Diversity[8]

	Companies with Less than 10 Preferred Providers	Companies with 10 or More Preferred Providers	P-value
Firm's commitment to diversity	2.40 (N=65)	2.95 (N=74)	$Pr(|T| > |t|) = 0.0135$

(Commitment to diversity measured on a scale from 1 to 5.)

because "adding" a minority lawyer or firm often means "taking business away" from one of the company's preferred providers (Wilkins 2008).

Indeed, given all of the focus on economics and competitiveness issues in law firms in recent years, perhaps the most surprising result to emerge from this aspect of our survey is the relative weight that GCs claim to attach to a firm's diversity vis-à-vis other, more highly touted law firm characteristics. Thus as Figure 2.3 underscores, GCs state that they view a law firm's commitment to diversity as being as important as the firm's overall size and internal quality control systems – and significantly more important than factors such as whether the firm has an office in a particular jurisdiction or its overall financial performance, factors that managing partners have traditionally spent considerably more time worrying about than diversity. Indeed, as our qualitative interviews reveal, the issue that managing partners tend to focus on the most in recent years – maintaining high profits per partner and other indicia of financial performance – are viewed by many GCs as "not important at all" to their hiring decisions, or worse as counting against a given law firm being hired. As one interviewee wryly noted: "My goal is not to buy every partner a Mercedes Benz" (Confidential Interview).

Moreover, given the typical profile of the lawyers who rise to the level of GC in S&P 500 companies, it is also predictable that these experienced players rely heavily on their own judgment and experience in assessing the factors that they consider important in hiring counsel for very significant matters. To test this proposition, we asked survey respondents where they obtained the information that they used to

[8] The average company in our survey gives 80% of its legal work to ten law firms (Coates et al. 2010).

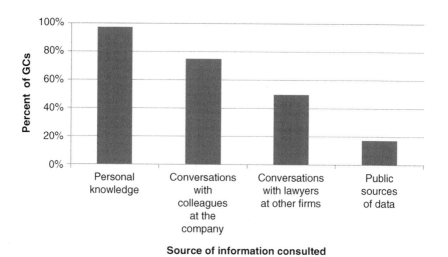

Figure 2.4 Sources of Information

select the last law firm the company hired from among four options: personal knowledge, conversations with others in the company, conversations with informants outside of the company, and publicly available sources of data. Respondents were asked to check all that apply. Figure 2.4 displays our results.

Given that most GCs now have significant experience – frequently including many years working in law firms before moving in-house – we were not surprised to see that virtually all respondents reported that they relied on their own personal knowledge of the legal market when selecting outside counsel for very significant work. Indeed, the only surprising aspect of this particular result is that approximately 3% of GCs did not rely at least in part on their own personal knowledge the last time they selected outside counsel. Although there is no way of knowing for sure, we suspect that this is an artifact of the increasing specialization of the market for high-end corporate legal services that makes it difficult for even the most sophisticated consumer to know "the best" provider in every legal area. This specialization makes the fact that 97% of GCs do claim to have personal knowledge about the outside counsel that they hire even more remarkable – a fact that we will discuss next.

Nor is it surprising that 75% of GCs supplement their personal knowledge with conversations with lawyers and business leaders within the company. One of the principal goals of the in-house counsel movement was to increase the breadth and depth of in-house know-ledge (Wilkins 2010). One would expect GCs to rely heavily on this expertise, as well as to at least consult with business leaders who often have their own relationships with outside counsel.

What is surprising is how few GCs consulted with anyone else. As Figure 2.4 underscores, only 50% of GCs consulted with anyone outside of their companies to collect information about the charac-teristics or quality of the law firms that they hired for very signifi-cant work. Even more importantly, only about one-fifth of GCs admitted to looking at any of the many existing public sources of data about law firm quality before making their decisions. Consider-ing the prominence that lawyers and law firms give to displaying their rankings in Chambers & Partners, the American Lawyer, and other prestigious rating services on their websites, this relatively low percentage suggests a fundamental mismatch between law firm marketing and the purchasing decisions of corporate clients, at least for important work.

More importantly for present purposes, the fact that the majority of GCs rely exclusively on their own knowledge and the advice of those with whom they are already close when making important legal pur-chasing decisions underscores that this is still a very insular process. Once again, as diversity advocates have long emphasized, insularity tends to breed homogeneity. Countless studies by cognitive psycholo-gists demonstrate that, even in the absence of conscious bias, people are most likely to see "quality" in those who remind them of themselves (Banaji and Greenwald 2013; Kang and Lane 2010). This is particu-larly true where the decision makers are acting under time pressure with relatively little information, and where the stakes are high (Banaji and Greenwald 2013); in other words, precisely the conditions that typic-ally characterize legal purchasing decisions in very significant matters. Given this reality, it is once again predictable that even GCs who express a sincere commitment to placing diversity among their top criteria when selecting outside counsel might behave differently when making actual purchasing decisions in high stakes matters.

3   Second is better than nothing – but unlikely to produce great change

In sum, our survey reveals that diversity is a solidly second order consideration for the average GC of a large company when hiring law firms for very significant work. Once again, the impact of this finding should not be underestimated. In close cases where firms are similar on "results in similar cases," "reputation," and "prior relationship," a secondary factor such as commitment to diversity could very well tip the balance, even if GCs tend to view this consideration as only "somewhat important" in the abstract. Indeed, many law firms have a difficult time distinguishing themselves on the primary factors identified in our survey – as one typical GC we interviewed succinctly put it: "Law firms spend too much time telling you how good they are. But if you weren't good I wouldn't be talking to you!" (Confidential Interview). Second order considerations can thus potentially provide "visible rankable signals" of quality that can sometimes prove to be decisive (Wilkins and Gulati 1996). As another GC put it: "I think there was a firm or two that was on the bubble that made it on to the list of eight because of strengths in diversity and pro bono and civil justice reform. They really stood out on these issues" (Confidential Interview).

Nevertheless, these results also confirm the frustration that many minority and female lawyers have expressed about initiatives like the Call to Action ever since GM's Harry Smith wrote the first letter seeking to improve law firm diversity through demand-side pressure. Summing up this frustration, a black GC in a major company who had recently left a large law firm put the point bluntly: "I think people are lying when they tell you that [diversity] is at the very heart of outside counsel selection process ... I never got selected because [a company] was trying to increase the diversity of their pool of providers" (Confidential Interview).

Even companies that claimed to value diversity often were candid about the fact that they were unlikely to terminate a relationship on this basis. As the GC of an investment bank put it "I don't think we have ever terminated a relationship exclusively because they have not been able to achieve the right kind of diversity mix" (Confidential Interview). Instead, the GC went on to say, "we hope that by asking [about diversity] that we at least continue to keep the pressure on firms in general to develop their diversity programs" (Confidential Interview).

In the end, our data confirm what many have long argued. When the stakes are high, diversity considerations will frequently be swamped by other factors that decision makers consider more important. To put the point somewhat crudely, when a CEO such as Lloyd Blankfein of Goldman Sachs or Jamie Dimon of J.P. Morgan Chase receives a subpoena to testify before Congress, he is unlikely to run out of his office screaming: "Get me the most diverse team of lawyers you can find!" Instead he will virtually always say: "get me the *best* lawyers you can find." While there is no inherent *contradiction* between diversity and merit, many of the GCs currently making legal purchasing decisions are not convinced that there is an inherent *positive relationship* between diversity and merit either (Wilkins 2004). The fact that 45% of our respondents claimed that diversity was either "not very important" or "not important at all" in hiring law firms for very significant work is stark evidence of this skepticism.

One of the things that distinguish CPP from other similar studies, however, is that ours is a relatively large sample. We therefore are able to compare respondents along a number of dimensions without losing the ability to generate meaningful results. As just indicated, 45% of respondents gave very little weight to diversity considerations. But this leaves 55% who report that a law firm's commitment to diversity is at least "somewhat important," with several suggesting that it is "important" or even "very important." Indeed, some of our interviewees stated that they not only used diversity as a very important criterion in hiring, but provided examples of where this factor was determinative in ending an important law firm relationship. As one respondent bluntly stated: "I have terminated a law firm over a disagreement with our view on the importance of diversity. We said it was important and they said it was not important to them, so we said thank you for being honest!" (Confidential Interview).

This variation in GCs' views about the importance of diversity raises an important – but difficult – question. Why do some GCs appear to value diversity much more highly than others in making legal purchasing decisions? Although much of this variation is undoubtedly due to the personal preferences and values of particular GCs, we wanted to know whether there were any more objective differences relating to characteristics of the company, GC, or decision making process that might help to explain this variation. The next part examines what our data tell us about how those GCs that valued diversity more highly differed from those who did not.

V WHY SOME GCS VALUE DIVERSITY MORE THAN OTHERS

To explore why some GCs are more likely to value diversity than others, we examined data on four hypotheses. The first follows directly from the logic underlying the Call to Action and other demand-side diversity initiatives. These initiatives start from the assumption that companies with a strong commitment to diversity will be more likely to convey that commitment to their outside law firms in a manner that will produce change. We therefore examine several indicia of a company's commitment to diversity to see whether those organizations that rank highly on these measures are also more likely to rank diversity more highly on the list of factors that they consider in making very significant law firm hiring decisions.

Our second hypothesis builds on one of the main reasons why many people believe that companies have become committed to diversity in the first place. As diversity advocates frequently point out, corporate America is far more diverse – with respect to both the demographics of the legal department and the organization as a whole – than the typical corporate law firm (Smith 2013). This increasing diversity, advocates assert, is driving companies to press suppliers such as law firms to focus on diversity as well. We test this hypothesis by examining whether companies that rate highly on various internal diversity metrics are also more likely to value diversity highly when hiring outside counsel for very significant matters.

The third hypothesis is related to another reason why companies arguably are ahead of law firms in their attention to diversity: visibility, Prominent organizations, whether in the private or the public sector, face important pressure to "look like America" with respect to the demographics of both their rank and file workers and their leadership. Organizations that fail to do so are subject to potential sanctions, either in the courts or in the court of public opinion. We therefore examine whether companies that are more visible, or have had visible issues with diversity, are more likely to value diversity more highly when making legal purchasing decisions.

Our final hypothesis examines whether the value a company places on diversity in hiring decisions is related to other aspects of the way that the company hires and fires law firms. Specifically, we ask whether companies that are less "insular" in their approach to law firm hiring, or less "satisfied" with existing relationships are more likely to value diversity more highly when making new hiring decisions in very significant matters. The next four sections explore each hypothesis in turn.

1 Commitment matters, but the more tangible the better
Are companies that have made an express commitment to diversity issues, or otherwise demonstrated a strong desire to promote the

TABLE 2.2   Perceived Importance of Diversity, Call to Action
Signatories vs. Others

	Not Important at All	Not So Important	Somewhat Important	Important	Very Important	Total
Signatories*	1	6	3	5	5	20
	(5%)	(30%)	(15%)	(25%)	(25%)	(100%)
Nonsignatories	34	22	31	24	8	119
	(29%)	(18%)	(26%)	(20%)	(7%)	(100%)

* If a company made a Call to Action signatory responses as of
December 1, 2004 (source: www.mcca.com/index.cfm?fuseaction=page
.viewpage&pageid=803)
Difference in the means between two groups in their ratings of a firm's
commitment in diversity is significant in the two-tailed test (3.35 for signatories
vs. 2.58 for non-signatories, p-value = 0.014)

interests of women and minorities, more likely to value a law firm's
commitment to diversity when hiring outside counsel for important
work? The question is not a frivolous one. Although it might seem
obvious that a company that expresses a strong commitment to diversity would be more likely to report that it is acting on this commitment,
there is unfortunately far too much evidence that signing pledges like
the Call to Action or receiving "diversity awards" is often simply
window dressing designed to put a more acceptable face on business
as usual. As indicated in Part II, a standard complaint by minority
lawyers about prior efforts similar to the Call to Action has been that
companies simply sign the pledge and do nothing. Indeed, those
responsible for getting GCs to endorse both the Pierce Letter and the
Morgan Letter have acknowledged that their policy was to take no
action against companies who did just that – not even taking their
names off the list of signatories (Wilkins 2004). It is therefore worth
examining whether our survey provides any evidence that the Call to
Action has produced more tangible results, at least with respect to the
value that GCs say that they place on diversity when they are not
expressly primed to tout their commitment to this issue.

To test this proposition, we compare the responses of companies in
our sample that signed the Call to Action with those that did not.
Table 2.2 indicates that at least with respect to the way that GCs
describe how they make hiring decisions in very significant cases, the

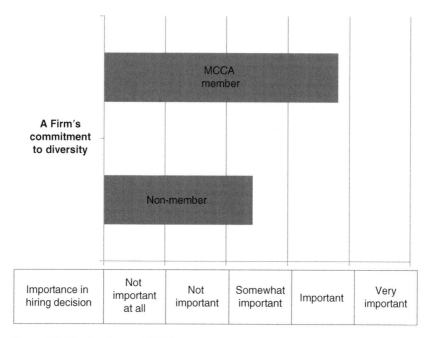

Figure 2.5 Membership in MCCA

Call to Action has fared better than some of its predecessors. Although the total number of signatories is small, those in our sample who have signed the Call to Action are significantly more likely to rank diversity as being either "important" or "very important" than those who did not sign. Assuming that GCs act on the basis of their stated preferences – once again, something that our study cannot determine – this increase in importance could tip the balance in favor of hiring firms with a demonstrated commitment to diversity for companies that have signed the pledge.

To test whether signing the Call to Action is more important than other ways in which a company might signal its commitment to diversity, we contrast the implications of signing the Call to Action with those of a company's decision to participate in another high profile diversity initiative: the Minority Corporate Counsel Association (MCCA). Figure 2.5 compares the value that companies who are and are not members of MCCA place on diversity. As with signing the Call to Action, becoming a member of MCCA is significantly correlated with a GC's likelihood of reporting that diversity was an important consideration in his or her last legal purchasing decision in a very significant matter. Indeed, being a member of MCCA appears to have an even greater impact on a GC's articulated preference for diversity than simply signing the Call to Action, with MCCA members assigning an average importance of 3.81 to this factor as compared to the 3.35 reported by signatories to the Call.

Although our data do not allow us to determine why companies that join MCCA appear to be even more likely than signatories to the Call to Action to value diversity highly when making law firm hiring decisions, aspects of these two forms of commitment might help to explain the difference. For example, there is considerable evidence that the higher and more sustained the level of commitment, the more likely it is to be translated into tangible action – particularly if the commitment involves a precious resource such as money or time (Ayres 2010; Thayler and Sunstein 2009). Like its predecessors, the Call to Action simply requires a signature, and an electronic one at that. There is nothing else required to keep the company's status "current," nor are there any benefits from "membership" other than an opportunity to affirm one's commitment to the cause. As Richard Palmore concedes, "the Call to Action was not an attempt to tell companies to act and react in a certain way" (Frater 2007). Rather, Palmore's "philosophy was that each company had to figure out how to implement the ideal" (Frater 2007). On the other hand, MCCA membership requires a company to pay dues, and gives the GC and other members of his or her department access to a broad range of information about bench-marking and best practices. As it boasts on its website: "The Minority Corporate Counsel Association (MCCA) is the premier source of learning, knowledge and future-oriented research on diversity and inclusion for the in-house legal profession. We provide resources, education, ideas and networking to enhance the power and perform-ance of the legal community" (Minority Corporate Counsel Associ-ation 2015). Given these differences, it is not surprising that companies who have made this deeper level of commitment also report placing more emphasis on diversity when selecting outside counsel.

2   Demographics matter as well – but the more senior the better

As we suggested at the outset, there is a reason why Richard Palmore has become such an effective champion for these issues. As one of the first black lawyers to both achieve partnership in a major law firm and become the GC at a major company, Palmore understands firsthand the importance of effective demand-side pressure to improving law firm diversity. Increasingly, Palmore is not alone. As of 2014, 113 of the GCs in the Fortune 500 are now women (Lum 2014). Fifty-four of these GCs are now racial minorities (Lum 2014).

In our interviews, we came away with the clear impression that women and minority GCs were much more likely to bring up diversity independently, and to discuss it as being more important, than were their white male counterparts. As the same black GC who expressed skepticism about corporate diversity initiatives when he was a lawyer put it: "I have probably recycled twenty or thirty job searches because the pool wasn't diverse enough. In some circumstances it was successful, but the amount of effort that's associated with it is really very, very substantial. We have made major strides in increasing the diversity of our law firms and leadership team" (Confidential Interview).

Given statements such as this, we wanted to compare the value that female and minority respondents to our survey placed on diversity in hiring decisions with the rankings of their white male counterparts. Unfortunately, the number of female and minority respondents to our survey was too small to draw any statistically meaningful conclusions. Interestingly, however, the small amount of evidence we have suggests that female and minority GCs appear to be no more likely to value diversity highly than their white male counterparts when ranking factors that influence outside counsel hiring in very significant matters. Although many may find even this tentative result surprising given the important role that many female and minority GCs have played in pursuing diversity, these lawyers also face important constraints in pushing diversity objectives, particularly when the stakes are high (Wilkins 1999). These constraints, however, are likely to be less binding in situations where a female or minority GC also has the support of top management in pursuing this objective (Heineman 2008). We therefore examine whether increased diversity in other parts of the organization's leadership affects the importance that a company places on a law firm's commitment to diversity.

Specifically, we look at two places within the corporate hierarchy where women and minorities might play an important role in setting the organization's priorities regarding diversity: the board of directors and the company's Named Officers and Executives (NOEs) as identified in its filings before the Securities and Exchange Commission (Gine 2007). Because of the difficulty of identifying race from the publicly available information at our disposal, we confine our analysis to whether the presence of women either on the board or among the company's NOEs affects the value that a given GC places on law firm diversity in legal purchasing decisions in very significant matters.

Not surprisingly, many of the companies in our sample neither had female board members as of 2006–7, nor women listed among the company's NOEs. Moreover, among those that did have female representation in these positions, that representation was often quite small. This token representation of women in leadership appears to have little or no impact on the GCs evaluation of the importance of diversity. For example, companies with only one female board member, or less than 10% female NOEs, were statistically identical in the weight that the GC accorded to a firm's commitment to diversity to companies with no women in these roles.

However, as the percentage of women on the board or top management increases, so does the weight that the GC states that he or she gives to law firm diversity in making hiring decisions in very significant cases. Table 2.3 and Figure 2.6 present these findings. Table 2.3 compares companies in which there are two or more female directors to companies with one or zero. The result is a more than 50% increase in the importance that the company's GC claims to place on diversity in hiring outside counsel. As Figure 2.6 underscores, the effect of having a greater number of women among the company's top executives is even more significant. When women constitute 10% of top management, the company's GC is more than twice as likely to rate diversity as important. In the admittedly rare circumstances where women

TABLE 2.3   Board Diversity

	Companies with Multiple Female Directors	Others	P-value
Pro Bono	2.31 (N=16)	1.73 (N=118)	$(\Pr(T > t) = 0.0186$
Firm's commitment to diversity	3.44 (N=16)	2.56 (N=118)	$\Pr(|T| > |t|) = 0.0113$
Ethical infrastructure	3.31 (N=16)	2.55 (N=118)	$\Pr(|T| > |t|) = 0.0259$
Results in similar cases	4.19 (N=16)	4.56 (N=118)	$(\Pr(T > t) = 0.0272$
Size of firm	3.50 (N=16)	2.84 (N=118)	$(\Pr(T > t) = 0.0051$

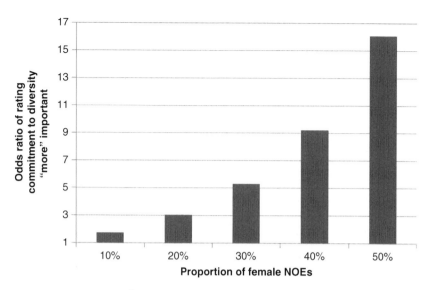

Figure 2.6 Female NOEs[9]

represent 50% or more of the company's top executives, the GC is a whopping 16 times more likely to value diversity as compared to companies with no female NOEs.

These findings are consistent with two standard arguments in the diversity literature. First, they underscore that diversity in an organization is more likely to make a difference once it reaches a "critical mass" (Kramer, Konard, and Erkut 2006). A single woman in the boardroom or in an executive office faces many barriers to changing the accepted ways of doing business. These barriers are often reduced if there is another woman in a position of power to support these initiatives.

---

[9] This figure is obtained by estimating an ordered-logit model to predict odds of rating a firm's commitment to diversity more important by one scale (e.g. "not important at all" to "not so important"; "somewhat important" to "important") with including a set of indicators of consulting with external sources of information in hiring decision, having termination experience, being an MCCA member, and making Fortune 500 list, as well as key figures such as legal budget, proportion of legal spending dedicated to outside counsel, number of internal counsels, number of preferred providers, and number of law firms in use. A company's industry and location are also controlled for in the model. In this model, the coefficient of the proportion of female NOEs is 5.5547. Based on this coefficient, odds of rating commitment to diversity more important by one scale becomes 16 to 1 when female executives consist of 50% of a company's NOEs. (exp [5.5547×0.5]=16.08). The odds ratio becomes even greater when we use the coefficient provided in the model in Table 2.5.

Indeed, even those who are skeptical of the importance of this cohort effect nevertheless concede that the place where it is most likely to have an effect is in the area of "employee relations," which plausibly covers issues of diversity (Broome, Conley, and Krawiec 2011: 1080).

This latter conclusion is bolstered by our data indicating that women who assume leadership positions may be on average likely to value different things than their male counterparts. Thus, in addition to being strongly correlated with the GC's commitment to diversity, Table 2.3 indicates that the number of female board members is also predictive of the value that the GC is likely to place on other factors, including the firm's commitment to pro bono work and its ethical infrastructure (e.g., whether the firm has an ombudsman or other mechanism for surfacing and resolving ethical problems). Indeed, although all GCs pay significant attention to the first three factors identified in Figure 2.3 – results in similar cases, reputation, and prior relationship – companies with two or more female board members are significantly *less* likely to value results in similar cases than those companies without significant female representation on the board. Although one should be very careful not to read too much into this kind of broad correlation (Dobbin and Jung 2011: 809–838) the fact that a GC's view about diversity is often clustered with other factors may foreshadow an important trend in how these decision makers are likely to evaluate law firms in the coming years, as we argue in Part VI.

3 Visibility increases scrutiny – and commitment

Sociologists have long argued that organizations that have a more secure place in prestige and profit hierarchies have more room to take risks in deviating from established practices, although they also may have less incentive to do so (Phillips and Zuckerman 2001). We therefore wanted to see whether consistent with this view, the GCs of larger or more successful companies are more likely to state that they value diversity than the GCs of other companies. Our data provide some interesting support for this theory.

Figure 2.7 compares the companies in our sample that are also among the Fortune 500 with those that are not.[10] As the data shows, Fortune

---

[10] To qualify as part of the Fortune 500, a company needs to satisfy the following conditions: (1) A stock must be publicly traded on the New York Stock Exchange, the American Stock Exchange, or the Nasdaq National Market; (2) It must have a minimum average daily trading volume of 100,000 shares during the 25 consecutive

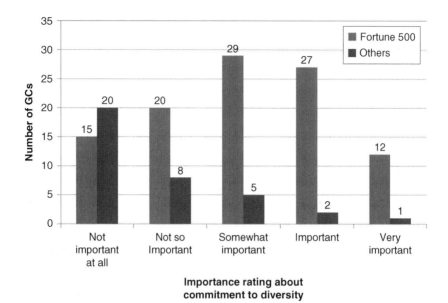

Figure 2.7 Fortune 500 vs. Other Companies

500 firms are arrayed along a normal bell-shaped curve around viewing diversity as somewhat important. However, S&P 500 firms that are not in the Fortune 500 are significantly more likely to view diversity as only marginally important or not important at all – and very unlikely to view this factor as important.

This result is not explained by size alone. Fortune 500 firms do tend to be larger than S&P companies not listed in that index, and they also do tend to use more law firms on average and have more preferred providers. As indicated earlier, companies with more preferred providers tend to place more weight on diversity, arguably because they have more freedom to do so. But even when we account for size, the correlation between being in the Fortune 500 and the GC's likelihood of ranking diversity as an important factor when making legal purchasing decisions persists.

trading days preceding initial inclusion; (3) It must have a minimum reported price equal to or in excess of $5 per share during that period; and (4) The company must have a minimum market capitalization equal to or in excess of $100 million during that period (Carty and Blank 2003).

TABLE 2.4 Companies that Have Been Sued vs. Those that Have Not

	Experienced Discrimination Lawsuits	NOT Experienced Discrimination Lawsuits	P-value
A firm's commitment to diversity	3.12 (N=41)	2.51 (N=98)	$Pr(\|T\| > \|t\|) = 0.0113$
# of employees	153 (N=40)	30 (N=95)	$Pr(\|T\| > \|t\|) = 0.0001$

Once again, our data cannot definitively answer why the GCs of Fortune 500 companies say that they care more about diversity than the GCs of other large organizations. The presence of this significant difference, however, does suggest that some of the factors previously identified by diversity theorists in the corporate context are indeed important. Not only do Fortune 500 companies tend to be larger in revenues, but they also are likely to have more employees, shareholders, and customers than other companies of similar size. All of these factors make these companies more visible, and therefore arguably more sensitive to being accused of failing to make progress on diversity goals. This is particularly true since accusations can often turn into lawsuits.

To test this proposition, we compared companies in our sample that had recently experienced important discrimination lawsuits with those who had not experienced such suits. As Table 2.4 indicates, companies that have recently been sued are significantly more likely to rate diversity as being more important than companies who have not been sued. Indeed as Figure 2.8 underscores, almost 50% (20/41) of the companies that experienced lawsuits answered that a firm's commitment to diversity is important or very important whereas less than a quarter (22/98 = 22%) of the companies that did not experience lawsuits placed a law firm's commitment to diversity in one of these categories.

The fact that some of the most important proponents of corporate demand-side diversity initiatives – for example., Wal-Mart, General Motors, Sears, McDonald's – are consumer-facing Fortune 500 companies that have faced highly visible employment discrimination litigation in recent years suggests that there is something to this correlation (Levit 2008). In addition, since companies in our sample that are not also in

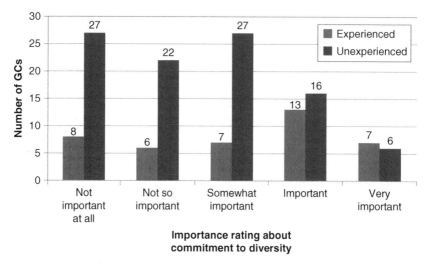

Figure 2.8 Discrimination Law Suits

the Fortune 500 also tend to have smaller GC offices and fewer preferred providers suggests that the relationships that these companies have with their outside counsel may be stickier and therefore more resistant to change around issues of diversity than the relationships in Fortune 500 companies. This brings us to our last hypothesis.

4   Breaking up the old relationships – part two

As Figure 2.4 indicates, legal purchasing decisions in very significant matters tend to be based on insular and limited information. GCs rely very heavily on their own personal knowledge and the knowledge of their immediate colleagues. Most pay relatively little attention even to the opinions of colleagues outside the company, let alone to publicly available data such as rankings. This inward focus undoubtedly reinforces the importance of existing relationships – and the relative unimportance of factors like diversity.

There are, however, a significant minority of GCs in our sample who claim to place more emphasis on "external sources," such as conversations with others outside the company or public rankings. Consequently, we can compare respondents who took an "internal" approach to legal purchasing decisions in these matters based exclusively on their own knowledge or the advice of those inside the company, with those who took a more "external" approach by also consulting informants outside of the organization or publicly available

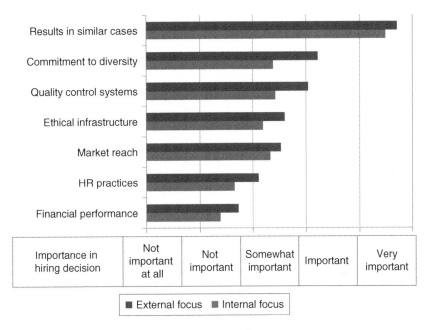

Figure 2.9 Internal vs. External Focus on Hiring Criteria

sources of information.[11] As Figure 2.9 indicates, GCs with "external" focus value diversity significantly more highly than their more inward looking peers. Indeed, with the exception of the three most important hiring criteria identified in Figure 2.3 – results in similar cases, reputation, and prior experience (which for ease of exposition we represent collectively in this Figure as "results in similar cases") – this group rates *every other firm level factor* more highly than those GCs who look exclusively inward. The differences are particularly great with respect to whether a law firm has effective internal quality control systems and whether it has effective ethical infrastructure to surface and report ethical problems – a similar clustering to the one reported previously with respect to the effect of having two or more female board members.

Nor, as Figure 2.10 documents, is this the only significant difference between internally and externally focused GCs. Although both sets of GCs terminate important law firm relationships infrequently (as documented in Figure 2.1), those who are more externally focused terminate

[11] No respondents relied exclusively on external sources.

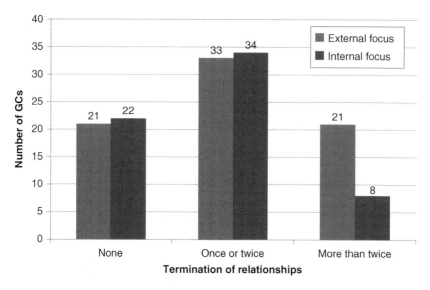

Figure 2.10 External Focus and Termination of Important Law Firm Relationships

these relationships significantly more often than those who look only internally when hiring outside counsel.

Moreover, those GCs who do terminate important law firm relationships frequently (two or more terminations within the three year period) are also significantly more focused on internal management issues. Figure 2.11 documents this relationship. GCs who have not terminated an important law firm relationship during the three year period overwhelmingly reported that internal quality control systems (e.g., cross-checking work product, close monitoring of associates) were at best "unimportant" in hiring law firms for very significant work, with 40% reporting that such issues were "not important at all." This finding is consistent with the early focus groups that we conducted before designing the survey, in which GCs overwhelmingly said that they considered such internal quality issues solely the responsibility of the law firm. But as Figure 2.11 highlights, those GCs who have recently found themselves in the position of terminating an important law firm relationship two or more times in the last three years report a very different attitude toward these internal controls. Fully two-thirds of all GCs who have experienced frequent law firm terminations rate internal quality control systems as being at least "somewhat important," with almost 30% rating these issues as "important" or "very important."

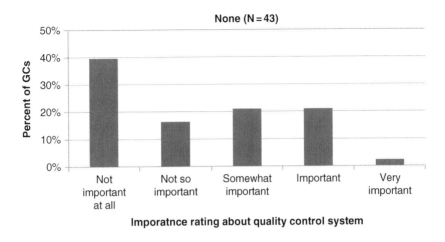

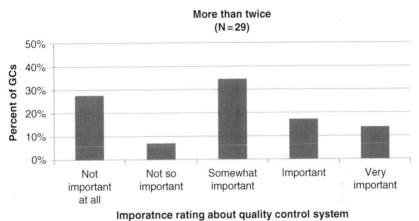

Figure 2.11 Termination of Relationships on Quality Control Systems

Given how the survey was constructed, we cannot say in which direction the causal arrow goes. Thus, one way to explain this difference is that GCs who find themselves in the position of having to terminate important law firm relationships that were formed primarily on the GC's own knowledge or the views of other members of the legal department are more likely to be interested in gathering additional information from knowledgeable informants outside of the company or publicly available sources of data when they make their next legal purchasing decision. Alternatively, it is plausible to imagine that when a GC who has not put much stock in rankings or the opinions of others outside of the company browses Chambers & Partners or talks to other

GCs and is surprised when he or she does not hear or see good things about the law firm that they typically use, that this GC will be more likely to look more closely at the performance of these established firms in a way that might lead to their termination. In either case, greater external focus is associated with higher rates of termination, which in turn are associated with a willingness to look beyond personal and institutional knowledge in making hiring decisions. And, as Figure 2.9 indicates, greater reliance on "external" factors such as the opinions of others or published rankings in turn produces greater attention to the internal structure and operation of law firms, including the firm's commitment to diversity – at least as articulated by the GC in describing how the company hires law firms in very significant matters. As indicated in Part II, the Call to Action has played a key role in creating an external environment in which discussions about diversity and diversity rankings are ubiquitous, thereby further encouraging those GCs who look externally when hiring outside counsel to place even more emphasis on this consideration. The facilitation of this feedback loop may turn out to be one of the primary benefits (albeit indirect) of diversity initiatives such as the Call to Action.

5   Interaction effects

To further explore the connections between our four hypotheses, and the relationship between these hypotheses and other variables that plausibly might affect a firm's commitment to diversity, we constructed an ordered logit model. Table 2.5 describes the model and presents its results. The first three cells describe three different combinations involving the interaction between whether a GC displayed "internal" versus "external" focus, and whether he or she reported that the company had terminated an important law firm relationship during the preceding three years: "external – termination," denotes GCs with an external focus who had terminated at least one important law firm relationship in the last three years; "internal – termination," denotes GCs with an internal focus who had made such a termination; and "internal-no termination," denotes internally focused GCs who had not made such a termination.[12] Cells (4)–(14) test the effects of eleven

---

[12] Our sample contains: (1) fifty-four GCs who have external focus and have terminated law firm relationships; (2) forty-two GCs who do NOT have external focus but have terminated law firm relationships; and (3) twenty-two GCs who do NOT have external focus and have NOT terminated law firm relationships frequently. We did

TABLE 2.5   Regression of External vs. Internal Focus and
Terminations

Dependent Variable	Importance Rating About Commitment to Diversity
(1) External – termination	2.69
	(0.8536)**
(2) Internal – termination	0.1839
	(0.7585)
(3) Internal – no termination	−1.7124
	(1.4016)
(4) MCAA Sponsor	3.7106
	(1.1149)**
(5) % Female NOEs	7.9567
	(1.9780)***
(6) Number of employees	0.0052
	(0.0042)
(7) Fortune 500	2.7605
	(0.8470)**
(8) Legal budget	0.0045
	(0.0049)
(9) % spending on outside counsel	0.0290
	(0.0149)
(10) # law firms in use	0.0029
	(0.0031)
(11) # preferred providers	0.0008
	(0.0266)
(12) # lawyers in the legal department	0.0009
	(0.0069)
(13) Industry-fixed effect	YES
(14) Location-fixed effect	YES
(15) N	109
(16) Pseudo R^2	0.3704

*** $p < 0.001$, ** $p < 0.01$, and * $p < 0.05$.

other variables in predicting the value that a GC claims to place
on diversity in hiring outside counsel in very significant matters:
(4) whether the company is a member of MCCA; (5) the number of
female NOEs listed in the company's public filings; (6) total number
of employees; (7) whether the company is listed in the Fortune 500;

not include the last possible combination "internal–termination," (twenty-one
GCs) as this is used as a baseline category, with which the odds of rating commitment to diversity more by one scale for each group is compared.

71

(8) total legal budget; (9) the percentage of that budget spent on outside counsel; (10) the total number of law firms the company reported using at the time of the survey; (11) total number of preferred providers the company reported having; (12) size of legal department; (13) the company's industry group; and (14) geographic location. Cells (13) and (14) are included to control for any industry- and location-specific factors that might affect views on diversity. Cells (15) and (16) report the total number of companies in the model (109)[13] and the degree to which the model fits our data (0.3704). As Table 2.5 demonstrates, the Model provides strong support for each of our four hypotheses, while further clarifying the relationship between them in predicting the value that a given GC claims to place on a firm's commitment to diversity when hiring outside counsel in very significant matters.

The first three cells examine our fourth hypothesis: that companies that are less insular in their hiring practices and less satisfied with the performance of their existing outside counsel are more likely to value diversity highly when hiring lawyers. As Figure 2.9 demonstrates, externally focused GCs are significantly more likely than internally focused GCs to highly value diversity. In this regression, we test whether this finding is affected by whether the GC has also recently terminated a firm. We therefore compare both externally and internally focused GCs who have experienced at least one law firm termination, and internally focused GCs who have no termination experience during the relevant period, with a reference group of externally focused GCs who have also not experienced terminations. As we see in cell (1), GCs who have an external focus and have experienced at least one law firm termination are significantly more likely to value diversity than those who have not experienced a termination. In contrast, internally focused GCs do not differ from the reference group, whether they have (2) or have not (3) experienced a law firm termination during the relevant period.

These results place an important gloss on the finding in Figure 2.9 that external focus increases the value placed on diversity. Although external focus is clearly important, those GCs who have also terminated a firm relationship within the last three years are especially likely to value diversity. Moreover, given that external focus is also correlated with the likelihood that a GC has experienced multiple terminations,

---

[13] For the purpose of this analysis, we eliminated any company that had missing data for any of the variables we considered. This resulted in our overall sample size being reduced from 139 companies to 109.

and that as Figure 2.11 demonstrates, terminating law firm relationships is also correlated with a greater emphasis on internal quality control systems, these findings have important implications that reach far beyond the issue of diversity. Specifically, they provide further support for the view that as the traditional insular model for hiring law firms becomes increasingly destabilized – in part, as a result of GCs' greater willingness to consult more external sources of information, and to terminate existing relationships based on that data – there will be growing pressure to create even more objective criteria for hiring outside counsel in significant matters (Wilkins 2015). We return to this overall trend in Part VI.

Cell (4) examines our first hypothesis, that the level of a firm's demonstrated commitment to diversity is likely to affect the GC's views. Specifically, Cell (4) further supports the results in Figure 2.5 that a company's membership in MCAA significantly increases the likelihood that the GC will highly value firm diversity, even when controlling for other factors. In fact, the model indicates that this factor is even more important than Figure 2.5 suggests. Controlling for the other factors in the model, if a company that is not a member of MCCA were to join the organization, the model predicts that it would increase the odds of the GC rating diversity a full point higher (e.g., from "somewhat important" to "important") by an astounding 40 times ($\exp[3.71\times1] = 40.85$). Clearly, belonging to an organization that requires both a financial commitment and offers important services can play a large role in at least elevating reported emphasis on diversity.

This finding has important implications for future diversity initiatives – including, ironically, Richard Palmore's own effort to continue what he started with the Call to Action. In 2008, Palmore founded the Leadership Council on Legal Diversity (LCLD) (Leadership Council on Legal Diversity 2015). Building on the momentum of the Call to Action, Palmore has created an organization that combines the success of signing up important companies (and now also law firms) that he achieved through the Call with the commitment and programing found at MCCA that the Call to Action did not include. Thus in addition to paying significant dues, companies and law firms wanting to join LCLD must commit to having the GC or managing partner personally be involved in LCLD's activities. Moreover, like MCCA, LCLD hosts a number of events designed to provide its members with information about best practices and to reinforce their commitment to achieving diversity goals. LCLD even offers fellowship programs in which GCs and managing partners identify promising women and minority candidates in their respective organizations and groom them for leadership roles. Although LCLD has only been fully operational for a few years, judging from the number of high profile GCs who are actively participating in the organization's activities, this initiative seems likely to do even better than MCCA at raising the salience of diversity issues among its members. Of course, as with all of the diversity initiatives we discuss in this chapter, whether this increased salience actually translates into increased law firm diversity remains to be seen.

Cell (5) examines our second hypothesis: that demographic diversity, particularly in leadership positions, has a positive effect on whether the GC values a firm's commitment to diversity when hiring outside counsel in very significant matters. Specifically, the model examines the effect of having a greater percentage of female NOEs on the value the GC claims to place on diversity. Consistent with Figure 2.6, the positive coefficient in cell (5) indicates that even taking account of other variables, this factor remains highly significant. Just as in other areas where organizations are trying to change their cultures, diversity in leadership appears to influence actors farther down the organizational chain of command.

Finally, the model in Table 2.5 also provides support for our third hypothesis: that higher company visibility increases the likelihood that the GC will highly value diversity. The positive coefficient in cell (7) indicates that even controlling for other factors, the GC of a Fortune 500 company is significantly more likely than the GC of a lower-profile S&P 500 company to report highly valuing diversity.

With the exception of these four factors – the combination of external focus and frequent terminations (1), MCCA membership (4), the percentage of female NOEs (5), and being a Fortune 500 company (7) – none of the other variables of interest in our model rise to the level of statistical significance. Of particular interest is the fact, as represented in cell (11), that after controlling for other factors, the number of law firms on a company's list of preferred providers loses its significance as a factor in explaining the value placed on diversity. As a result, while Table 2.1 does provide support for the oft-repeated claim by diversity theorists that the move toward reducing the number of preferred providers also reduces opportunities for minority and women lawyers, this trend may in the end be less important than other factors that incentivize GCs to change the way that they purchase legal services (external focus coupled with frequent terminations), or to value diversity more highly within existing relationship (e.g., membership in MCCA or similar organizations, having a meaningful percentage of women and minorities in top leadership positions, and/or the heightened concern about public perception that comes from being a more visible company).

Needless to say, understanding the precise relationship among these factors, as well as the role played by the issues of commitment, demography, visibility, and destabilization of existing relationships, will require far more in-depth analysis than we have offered here. Rather than providing a detailed conclusion, therefore, we close with some tentative thoughts about what this complex circle of information, expectation, and action might have to say about the important shift currently underway in relationships between large companies and law firms – a shift produced in part by demand-side diversity efforts such as the Call to Action.

VI THE FUTURE IS CALLING

One of the things that we found most striking about our initial focus group discussions for this project was how uninterested GCs were in the internal operation of the law firms to whom they give millions of dollars of business. The prevailing view seemed to be that things like compensation, assignment, and monitoring systems were the firm's problem. All the GC wanted was results – at discounted prices.

Ironically, diversity initiatives like the Call to Action were the rare exception to this rule (Wilkins 1998). With respect to these initiatives, GCs at least claim to be interested in the internal hiring and promotion practices of firms, in order to ensure that these suppliers are meeting their diversity targets. Scrutiny around these issues has become more intense, moving beyond simple numbers counting to active investigations into hiring, assignment, and mentoring systems.

A small but significant group of GCs are beginning to apply this same kind of scrutiny to other law firm practices, looking beyond simple billing to examine carefully things like assignment practices, training, compensation, and quality controls. This practice is being driven by evolving relationships between companies and law firms that increasingly resemble the relationships that companies have with other important suppliers (Wilkins 2010). These new relationships differ significantly from the bilateral monopolies that used to characterize the relationship between companies and their most important law firms, where one firm would do virtually all of a given company's legal work in return for the implicit promise that the firm would not represent major competitors. But these relationships also differ significantly from the assumed spot-contracting model of "we hire lawyers not firms." Instead, companies and their primary law firms are moving toward a "strategic-partnership" or "keiretsu" model in which the two parties both cooperate and compete to achieve a set of shared objectives, while simultaneously pursuing their separate institutional goals (Wilkins 2010).

To achieve this balance, companies and law firms are blurring organizational boundaries to share information, ideas about best practices, and even personnel to build mutual learning and trust. But, in the words of the Russian proverb Ronald Reagan famously applied to negotiations with the former Soviet Union, the motto of this new partnership is "trust, but verify" (Watson 2011). As a result, both companies and firms are under increasing pressure to develop visible and objective metrics of quality that each side can rely on to ensure that the other party is fulfilling its commitments to the joint endeavor, while being willing to open their internal practices to inspection and influence by the other party to promote mutual gain.

For companies that have moved to this new model, seeking to influence a law firm's commitment to diversity is just one piece of building a deeper and more collaborative relationship in which both law firm and company practices are subject to mutual deliberation and debate. As one GC stated when summing up what he says he expects from the law firms he hires: "We'd be more likely to hire you if you were at a firm where we thought that we liked the firm's structure ... the firm's cultural mores around responsiveness, around conflicts, around diversity, around quality of service, and around pricing, those sorts of things" (Confidential Interview).

Intel's relationship with its primary outside firms underscores just how important this trend has become. Rather than simply exhorting the firm to care more about issues such as diversity, professional development, and pro bono – and threatening to cut off work if the firms fail to perform to the company's satisfaction – Intel has instituted a series of policies and practices designed to get both the company and its law firms to understand the true benefits and costs of seeking these objectives. Under Intel's model, lawyers from the company and from the company's primary outside law firms work collaboratively to ensure that each side understands the reasons why Intel cares about these issues, as well as the difficulties that law firms may experience in achieving these objectives, all within a framework in which Intel continues to push firms to reduce legal costs and the firms continue to pursue profits (Heineman, Lee, and Wilkins 2014).

This new model of strategic "cooptition," as business school scholars have come to refer to the practice (Loebbecke 2009), has the potential to reshape the relationship between companies and their outside firms. And if this happens, an important part of the credit (or for some who worry about the implications of creating too much interdependence between companies and law firms, the blame) for this new reality will belong to visionaries like Richard Palmore, whose Call to Action has helped to sow the seeds for a new and more complex collaboration between companies and law firms.

REFERENCES

Ayres I. 2010. *Carrots and Sticks: Unlock the Power of Incentives to Get Things Done*. Bantom Books New York: New York.

Banaji M R and Greenwald A G. 2013. *Blindspots: Hidden Biases of Good People*.

Broome L L, Conley J M, and Krawiec K D. 2011. Does Critical Mass Matter? *Views from the Boardroom, Seattle University Law Review*, 34:1049–1080.

Call to Action 2004. [1] www.acc.com/vl/public/Article/loader.cfm?csModule= security/getfile&pageid=16074

Carty C M and Blank H D. 2003. The Fortune 500 vs. The S&P 500. Financial Advisor. Accessed April 12. www.fa-mag.com/component/content/article/624.html?magazineID=1&issue=28&Itemid=73

Cheserant C and Harnay S. 2013. The Regulation of Quality in the Market for Legal Services: Taking the Heterogeneity of Legal Services Seriously. *The European Journal of Comparative Economics*, 10(2): 267–291.

Connell A G. 1997. *The Lawyers' Committee for Civil Rights Under Law: The Making of a Public Interest Law Group*: 96–108 (unpublished PhD dissertation, University of Maryland at College Park) (on file with the Harvard Law School Library).

Coates IV J C, Destefano M, Nanda A, and Wilkins D B. 2010. Hiring Teams Lawyers, and Firms: Evidence of the Evolving Relationships in the Corporate Legal Market. *Law & Social Inquiry*.

Coyoca L E. 2010. The Diversity Dilemma: Another Victim of the Bad Economy? https://apps.americanbar.org/litigation/committees/corporate/docs/2010-cle-materials/11-diversity-dilemma-another-victim-bad-economy/11a-diversity-dilemma.pdf

Dinovitzer R, Nelson R L, Plickert G, Sandefur R, and Sterling J S with Adams T K, Garth B G, Hagan J, Wilder G Z, and Wilkins D B. 2009. *After the JD II: Second Results from a National Study of Legal Careers.* Chicago, IL: American Bar Foundation.

Dobbin F, and Jung J. 2011. Corporate Board Gender Diversity and Stock Performance: The Competence Gap or Institutional Investor Bias? *North Carolina Law Review* 89(3): 809–838. Accessed April 12. www .wjh.harvard.edu/~dobbin/cv/workingpapers/Board_Diversity_and_Per formance_07_01_10.pdf)

Frater E. 2007. A Call to Action Continues: General Counsel Still Leading the Way, www.mcca.com/index.cfm?fuseaction=page.viewpage&pageid=1618

Fritz A. 2002. Corporate America Commits to Diversity, Memphis Law, www .memphisbar.org/magazine/aaugust02/corporateamerica.html, last visited January 1, 2004, cited in Wilkins DB 2004, at 1556, n. 46.

Gine M. 2007. Compustat Executive Compensation Database. Accessed April 12. http://wrds-web.wharton.upenn.edu/wrds/support/Additional %20Support/WRDS%20Presentations/_000user2007/executive_com pensation.pdf

Heineman B W. 2008. *High Performance with High Integrity: Memo to the CEO,* Harvard Business School Press, Boston MA.

Heineman B W, Lee W R, and Wilkins D B. 2014. Lawyers as Professionals and as Citizens: Key Roles and Responsibilities in the 21st Century, https://clp.law.harvard.edu/clp-research/legal-practice/professional ism-project/

Hunter M. 1963. Lawyers Promise Kennedy Aid in Easing Race Unrest. *New York Times*: 1.

Gilson R. 1990 The Devolution of the Legal Profession: A Demand Side Perspective. *Md. L. Rev.*, 49: 869.

Institute for Inclusion in the Legal Profession. 2011. The Business Case for Diversity: Reality or Wishful Thinking.

Kang J and Lane K. 2010. Seeing Through Colorblindness: Implicit Bias and the Law. *University of California at Los Angeles Law Review*, 58: 465–520.

Kramer V W, Konrad A B, Erkut S. 2006. *Critical Mass on Corporate Boards: Why Three or More Women Enhance Governance,* 11 WELLESLEY CTRS. FOR WOMEN REP. 3 (2006), *available at* http://vkramerassociates.com/ writings/CriticalMass ExecSummary%20PDF.pdf

Levit N. 2008. Megacases, Diversity, and the Elusive Goal of Workplace Reform. *Boston College Law Review*, 48:

Leadership Council on Legal Diversity 2015, last visited April 26, www .lcldnet.org/about/.

Levs M L. 2004. Sara Lee's General Counsel: Making Diversity a Priority, www.mcca.com/index.cfm?fuseaction=page.viewpage&pageid=803.

Lin A. Nov. 6, 2003. Just Like Any Vendor, Law Firms are Asked to Compete for Business on the Web. New York Law Journal.

Loebbecke C. 2009. "The Future of Innovation … The Benefits of Being Realistic." in *The Future of Innovation* (Von Stamm B and Triflova A eds.).

Lum L. 2014. Women and Minorities as General Counsels, Diversity & the Bar, December 2014, www.diversityandthebardigital.com/datb/november_december_2014#article_id=529114

Mahoney B. 2013. Diversity a Business Necessity for Law Firms, Experts Say. Law360, www.law360.com/articles/462401/diversity-a-business-necessity-for-law-firms-expert-says.

Minority Corporate Counsel Association. 2009. Examining the Role of the Law Firm Diversity Professional, www.alanet.org/diversity/MCCAExaminingLawFirmDiversityProfessionalsReport.pdf

2014. Is the Call to Action Working? *Diversity Matters*. www.bakerdonelson.com/is-the-call-to-action-working-04-21-2011/

July 29, 2014. DuPont, General Mills, Verizon and Walmart Launch "*Engage Excellence*" Minority Lawyer Inclusion Incentive Program: One Answer to the Call to Action, www.mcca.com/index.cfm?fuseaction=Feature.showFeature&featureID=504.

2015. Why Join MCCA?, www.mcca.com/index.cfm?fuseaction=Page.ViewPage&pageId=2147.

Phillips D J and Zuckerman E W. 2001. Middle-Status Conformity: Theoretical Restatement and Empirical Demonstration in Two Markets. *American Journal of Sociology*, 107(2): 379–429.

Rosen R E. 1989. The Inside Counsel Movement, Professional Judgment, and Organizational Representation. *Indiana Law Journal*, 64: 479.

Sander L. March 2006. *In-House and Outside Counsel: Building a Solid Relationship*, Chicago Lawyer.

Smith B. 2013. Raising the Bar: Exploring the Diversity Gap Within the Legal Profession.

Smith J. May 4, 2014. Female Lawyers Still Battle Gender Bias: Despite Advances, Women Still Lag Behind Men in Billing Rate, Leadership Roles. Wall Street Journal.

Thayler R H and Sunstein C R. 2009. *Nudge: Imporving Decisions about Health, Wealth, and Happiness*. Penguin Books New York: New York.

Triedman J. May 2014. *The Diversity Crisis: Big Firms Continued Failure*, American Lawyer.

Watson W D. 2011. Trust, but Verify: Reagan, Gorbachev, and the INF Treaty. *The Hilltop Review*, 5: 22.

Wilkins D B and Gulati G M. 1996. Why Are There So Few Black Lawyers in Corporate Law Firms—An Institutional Analysis. *Cal. L. Rev.*, 84: 493.

Wilkins D B. 1998. Do Clients Have Ethical Obligations to Lawyers? Some Lessons from the Diversity Wars. *Georgetown Journal of Legal Ethics* 10: 855.

1999. Partners without Power? A Preliminary Look at Black Partners in Corporate Law Firms. *Journal of the Institute for the Study of Legal Ethics* 2: 15.

2004. From "Separate is Inherently Unequal" to "Diversity is Good for Business": The Rise of Market-Based Diversity Arguments and the Fate of the Black Corporate Bar. *Harvard Law Review* 117: 1548.

2008. "If you Can't Beat 'Em, Join 'Em!" The Rise and Fall of the Black Corporate Law Firm, *Stanford Law Review* 60: 173.

2010. "Team of Rivals? Toward a New Model of the Corporate Attorney-Client Relationship. *Fordham L. Rev.* 78: 2067.

2015. Law firms, in *International Encyclopedia of the Social and Behavioral Sciences*, 2nd edn. (Wright J D, editor-in-chief), vol 13, p. 578.

DIVERSITY AND TALENT AT THE TOP

Lessons from the boardroom

KIMBERLY D. KRAWIEC, JOHN M. CONLEY, AND LISSA L. BROOME[1]

I INTRODUCTION

Corporate boards lack significant diversity. The numbers have improved over the years, but have moved relatively little in the last ten years. The percent of board seats held by women in Fortune 100 companies increased from 16.9% in 2004 to 19.8% in 2012, while the percent of board seats held by minorities (including female minorities) increased from 14.9% in 2004 to 16.3% in 2012.[2] There is a great deal of discussion in the popular press about the lack of board diversity and the need for more diverse boards, with some European countries having mandated board gender diversity quotas. We began this project with these numbers as a backdrop and an interest in two related questions: why do corporate boards pursue diversity (defined in terms of gender, race, and ethnicity) – even to the limited extent that they

---

[1] Kimberly D. Krawiec, Kathrine Robinson Everett, Professor of Law, Duke Law School; John M. Conley, William Rand Kenan, Jr. Professor of Law, University of North Carolina School of Law; Lissa Lamkin Broome, Wells Fargo, Professor of Banking Law, University of North Carolina School of Law. The body of this article was prepared for publication in the University of Illinois Law Review, Kimberly D. Krawiec, John M. Conley, and Lissa L. Broome, "The Danger of Difference: Tensions in Directors' Views of Corporate Board Diversity," 2013 *U. Ill. L. Rev.* 919 (2013).

[2] These numbers were compiled by The Alliance for Board Diversity, www.catalyst .org/system/files/2012_abd_missing_pieces_final_8_15_13.pdf. More recent figures on the percent of female directors in Fortune 500 companies indicate a similar trend: 14.7% in 2005, 15.7% in 2010, 16.1% in 2011, and 16.6% in 2012. www.cattalyst .org/knowledge/statistical-overview-women-workplace.

do – and what difference might diversity make to how boards work? There has been substantial quantitative research on the second of these questions, and the results can fairly be described as mixed.[3]

Our research has employed a qualitative interview strategy to pursue both questions. We have interviewed fifty-seven people with direct experience with corporate boards, as directors, executives, consultants, regulators, or proxy advisors. Fifty of these serve or have served as directors of publicly traded corporations. Using a method rooted in anthropology and discourse analysis, we have worked from a general topic outline and conducted open-ended interviews in which we encouraged respondents to raise and develop issues of interest to them.[4] The interviews have typically lasted forty-five to ninety minutes. With transcripts of the recorded interviews in hand, we then – as a group – listen to them again, analyzing them qualitatively with a focus on the themes that the respondents identify, the emphases that they give them, the stories (or narratives) that they tell, and the details of the language that they use. We also thematically code the transcripts and use sorting software to get another, complementary view of the frequency and distribution of the various themes.

Two overarching themes have been pervasive in our interviews: First, there is near-unanimous agreement (with only one clear dissenter) that board diversity is a good thing, a valuable outcome that is worth striving for. But second, it is very difficult for our respondents to provide examples from their experience of when board diversity has made a tangible difference. We have heard abundant stories about when other kinds of diversity – what might be called functional diversity: different business backgrounds and skills, for example – have made a difference in how effectively boards do their work. But pressing respondents for comparable stories about demographic diversity has yielded very little beyond awkward silences. Respondents have sometimes commented on that very awkwardness, noting how difficult it is to talk about gender and – especially – race making a difference without engaging in essentializing or stereotyping.

But even if they have found it difficult to give concrete examples of the benefits of director diversity, our respondents have provided

---

[3] We have reviewed this research in Lissa L. Broome, John M. Conley, and Kimberly D. Krawiec, "Dangerous Categories: Narratives of Corporate Board Diversity," 89 *N.C.L. Rev.* 761, 765–66 (2011).

[4] For a lengthier description of our research methods, see ibid. at 768–77.

well-developed (and perhaps well-rehearsed) conceptual arguments. We have been repeatedly struck by the similarities between these arguments and those advanced by Justice Powell in his famous opinion in *Bakke* (which appeared to have injected "diversity" in its present sense into the public discourse).[5] Like Justice Powell, our respondents suggest that demographic diversity is a proxy for different experiences, sensibilities, and points of view.[6] Just as he argued that, as a consequence, the discourse in a diverse classroom would be broader and deeper, our respondents contend that diverse boards will engage in richer and more productive debate and examine business problems in more comprehensive ways.[7] For legal reasons, Justice Powell did not argue for diversity on remedial or compensatory grounds.[8] In an interesting convergence, only a few of our respondents made arguments for board diversity that were grounded in social justice and fundamental fairness.

Throughout the study, we have been struck by some connections to the parallel issue of diversity in the legal profession. These connections are particularly evident in the case of private law firms, which, like business corporations, are profit-driven entities. Study after study has reported that the legal profession has become much more diverse at the

[5] Regents of Univ. of Cal. v. Bakke, 438 U.S. 265 (1978). The decision rejected a race-conscious admissions program at the UC-Davis medical school. But Justice Powell, in an opinion, that only he signed, advanced the notion that race could be *a* factor in state university admissions, because of the value of diversity. He seems to have borrowed the concept of diversity from an amicus brief submitted by Harvard and other elite universities. Ibid. at 316, 322–23. For a discussion of the impact of the *Bakke* case on public discourse about diversity, see John M. Conley, Lissa Lamkin Broome, and Kimberly D. Krawiec, "Narratives of Diversity in the Corporate Boardroom: What Corporate Insiders Say about Why Diversity Matters," in *Discourse Perspectives on Organizational Communication*, 201, 205–08 (Jolanta Aritz and Robyn C. Walker, eds. 2012).

[6] Justice Powell wrote that "[a]n otherwise qualified medical student with a particular background – whether it be ethnic, geographic, culturally advantaged or disadvantaged – may bring to a professional school of medicine experiences, outlooks, and ideas that enrich the training of its student body." Regents of Univ. of Cal. v. Bakke, 438 U.S. 265, 314 (1978).

[7] Justice Powell argued that diversity would promote a "robust exchange of ideas." Ibid. at 313.

[8] Because there was no evidence of then-current discrimination at UC-Davis, a remedial or compensatory rationale would have been constitutionally inappropriate. See Conley, Broome, and Krawiec, *supra* note 3, at 206–08 (discussing this and other aspects of the Powell opinion).

entry level over the past twenty-five years.[9] But the same data indicate that, especially in large private firms, women and minority lawyers have been less successful in reaching the senior partnership ranks and participating in firm management – in other words – in reaching positions roughly analogous to corporate directorships.

Like their counterparts in the upper reaches of the corporate world (the people we interviewed for this project), law firm partners are reported to be nearly unanimous in their endorsement of the principle of diversity.[10] Their reasons for believing in diversity are also similar to some the arguments made in favor of corporate director diversity: the

---

[9] According to American Bar Association data, for example, female enrollment in J.D. programs broke the 30% barrier in 1978 and has held steadily in the high 40s since the late 1990s. American Bar Association Section of Legal Education and Admission to the Bar, Statistics, available at www.americanbar.org/groups/legal_education/resources/statistics.html (visited March 5, 2013); the specific data we cite can be found at www.americanbar.org/content/dam/aba/administrative/legal_educa tion _and_admissions_to_the_bar/statistics/jd_enrollment_1yr_total_gender.auth checkdam.pdf (visited March 5, 2013). Yet according to a National Association of Women Lawyers Survey, female representation among large law firm partners has plateaued at or slightly below 20% – and at about 15% if the criterion is equity, or "real," partners. National Ass'n of Women lawyers and NAWL Foundation, Report of the Seventh Annual NAWL National Survey on Retention and Promotion of Women in Law Firms (2012), available at http://nawl.timberlakepublishing .com/files/NAWL%202012%20Survey%20Report%20final.pdf (visited March 5, 2013). That survey also reports that women occupy only 20% of the seats on firms' highest governance committees, and only 4% of the firms have female managing partners. The ABA reports that minority enrollment in law schools reached 10% in 1982 and increased steadily to reach 25% in 2010. But according to the NALP, the national association for legal career advisors, minority representation among law firm partners reached 5% only in 2003 and has since increased to only 7.9%. See NALP, Minorities & Women, available at www.nalp.org/minoritieswomen (visited March 6, 2013) (our minority representation statistics are derived from individual yearly NALP reports, available through this website). For a review of earlier data, see John M. Conley, "Tales of Diversity: Lawyers' Narratives of Equity in Private Law Firms," 31 L. & Soc. Inquiry 831, 838–40 (2006).

[10] Studies addressing the issues discussed in this paragraph include Conley, *supra* note 7; Devon W. Carbado and Mitu Gulati, "Race to the Top of the Corporate Ladder: What Minorities Do When They Get There," 61 *Wash. & Lee L. Rev.* 1645 (2004); Elizabeth Chambliss and Christpoher Uggen, "Men and Women of Elite Law Firms: Reevaluating Kanter's Legacy," 25 L. & Soc. Inquiry 41 (2000); David B. Wilkins, From "'Separate Is Inherently Unequal' to 'Diversity Is Good for Business': The Rise of Market-Based Diversity Arguments and the Fate of the Black Corporate Bar," 117 *Harv. L. Rev.* 1548 (2004); David B. Wilkins, "Doing Well by Doing Good? The Role of Public Service in the Careers of Black Corporate Lawyers," 41 *Houston L. Rev.* 1 (2004).

firm functions better, the clients demand it, and competition requires that a firm leave no talent pool untapped. In explaining the relative lack of diversity at the senior and management levels, lawyers often gravitate to a version of the "pipeline" argument that we report in this study. With respect to minorities, big-firm lawyers often cite the relative paucity of entry-level candidates who meet their law school grade-centered selection criteria.[11] Private-firm lawyers also emphasize factors that may lead women and minorities to lose or drop out of the never-ending law firm tournament, including family obligations, the lack of mentorship and sponsorship within the firm,[12] the inability to get career-building high-value work from senior lawyers,[13] the demands of public service, and the attractions of public-sector and in-house work.

In the remainder of this chapter we will set out and analyze the most important themes that have emerged in our director diversity research. In the Conclusion, we will also offer some further thoughts about what light our project might shed, at least indirectly, on diversity in law firms.

II DIVERSITY IS GOOD, BUT IT IS HARD TO SAY WHY

With the exception of one clear dissenter (and two "soft yesses," who said that diversity could not hurt), everyone we interviewed gave diversity an unequivocal endorsement. Almost everyone thus agrees that diversity is a good thing, and that corporate boards should pursue it. Just why diversity is good has proved to be a more complex question. In fact, we heard repeatedly that the value of diversity is simply taken

---

[11] Louise Ashley and Laura Empson, this volume (discussing use of educational credentials, including study at elite universities and performance at those universities as ways to select the most talented job candidates for law firms, accountancy firm, and investment banks in the U.K.).

[12] Forrest Briscoe and Andrew von Nordenflycht, this volume (noting research finding that females and minorities have less access to social networks within the workplace than white men).

[13] Ibid. (finding in research of billing records at a large law firm that female and minority attorneys who worked with partners near retirement – a strategy of inheriting clients from retiring partners – did not experience an increase in billings following the retirement as did white male attorneys and instead experienced a decline in client billings).

for granted and rarely if ever discussed. This comment from a white female director is typical:

Text 1

Q: Okay and as the Board and the committee has discussed this [the need to add diversity to the board], do they talk about why it's important to have some minority representation?

A: No, never.

Q: Really? But everybody seems to be on board with it.

A: Yes, yes.... And this is exactly the same when we talk about women in higher management in the company, minorities in the company itself. There's an unstated assumption that we need to be doing better or we're doing better or whatever it is that we're looking at. Since it's not stated, I would hate to say what I thought other people were thinking in their heads. I mean I don't have any idea.[14]

A minority male director had a similar view:

Text 2

Q: Why – what do people say about why you need a woman?

A: You know, it's unspoken. It's interesting. It's an unspoken agreement that it's just unseemly that we don't have one.[15]

Despite their ambivalence, our interviews did yield many theories on why board diversity is valuable. The theories that our respondents advanced include the following:

• Perhaps the most pervasive justification we have heard is that diverse boards engage in richer and ultimately more effective discussion and debate.

---

[14] 79. We promised all of our interview subjects that we would not identify them, either directly or indirectly. Accordingly, the only citation we can provide for each quote is the number we have assigned to the particular speaker's interview. Any further descriptive information about the subjects that we are able to furnish consistent with our promise of anonymity can be found in the text surrounding the various quotes. We have provided the interview numbers in case readers are interested in tracking multiple statements by particular subjects. (e.g., subject number 81, cited in the following footnote, is quoted and cited on four separate occasions.) Some readers may also be interested in when we did the various interviews, so we have provided the dates of each interview, by interview number, in the Appendix. When an ellipsis appears in an interview quotation, it indicates that we have deleted some material from the quotation, rather than a pause in the respondent's speech.

[15] 81.

This sentiment is expressed in a variety of ways: people of diverse backgrounds bring different perspectives, experiences, concerns, and sensibilities to the boardroom; people of diverse backgrounds are more willing to question and dissent from the status quo; and diversity in the boardroom minimizes what one respondent called "the danger of group think," which can ensue when everyone has had the same set of formative experiences.

- Directors of diverse backgrounds ensure that the perspectives and concerns of often-ignored constituencies are represented in board discussions. These can include female and minority customers; rank-and-file employees (to whose needs female and minority directors are said to be better attuned than white males); female and minority prospects for executive positions and future board seats; and communities that a company's business may affect.

- A related theory is that the presence of female and minority directors sends signals to various constituencies about a company's values. Those constituencies include employees at all levels, customers, communities, regulators and other government actors, and the public.

- Female and minority directors can help in unique and tangible ways with marketing, customer relations, and employee relations.

- A company that does not have a diverse board is failing to tap into a significant part of the relevant talent pool, and is therefore likely to be less effective.

- Very rarely, our respondents have said that pursuing diversity is simply the right thing to do, as a matter of fundamental fairness or making up for the historical record of discrimination and exclusion at the highest levels of corporate management.

As we will emphasize repeatedly, concrete examples that validate these various theories have been very hard to find. In subsequent sections we will illustrate this point with reference to particular theories, and offer our thoughts on why examples prove to be so elusive.

III   DO DIVERSE BOARDS WORK BETTER?

As we have noted, a frequent argument for diverse boards is a functional one: they work better, in the sense that a diverse membership brings different perspectives, sensibilities, and experiences to the table and, consequently, engages in a richer discussion of issues. Concrete examples of this richer discussion have proved elusive, however. With respect to the dynamics of discussion and debate, respondents struggle with the question of whether women or minorities behave differently than white men in the boardroom *because of their gender or race*. We have heard, for example, that women are more likely to be attuned to the human impact of board decisions – comments that evoke the cultural feminism of Carol Gilligan.[16] But, overall, questions about demographically correlated differences in interactive behavior tend to evoke comments about the dangers of stereotyping, and sometimes self-evaluative remarks about what one can and cannot say.

Some respondents suggested that women bring a different style of discourse, discussion, and debate to the boardroom. Others made the point that women come to a board with different life experiences and, consequently, different "priorities." But, in each case, respondents often struggled for specifics, or equivocated or apologized for stereotyping.

We were told of specific instances where a director's gender or race might have led him or her to raise an issue or provide information that the board would otherwise have missed. Many of these seemed trivial, matters that should have been obvious to lower-level marketing people – and particularly trivial considering that they were the first examples given in response to our request for illustrations of richer discussion. On two different occasions, respondents have told us of African-American directors advising the board on the dining-out preferences of African-American families. We have also heard instances of female directors explaining the difficulties faced by mothers out shopping with their children.

There were also dissenting views, as exemplified by the comments of the minority male director of a restaurant company quoted previously in Text 2:

> **Text 3**
>
> A: At least in the restaurant business I'm not so sure that's necessarily true. Yes, you need it at the company level so you can understand tastes and food preferences and things like that. But boards have nothing to do with helping restaurants figure out tastes and food preferences, right?
>
> Q: That's interesting, because I feel like we've gotten some anecdotes of that sort, and they surprised me, for that reason. It was sort of – wow, that's a board-level discussion? So in your experience that is not a board-level discussion.

---

[16] Carol Gilligan, In *A Different Voice: Psychological Theory and Women's Development* (1982).

A: We go out of our way – I mean, of course, we kibitz and go, "I'll tell them I didn't like the sandwich," or whatever, or, "I think they're missing something." And the CEO goes, "Very nice for you to tell me that. Who are you? You don't sell a thousand of these a day. You have no idea.". . . That's not our job. We pay people to figure that out. If we thought we could figure it out, something's wrong with our company. Right? If it becomes our job we made a big mistake.

Q: Right. Right.

A: Now, I could imagine like a Nike or whatever having some – because you attract spectacular marketing genius-level people to your board, that they might come up with a perspective or strategic perspective that is helpful, right? I could see that. I could see that. But – I could see that. But, boy, is that going to be rare. That shouldn't be a board's job, because it's kind of a once in a blue moon, and it could've just as easily happened because of the comment card you got and the CEO – so I think unless you have an agenda, right, some sort of macro agenda that you want to see implemented through the board level, right, and you think that agenda is going to be more likely to be implemented because of certain kinds of people on the board. The idea that you're improving XYZ because of – I think that's farfetched, and I don't think that's really the board's job. That's my sense.[17]

Echoing the previously discussed argument about female empathy, some respondents contended that female or minority board members are better able to empathize with corporate employees, and were more likely to raise concerns about their welfare in the boardroom. Female and minority board members were also said to aid in the recruitment, retention, and promotion of women and minorities, especially at the senior management levels, and to argue for inclusiveness in executive succession. A white female director, for example, said this (notice that, like many other respondents, she "hate[s] this stereotyping"):

Text 4
Q: Do you think there are issues or kinds of issues that women or minorities are more likely to raise or push in the boardroom than white men might be?

A: Boy I hate this stereotyping but I think, because I think there are some white men who would do this too but I think issues related to human resources and how people in the ranks are feeling and that kind of thing are much more likely to be brought up by a woman. I'm still

[17] 81.

kind of a lone voice when it comes to considering your sales force of [thousands] as a potential strategic advantage or the opposite and, therefore, what are our strategies associated with that? I mean I'm like a broken record on that . . .

A: Well it means you've got [thousands of] people out there representing you as a company and if you don't invest in them, I mean they're touching the customer so they can either make you more effective or they can keep you from being as effective as your other strategies indicate because you have to do everything through them so I think they should be much more a part of the conversation. How are they compensated? How are they trained? How are they motivated? How do they feel? That's just not the kind of thing that I normally hear a board colleague bring up or make very important. When there's a problem, yes.[18]

A final point is that some respondents have suggested that attention to board diversity is something of a luxury reserved for good – or at least normal – times. When a company is in crisis mode, fighting for its life, interest in diversity disappears. While diversity may be good, in other words, it seems not to be essential to survival. A question that arises by implication is whether diverse board members are fully in the loop in times of crisis, when, we are told, decision-making is likely to be in the hands of a few especially experienced directors. The minority male director quoted in Texts 2 and 3 summarized this theme succinctly:

Text 5
Companies go through good times, they go through great times and they go through times that are not so good through major transformations. Companies that are in textiles, furniture, tobacco are in major transformations and so I don't think those companies are going to be focused on gender issues or racial issues as much as they are some of the more operational type issues.[19]

IV GETTING ALONG VERSUS AVOIDING GROUPTHINK

Our respondents told a strong and consistent story regarding the importance of "getting along" and collegiality in the boardroom. All of our respondents emphasized – quite emphatically – that the board could not properly do its job if it spent time on resolving tension or

[18] 83.   [19] 81.

unconstructive arguing, or if one or more directors failed to conform to the prevailing corporate culture. Our respondents did not contend that boards should never disagree, but emphasized that such disagreement should be cordial and follow the prevailing corporate cultural norms of engagement.

For example, a white female director contrasted the collegial and cooperative atmosphere of the boardroom with the more competitive corporate working environment:

Text 6

And, in fact, one of the things I like about my board work, as opposed to working full time in a corporation at this point, is that the dynamics and the politics are very different than they are as an individual contributor or as an employee of the company. It's a much more collegial and, therefore, in my opinion, a much more pleasant experience because it's really all about the dynamics among the board. You're not really competing with them for position or the next promotion or for, you know, visibility. You're all in it together. And that's key to making these boards work.[20]

A white male director with many years of board experience, who is also a university professor, elaborated on boardroom norms of collegiality and consensus:

Text 7

The object is to reach an agreement to do something, so there's a kind of consensus norm, so there's a very strong pressure to get with the program. You're not supposed to hide what it is you have to say, but once you make an effort to persuade somebody and it's not going that way, you're supposed to think, "Well, there are reasonable positions on the other side by reasonable people," so there's no dissent norm. That would be totally bizarre in a company. Once you say your piece in a concise way, if it's not going to go that way, then when it comes to a vote, you're a yes unless it's a matter of conscience, which it hardly ever really is.[21]

Our respondents also emphasized the importance of collegiality and consensus in the board's interactions with the CEO. Indeed, this relationship is so important that many of our respondents characterized the role of the CEO in selecting board members as something

[20] 23.   [21] 95.

approaching a veto power, despite recent corporate governance interventions that emphasize the board's independence from the CEO.[22]

These stories of collegiality, consensus, and getting along are in some tension with two other, related, stories: about the importance of avoiding "groupthink," and the need for the board to act as an independent check on behalf of shareholders rather than simply rubberstamping management actions. "Groupthink" has been defined by the psychologist, Irving Janis, as a mode of thinking that arises when a decision-making group is so cohesive that its members become reluctant to criticize, even in their own thinking, the judgments, and ideas of their colleagues and leaders.[23] Members seek to be amiable and establish concurrence on important issues, with no conflict or infighting.[24] One proposed solution to the tendency toward groupthink is diversity within the group, either of observable characteristics (such as race, gender, and ethnicity) or of unobservable characteristics (such as ideology, experience, or viewpoint).[25]

Much research on group decision-making has focused on the problem of countering groupthink, with mixed results in the case of observable characteristics.[26] As we discuss in prior work, this significant body of research on heterogeneity in groups predicts both positives (more and better information, the consideration of more alternatives, and higher-quality decisions), and negatives (a reduction in group cohesion, and an increase in member dissatisfaction and turnover) in the case of race and gender diversity.[27]

Our respondents frequently asserted both the avoidance of groupthink and an ability to facilitate board independence as rationales in

---

[22] A board's nominating committee must be composed of independent directors, which means that the company's CEO may not be a member. NYSE LISTED COMPANY MANUAL § 303A.04(a) ("Listed companies must have a nominating/ corporate governance committee composed entirely of independent directors.").

[23] Irving Janis, *Victims of Groupthink* 9 (1972) (defining groupthink as poor decisions made by a group as the result of pressure from the group that resulted in reduced moral judgment and eliminated a reality check).

[24] Ibid.

[25] Francis J. Milliken and Luis L. Martins, "Searching for Common Threads: Understanding the Multiple Effects of Diversity in Organizational Groups," 21 *Acad. Mgmt. Rev.* 402 (1996) (discussing this idea and analyzing studies on point).

[26] Lissa L. Broome, John M. Conley, and Kimberly D. Krawiec, "Dangerous Categories: Narratives of Corporate Board Diversity," 89 *N. C. L. Rev.* 759, 765–67 (summarizing this research).

[27] Ibid. at 765.

favor of race and gender diversity. Yet, as noted, these rationales are in tension with our respondents' even more frequently asserted contentions that boards must get along with each other and senior management, be collegial, and avoid confrontation.

For example, one respondent, a proxy advisor with substantial experience in board and corporate governance issues, told us that most of the investors whom his company advised did not take board diversity seriously, as they did not believe it improved shareholder value. Among those that did, however, the most important reason was likely the avoidance of groupthink:

> **Text 8**
> I think people know especially on the risk side that whenever you get anything involving sort of groupthink, everybody in the room having the same background, group of experiences and so forth that that is an absolute breeding ground for risk, for problems to occur.... and I think by and large the folks that believe that diversity is important put a very high value on it for that exact reason that they think this creates greater, frankly, psychological independence in the board room. It creates more viewpoints in the boardroom and that leads to better decision making I think and I think that's a change from certainly fifteen or twenty years ago when I think it was purely viewed in terms of sort of social equity issues about increasing participation by women and minority group members on boards of directors and I don't see that as much today.
>
> I think the arguments in favor of board diversity are much more sophisticated today and that we're really talking about trying to help boards to provide stronger oversight. We're trying to help boards to eliminate the possibility of groupthink I think.[28]

A white female director specifically mentioned her own role in avoiding groupthink in connection with a CEO succession decision. A group of directors (the "real champions") seemed to be suppressing dissent and pushing the board toward a particular candidate until our respondent intervened and insisted on closer scrutiny. She characterized her proposal as one "that I don't think a white male would have suggested," and thus evidence of the benefit of board diversity.

The white male respondent quoted previously in Text 7 attempted to reconcile the seemingly conflicting values of avoiding groupthink and fostering consensus:

[28] 36.

Text 9

Q: Could you talk a little bit about the consensus norm? As you know, academics love to talk about groupthink and the like. Is this a productive norm or does it have costs? I'm not suggesting that people should sit around and argue all day the way they might in a faculty meeting, but does it, in your view, makes decision-making better, worse, no effect?...

A: I think it's helpful. Why would it be helpful? It's because you're doing more than reaching a decision. You're managing. If you look at the Delaware Corporation Code in Section 141, it says the job of the board is to manage the company, so that includes lots of things, like coming to a decision, but it's also an oversight role, a monitoring role and you're implementing something ....

The corporate analog is once we agree on a policy, I'm supposed to help implement it. I can't sabotage it ongoing. I think the consensus norm relates to that. If you don't feel censored, if you feel like you can talk, which in my experience people can talk and say what they think and then, it turns out that the company wants to go in a certain direction, then my job is to help make it work. So, what's the point of saying no then? It's going to go through. It should be 12–0 rather than 10–2. I mean, basically then what I'm signaling when I say yes is, "Okay. I had my shot. I couldn't persuade you people. Now I'm going to help make it work." That's my job. That's, I think, what [the] unanimity norm does. It isn't total. I've seen it violated once or twice, but for the most part, you try to do it.[29]

To be clear, our respondents do not contend that boards should never disagree, only that such disagreement should be cordial and follow the prevailing corporate cultural norms of engagement. Nonetheless, we heard a number of stories of board members who did not work out, due to "asking hard questions" in an "aggressive" manner, and of boards that were ineffective, because of "unproductive" disagreement. According to our respondents, however, such instances are rare – board members who find themselves out of step with prevailing board norms of consensus either resign or are asked to leave the board.

V FITTING IN VERSUS THE OUTSIDER ROLE

The prior section discussed stories of substantive agreement and disagreement in the boardroom. They highlighted the importance attached by directors to a collegial and productive boardroom environment (both among the board and between the board and

---

[29] 95.

management), and adherence to the consensus norm that pervades the boardroom. Related to those stories are narratives at another level, about the efforts of individuals to look, speak, and behave like directors. In other words, this section discusses the pains taken by directors to "perform" the social role of director, in the sense of presenting oneself in a way that is appropriate to time, place, and audience.[30] All directors, regardless of race or gender, emphasize the importance of being perceived by board colleagues as competent and intelligent – that is, as a "real" director. Directors thus give careful thought to the way in which their questions, comments, behavior, and even their dress are perceived by other board members.

Though a few of our female and minority respondents reported feeling like an outsider, even after a long period of service on a board, most did not. Rather, most said that they were treated well and respected, although this sometimes had come only after an adjustment period during which the director observed the behavior, dress, and demeanor of others; learned the substance of the company's business and the work of the board; and gradually became integrated into the boardroom culture. Though this observation and adjustment period was mentioned more often by female and minority respondents than by white males, some white male directors emphasized that it would be normal for any new director to ease slowly into a new boardroom, spending more time at the beginning listening and learning than actively participating and asking questions.

The white male director quoted in Texts 7 and 9 previously, for example, discussed at some length his efforts to overcome his outsider status as an academic. According to him, it would be normal for any director to experience an adjustment period when joining a new board. However, his adjustment period, which he lessened somewhat by reading about boards and asking other directors about proper behavioral norms, was more difficult because of his new colleagues' preconceptions about professorial behavior:

[30] The performance perspective derives in large part from the work of the sociologist Erving Goffman, who thought about everyday social behavior by analogy to theatrical performances. That is, the social actor, like the skilled dramatic actor, takes on a role, develops a belief in it, and crafts a performance that is appropriate for the audience and mindful of the entire social context. Erving Goffman, *Frame Analysis: An Essay on the Organization of Experience* (1974); Erving Goffman, *The Presentation of Self in Everyday Life* (1959).

Text 10

Q: Let me focus on the word behave [which respondent had just used]. You're talking about substantive positions on issues, but was there a behavioral side to this that they thought you'd act and interact in a particular way?

A: I think people were worried that I would be giving lectures. They thought I might be a little snobby because I was a [name of university] professor. There are very different norms in board meetings about how you talk and how much you talk and how you reach consensus. The difference between a faculty meeting and a board meeting is very, very large. I thought they were worried that I would mis-fit. But I'd read enough about what goes on and tried to pick things up and ask people I knew who were directors and so, I behaved like a director. That is, I thought my job was to behave like a director if I was a director, but they were initially concerned that I would behave like their view of what a professor would behave like.

Q: Were you able to jump right in behaving like a director or did you have to hold back for a while? How did that work?

A: I had to hold back forever compared to being on a faculty.... I had to essentially behave differently. Looking back, I don't think I screwed it up too much at the start, but I was very self-conscious at the start of how I had to behave. I talked much less at the start than I do now, so I was really trying to be careful about it.

Q: Is that common, do you think, for all new directors, meaning when you've just come onto a company or was it because you were coming from a different environment?

A: I think it is common for new directors to be a little reticent and I was like – I wouldn't say I was doubly in any precise sense reticent – but I was conscious that it wasn't only that I didn't know the industry. It was that I also had to learn how to behave which other people didn't really have.[31]

Female and minority directors are especially likely to report working hard at managing the impressions of other board members, putting colleagues at ease, and fitting into the boardroom environment. For example, this white female director spent "several years" adjusting to the male-dominated culture of one boardroom.

Text 11

Right. But I'll tell you something else. It took me several years to be comfortable at this board, partly because it was – the culture was so

---

[31] 95.

male – not just male dominated, but a particular kind of culture, and because I didn't know it.[32]

An African-American female director whose professional and educational background was also quite different from those of most directors told the following story of her successful efforts to gain the trust and acceptance of her new board colleagues:

Text 12

[I]n being on the board at [company name], I've consciously forced myself out of my comfort zone because I knew I had to know these people and learn who they are and interact with them and so after the conclusion of the board meetings, I found myself looking around and I was saying why am I always the last person here and that was a conscious decision that I had made. I hung around and I talked to people and got to know them and that paid off because they felt comfortable with me. They felt comfortable calling me up and saying let me bounce something off of you. They felt comfortable saying I'm going to sit beside [name of respondent] at the meeting today and so that maybe my biggest success on that board was letting them know who I was and letting them know we're all on the same team and I wasn't that student who always raised my hand. I knew the answer.. . .

I would get there early because I realized that some of them got there early. If the meeting started at two, they were there at twelve. So I started coming early and have lunch with them in the cafeteria so I kind of developed my little group. I knew they were going to be there and I would sit at the table and talk with them and understood what the rituals were. Then they would all go to another little area and read the papers and sit and talk. And so you talk about – you have a board meeting, but then they go out to the parking lot and talk. I began to understand that decisions were not only made in the board room but they're made somewhere else and so if I hadn't stepped outside of my comfort zone, I would never have known that.[33]

Notice, however, that this acceptance as part of the group came only with time, and only after continued efforts from our respondent. Though the other directors made no overt attempts to exclude her, neither did they inform her of unofficial group norms, such as arriving early to lunch together, despite the fact that informal board business sometimes occurred during these gatherings:

[32] 41.   [33] 43.

Text 13

Q: But nobody came up to you and said, "Hey [identifying director information], come a little early next time because we have lunch in the [company cafeteria]?"

A: Uh uh. They didn't.... Then after a couple of times they began to look for me and we're going to lunch and so we had our table that we sat at and so I just kind of learned how to click with the group.

Q1: Have you done that your whole life, worked hard to fit in to whatever group you're in?

A: I have.[34]

As in the discussion of groupthink in Section IV, our respondents' accounts reflect a certain tension. That is, female and minority directors are valuable in part because of their "outsider" status – their independence from management and other board members, by virtue of their demographic difference – which can reduce groupthink and increase board independence. Yet at the same time all board members are explicitly screened on the basis of their fit with the rest of the group. As the evidence in this Section reveals, rather than embracing their outsider status on the board, female and minority directors report an understandable desire to fit in, to be perceived as just another board member who is competent and valued for her skill set and other substantive attributes, rather than for her gender, race, or ethnicity.

One white male respondent explicitly addressed this tension, in response to a question from us. As Text 14 demonstrates, there is no simple resolution; indeed, there is probably no resolution at all. One must be simultaneously similar and different. Similar enough to be taken seriously and to be able to work effectively in the particular board environment, yet able to maintain whatever distinct perspective might give diversity its salience:

Text 14

Q: One other thing that interests me is we've talked a little bit about people of different backgrounds, demographic backgrounds perhaps bring a different point of view but I wonder if there's pressure on a woman or a person of color when coming onto a board to act just like the white guys who have always been on the board. Do you think there's a conformity pressure that dilutes the value of difference?

[34] 43.

A: There probably is but it doesn't have anything to do with that it's a group of white guys or a group of older guys or a group of conservatives. It just has to do with if a Mormon goes into a biker bar [chuckle], nobody has to say a word and truly not mean anything but you're just there and everybody instinctively as a human take their cues. Culture is, the McKinsey definition is just how do we do things around here? So how do you disagree with a CEO? In some companies the director will go, "I think that's bullshit," and in some companies that would be like throwing mustard on his shirt. In other companies you'd say have you thought about this and pose it like that so that's where the pressure is, is to kind of find the way that things are done effectively and act in that. Now that then gets to this complicated question of well, why are they acting the way they're acting? Is it because they're all white men or whatever it might be? But that could be answered yes because they're all white men but the pressure is not to be like an old white man. It's just to adopt the norms of how things get done and that's no different than it is in the school or my seven year old's kindergarten or wherever it is.[35]

VI CRITICAL MASS VERSUS THE FIRST AND ONLY

Closely related to the problem of fitting in versus being an outsider in the boardroom is the issue of critical mass: the theory that women and racial or ethnic minorities are unlikely to have an impact in the boardroom until they grow from a few tokens into a considerable minority of the board.[36] In contrast to other recent qualitative research on corporate boards, we find limited support among our respondents for critical mass theory.[37]

Some female respondents expressed the view, consistent with Rosabeth Moss Kanter's original articulation of critical mass theory,[38] that having more women on the board increased their comfort level. We also heard stories of the stresses associated with being the first and only female or minority board member, including the pressure to work harder; automatic visibility; and the heightened scrutiny that comes

[35] 45.

[36] Lissa Lamkin Broome, John M. Conley, and Kimberly D. Krawiec, "Does Critical Mass Matter? Views from the Boardroom," 34 *Seattle U. L. Rev.* 1049 (2011) (discussing critical mass in detail).

[37] Compare Vicki W. Kramer et al., *Critical Mass on Corporate Boards: Why Three or More Women Enhance Governance* (Wellesley Centers for Women 2006) (concluding that a critical mass of women improves corporate governance), *with* Broome, Conley, and Krawiec, *supra* note 40 (finding more limited support for critical mass theory).

[38] Rosabeth Moss Kanter, *Men and Women of the Corporation* 206–42 (1977).

with it; being viewed as the sole representative of an essentialized conception of female or minority interests; and anxiety about making it harder for future female or minority candidates.

One white female – and obviously well-read – board member cited both Kanter and Vicki Kramer's Wellesley study[39] of critical mass in response to a question regarding what it felt like to go from being the lone woman on a board to one of three women directors:

> **Text 15**
>
> [I]f you hadn't seen [Vicki Kramer's] work, I wanted to be sure to mention it. But I would have figured that you would, and I'm glad you have. I think she's right: I think there is a feeling that when you have two or certainly three women on the board, then some of the pressure to represent all women, or some of your token visibility in the Rosabeth Moss Kanter sense goes away. I think it makes a difference, yes....
>
> And I do recall, to go back to your earlier question that when I was the only one on the [name of company] board ... it did feel like I was continually representing something, or being a token. And that didn't feel nearly as good as being part of a group of two or three.[40]

Yet our respondents' critical mass narratives were often in tension with their professed comfort with their first and only status. Many of our respondents tend to view themselves as trailblazers – often the first and only female or minority at many important career stages. They exhibit pride in the notion that they are highly qualified corporate directors, accustomed to their outsider status, and needing no additional reassurance or support from the presence of other members of their demographic group. All report an ability to function as effective directors even when the sole female or minority in the boardroom. Moreover, with the possible exception of employee relations, our interviews do not support theories that a critical mass of female directors will produce different, or distinctly feminine, outcomes.

A white female director expressed the point well, in response to a question about how it felt to be the first woman on a particular board:

> **Text 16**
>
> Well that's been my journey so I didn't really feel any different than my entire career [laughter] because when you start your career in the late seventies and early eighties you're the first woman at anything. At [name of company] I was the first woman general manager, first woman brought

---

[39] Kramer et al., *supra* note 41.   [40] 60.

into the management training program, first woman vice-president, you know, those types of things and so it kind of had been my journey so it didn't feel any different than the other things that I had done. I guess probably one of the things that I'm most proud of is that I haven't stayed the only woman on any of the boards that I've joined and that I'm very proud of because I think sometimes companies say, "Well, we've got ours," and they don't pursue it so.[41]

Though both female and minority respondents provided insight on their first and only status, or about tokenism more specifically, very few of our texts address the issue of a critical mass of minority (as opposed to female) directors. In part, this reflects the simple fact that it is hard to find a public company with multiple minority directors. And even when one is found, the minorities may be from different demographic groups, such as African-Americans, Asians, or Hispanics.

VII SIGNALING VERSUS MEANINGLESS PUBLIC RELATIONS

There are also stories that suggest that a diverse board may signal customers, employees, shareholders, and other constituencies such as communities, regulators, or activists about a company's values. When pressed, no one ultimately claimed to believe that customers are aware of who is on the board. However, some recognized that when others – perhaps particular activist groups – point out a lack of diversity, consumers in the underrepresented demographic group might decide to take their business elsewhere. This point was suggested by a white female director of a manufacturing company, when asked what she would say to a skeptical white male board member about the value of diversity. Her response referred to employees as well as customers as recipients of the signal:

Text 17
[I]f we can look like the people who are buying our products, it will show that we respect them and they will either work harder for us and say yup those people respect my opinion because look they have an African American on the board and he speaks for me because I'm an African American or they have women on that board or they have a Chinese

[41] 57.

person on that board and our public will look at us and say they're dedicated to making sure that all voices are heard at that company. The price is the same but company X doesn't have any women or any people of color. I'm going to buy from this company because they are showing that they respect global vision and they respect a lot of people's voices and that's what I would say to this man.[42]

A white male director made a similar point and also referred to employees along with customers:

Text 18
I think it's important for business reasons also because your customers and your employees look at the board and they would like to have representation on the board from their social climb or race or whatever so I do think it's important but it's not the determining factor. The determining factor is whether they're qualified to be on a public company board or not.[43]

We heard skepticism about the extent to which employees actually pay attention to the composition of the board. Nonetheless, some of our respondents are convinced that employees do pay attention and respond to board diversity, perhaps by taking away the message that the company offers opportunity to all. Senior executives who interact with the board on a regular basis are surely aware of the board's demographic composition, and some board members believe that women and minority executives are heartened to see diversity in the body that selects the CEO. We have also heard stories about rank-and-file workers having a positive reaction to board diversity when they were made aware of it. Many of the companies represented in our interview sample did go to some lengths to inform employees of board composition, especially when there was some diversity on the board. Pictures of the board as a group or individually were displayed in the company's annual report, in announcements to employees, and in videos distributed to employees to tout board diversity. In several instances, the effort to connect board members and employees was direct, with the company arranging meetings between a female director and female employees or a minority director seeking to make contact with minority employees. A white female director reported on the effect one such meeting had on the female employees:

[42] 50.   [43] 93.

Text 19

Well, they at least had somebody who was listening. And I guess it had a good effect. It really took a regime change, though, for it to really begin to show up, that there really was interest in top management. I mean, the message came back loud and clear, and everyone decided they were going to do something about making women feel that there was a place for them in top management. But it really took a while for it to come through and.... I was the messenger of that message.[44]

Another white male director observed, however, that the composition of senior management sent a much stronger signal to employees than the composition of the board:

Text 20

[T]he composition of our senior management is four times as important as the composition of the board. That's where the cue is taken is of the CEO and the CEO's direct reports so you could have the most diverse board in the world and if you've got a monoculture of CEO and direct reports, that board doesn't matter very much in the perception of employees.[45]

A minority male director, quoted earlier in Texts 2, 3, and 5, discussed his company's store-level sales associates, but thought that the company had never considered them as recipients of a diversity signal:

Text 21

I would say that the majority of our store-level employees are African American, probably. And so that's interesting. I don't think anyone's ever viewed it as an issue, from that perspective, although you would think we ought to, right?[46]

In only a few cases was shareholder pressure regarding the board's diversity mentioned in our interviews, and in those cases the pressure came from institutional investors:

Text 22

Q: You said earlier that you thought investors might care. What type of investor do you think cares? I'm assuming it's not the hedge funds.

A: Well maybe. I mean it's institutional investors. Yeah. I think they're looking at these things. Probably it doesn't rank very high on their list of things they look at but yeah.[47]

[44] 55.   [45] 45.   [46] 81.   [47] 56.

Regulators, communities, and specific interest groups may also be the recipients of the signals sent by diversity in the boardroom. There may be a sense in some regulated industries that the government regulator is aware of the demographic composition of each company's board and may look more favorably on a company with a demographically diverse board.

Signaling is a complicated phenomenon, however, and especially so in the case of board diversity.[48] In particular, signals must be credible: that is, recipients must be able to differentiate "cheap talk" – meaningless public relations – from meaningful information. Moreover, while such signaling could be a significant reason for and effect of board diversity, it says nothing about whether diversity affects how boards actually function. It is this improved board functioning – rather than signaling – that was most often raised by our respondents as the primary benefit of board diversity.

VIII IF BOARD DIVERSITY IS GOOD, WHY ISN'T THERE MORE OF IT?

As we have repeatedly noted, almost all respondents said that board diversity was beneficial, and many expressed a desire to see more of it. When we asked why boards were not more diverse, the response almost always related to the talent pool. Many thought it was just a matter of time before more women and minorities gained sufficient experience at the appropriate corporate level to be qualified for and considered for board service. A white male board member gave what seemed to be the standard explanation:

Text 23
Well the easy answer is because there's not enough qualified people but I think that's a copout. I think that a lot of work needs to be done in educating boards and the CEOs to get on the ball here. It's frustrating to me at times that more progress hasn't been made in the forty years that I've been doing this and I don't have an excuse for it other than there's not enough pressure, if that's the right word, being placed on CEOs for upper level management considered female or minority. I think we're getting a larger and larger pool of qualified talent every year. I mean it

[48] Signaling is discussed in more detail in Lissa Lamkin Broome and Kimberly D. Krawiec, "Signaling Through Board Diversity: Is Anyone Listening?" 77 *U. Cin. L. Rev.* 431 (2008).

takes twenty to twenty-five years to get somebody to the level of experience of a [name of a white male director]. You don't get that in five years so it's an ongoing process and I would say probably we didn't wake up until the eighties in getting people educated and into first level management positions so that they could go further so I think maybe now we're starting to see the results of that and that's why there's more qualified people coming but I don't have any excuse for why there's fifteen percent of the people on boards or management.[49]

A few respondents acknowledged that boards would need to look beyond CEOs and retired CEOs – the preferred background in many board searches – to find women and minority candidates. These respondents suggested CFOs (for their financial expertise) or division presidents, COOs, or others with significant responsibility for profit and loss as places to look for candidates.

Some respondents assumed that the pipeline for female board members would fill faster than that for minorities, perhaps by virtue of the fact that fifty percent of the population is female. As a white female director put it:

Text 24
I would say there are fewer salient racial minority leaders who are brought to our attention, than women. And I'm not quite sure why that would be. But we had a harder time deepening our list of minority candidates than women, even though, in the end, I think we had some very strong minority representatives. So, it may be that there are just fewer people who come to mind, or it may be that as a woman I was more aware of the women I wanted to suggest.[50]

Only a few respondents appeared to have carefully considered why the pipeline was not fuller, and whether those conditions would change in the coming years.

Perhaps the reason for the lack of increased board diversity is as simple as the perception by some board members that a board that has a woman or two and perhaps a minority is a diverse board, necessitating no further efforts to find female or minority candidates. In response to the question of why the level of board gender diversity is not higher, given the apparent support for greater diversity among board members themselves, a diversity advocate who participates in training programs for women seeking director positions stated:

[49] 93.   [50] 60.

Text 25

Well because I think diversity becomes like a check the box thing. You know what I mean?

Q: So one is enough?

A: One is enough....[51]

A white male director who identified himself as a diversity advocate gave a similar response, but was optimistic about the future:

Text 26

I think we've stalled. I think we've gotten one of those, and one of that, and maybe we'll get two, but I think we're going to get over the hump, one, because I think the pool is so much larger today, which is all products of what is happening in society.[52]

But the notion of stalling may have another dimension: that is, the economy may be causing future directors to stall out on the preferred career path before becoming board-ready. In the words of another white male board member:

Text 27

One of the things that's holding [greater board diversity] back is the economy and companies aren't doing as well. Companies are retrenching. Management ranks are shrinking. They're not growing. You don't have the people going up in the organization that you did maybe five years ago so that certainly is not helping the situation at all. Also, boards are becoming smaller.[53]

There is also relatively low turnover on corporate boards. In the absence of a contest for control, the election of directors by shareholder proxy is largely a *pro forma* process in which boards are self-perpetuating. Thus, directors usually leave a board only when they decide to step down on their own or face a mandatory retirement age imposed by the board. This lack of board turnover leads to relatively few opportunities for new board members, including women and minorities.

IX CONCLUSION: WHY ARE RACE AND GENDER SO "DANGEROUS"?

During the course of this project we have come to think of gender, race, and ethnicity as "dangerous categories" because our respondents have

[51] 49.   [52] 69.   [53] 93.

had so much difficulty talking about them. On the one hand, with only one or two exceptions, everyone we interviewed has agreed that attention to diversity along these demographic axes leads to a better boardroom. But on the other, just about everyone has struggled to articulate precisely why this is or should be true. A related manifestation of the danger is the awkwardness that so many respondents showed in discussing whether directors from diverse categories really *are* different. That is, many people argued – often strongly – that diversity produces different perspectives, sensibilities, and points of view. But many of those same respondents also stressed with equal vehemence that all directors are really the same, with their performance based solely on their personal abilities and professional qualifications. Significantly, we observed this phenomenon across the entire demographic spectrum of the people we interviewed.

Perhaps this tension reflects a fear of saying that people of diverse demographic backgrounds are different in some meaningful way. Those who are not members of traditionally unrepresented groups do not want to be seen as stereotyping or essentializing by identifying particular unique attributes of members of those groups. At the same time, those who are members of the traditionally unrepresented groups have an interest in presenting themselves as being selected for board service because of their professional merit without regard to their gender, race, and ethnicity. Thus, neither group is comfortable discussing potential differences between men and women, between blacks and whites, or between Hispanics and non-Hispanics. As a result, though our respondents assert that diversity matters because female and minority directors bring something "different" to the table, they are uncomfortable with discussing in any detail what those differences are.

To illustrate, an African-American female board member strongly denied that her contributions to the board were based on race or gender:

Text 28

Q: You talked before about reasons for diversity. In your time on the [name of company] board, can you think of any specific instances where you think you made a contribution that might reflect on the fact that you were a woman or a minority that somebody else with a similar skill set to you who was a white male wouldn't have made?

A: No. I don't. I don't think that I ever brought anything to the table where there were any social issues or other issues that I brought a different viewpoint to the table or a different perspective because

I was a minority or because I was a woman. Every decision that I made had to do with it was a business decision in terms of strategy, exercising independent judgment, really evaluating everything to make sure that whatever vote that I cast, whatever way or the other, it had been weighed sufficiently.[54]

Another African-American female director echoed the first woman's comments:

Text 29
Q: Can you give us any examples of where you think you made a particularly important contribution in the board room and that perhaps a white male would not have had that same insight or same contribution?

A: Well, I think that I make a contribution across the board on all aspects of the items we cover – strategy, finances, compensation, governance – really, all the big issues that we cover as a board. I'm not on any Audit Committees, but I think I make a contribution with respect to the financial state of the business, because I always have an option, very often I'm agreeing with that of management, or with that of other board members; if I disagree, I give them the reasons why. I would say that I don't think there are too many glaring examples, but I can say that I never forget two things – one, that my principal constituency base is the shareholders, and that is *all* the shareholders, so is this something that's reasonable for the shareholders. So, for example, I'm a person who's thoroughly opposed to tax gross-ups because that's just giving away corporate money, and I feel like we pay our executives well enough that they can pay their taxes like everybody else, like you and I do, which is out of our income – I'm just opposed to it. So across the board I vote against that. I have sometimes been voted down, so the vote will be 12 board members; it'll be 11 to 1. That's fine, just put it in the record. They don't want to put it in the record. That's not a *black* thing, you have to understand that.[55]

White male directors were similarly unwilling or unable to articulate unique contributions from female or minority directors:

Text 30
Q: Going back to when you got the two women on the board, are there any anecdotes or examples that you can think of, of specific contributions that either one of them made to board discussion that they had a different insight or a different way of looking at things?

[54] 43. [55] 59.

A: You know, I don't really think so. I mean I can't really think of anything in specific. But the thing that I remember more about the two of them as females, they were just as vocal during board meetings and on certain issues, if not more vocal, than some of the male board members we had.[56]

But denying difference may be dangerous as well. If there are no relevant differences between women and minorities and white males in the board room, then why are women and minorities not more equitably represented on corporate boards?

A telling clue came in response to what was usually one of our last questions: "Are there other directors you know, that you think we should talk to?" In almost all cases, respondents provided the names of women or minority directors. Very few referred us to white men, even though they constitute the majority of directors, and even though we always mentioned that our study was not limited to female and minority respondents. Indeed, we often specifically requested the names of white males, in an attempt to garner a representative sample of directors. Are women and minorities assumed to be the only ones who have thought about diversity or who would be willing to take the time to talk about the impact of board diversity? If so, then this adds another tension to our respondents' stories: though almost all insist that diversity is good and important, the assumption is that only female or minority directors would have any interest in discussing it.

A final example that epitomizes just how dangerous – and incoherent – discussions of race and gender in board selection can be came from a highly experienced white male director. We discussed one board's perceived need to diversify by adding an African-American director. He began by stating that the board in question had made a "conscious decision" to seek an African-American candidate. Yet even though race was a "big, big plus factor" only one of three finalists was African-American – and "not because of color":

Text 31
Q: And was this a fairness or responsibility argument again that we need to have an African American on the board?

A: Well it was a conscious decision by the board that we felt given equal qualifications we would prefer to have a minority and specifically if we could an African American.

[56] 87.

Q: And was that more just sort of you felt it was the right thing to do or because of specific business imperatives?

A: No. It was the right thing to do.

Q: The right thing to do. Okay.

Q: Was the search limited by that as a factor or was it an open search with that as a big plus factor?

A: It was an open search with that as a big, big plus factor and we narrowed it down to ten people. I think half of them were African Americans and a couple of them were Hispanic. No. I shouldn't say that. Three or four were African Americans, two or three were Hispanic. There was one Oriental and I think there were a couple of females. We interviewed the top five and [an African American male] came out on top. Incidentally, the number two person was a white male. The number three person in the whole thing was a female.

Q2: So despite the strong plus for an African American candidate, really only one of the top three was an African American.

A: Only because of qualification and not because of color.[57]

While pursuit of diversity may be fraught with ambiguity, the outcome of that pursuit is not. The numbers are inescapable: boards are *not* diverse along gender or racial grounds. During the course of our interviews we heard many concrete ideas for improving those numbers, including:

- Define qualifications more broadly. Include other C-suite executives besides the CEO as well as division presidents and leaders from government service, accounting, retired military, and academia.
- Do not require prior public company board experience.
- Limit some searches to women or minority candidates.
- Identify the skill sets needed for new board members and then look specifically for women or minorities who have that skill set, rather using diversity as a "plus" factor.
- Value different perspectives that could be provided by someone with different industry experience (e.g., technology or mining firms going outside of these industries), or from a younger person with experience with social media or other emerging technologies that older directors may not be familiar with.

[57] 93.

- Work on structural issues that may impede the advancement of women and minorities in corporations.
- Consider ways to "refresh" the board, and create opportunities for new board members including women and minorities, by imposing mandatory retirement ages, rigorous board assessment, or some form of term limits, including deeming a long-serving director as no longer satisfying the requirements to be deemed an independent director.

It remains to be seen, of course, whether these ideas will be implemented to any significant extent and, if so, whether they will lead to greater diversity. If that does happen, the next – and ultimately most interesting – question will be whether and how increased diversity changes boardroom dynamics. Based on the evidence of this study, it could go either way. Perhaps diversity really will produce different perspectives that lead to richer discussion, less groupthink, and better-informed decisions. But it is also possible that the pressure to fit in and reach consensus, and the concomitant fear of contentious debate and divisive votes, will overwhelm the potential value of difference. If that happens, tomorrow's boards could look different while continuing to reproduce yesterday's status quo.

As a final thought, we return to the law partnership-corporate director parallels we suggested in the Introduction. First, the topic of diversity is probably as dangerous in law firms as in the corporate context. The idea of diversity to satisfy the demands of corporate clients is broadly accepted, if cynically self-interested. It is also plausible that firms that represent individuals (e.g., small plaintiff's firms) might want lawyers with obvious demographic connections to a diverse clientele. But beyond that, we suspect that it is hard to say – in every sense of that phrase – why diversity should matter in a law firm, especially a large one that specializes in business matters. Do lawyers think that they work more effectively in teams with racial and gender diversity? Is groupthink a problem in handling mergers or intellectual property litigation? Do law firm partners think that female and minority lawyers have unique perspectives on legal problems? And if they did think so, would they say it?

Some of our bullet-point recommendations for improving director diversity might also be adapted to the law firm context. For example, the idea of defining qualifications more broadly has a clear analog: selective legal employers could almost certainly reduce their obsession with law school grades without any effect on the quality of their legal work.[58] Law firms and their recruiters could also work more assiduously in identifying women or minority candidates with the skill set being sought in a new or lateral attorney to ensure that there is a wide and deep pool of candidates, rather than just listing diversity as a "plus" factor in the hiring decision. Even more obvious is the need for law firms to "work on structural issues that may impede the advancement of women and minorities," in particular the lack of mentors and in-firm sponsors and the uneven distribution of high-value work.

The lack of turnover on boards may also be an issue in law firms. As economic forces change the market for legal services, the traditional pyramid of one partner to three associates in law firms is under pressure. Many firms no longer hire large classes of incoming associates, instead favoring less and more targeted lateral hiring from other firms. As associate ranks dwindle, the number of new partners made by promotion from within is likely to decrease, with potentially detrimental effects on the ability of women and minorities to increase their relative representation in the ranks of law firm partners. Law firms may also need to address ways to make room for women and minorities at the highest level of law firms.

Just as in the director context, however, it remains to be seen whether these ideas will be implemented and, if they are, whether they will lead to greater diversity. If they do, it will be equally interesting to see if they lead to any material change in the dynamics of law practice and the quality of legal work.

APPENDIX

Transcript Number Date (Text)

09 07/30/07 (Text 1)
23 11/30/07 (Text 6)
36 04/22/08 (Text 8)
41 05/07/08 (Text 11)

---

[58] Lisa Webley, et al., "Access to a Career in the Legal Profession in England and Wales: 'Race', Class and the Role of Educational Background," 2013 *ABF Symposium* (finding in qualitative study of women and minority lawyers in England and Wales that the University attended was a powerful indicator of successful entry into the profession, whereas grades achieved became relevant only if the entrant had met the first requirement of attending an elite university).

43 05/18/08 (Texts 12, 13, 28)
45 08/08/08 (Texts 14, 20)
49 09/24/08 (Text 25)
50 10/03/08 (Text 17)
55 11/14/08 (Text 19)
56 11/14/08 (Text 22)
57 12/12/08 (Text 16)
59 02/18/09 (Text 29)
60 05/21/09 (Texts 15, 24)
69 11/19/09 (Text 26)
81 04/07/11 (Texts 2, 3, 5, 21)
83 08/25/11 (Text 4)
87 12/14/11 (Text 30)
93 01/11/12 (Texts 18, 23, 27, 31)
95 03/30/12 (Texts 7, 9, 10)

EXPLAINING SOCIAL EXCLUSION AND THE 'WAR FOR TALENT' IN THE UK'S ELITE PROFESSIONAL SERVICE FIRMS

LOUISE ASHLEY AND LAURA EMPSON

INTRODUCTION

There is a belief current within many organizations today that they are engaged in a 'war for talent'. Attention to this feature of organizational life is generally traced to publication of a book by the same name, by a group of McKinsey consultants in 2001 (Michaels, Handfield-Jones and Axelrod, 2001). The *War for Talent* advocates that top firms should develop a 'talent mind-set,' defined as a deep-seated belief that having better talent at all levels is how an organization can outperform its competitors. This mind-set has encouraged organizations to focus on attracting only the very 'best of the best' within the labour market, a task which has apparently become more challenging as the demand for great talent outstrips supply (Michaels et al., 2001). In the context of an apparent scarcity of top talent available to organizations, scholars and policy makers have suggested that one solution is to diversify their supply. Initiatives designed by elite professional service firms (PSFs) and charities to broaden access to the sector according to social background have been positioned as a means to improve the supply of talented graduates, whilst also rectifying their historic tendency to exclude on the basis of social class (Ashley, 2010; Ashley and Empson, 2013; Cabinet Office, 2009; Cook, Faulconbridge and Muzio, 2012; Sommerlad, 2011).

Based on a qualitative study of five elite PSFs in the UK, this study interrogates the concept of the 'war for talent' and questions its effects. We ask: *how have recruitment and selection processes implemented by elite*

PSFs helped to construct the 'war for talent'? On the basis of these findings, we discuss to what extent the 'war for talent' can be reconciled with the professed commitment to improved diversity and inclusion on the basis of social class in elite PSFs.

To date, the notion that a 'war for talent' exists within professional labour markets has been treated uncritically within the academic literature and the effects of this battle have been under-theorized (Gardner, 2002; Hiltrop, 1999; Ng and Burke, 2005; Somaya and Williamson, 2008). However, given its apparent salience in the practitioner context, critical engagement with the 'war for talent' is essential (Lewis and Heckman, 2006). In this study, we show that the key challenge faced by elite PSFs with respect to graduate recruitment and selection is not an absolute scarcity of talent, but an increasing abundance of qualified graduates, as a result of the expansion of higher education in the UK. In this context, leaders within elite PSFs find it difficult to accurately identify potential. They have responded by defining 'talent' according to an increasingly narrow set of educational credentials, confined to a small set of degrees, obtained from a limited set of elite universities.

We suggest that a perceived 'war for talent' arises, at least in part, because most elite PSFs in the UK have identified the same 'ideal type' of graduate candidate, and subsequently compete with each other to recruit and select individuals from this relatively small pool. Ownership of these credentials tends to be heavily concentrated amongst more economically privileged students and as a result, this approach creates the conditions for inequality and exclusion. This finding has important implications for the likely success of diversity and inclusion programmes which in principle at least, seek to achieve opposite goals.

In the remainder of this chapter, we develop our argument as follows. First, we describe the theoretical perspectives that have been used to explain social exclusion across the professions and outline the construction of the 'war for talent', which has arguably become the new orthodoxy in management practice (Gladwell, 2002). Second, we describe the methodology for our qualitative study. Third, we describe the findings from our empirical research. We conclude by considering the theoretical implications of our findings, and argue that policies designed to address exclusion on the basis of social background within elite PSFs are unlikely to be successful unless and until they arrive at a new definition of 'talent'.

THEORETICAL CONTEXT

We start by synthesising previous empirical research, which has attempted to explain social exclusion within the professions and the key theoretical frameworks employed in this context. Next, we describe the adoption of the diversity and inclusion agenda in the professions alongside the historical development of the 'war for talent'.

Social exclusion and higher education

Recent concern with access to the professions in the UK according to social background can be traced to the publication of the *Cabinet Office Panel for Fair Access to the Professions* (2009). This reported that students from less privileged socioeconomic backgrounds continue to face significant difficulties with respect to entering the elite professions. In the UK, this problem is particularly acute within the legal sector where solicitors born in 1970 grew up in families with an average income 65 per cent higher than the UK average (Cabinet Office, 2009). The accountancy sector has experienced a significant decline in social mobility over the past thirty years. Whilst accountants born in 1958 grew up in families with an income close to the national average, those born in 1970 grew up in families with an income 40 per cent above the national average. Whilst there is less data available than in other elite occupations, evidence of social exclusion also extends to the financial services sector. For example, during 2011, The Sutton Trust examined the educational background of over 7,000 of what they call the UK's 'leading people' and found that 57 per cent of those in financial services had attended fee-paying schools (The Sutton Trust, 2012). This compares to 7 per cent of the UK population.

Social mobility and access to the professions has declined during the same period as higher education has dramatically expanded in the UK. Thus, whilst in the 1960s there were only 200,000 students in university (Dearing, 1997), today there are more than 2 million students in the UK's universities (www.hesa.ac.uk/pis/urg). The expansion of higher education has been justified by successive UK governments in relation to a human capitalist perspective, which posits a relatively straightforward relationship between education and success (Becker, 1975; 2006). This relationship, its proponents argue, leads to merito-cratic labour markets which achieve equality of opportunity because ascribed characteristics that people acquire automatically as a result of family background become less important than achieved characteristics such as educational qualifications (Jackson, 2001). In practice, however, the expansion of higher education in the UK has benefitted mainly the middle-classes (Greenbank and Hepworth, 2008). This is partly because this expansion has been accompanied by a significant division between prestigious 'old' universities[1] (including the 'Russell Group') which are predominantly populated by students from relatively privileged backgrounds, and less prestigious 'new' universities, which recruit higher numbers of students from less privileged backgrounds. For example, the proportion of young, full-time undergraduate entrants to Russell Group universities from less advantaged social backgrounds was 19 per cent in 2011/12 (SMCPC, 2013), which compares to just under 33 per cent for all universities in the UK in 2013/14 (www.hesa.ac.uk/pis/urg).

Studies have shown that this division is not necessarily a reflection of lesser ability, but of unequal access to resources and effective teaching (Metcalf, 1997). Nevertheless, it has the effect of limiting access to the professions for less privileged students, as most elite firms exert a strong preference for graduates educated at 'old' universities, particularly the Russell Group (Ashley and Empson, 2013; Cook et al., 2012). Indeed, research published in 2013 asked leading graduate employers which universities in the UK they had formally targeted for graduate recruitment promotions during the previous year. The results show that 43 per cent of these top employers, which included elite professional service firms, focused their efforts on an average of 15 or fewer universities, and that the top five universities targeted by the largest number of leading graduate employers are Warwick, Nottingham, Manchester, Cambridge

---

[1] The expansion of higher education in the UK was particularly facilitated through the creation of a number of 'new' universities, ex-polytechnics which became universities under the Further and Higher Education Act in 1992. Today, 52 per cent of school leavers attend university in the UK, compared to 16 per cent in 1989. However, a distinction remains between 'old' universities and new universities. The former are pre-1992 institutions which are commonly considered more prestigious than post-1992 or 'new' universities. The Russell Group is a self-selecting consortium of twenty-four leading old universities including Oxford and Cambridge ('Oxbridge'), which is often used as shorthand for the UK's most prestigious universities, a designation relating in part to their strong research output and higher entry requirements. Typically, Russell Group universities will require students to have 360 UCAS points (at least three A grades in their A-levels), which is achieved by one-tenth of all A-level students each year, or approximately 115,000 students. A-levels are the exams taken by students in the UK during their final year at school.

and Bristol, all of which are members of the Russell Group (www.high
fliers.co.uk/download/GMReport13.pdf).

The relationship between higher education and social exclusion has
been theorized extensively by Pierre Bourdieu, who suggested that the
major role of the education system is the reproduction of the culture of
the dominant class, who have the power to impose and legitimate
meanings, and to define their own culture as the basis for knowledge
in the education system. Students from more privileged backgrounds
are subsequently advantaged because they are more likely to have been
socialized in the dominant culture, and thus to achieve higher educational attainments. Bourdieu (1972; 1984; 1985; 1988) further characterized society as divided in to fields or domains of power, within which
an individual's success will depend in part on their access to, or
ownership of, various forms of capital (Bourdieu 1991). Arguably the
most significant forms of capital are *social capital*, which is generated by
relationships and can broadly be defined as the values and networks
passed down from friends and family, and *cultural capital*, which exists in
three forms: embodied capital refers to properties of the self, which are
usually transmitted from the family through socialisation; objectified
capital is represented by cultural goods; institutional capital is represented by academic credentials and qualifications, which are recognized
by institutions, including the labour market. What can constitute
cultural capital are those symbolic goods which the elites of the field
recognize as such through 'cultural authorization' (Young, 1990).

A related approach makes an explicit association between social
exclusion and the *expansion* of higher education, with the latter theorized as a 'positional good' (Saunders, 2006). According to this interpretation, it is hypothesized that faced with a growing abundance of
similarly qualified graduates, employers have increasingly turned to
other markers to define quality, including educational, institutional
and embodied capital. Again, since these forms of capital are both
arbitrarily legitimated and typically associated with the possession of
relative wealth, the expansion of higher education has not had the
anticipated effect of opening up the labour market on more equitable
terms overall. Brown (2003) describes a difference between 'ranking'
and 'rigging' strategies of social groups within a competitive labour
market, where ranking refers to the ability of individuals to mobilize
social, cultural and economic assets to secure a labour market advantage, whilst 'rigging' refers to the ability of social groups to influence the
rules of the competition and so 'rig' the game in order to favour people

like themselves by, for example, determining the particular validity of certain extra-curricular activities (Gordon, 2013).

Scholars working within the neo-Weberian tradition also adopt a critical perspective in relation to social exclusion. A body of theoretical and empirical work has been developed here which suggests that the high status historically enjoyed by the professions has been secured through exclusivity, which in turn depends on the construction of both professionals and professional knowledge as distinctive, valuable, and reserved for the few and the finest (Ashcraft et al., 2012: 473). The concept of the 'professional project' has been influential here, and presents the process of professionalism as an 'attempt to translate one order of scarce resources – special knowledge and skills – into another – social and economic rewards' (Larson, 1977: xvii). When the possessors of a certain body of abstract knowledge can standardize and control the dissemination of the knowledge base, they can dominate their market and enter a 'regulative bargain' in which occupational closure is sanctioned by the state (Macdonald, 1995: 10). This will allow them to further restrict access to their knowledge base and control the number of members on the basis of formal barriers, including qualifications and credentials, and by supervising the 'production of producers' (Larson, 1977: 71).

However, the construction of professional knowledge as both scarce and valuable is not stable (Macdonald, 1995). Specific challenges to the professions over the past twenty years include the development and growth of large, multinational PSFs, a trend encouraged and facilitated by globalization, and leading to a significant fragmentation of the professions (Faulconbridge and Muzio, 2008). Over the same period a move towards graduate entry has contributed towards the social standing of many elite professions, yet simultaneously caused professional bodies to lose control over their supply side, as a result of democratization and diversification of the student body. Again, this challenge can be related in part to the expansion of higher education over the past thirty years in the UK. This development has supplied the labour force required by the increasing numbers of very large, multinational firms (Derber, 1982) but has also led to some diversification away from the white, male, middle-class norm.

Scholars working within the neo-Weberian tradition have adopted Bourdieusian (1984; 1985; 1988) theory to explain how occupational closure is specifically operationalized against this backdrop, using informal rather than formal barriers to entry alone. They suggest that whilst relevant credentials and qualifications are relatively abundant, an illusion of scarcity within the professional labour market is maintained as firms exert strong preferences for graduates with certain types of legitimized embodied capital, and through the commodification and inflation in the value of traditional markers of elite status defined as institutional capital, in particular in the UK, a degree from Oxford or Cambridge (Sommerlad, 2011). As such, though the precise explanation may vary, most relevant theoretical frameworks suggest a relationship between social exclusion from the professions, the expansion of higher education, and unequal access to the forms of capital. We show next how the impact of these processes has been tacitly recognized by the UK government and professional regulators, such that PSFs have been expected to respond (Cabinet Office, 2009; Social Mobility and Child Poverty Commission, 2013.)

Diversity, inclusion and the talent agenda

Publication of the *Cabinet Office Panel for Fair Access to the Professions* in 2009 drew attention to the issues of social mobility and access to the professions. This led to a report entitled '*Unleashing Aspirations*', which offered over 100 recommendations at a societal and organizational level, based on apparent 'best practice', in order to encourage change within the professions, which was followed in 2012 by the *Social Mobility Toolkit for the Professions* (Spada, 2012). This latter document is positioned by its authors as a common framework for measuring social mobility within the professions. The toolkit also provides practical recommendations for employer organizations, professional bodies and regulators on how they can develop social mobility. In 2013, the UK's Social Mobility and Child Poverty Commission, which had been established by the coalition government the previous year, published a report entitled '*State of the Nation*,' which summarized progress towards improved social mobility, including access to the professions.

In each publication, change is said to start at the societal level and recommendations are designed to recognize that relative disadvantage starts at a young age. However, a key goal is to widen participation to elite universities, so that more people from less privileged backgrounds attend the institutions from which leading PSFs select. At the macro-level, universities are encouraged to offer bursaries and scholarships for less privileged students and indeed, since the implementation of the new fees regime in the UK, this has become a condition for funding. For professional firms, recommendations include the suggestion that they should address a lack of social capital amongst less privileged students by providing mentoring and paid internship opportunities. PSFs are also encouraged to open up more routes for non-graduate entry.

Partly in response a number of initiatives have been designed across the professions to encourage diversity and inclusion on the basis of social background. Within the legal sector initiatives include educational charity The Sutton Trust's 'Pathways to Law'. An additional programme, Prime, is a consortium of leading UK law firms aiming to improve access to the law for less privileged students, with Access Accountancy having similar goals in that sector. Charitable body the Social Mobility Foundation works across the professions to deliver their programmes, which seek to improve access on the basis of social background to a range of sectors including accountancy, law and financial services. The common goal of these programmes is to identify students who are under-privileged using a range of socioeconomic measures, but who are otherwise suitably qualified for a professional career according to academic criteria. Eligible students are subsequently provided with support, mentoring and skills training, which it is intended will help them to access an elite university, and also internships, which are considered a critical pathway to eventual employment at an elite PSF.

The adoption of these and other initiatives has been encouraged by the UK government and regulators in relation to a 'business case' based primarily on the attraction and retention of diverse talent. For example, the report published by the Social Mobility and Child Poverty Commission (2013: p. 227) and cited here claims that 'there is both a business case and a fairness case ... unfair practices deny businesses access to talent'. Business case arguments have also been employed by the charities operating these initiatives and by the firms who adopt them. For example, in exhorting law firms to join their programme, Prime's publicity material states that: 'By opening the doors to the profession you will also be opening your firm to real talent, broadening the pool from which to hire the professionals of tomorrow'. In 2012, a partner at leading law firm Allen & Overy predicted that: 'The increased heat in the war for talent will result in the production of a truly diverse workforce. This will lead to a final assault on the last great prejudice – class'[2]. In 2010 the Chief Executive of the Social Mobility Foundation, was quoted as saying that: 'There is a veritable war for

[2] www.allenovery.com/SiteCollectionDocuments/Employment%20Report.pdf#page=12&zoom=auto,0,313

talent ... [law firms are] interested in making the legal profession accessible to those from lower socioeconomic backgrounds, but their primary aim is to source talent'.[3]

Within the banking sector, one leading investment bank has given its diversity and inclusion committee the moniker 'War for Talent Committee'. Within the accountancy sector, in 2012 the chief executive of the Institute for Chartered Accountants in England and Wales, Michael Izza, said that the accountancy profession was *leading the way* in driving social mobility and positioned diversity efforts in relation to a highly competitive marketplace, for both people and business. He said: 'If we are to compete in a tough global marketplace with better-qualified people and stronger skills, it's vital that government continues to work with business and the professions so that we can all take advantage of the economic opportunities this will bring. The accountancy profession is ready to play its part'[4].

Recruiting and retaining a more diverse talent base is then expected to offer organizations a key competitive advantage given apparent limitations of supply (Brown and Tannock, 2009; Barnett and Hall, 2001; Cox and Blake, 1991). As such, these initiatives are clearly associated with the so-called 'war for talent', the term coined by a group of McKinsey consultants in 2001 (Michaels, Handfield-Jones and Axelrod, 2001). The *War for Talent* was the result of extensive research by consulting firm McKinsey amongst large US corporations, which aimed to establish how top-performing companies differ from their peers. The consultants leading the project concluded that success in the modern economy depends upon developing a talent 'mind-set', defined as a 'deep-seated belief that having better talent at all levels is how you outperform your competitors' (Michaels et al., 2001: 22).

Proponents of the 'war for talent' ascribe to human capital theory yet also develop the relationship proposed in this context between learning and earning. They focus on the need to differentiate employees based on performance and to attract and nurture so-called 'A-players' who are in the top ten per cent of talent available (Brown and Tannock, 2009; Smart, 2005; Robertson and Abbey, 2003). A strong focus on attracting and rewarding only the very 'brightest and the best' is arguably both cause and effect of a situation in which

[3] www.legalweek.com/legal-week/analysis/1598104/training-education-the-talent-grab
[4] www.accountancyage.com/aa/news/2180822/accountancy-follow-lawyers-social-mobility#ixzz2MBpRFcmA

organizations operate in scarcity mode with regard to talent (Beechler and Woodward, 2009; Rowley and Jackson, 2010). This scarcity has been attributed in part to demographic changes and also to the rise of the knowledge economy in which human assets are said to have become a critical feature of organizational performance (Pink, 2001).

Some commentators from a more critical perspective have noted that McKinsey's key case study for the talent mind-set was Enron which, as history has shown us, is not a company noted for its long-term ethical or indeed commercial success (Gladwell, 2002; Eichenwald, 2005). Writing specifically in relation to higher education and the 'global war for talent', Brown and Tannock (2009) suggest that the latter is a construct which contributes towards social, economic and educational inequality. They argue that the relatively vague definition of 'talent' used by many corporate employers may give them leeway to 'make self-interested and unfair recruitment and promotion decisions', and that talent as conceived by business elites in the global war for talent is narrowly defined in terms of formal educational credentials, market value and business interest (Brown and Tannock, 2009: 387).

The ambiguity associated with definitions of 'talent' is reflected in the literature where sometimes talent refers to the entirety of an organization's workforce, but often relates to only the top ten per cent of performers within an organization (Beechler and Woodward, 2009; Rowley and Jackson, 2011). Precisely who fits into that category is though uncertain. For example, Michaels et al., (2001: xii) call talent the 'sum of all our abilities', whilst at the same time state that it 'eludes description: you simply know it when you see it'. Widely adopted within the practitioner context, the academic literature has also accepted the notion that a 'war for talent' exists, and as a result the effects of this battle have been under-theorized (Gardner, 2002; Hiltrop, 1999; Ng and Burke, 2005; Somaya and Williamson, 2008; Tymon and Stumpf, 2001). In the remainder of this paper, we explore the relationship been the 'war for talent', diversity and social exclusion, based on data from five elite PSFs.

METHODOLOGY

This paper draws on two sequential studies. The first, conducted in 2010, was intended to examine the introduction, development and implementation of diversity and inclusion programmes in the context of large international PSFs in the UK. Though social class was not the only diversity strand addressed in this study, it emerged as an important theme early on, as did the relationship with 'talent'. In order to investigate this relationship in detail, this study was followed up during 2012 with a study which examined social class, the 'war for talent' and access to a large investment bank based in the City of London. In further detail, the sequential studies can be broken down as follows:

Phase 1: Focused on assessing the value of diversity strategies as a means to widen access in leading PSFs. The central question guiding the study was: *can diversity deliver fair outcomes where equal opportunities have not?* This study consisted of in-depth case studies of the London offices of two law firms of which one was in the top ten by turnover in the UK, three accountancies all of which are in the 'big six' leading firms in the UK and one management consultancy. Similar themes were evident at each of these firms. However, the focus here is on the 'war for talent' at the most prestigious elite PSFs in the UK. Since the management consultancy we studied and one of the law firms arguably fall just outside this definition, they are not reported on here.

Phase 2: The second phase of the research extended our analysis to a large investment bank in the City of London, and focused specifically on social class. The key question here was first: *how and why does this firm discriminate within the graduate labour market on the basis of social class?* Second: *what is the likely impact of diversity and inclusion programmes implemented by the firm to address social exclusion?*

Development of research questions

The purpose of the first study was to understand the impact of diversity and inclusion agendas across a range of axes. Consistent with the grounded nature of the study, interviewees in the first phase of the study were not asked about class directly. However, the issue was comprehensively discussed in relation to two general questions. The first was: *what is the biggest diversity challenge for your firm?* The second was: *to what extent do ethnic minorities experience challenges that white people do not in this firm?* Often, because of the intersections between ethnicity and class, the latter would come up in response to the second question. Interviewees would then talk about this in relation to either recruitment or career progression or sometimes both. Class was also discussed in the context of other people's experiences and the interviewee's perceived views of client expectations. In the second phase of the research, the issue of class was addressed directly through a series of

TABLE 4.1   Sample Group at Case Study Firms

	Mars Bank			Moon Accounting			Star Accounting			Planet Accounting			Galaxy Law			Total
	MD	VP	SM	P	D	SM	P	D	SM	P	D	SM	P	SA	JA	
M	4	5	2		2	1	3	1	4	5	3	1	6	5		42
F		2	4	4	1	3	1	2	5	3	2	2	3	5	1	38
T	17			11			16			16			20			80

questions, which were designed specifically to understand if, how and why the firm discriminated on the basis of social class within the graduate labour market, and the likely impact of diversity and inclusion programmes to address this situation.

Data collection and analysis
A total of eighty interviews were conducted in the five case study firms we report on here (Table 4.1). Interviews took place on the organisations' own premises and were recorded for transcription and detailed field notes were taken. At all five firms, interviewees were purposively selected with a particular emphasis on senior staff who had previous and/or current responsibility for graduate recruitment and selection, and/or with responsibility for agendas aimed at diversity and social inclusion. All interviews were conducted by the first author, face-to-face and took up to one hour.

We also examined the corporate websites of the six largest English law firms in the UK, the six largest investment banks, and the six largest accountancy firms, which are counted amongst the most prestigious and largest graduate employers in the UK (Highfliers, 2013),[5] with the intention to understand how these firms present and design their approach to graduate recruitment, selection and to social inclusion. Corporate websites are an important source of information about these specific areas and the specific principles and values espoused by elite PSFs. They also provide details of the graduate schemes available, along

[5] Law firms included Clifford Chance, Linklaters, Freshfields Bruckhaus Deringer, Allen & Overy and DLA Piper International; accountancy firms included EY, KPMG, Deloitte, PWC, BDO and Grant Thornton; investment banks included Goldman Sachs, Morgan Stanley, J.P. MorganChase, Bank of America Merrill Lynch and Deutsche Bank.

with the skills, qualifications and competencies for which the firm looks, and information on how and when a candidate should apply. Since almost all applications are nowadays submitted on-line, candidates must by necessity visit the graduate careers pages on a potential employer's website.

The data collection and analysis was designed to reveal how assumptions about social class, underlying values and behaviour, were justified and explained particularly with respect to talent. We searched for references to graduate recruitment; to graduate selection; and to diversity and social inclusion. References to graduate recruitment were coded as relating to an 'abundance' of applicants compared to those describing 'scarcity'. The vast majority were in the former category. References to graduate selection were analysed in order to identify how talent is identified and defined in practice within elite PSFs and were subsequently coded and mapped onto sub-categories according to the various forms of capital. Overall, the analysis followed an iterative process, repeatedly moving between extant theory on diversity and inclusion and interview data.

FINDINGS

In this empirical section, we ask: *how have recruitment and selection processes implemented by elite professional service firms helped to construct the 'war for talent'?* We suggest that in the context of a growing abundance of suitably qualified graduates in the labour market, our case study firms have sought ways to manage this volume and narrow the field. This is achieved by focusing on an 'ideal candidate' who is typically selected according to a range of indicators of cultural capital, within which a relatively narrow set of educational qualifications proves particularly important. This strategy leads to social exclusion as ownership of this legitimated set of educational credentials tends to be concentrated amongst relatively privileged students. In our concluding discussion we consider the implications of our findings including to what extent the 'war for talent' can be reconciled with the professed commitment to diversity and inclusion in elite professional firms?

Narrowing the field

Corporate websites belonging to the firms we examined emphasized their aim to recruit only the 'brightest and the best' whilst claiming that they seek to achieve this goal according to objective measures of merit and irrespective of social or educational background. In practice, all five of our case study firms expect candidates to have completed relevant work experience in order to secure a job, ideally at the same firm or at the least within the same sector. In order to secure an internship and an eventual graduate trainee position, students are required to complete an extensive application process, usually including on-line numerical and verbal reasoning tests, and a 'competency based' telephone interview. If the candidate is successful, they may be invited to an assessment centre, where they will be interviewed again, this time in person, and take part in a series of team-based exercises and further tests.

Candidates are also screened at an early stage in the selection process on the basis of academic credentials. Despite some variation between firms, elite PSFs typically expect upwards of 340 UCAS[6] points at A-level (or equivalent qualification) depending on the scheme to which students apply and the practice area. Applicants are also expected to receive an upper second or first class degree (achieved by approximately sixty per cent of university students in the UK each year) and firms which have more than one graduate programme also state that certain schemes have preferences for relevant degrees. However, in all other respects, elite firms suggest that a candidates' academic credentials will be judged equally with no regard to the awarding institution and indeed, an applicant's choice of university is not mentioned as a relevant factor on the case study firms' websites at all. This rhetoric was replicated by some interviewees:

> We don't discriminate against universities at all and we will take them from any university if they have done a relevant degree and they've got 2:1.
>
> M6, Partner, Planet Accounting

However, even after candidates have been screened on academic credentials and a range of competency based criteria during the selection process, most elite PSFs continue to experience a significant oversupply of potentially qualified candidates. In this context, according to

---

[6] UCAS is an acronym for the Universities and Colleges Admissions Service. The UCAS Tariff is a means of allocating points to compare post-16 qualifications used for entry to higher education and was developed to help students make application choices, which match their qualifications and to provide information to universities and colleges about a wide range of qualifications.

our interviewees identifying the most talented candidates is difficult, costly and time-consuming, if it is possible at all. For example, Mars Bank's graduate recruitment manager explained that the firm aims to recruit 'top talent' yet simultaneously acknowledged difficulties with this objective, saying *whatever top talent means*. Peers at both Moon Accounting and Galaxy Law also referenced the challenges associated with identifying potential amongst an abundance of skilled applicants:

> It's simply supply and demand. There are far, far more people applying with appropriate academic grades than there are places and therefore it's how much time and effort you are willing to invest in finding the very best ... [selection] is more problematic now than ever, just because of the supply coming through.
>
> M4, Galaxy Law, Head of Graduate Recruitment

> You need ability, but how do you judge it? How you cope with the numbers in the marketplace is just beyond me.
>
> F2, Partner, Moon Accounting

A key task with respect to selection is therefore to find ways in which to discriminate on an apparently legitimate basis amongst applicants and narrow the field to more manageable proportions. Interviewees with experience of or responsibility for graduate recruitment acknowledged that, when deciding where to focus attraction efforts, and who to select for assessment centres, interviews or internships, an applicant's university becomes critically important, with only a very limited number of institutions perceived as acceptable:

> We are in a position to have the opportunity to select ... the way it works in terms of the recruitment process, is you will have your list of good universities ... you look at Oxford, Cambridge, Imperial, LSE, Warwick, and then as you gradually go down it is less and less, people will not actively recruit ... because even that group of universities gives you a huge amount of applications.
>
> M11, Managing Director, Mars Bank

> The recruitment strategy has certainly changed quite dramatically. It's primarily from Russell Group universities now.
>
> F3, Head of Diversity, Galaxy Law

This preference for students from particular elite universities is facilitated as each firm has developed specific relationships with a small group of institutions, from where applications are encouraged. This preference is enacted via the so-called 'milk-round', during which large corporate employers make visits to the universities from which they wish to encourage applications for internships and summer vacation work, and offer aspirant professionals at these firms help and advice such as mock interviews and coaching in psychometric tests to help them navigate the selection process. Though this assistance by no means guarantees success, it arguably places these students at a considerable advantage compared to those educated elsewhere.

Interviewees at all five firms underlined that their organization visited only a small sub-set of Russell Group universities, from which they were subsequently particularly likely to select new staff:

> We're trying to be more focused on less universities because we think that will give us a greater opportunity to find the stars ... Russell Group and Oxbridge ... it's about being more focused and trying to get the best people.
>
> M4, Galaxy Law, Partner and Head of Graduate Recruitment

> We go to everything from the Oxbridge to ... we go to quite a few, ummm, [names two Russell Group universities].
>
> M12, Director, Mars Bank

At Galaxy Law the recruitment process for graduates is relatively uniform across the firm, as all new recruits initially join the same training programme before deciding where to specialize upon qualification. In contrast, at Moon Accounting and Mars Bank for example, the recruitment process differs slightly according to the department, as does the expressed preference for graduates with particular credentials. This variation was most marked at Mars Bank where for example interviewees within the investment bank division recite a different list of preferred institutions compared to the private bank. However, neither of these lists is made public and these preferences do not appear to relate solely to the relative prestige of the institutions, but also to a more idiosyncratic emphasis on the universities and indeed faculty with which each division had a historical relationship:

> I went to see an MD in the investment bank sort of post [and] he asked to see my CV, and looked at it and said, 'That's a pile of crap. We don't recruit from [that university]', and threw it away ... I mean the fact that [it] was a Russell Group university it had no bearing on him ... There are a core group of universities that they recruit from for front office roles in the bank and that won't change.
>
> M6, Vice President, Mars Bank

Risk, reputation and corporate realities

These relatively narrow recruitment and selection strategies were explained primarily by interviewees in relation to the need to impose a strict process given the sheer volume of applications, and in turn, as a means explicitly to reduce the costs of recruitment. However, selecting graduates from elite institutions is considered to offer a number of additional, though related, benefits. First, focusing on a small number of institutions with high entry standards is thought to significantly reduce risk in the graduate selection process, and result in new recruits who represent a 'safe bet':

> Selection ... is the problem, it's not recruitment ... we cannot inter-view everyone. So we take the safe option, of looking at the good degrees from the good universities, knowing that we've automatically guaranteed ourselves a certain minimum standard.
>
> M4, Managing Director, Mars Bank

> If I looked at promotions we'd never look at whether you've got a degree. Proven experience is more important, definitely. At graduate level we do because you need a means ... it's more of a blunt selection process. Any other level we do it based on that they can do the job.
>
> M8, Partner, Planet Accounting

> Imagine you have a thousand applicants from Oxford ... we have people from Oxford screening people from Oxford. So the fact that you were there means that ... you are in a better position to assess whether he was actually good, relative to his peers, or bad.
>
> M11, Managing Director, Mars Bank

Second, selecting graduates from elite institutions is considered by interviewees to protect the status and image of the elite firms involved and offer the firm, and their clients, the reassurance that they have appointed the very 'best of the best'. In contrast, recruiting graduates from lower tier universities, even where they may be highly intelligent, represents a perceived risk that the firm itself will be considered a lower tier institution. This strategy is also considered by interviewees to help ensure similarity between professional advisors and their clients and to ensure that professional networks are based on close relationships and high social status.

> Where you sell knowledge ... it's very hard to take the risk on that ... I think the natural inclination, just as our clients would go to who they perceive to be the best law firms, to provide the best service, for us when we're looking to recruit ... you're going to try to get the best. That's

business sense. So naturally you would go to your old stomping grounds, the established universities, people where you've recruited from before.

M2, Partner, Galaxy Law

... if you've got a CEO of a business, he wants to be speaking to somebody who he thinks has been brought up and educated in the right way, and is very personable with him. That's not to say that that person is any better or worse than someone from a sort of lower social strata, who might be fifteen times more intelligent, but the CEO probably won't think that's the right person.

M6, Vice President, Mars Bank

There are firms within firms, you know? Corporate finance would be a good example where by and large because of the nature of the people who they have as their clients, the investment managers and you know former stockbrokers ... you'll probably find a greater proportion of our people coming from a similar background ... without that there's a risk ... you know, of not making a connection.

M7, Partner, Star Accounting

The selection process in relation to graduate recruitment is by its nature exclusive, given a high number of applicants for relatively few places. However, an important finding of the current research is that most elite PSFs have identified the same 'ideal type' of graduate candidate, which rests heavily on a small sub-set of elite universities with which they are most familiar and, often, a set of specific degrees. They subsequently compete to attract this 'ideal type' of candidate, both with their peers across the professions and, with most intensity, their competitors within the same field:

There has been this narrowing towards selecting from the top universities-all the banks are in competition, you know, gunning for that small pool of talent.

M5, Manager, Mars Bank

The precise impact of this process on social exclusion cannot be easily quantified as currently relatively few firms or sectors release data on the socioeconomic background of their graduate applicants in relation to those that they recruit. However, a recent study conducted by the SMCPC (2015) found for example that at 'Big Four' accountancies typically 40–50 per cent of applicants and 60–70 per cent of new appointees to graduate schemes had attended 15 or fewer elite Russell Group universities. At the same firms, just 30 per cent of new graduate trainees had attended a non-selective state school in the UK, compared to almost 90 per cent of the population.

Interviewees in the current research did suggest that the recruitment and selection process has a number of less positive implications for both organizations and individuals. Starting with the latter, interviewees recognized that many intelligent and talented people from less privileged backgrounds do not attend the institutions from which their firms currently recruit and are excluded as a result, no matter how great their skills and aptitude. With respect to the impact on the organization, at all five case study firms, interviewees acknowledged that current recruitment strategies limit the range of cognitive styles and approaches within the organization. Focusing on a small group of institutions, and a particular set of qualifications, was acknowledged as a relatively blunt tool which does not necessarily deliver people with the most appropriate skills and aptitudes for different lines of business. For example, at Moon Accounting interviewees explained that the complexity of the firm means that different departments have many different requirements of graduate employees, but that the current selection strategy expects the same academic standards from all. Interviewees also underlined that there is a relatively uncertain relationship between pure IQ and the capability to perform in a commercial environment, which requires a number of additional skills and competencies, and that the current strategy may also exclude the type of people who bring additional creativity and the potential to innovate:

> [Selection] tends to be from the top tier of universities . . . not the old polytechnics . . . the challenge I have is that for a lot of the people who do technology degrees, the type that I did and what my friends did, they are the kind of people that I wouldn't mind having in Moon Accounting . . . saying you must have a 2:1 from Cambridge in Maths to do Accountancy doesn't interest me, it doesn't fit my model.
>
> M8, Senior Manager, Moon Accounting

> When meeting people here, you'll get this 'yes but we've got to have these people from Oxford and Cambridge'. But you know you can look at all of the research and you can look at employability studies and things like that, there is no direct evidence to show that people from Oxford and Cambridge do better based on merit. We are not an academic institution, we want people who have got hunger and who have got business sense and commerciality, we don't need people who can memorise a hefty law tome.
>
> F3, Head of Diversity, Galaxy Law

Process and volume have meant that individual characteristics are less accommodated ... we satisfy our criteria recruiting the "best" people ... we're recruiting to a set of [academic] standards and in fact we just recently increased those standards ... but in terms of our ability to accommodate, you know, the sort of the people who might actually benefit our business, we've lost that.

M10, Partner, Moon Accounting

However, the prospect that elite PSFs will make substantial changes to their recruitment and selection practices was considered by the majority of interviewees to be as unlikely as it is unnecessary:

There is an understanding that the pool of talent can only be widened by policies of diversity, but the reality is in terms of talent we get far more people apply to us than we can ever take on.

M3, Partner, Galaxy Law

Widening access is not going to be a priority because there are just so many graduates that we've got more than we could ever need.

F2, Partner, Planet Accounting

From this perspective, one senior manager (F2) from Mars Bank concluded that: *The war for talent is bollocks! ... Absolutely shite!'*

CONCLUSION

This paper has sought to show how recruitment and selection processes implemented by elite PSFs helped to construct the 'war for talent'. We have demonstrated that faced with an over-abundance of suitably qualified graduates, our case study firms find it difficult to accurately identify potential. One response has been to define 'talent' according to an increasingly narrow set of educational criteria, in other words c.340 UCAS points or equivalent and a 2:1 or above from an elite university, almost always within the Russell Group and ideally Oxford or Cambridge. However, even according to those criteria the number of potential applicants remains high, compared to the number of positions available. To further reduce the size of the field, case study firms have defined talent more narrowly still, including by focusing particularly on a smaller sub-set of elite universities with which they are most familiar and often, a set of specific degrees. An important characteristic of the 'ideal type' of candidate constructed as a result is that it appears similar across all the case study firms and, according to interviewees, across the elite professional service sector.

This strategy means that an initial context of abundance in terms of the supply of potentially suitable graduates is translated into a context of relative scarcity. The perception that there is a shortage of top talent is further supported as most elite PSFs compete to attract the same type of candidate, both with their peers across the professions and, with most intensity, their competitors within the same field. Interviewees who took part in the current research recognize that this strategy has a negative impact on social inclusion, given that the elite institutions from which these firms select tend to be heavily populated by people from more privileged backgrounds. They acknowledged that by defining 'talent' in such narrow terms, the case study firms also exclude many talented people with potentially more drive, ambition and aptitude to succeed than their more traditional peers. However, the current strategy appears to sit comfortably with a more powerful argument in favour of the status quo, namely that selecting students with strong academic qualifications from elite education institutions is an important means to reduce organizational risk.

In making these arguments, our intention is not to suggest that a 'war for talent' is entirely a construction. Knowledge based organizations in today's economy will continue to seek to attract the very best talent available. However, we suggest that the intensity of this battle is significantly enhanced because of the tendency of PSFs to construct talent as though there is an absolute shortage of supply, rather than a relatively narrow definition. Furthermore, whilst in theory the 'war for talent' has been associated with meritocracy, in practice we suggest that by defining talent in such narrow terms, this battle has in fact helped to create the conditions for inequality and social exclusion.

That this paradoxical situation is allowed to persist might be partly explained if we consider that tapping into a more widespread narrative of scarcity offers symbolic and material advantages to elite PSFs. The expansion of higher education means that the UK is training more potential professionals than ever before, a fact that is tacitly acknowledged by both our interviewees and corporate literature. The latter tends to underline the highly competitive nature of the recruitment and selection process, in which context there are many more suitably qualified applicants than available graduate positions. Utilising the legitimized belief that there is a 'war for talent' may help the professions to suggest that the skills and abilities necessary to perform within this particular context are nevertheless both valuable and rare (Ashcraft et al., 2012.)

On this basis, it is also important to question the role of the 'war for talent' in relation to seemingly progressive policies aimed at social inclusion. Corporate literature relating to programmes aimed at diversity and social inclusion within the professions appear to suggest that a shortage of talent can be used as a key motivating factor, encouraging firms to redefine what 'good' looks like. In theory then, this business case may lead to more fair outcomes. In practice however, a brief analysis of the aims and activities of diversity and inclusion programmes reveals that this objective is carefully limited and controlled. For example, a key goal of social inclusion programmes is to help less privileged students conform to existing expectations within elite firms, by supporting them into elite universities and providing them with coaching and training to develop the type of social and cultural capital necessary to secure eventual employment. In other words, though attracting some potential applicants from non-traditional backgrounds, to have any chance of a securing a graduate position, these 'non-normative' students are expected to acquire essentially the same forms of institutional, social and cultural capital as their 'normative' peers.

Arguably, the limitations of the social inclusion agenda within the professions exemplify many of the problems associated with the diversity agenda in a more widespread critical literature (Lorbiecki and Jack, 2000). The business case for change is often considered particularly problematic on the basis that it is economically contingent (Barmes and Ashtiany, 2003; Dickens, 1999). This analysis would support our suggestion that social exclusion is perceived by many professionals to offer more obvious commercial benefits to their firms, than attention to social inclusion. In addition, although the diversity agenda has radical roots in identity politics and was originally aimed at transformative organizational change and the recognition of difference (Tomei, 2003) the current approach to social inclusion within the professions seems more heavily focused on a 'deficit model'. Accordingly, non-traditional applicants are expected to assimilate to existing organizational cultures, with little critical introspection within firms as yet around the emotional costs to individuals of doing so, or how organizational cultures set up unnecessary barriers to success.

It is no coincidence that many of the challenges of the diversity and inclusion agenda outlined earlier closely match those directed at the notional 'war for talent' developed by more critical scholars (Brown and Tannock, 2009). Rowley and Jackson (2011: 208) suggest that an analysis of *effective* talent management can be subsumed under discussions of 'managing diversity'. Certainly, both agendas are firmly embedded within the much wider backdrop of neo-liberalism, in which context a focus on the profit motive is said to regularly trump concerns with equality and social justice (Litvin, 2002). That even charitable organizations, whose remit is aimed at goals of diversity and social inclusion, have adopted the talent rhetoric may reveal the extent to which they too have been co-opted within this neo-liberal discourse. One result is that programmes aimed at social inclusion are diluted in their reach and depth, in order to achieve a type of 'exclusive inclusivity'. Though useful for a small number of under-privileged students, this approach may ultimately prove extremely limited in its progressive effect.

REFERENCES

Ashcraft, K. L., Muhr, S. L., Rennstam, J., & Sullivan, K. (2012). Professionalization as a branding activity: Occupational identity and the dialectic of inclusivity-exclusivity. *Gender, Work & Organization*, 19(5), 467–488.

Ashley, L. (2010). 'Making a difference? The use (and abuse) of diversity management at the UK's Elite Law Firms'. *Work Employment Society*, 24 (4): 711–727.

Ashley, L., and Empson, L. (2013). 'Differentiation and discrimination: Understanding social class and social exclusion in leading law firms'. *Human Relations*, 66(2), 219–244.

Barnett, R. and Hall, D. (2001). "How to used reduced hours to win the 'war for talent'". *Organizational Dynamics*, 29(3): 192–210.

Barnes, L., and Ashtiany, S. (2003). 'The diversity approach to achieving equality: Potentials and pitfalls'. *Industrial Law Journal*, 32(4), 274–296.

Becker, H. (1993). *Human Capital*. 3rd ed. Chicago: University of Chicago Press.

(2006). 'The age of human capital'. In *Education, Globalization and Social Change*. H. Lauder, P. Brown, J.A. Dillabough, and A.H. Halsey (eds): 292–294. Oxford: Oxford University Press.

Beechler, I., and Woodward, S. (2009). 'The global "war for talent"'. *Journal of International Management*, 15(3): 273–285.

Bourdieu, P. (1972). *Outline of a Theory of Practice*. Cambridge: Cambridge University Press.

(1984). *Distinction: A Social Critique of the Judgement of Taste*. London: Routledge and Kegan Paul.

(1985). 'The social space and the genesis of groups'. *Theory and Society*, 14 (6), 723–744.

(1986). "The Forms of Capital." Pp. 241–258 in *Handbook of Theory and Research for the Sociology of Education*, J. Richardson (ed.). New York: Greenwood.

(1991). *Language and Symbolic Power*. Harvard University Press.

Brown, P. (2003). 'The opportunity trap: Education and employment in a global economy'. *European Educational Research Journal*, 2(1), 141–179.

Brown P., and Tannock, S. (2009). 'Education, Meritocracy and the Global War for Talent'. *Journal of Education Policy*, 24 (4): 377–392.

Cabinet Office. (2009). *Unleashing Aspirations: The Final Report of the Panel on Fair Access to the Professions*. London: Cabinet Office.

Cook, A., Faulconbridge, J., and Muzio, D. (2012). 'London's legal elite: recruitment through cultural capital and the reproduction of social exclusivity in City professional service fields'. *Environment and Planning, A* 44: 1744–1762.

Cox, T., and Blake. (1991). 'Managing cultural diversity: Implications for organizational competitiveness'. *The Executive*, 5(3): 45–56.

Dearing, R. (1997). 'Higher Education in the Learning Society'. London: Higher Education Quality Council.

Dickens, L. (1999). 'Beyond the business case: A three-pronged approach to equality action'. *Human Resource Management Journal*, 9(1), 9–19.

Eichenwald, K. (2005). *Conspiracy of Fools: A True Story*. New York: Broadway Books.

Faulconbridge, J., & Muzio, D. (2008). Organizational professionalism in globalizing law firms. *Work, Employment & Society*, 22(1), 7–25.

Gardner, T. M. (2002). 'In the trenches at the talent wars: Competitive interaction for scarce human resources. *Human Resource Management*, 41(2), 225–237.

Gordon, D. A. (2013). *Employability and Social Class in the Graduate Labour Market*. Unpublished PhD Thesis, Cardiff University.

Gladwell, M. (2002). 'The talent myth'. *The New Yorker*, 22(2002), 28–33.

Greenbank, P., & Hepworth, S. (2008). Improving the career decision-making behaviour of working class students: Do economic barriers stand in the way?. *Journal of European Industrial Training*, 32(7), 492–509.

Hall, S., and Du Gay, P. (1996). *Questions of Cultural Identity*. SAGE Publications Limited.

Hiltrop, J. M. (1999). 'The quest for the best: Human resource practices to attract and retain talent'. *European Management Journal*, 17(4), 422–430.

Jackson, M. (2001). *Meritocracy, Education and Occupational Attainment: What Do Employers Really See as Merit?* Nuffield College Sociology Working Papers, Number 2001 – 03. (www.sociology.ox.ac.uk/materials/papers/2001-03.pdf)

Larson, M. S. (1977). *The Rise of Professionalism: A Sociological Analysis*. London: University of California Press.

Lewis, R. E., and Heckman, R. J. (2006). 'Talent management: A critical review'. *Human Resource Management Review*, 16(2), 139–154.

Litvin, D. R. (2002). 'The business case for diversity and the "Iron Cage"'. In *Casting the Other: The Production and Maintenance of Inequalities in*

Work Organizations. Czarniawska, B., and Hopfl, H. (eds.). London: Routledge.

Lorbiecki, A., and Jack, G. (2000). 'Critical turns in the evolution of diversity management'. *British Journal of Management*, 11(s1), S17–S31.

Macdonald, K. M. (1995). *The Sociology of the Professions*: Sage Publications Limited.

Metcalf, H. (1997). *Class and Higher Education: The Participation of Young People from lower socio-economic groups*. London: CIHE.

Michaels, E., Handfield-Jones, H., and Axelrod. B. (2001). *The War for Talent*. Boston, MA: Harvard Business School Press.

Ng, E. S., and Burke, R. J. (2005). 'Person–organization fit and the war for talent: Does diversity management make a difference'? *The International Journal of Human Resource Management*, 16(7), 1195–1210.

Pink, D. 2001. *Free Agent Nation: The Future of Working for Yourself*. Warner Books, New York.

Robertson, A., and Abbey, G. (2003). *Managing Talented People: Getting on with- and Getting the Best from-Your Top Talent*. Momentum Wcze.

Rolfe, H., and Anderson, T. (2003). 'A firm choice: Law firms' preferences in the recruitment of trainee solicitors'. *International Journal of the Legal Profession* 10(3): 315–344.

Rowley, C., and Jackson, K. (2011). *Human Resource Management: The Key Concepts*. London: Routledge.

Saunders, P. (2006). *Meritocracy and Popular Legitimacy*.

Smart, B. 2005. *Topgrading: How Leading Companies Win by Hiring, Coaching, and Keeping the Best People*. Penguin Group, New York.

Social Mobility and Child Poverty Commission. (2013). *State of the Nation 2013: Social Mobility and Child Poverty in Great Britain*. London.

(2013) *Higher Education: The Fair Access Challenge*. London.

(2015). *A Qualitative Study of Non-Educational Barriers to the Elite Professions*. London.

Somaya, D., and Williamson, I. O. (2008). 'Rethinking the 'war for talent'. *MIT Sloan Management Review*, 49(4), 29–34.

Sommerlad, H. (2011). 'Minorities, Merit, and Misrecognition in the Globalized Profession'. *Fordham L. Rev*, 80, 2481.

SPADA. (2012). *Social Mobility Toolkit for the Professions*. London: Professions for Good.

The Sutton Trust. (2005). *The Sutton Trust Briefing Note: The Educational Backgrounds of the UK's Top Solicitors, Barristers and Judges*. London: The Sutton Trust.

Tymon, W. G., and Stumpf, S. A. (2003). 'Social capital in the success of knowledge workers'. *Career Development International*, 8(1), 12–20.

Young, I. M. (1990). *Justice and the Politics of Difference*. Princeton: Princeton University Press.

2

ENTERING PROFESSIONAL CAREERS
Barriers, ladders, and basement doors

TYPECAST SOCIALIZATION

Race, gender, and competing expectations in law school

YUNG-YI DIANA PAN

> I can't think fast enough to say it properly with the right
> vocabulary so I'll be taken seriously, because already they
> look at me as a woman of color . . . So anything I say out
> of my mouth needs to be top notch, I guess in the way
> that I am saying it and portraying it because that is going
> to be additional fire. An additional reason for them to
> say, "you see? They're not good enough to be here."
>
> Elina, Chicana

In 2012, a report by the *American Bar Association Commission on Women in the Profession* found that women of color, relative to white men, white women, and men of color, have the highest attrition rate of any group of attorneys; are more likely to experience exclusion in the profession based on gender or race stereotyping; are more likely to feel compelled to make adjustments to fit into the workplace; and are more likely to report dissatisfaction with work and have limited access to high profile clients.[1] Though not necessarily surprising, these findings appear incongruent for a profession that has experienced tremendous growth in the number of women of color over the past two decades.[2] These findings, coupled with Elina's comment previously, hint at the internal struggles faced by Asian American women and Latina law students while undergoing professional socialization.

Asian American women and Latina law students report apprehension about their entrance into an elite, mainstream profession.[3]

---

[1] Women of Color include black/African Americans, Native Americans/American Indians, Latinos/Hispanics, and Asian Americans. Refer to ABA Commission on Women in the Profession, 2012.

[2] American Bar Association. 2011. "A Current Glance at Women and the Law (2000–2011)." Prepared by the Commission on Women in the Profession: American Bar Association. 2009. *Legal Education Statistics.*

[3] Asian Americans and Latinos comprise the bulk of post-1965 immigrants. Those who enter mainstream professions are primarily U.S. born, otherwise known as

141

Assumptions about family/work priorities, and gendered expectations embedded in the legal culture affect how these women think about their futures in this demanding career. As a result, Asian American women and Latina law students internalize competing demands and expectations, which significantly affect how they understand their place within the legal profession.

Literature abounds on white women and black/African Americans in the legal profession and in law schools, but little attention has been paid to the *intersection* of race/panethnicity[4] and gender (Blair-Loy and DeHart 2003; Epstein 1983; Gilkes 1982; see also Payne-Pikus, and Seron in this volume). Recent scholarship identifies how various intersections affect experiences in the professions. In this volume, Carroll Seron's contribution assesses how the intersection of race, class, and gender color students' career trajectories in the science, technology, engineering, and math (STEM) fields, and Payne-Pikus et al., examine how such intersections leave black women attorneys feeling dissatisfied while working at large firms. The profundity of social isolation underscores the importance of understanding individual experiences at the intersections.

Webley et al., also in this volume, suggest that university prestige significantly affects access to a legal career in the United Kingdom, which correlates with socioeconomic background. The implications are significant, as Black and Minority Ethnics (BMEs) typically do not hail from higher SES backgrounds. Tomlinson et al.'s (2013) recent publication finds that minorities in law (white women and individuals of color) reproduce the structure of the profession rather than attempt to transform it as "most attempts to reform the system were not achieved through challenging the large corporate firms but, involved moving away from such environments and creating new alternatives" (p. 265). It appears then, minorities in law recognize the structural concerns, especially in corporate forms, and withdraw from them, rather than endure.

This chapter focuses on the experiences of Asian American women and Latina law students, who, as racialized immigrants, contend with racialization and other obstacles while incorporating into mainstream America. Racialization has been a part of the United States since the

second-generation in contrast to their first-generation foreign-born parents. For more discussion on post 1965 immigrant adaptation, refer to Portes and Rumbaut 2001, 2006.

[4] I use race and panethnicity interchangeably to characterize Asian Americans and Latinos as racialized members of umbrella categories.

country's inception, used to classify individuals who are a part of, and deviate from the White-Anglo-Saxon-Protestant population (Bonilla-Silva and Dietrich 2009; Feagin 2013; Frank et al. 2010; Golash-Boza 2006; Omi and Winant 2015). Individuals of heterogeneous ethnic backgrounds are grouped together, or racialized, based on ancestral geographic origin, phenotype, shared linguistic background, and/or similar experiences of prejudice and discrimination in the United States. Asian Americans and Latinos are no exception.

Focusing on these two particular groups underscore how the intersection of race and gender shape professional socialization. Some recent scholarship purports Asian Americans and Latinos joining the "white" racial category (Alba and Nee 2003; Lee and Bean 2004, 2007). This claim however, warrants investigation into these individuals' experiences as racialized individuals. If race does not in fact matter, one could adequately claim that the professional socialization of Asian Americans and Latinos mirror their white counterparts. But, as we will see, Asian American women and Latinas experience typecast socialization at the junction of race and gender.

Parental expectations further affect these women's experiences. Most of the Asian American women and Latinas have first-generation immigrant parents who harbor gendered expectations of their daughters. First-generation immigrant parents hailing from Asian and Latino backgrounds tend to be more conservative about raising girls as opposed to boys, which present particular demands on their children (Portes and Rumbaut 2001). Familial expectations then introduce another "variable" to the intersection of panethnicity and gender. I explore how multiple and intervening expectations affect these women's thoughts about their career trajectories. On the one hand, Asian American women and Latina law students look to the legal profession as a mechanism for upward mobility. On the other hand, they feel trepidation as they recognize the layers of expectations and demands with which they must contend.

These women of color law students learn how to perform in law school as aspiring lawyers, but also as gendered and racialized individuals. I argue that Asian American women and Latinas undergo "typecast socialization" where they absorb expected roles based on assumptions embedded within legal culture while contending with professional expectations, and heeding parental demands. I begin this chapter by situating typecast socialization among three sets of literature: women in the professions and tokenism; mentorship; and perceptions/stereotype threat. I then present the data and methods, and follow with a presentation of the findings. I conclude with discussion, conclusion, and recommendations to law schools.

WOMEN IN THE PROFESSIONS AND TOKENISM

Social scientists maintain steadfast interest in women's entry and acceptance into the professions (Blair-Loy 2003; Epstein 1983; Kanter 1977). In general, women and men do not experience compensation parity, and women professionals tend to be concentrated in "feminine" careers, such as nursing, teaching, and social work while men dominate medicine, law, and engineering – otherwise known as "masculine" fields (Abel 1989; Bolton and Muzio 2007; Cech et al. 2011; Yoder 1994). The women who break through the "glass door" and enter male-dominated professions experience tokenism by enduring more scrutiny from colleagues when compared to men, especially with regard to their career commitment (Kanter 1977). Gender tokens find more difficulty networking with their peers, which negatively affects retention in their chosen lines of work (Smith and Elliott 2002). Generally, these women contend with dual expectations – learning the decorum of male-dominated professions, and adhering to gendered roles on the part of their colleagues and families.

A masculine professional identity defined, and still defines the legal profession. Women law students are taught, implicitly and explicitly, to "behave like gentleman" where "learning to think like a lawyer means learning to behave and act like a man. As one male professor told a first-year class of women law students: 'To be a good lawyer, behave like a gentleman'" (Guinier et al. 1997: 29). But, it is not necessarily easy to become "gentlemen," since members of the legal profession hold assumptions about gender roles and appropriateness. Epstein (1992) notes that as tokens, women attorneys take part in the construction and reconstruction of gendered boundaries at work wherein "women who were (and are) tough faced the disapproval of both men and women colleagues and even of feminist attorneys, who faulted them for assuming a 'male model' of behavior (or for wearing clothing regarded as 'masculine' in style) and otherwise deviating from sex-role-appropriate attitudes" (p. 245). Although women attorneys may not always experience tokenism, their lack of integration into the profession remains stark. The previously-mentioned gendered segmentation reflects a larger structural understanding where women attorneys are expected to bring to the profession a better sense of communication and camaraderie (i.e., "feminine" characteristics), while simultaneously enduring reservations about their commitment to the profession given stereotyped family and childrearing responsibilities (Blair-Loy 2003; Wallace and Kay 2012).

Current scholarship describes a phenomenon that is unsurprising, but this literature is incomplete. While there have been some research addressing how the intersection of raced and gendered segmentation and tokenism affect professional women's experiences, the focus tend to be on black/African-American women, and do not include the lived experiences of Asian Americans or Latinas (Blair-Loy and DeHart 2003; Epstein 1983; Gilkes 1982; Keith 2009; with the exception of Watkins-Hayes 2009). In law, tokens who are "racially palatable" ascend the corporate legal ladder through a calculated process that requires appeasing the status quo, and competing with other individuals of color (Carbado and Gulati 2004). There is no doubt that those who "race" to the top must overcome obstacles to get there, but one wonders how the combination of being a woman and a racialized minority further compounds these experiences. If subscribing to a "male" behavior is expected on the part of white women, and becoming "racially palatable" is expected on the part of men of color, are women of color expected to accommodate a "racially palatable male" model? If so, what does this model look like from these women's perspectives? And, what do their role models demonstrate to them?

MENTORSHIP

As a part of professional socialization, seasoned attorneys mentor neophyte lawyers, directly or indirectly – serving as role models. The product of this mentoring relationship is one in which the latter benefits by assimilating professional norms and expectations. The social capital accrued propels the neophytes forward in their chosen careers. Research on mentorship in law firms however, finds different results based on gender. Specifically, men with senior mentors report higher earnings, fairness at work, and greater work satisfaction as advantages when compared with their women counterparts (Kay and Wallace 2009). Although women junior attorneys with multiple mentors report satisfaction with their careers, they do not report the sense of fairness experienced by men. How men and women capitalize on their relationships with mentors seems to qualitatively affect their work experiences.

Kay and Wallace's (2009) research suggests that it is not necessarily the gender of the mentor that affects how junior attorneys utilize social capital, but rather how these neophytes learn to access resources. While this may be the case, current research on law schools finds that the presence of women and minority professors positively contribute to the success of these target populations (Banks 1988; Fischer 1996). Prior studies indicate that a supportive classroom environment instills confidence for students to voice their opinions and ask questions when they do not adequately understand course materials. When professors call on men and women students fairly, and take the time to understand their questions or comments in class, the women students perform better than in other situations that appear to be more task-oriented (Fischer 1996). This type of qualitative outcome in the classroom allows women to be confident, thereby cultivating relationships with professors and peers – relationships that are beneficial to garnering social capital.[5] Not mentioned in this literature is how stereotype threat – or anticipatory perceptions – affects the way that men and women seek and utilize social capital.

ANTICIPATORY PERCEPTIONS

Confidence is important to cultivating professional success. Previous research finds that when compared with their women or nonwhite counterparts, white men tend to be more confident in the classroom (Clydesdale 2004; Costello 2005; Mertz 2007; Moore 2008; Schleef 2006). Recent scholarship on professional identities and role confidence find that an individual's expectations for her/himself influence how s/he perceives her/his abilities. Costello (2005) argues that professional students undergo an identity crisis as they balance a set of, at times contradictory, personal and professional expectations. Similarly, Cech et al., (2011) demonstrate that a lack of role confidence leads women engineering students to retreat from the STEM fields at greater rates than men. Women students are overwhelmingly concerned with how they will "fit in" with standard STEM professional roles. Although they may be fluent in the skillsets required to become good engineers, scientists, and mathematicians, the institutional setting and

[5] If "supportive" environments were found in law firms, junior attorneys in general could use their social capital in similar ways.

146

a hyper-masculine professional culture deter many women students from pursuing advanced degrees or careers in these fields.

Confidence in one's abilities and the lack of an aspirant role model creates a professional impact on whether certain individuals (i.e., women) will pursue or remain in a particular career. When women enter the professions, there are a set of expectations about their abilities on the part of colleagues and society at large. For one, professional women must adapt to competing schemas of devotions (Blair-Loy 2003). The more masculine "work devotion" schema requires an individual to devote one's time and emotional commitment to one's career. This form of devotion leads to a sense of competence, identity, belonging and meaning, and is typically ascribed to professional men. In contrast, the "family devotion" schema describes intensive mothering, emotionally absorbing, with a focus on child-care, and rearing. Being a professional woman requires bridging these two competing schemas: cultural expectations dictating what should be appropriate for women, and a masculine characterization of the world of work.

For law in particular, these competing schemas begin in law school. Clydesdale (2004) further finds that white, male law students are not only more confident in law school, but this confidence positively benefits their overall test scores.[6] Further, law students who are not white or male are less confident and do not perform as well on tests, and have lower bar passage rates (Sander 2004). This type of standardized "knowledge" serves as a stereotype threat haunting "atypical" students. White women and nonwhite students contend with the image that they are less qualified than their white, male counterparts to enter prestigious institutions, or that they are less adequate at school. Such students are then fearful that they may assume the stereotype that they do not belong, or cannot succeed in the chosen subjects of study (Steele 1997).

Additionally, studies on retention rates at law firms demonstrate that nonwhite lawyers are less confident in their abilities when compared with their white peers (Payne-Pikus et al. 2010; Tomlinson et al. 2013;

---

[6] According to Clydesdale (2004), "the typical (i.e., modal) first-year law student is a white male in his early twenties, who speaks English as his first language, attends law school full time, expresses high self confidence, possesses no physical or learning disabilities, is neither married nor has children, plans 0–9 weekly hours of paid employment during the first year, and comes from an above-average socioeconomic background" (pp. 724–725).

Wilkins 1997; Wilkins and Gulati 1996). For women, and especially women of color, this stereotype threat becomes another experience of "othering" where they are not only gender minorities in a masculine culture, but also racial minorities in a white professional space (Moore 2008). Asian American women and Latinas experience socialization into the legal profession that is unlike white and/or male attorneys as they not only contest industry standards, but also balance cultural expectations. Combined, these examples of stereotype threat affect Asian American women and Latinas' socialization into law.

Data and methods

The data come from a larger study that took place at two field sites, and consists of diary entries, non-participant observations, and interviews with 107 law students between 2009 and 2013. The two field sites are Western Tier 1 (WT1), and Metro Tier 4 (MT4). WT1 is a nationally ranked top-20-law school, while MT4 is a lower-tiered institution. I purposely chose these two divergently ranked law schools as field sites to capture differences in student demographics, as well as similarities across law schools without regard to ranking. I attended student organ-ization meetings, had formal and informal conversations with law students and law professors, and corresponded with students via email at both institutions. For the purpose of this chapter, I focus on conver-sations with sixty three women, primarily Asian Americans and Latinas. The sample of women respondents consist of twenty five Asian Americans, twenty two Latinas, nine white women, and seven other racially identified women (Refer to Table 5.1). Thirty-four women are from WT1, and twenty-nine are from MT4. All students were enrolled in law school full-time at the time of our interviews, and the break-down is as follows: 18 first-years (1Ls), 21 second-years (2Ls), and 24 third-years (3Ls).

TABLE 5.1 Women Respondents' Year in School

Race/Ethnicity	1L	2L	3L	Total
Asian American	3	10	12	25
Latina	9	8	5	22
White	3	1	5	9
Other	3	2	2	7
Total	18	21	24	63

I used an intentional snowball sampling method to recruit inter-viewees. Respondents were initially referred through law professors and other established contacts at each law school. Following these interviews, I asked respondents to refer me to peers within their small groups. Entering cohorts at these law schools are large and number in the hundreds, but students are assigned to small groups of peers with whom they take their first year courses. These groups are diverse – by race, ethnicity, socioeconomic background, and gender. The result of this intentional snowball sampling method led students to identify peers with whom they may associate, but do not necessar-ily have close friendships, thereby diminishing selectivity bias. I audio-recorded all interviews, transcribed the conversations, and maintained confidentiality by replacing identifiers (e.g., students' names, professors' names, places of internship, law schools, etc.) with pseudonyms.

Each interview lasted between 45 and 120 minutes, occurring mostly in cafés near the law schools; some interviews took place in classrooms or respondents' homes. The interviews addressed many topics, ranging from the respondents' family backgrounds, their reasons for involvement (or noninvolvement) in law student organ-izations, and why they chose to attend law school. Questions were designed in such a way that respondents answered them through storytelling without much prompting from me, the interviewer. All respondents were briefed on the purpose of the study, and most were eager to participate as they noticed a lack of literature about Latino and Asian American law students, and wanted their experiences documented for future generations of law students. In fact, women of color law students were the most enthusiastic, and almost always immediately contacted members of their small groups after our inter-views. These women maintained steadfast interest in the outcome of this study by asking me about my findings when I saw them on campus well after their interviews. Tables 5.2 and 5.3 provide the demograph-ics of the respondents.

The women of color law students' unwavering support of this study aroused initial analytic interest about the intersection of race and gender in law school. After open coding interview transcripts, I found a common theme among the women of color respondents – most spoke about their experiences as women by referencing their race and/or ethnicity, or vice versa. While some social inequality literature intersect race and gender, the implicit shared experiences among my

TABLE 5.2   WT1 Respondent Characteristics

Name	Year in School	Immigrant Generation*	Ethnicity/Race
Abby	1L	NB	Mexican/White
Araceli	2L	2nd	Mexican
Arely	1L	1st	Puerto Rican
Bryn	2L	2nd	Punjabi
Candice	2L	NB	White
Cindy	3L	NB	White
Clara	3L	NB	White
Debbie	2L	1.5	Chinese
Elina	3L	2nd	Mexican
Esperanza	2L	2nd	Mexican
Evellia	1L	1.5	Mexican
Felicia	1L	NB	Chicana
Jessica	3L	2nd	Filipina
Jocelyn	2L	NB	Korean/White
June	3L	2nd	Dominican
Jyoti	3L	2nd	Indian
Lucia	2L	2nd	Mexican
Lydia	2L	2nd	Taiwanese
Maisy	2L	NB	Chicana
Marcia	1L	NB	White
Marie	1L	1.5	Taiwanese
Marta	2L	1.5	Mexican
Mila	3L	2nd	Persian
Nancy	1L	2nd	Chinese
Natalia	2L	2nd	Mexican
Ofelia	1L	2nd	Eritrean
Olinda	1L	2nd	Mexican
Raquel	1L	2nd	Salvadoran
Sara	1L	2nd	Colombian
Selena	2L	2nd	Mexican
Smriti	1L	2nd	Indian
Stacey	1L	2nd	Korean-Argentinian
Supriya	1L	2nd	South Asian
Susan	3L	2nd	Filipina

* 1st denotes arrival to the United States as immigrants, 1.5 is immigration as a children between 7–13 of age, and 2nd means born in the U.S. to 1st generation parents. NB represents "native born," meaning their parents were born in the United States, thus they are 3rd generation plus Americans.

TABLE 5.3 MT4 Respondent Characteristics

Name	Year in School	Immigrant Generation*	Ethnicity
Andréa	2L	2nd	Mexican/Guatemalan
Angela	2L	2nd	Korean
Anjali	2L	2nd	East Indian
Asha	3L	1.5	Indian
Beatriz	3L	2nd	Salvadoran
Blanca	1L	NB	Mexican/Indigenous
Brittany	3L	NB	White
Elena	3L	3rd	Latina
Elise	1L	NB	White
Estelle	2L	2nd	Chinese-Vietnamese
Evelyn	3L	2nd	Filipina
Farrah	2L	2nd	Pakistani/Indian
Felicidad	1L	NB	Chicana
Helen	3L	2nd	Chinese-Vietnamese
Hollie	1L	NB	White
Itzel	3L	NB	Mexican
Jenna	3L	NB	Japanese
Jillian	3L	1.5	Chinese
Julia	3L	NB	White
KyungHwa	3L	1st	Korean
Leah	3L	2nd	Chinese
Lori	3L	NB	White
Luara	1L	NB	Chicana
Margaret	3L	2nd	Korean
Mina	2L	2nd	Korean
Noemi	3L	2nd	Salvadoran
Rose	3L	2nd	Chinese
Serafina	2L	1.5	White
Whitney	2L	1.5	Chinese
Zahra	3L	1.5	Persian

* 1st denotes arrival to the United States as immigrants, 1.5 is immigration as a children between 7–13 of age, and 2nd means born in the U.S. to 1st generation parents. NB represents "native born," meaning their parents were born in the United States, thus they are 3rd generation plus Americans.

respondents, as *minority* minorities, struck me as unique in the law school setting. I now turn to how these intersections result in typecast socialization for Asian American women and Latinas as they learn to become lawyers.

Findings: typecast socialization

Asian American women and Latinas relay that their race *and* gender affect how they experience law school, and ultimately how they think about their coming careers. I find in particular that women of color undergo "typecast socialization" wherein they perform roles expected of all law students, in addition to a set of gendered *and* raced ones. Goffman (1959) finds that individuals manage impressions depending on the actors present, and the regions/stages they utilize. Goffman's dramaturgical perspective illuminates the simultaneous performances with which women of color law students engage while learning to become lawyers. These women take on multiple identities as they perform for different actors – each of whom has expectations of them. Like their white and male peers, these women become fluent in the language of law, and worry about securing jobs after graduation. Yet, unlike their male and white peers, Asian American women and Latinas must also negotiate different assumptions about their politics and career devotion.

Kanter (1977) introduced "tokenism" to describe the experiences of women and nonwhite professionals. Tokens "sometimes had the advantages of those who are 'different' and thus were highly visible in a system where success is tied to becoming known. Sometimes they faced the loneliness of the outsider, of the stranger who intrudes upon an alien culture and may become self-estranged in the process of assimilation" (207). Tokens are burdened with traditional agents of professional socialization along with others due to their gender and race.

The ways that Asian American women and Latina law students experience their socialization depended on their beliefs about people's perceptions of them as women, and as nonwhite law students. Guinier et al., (1997) argue that women law students are expected to become "gentlemen" as they assimilate into their professional roles. Being gentlemen requires logical thinking, and particular professional demeanor. But, performing as law students means that these women must learn to become more than gentlemen – rather, white men, since that group dominates the profession's history and culture. These students then worry that being women of color will prevent them from achieving normative objectives, such as winning cases and becoming reputable among colleagues. When asked what constitutes a successful attorney, Jyoti, a first-year, South Asian American WT1 student says,

What makes me successful is the ability to take sides, question, answer fast, [and] answer effectively. And I think part of a lawyer's job is to tease out the underlying questions with his [or her] clients or the company. So, when clients come to you, their real legal problem is something. But, as a lawyer, you have to ask the right questions and you often realize their problem is actually something else. An effective lawyer can do that in minutes.

Jyoti describes the normative response that any law student, especially at highly ranked institutions, regardless of gender or race would provide when asked about criteria for success. Similarly, Sara, a first-year, Colombian American WT1 student responds this way: "Winning cases ... having respect among your colleagues. Yeah, that's about it, and just respect and the clients are happy with your work. That might go hand-in-hand with winning cases ... I guess just that they [clients] see you in the capacity that you're a good lawyer. If someone were to ask them about you, they would recommend you."

From these two women's immediate responses, one gathers that becoming successful translates to making a name for oneself, whether through winning cases, impressing one's clients and colleagues, or solving problems quickly. At first blush, it seems likely that these attributes of success mimic those of men and white students. However, Asian American women and Latinas contend with other expectations that complicate their socialization.

AN ANGRY MOMMY

Women professionals in general are presumed to fall in line with the family devotion schema (Blair-Loy 2003). But, they balance work and family obligations while keenly aware that male colleagues do not contend with the same pressures. Although the majority of the women in this study do not yet have children, their interactions with professors, peers, and practicing attorneys demonstrate particular gendered assumptions about their careers. Take, for example, Jyoti's reflection about an interview for a summer internship,

I went to one interview where the guy [interviewer] said straight out, "we're not cosmopolitan." Translation: we're not diverse. And, then he starts talking about how all the women left to do the "mommy" thing. So, I sat there, knowing he sees me as a south Asian female. And, I've had that experience at least once or twice more. Where it was that direct.

153

The interviewer here assumed that women will exit their careers to become primary caregivers for their children, and openly expressed his disdain for it. While other women respondents discussed such gendered interactions with male peers, professors, or alumni, only Jyoti described such an encounter with an interviewer.

Mostly, these women expressed apprehension about entering a demanding profession that may not be conducive with motherhood. They are not explicitly told about the expectations, but learn about them through organic interactions with peers and alumni. For example, Marta, a second-year Mexican American student says, "one of the biggest problems is how do I deal with having a family and at the same time, being a lawyer? A good lawyer. Because it seems like you do, in some ways, have to give up so much of your time to your career that it seems a little bit impossible to do both." And Arely, a first-year Puerto Rican American student, agrees, "It seems like there's a certain amount of hours you have to put in every week and when you're single and young, you can absolutely do that. But when you're married and you start having children, it starts becoming more and more demanding."

This high-stress, male-dominated culture affects these women students to the point where they experience anxiety just thinking about their future careers. June, a third-year Dominican American student explains:

> [I]t's really hard to be a working mom when you have billable hours and clients calling you all night and stuff. So that's one of the things that worries me the most. And actually, I just basically decided with my fiancé that I would probably only want to have one child because I don't think I could handle two and working full time. Basically, just the idea of having…I get stressed out! Even the idea of having two children, even though it's not going to happen for a little while, was like stressing me out! Because I just, I don't think I can do it …

We see here that these women law students are affected by images of seasoned women lawyers. Practicing male attorneys explicitly and implicitly make mention of women prioritizing motherhood over their careers, and women attorneys also express the difficulty of balancing work and family. The Asian American women and Latina law students, most of whom do not have children, are already worried about this balancing act. Some, like June, have decided that they will only have one child, or plan to have no children, if they intend to excel in their careers.

Aside from these gendered professional expectations, Asian American women and Latinas also deal with the "angry woman of color" image among their peers. This image is often ascribed to women of color who are critical of race and/or gender issues (Guinier et al. 1997). Many of the women in this study feel passionate about issues that concern disenfranchised communities, and often speak up in classrooms when other students are silent. But, they are also fearful that they may delegitimize their position among peers and instructors for seeming "angry." To remediate this concern, many Asian American women and Latinas attempt to manage the way others perceive them, such that they will not be presumed to be the "angry woman of color." Consider what Felicia, a first-year Chicana student has to say,

> I don't want to offend people and I also don't want to be the "angry woman of color"... People characterize other women or peers that speak on these topics [of race and gender] as angry, frustrated. They can't empathize with them. I think people have grown up in such segregated societies, and especially at this caliber of a school [WT1] and in graduate education, period. It's a pretty heteronormative, white student body... So, I'm pretty rational, pretty articulate, fact-based. I'm not talking with passion. But still, these issues are issues that I think my classmates and America in general, are uncomfortable with. So, with that discomfort comes stereotypes, and I think the "angry woman of color" [image] is definitely alive.

As a first-year law student, Felicia attempted to tamp down her passions to avoid being associated with these characteristics. Despite this, she believes the label has already been applied:

> My first semester, [I felt I] was pretty quiet. I took Torts, Property, Civil Procedure, and the legal writing class and really didn't speak up except in Property, which is a small class. And, I heard people saying that I was the "critical race theory" person when I felt like I really hadn't even begun to touch on what I could. So again, I've been very conscious about not speaking up about these issues. And yet with that, it's already translated.

Although she made an effort to curtail her comments in class, Felicia cannot shake the typecasting as an "angry woman of color" purely because, as she understands it, she is a woman, and a person of color who expresses her opinions. Bryn, a second-year South Asian American student echoes Felicia's sentiments:

> I don't think anyone wants to feel like they have to speak for their race or political position or that they have to out themselves that way. There's a real fear that your viewpoint will not be considered seriously

if you are "the angry black woman," or the "angry person of color," or the "crazy radical." And, there's a real fear in the first couple of months of being stereotyped that way because we're colleagues for life.

What Bryn shares here is that women of color must manage their impressions in order to build rapport with their peers. Despite this, they still feel stereotyped as "angry" the moment they open their mouths to speak about a raced or gendered topic, such as domestic violence or undocumented immigration.

As described, women of color law students contend with two presentations of self as they undergo professional socialization. On the one hand, they, like their peers who are men, attempt to embody the standard definition of "successful attorney" – winning cases, establishing a healthy client base, building a name for oneself, etc. On the other hand, they make an effort to avoid being seen as "angry" in the classroom for fear it will cast them in a stereotyped light often prescribed to women of color. Despite their efforts, they are typecast as budding attorneys who are passionate about particular social issues, and are therefore, undeniably "angry."

THE NONPROFESSIONAL CAREER

While Asian American women and Latinas may be perceived as "angry" in the halls of law schools, their parents do not think of them this way. But, this does not mean that their parents do not place pressures on them to succeed ... as women. Asian American women and Latina law students intend to make their parents proud through their educational achievements, but they also anticipate offering concessions on their eventual careers. For example, an interviewee's mother could not fathom why her daughter would want to pursue a law degree. Growing up in an impoverished neighborhood, Elina, a third-year law student who self-identifies as Chicana, feels fortunate that a high school teacher noticed her potential and nurtured her academically, encouraging her to attend college and eventually, graduate school. Elina's mother, however, did not understand why she would not just marry and have kids. Elina expresses, "I know that my mom doesn't understand. She doesn't get it. She still believes I'm going to eventually marry and have kids and she doesn't get why I'm doing this." As seen here, although Elina's mother did not actively discourage her from pursuing a law degree (or higher education all together), she expects her daughter to fulfill her "duty" to marry and have children. Similarly, Lydia, a second-year Chinese American student, considers her parents' expectations when speaking about her career plans:

> I think for both of them [parents], it's always been emphasized to have a family. So, for me, it's never been to think [of making] partner or think [of making] x amount of money. [My parents want me to] be happy, have a family. [For] my brother, it has always been, "you should support your wife," and for me, it's kind of less of a professional aspect. Like my mom is afraid I'm going to get too intimidat[ing] now.

Lydia's mother, while supportive of her daughter's educational and career choice, fears that with a JD, she may become "too intimidating" as a marriage prospect. Whereas Lydia's brother is expected to have a career to support his family, Lydia's degree seems less consequential. The ultimate goal on the part of Lydia's parents, it seems, is to marry, and not necessarily have a career.

Elina and Lydia both share frustrations not unlike other women of color law students. They grapple with parental expectations as they learn how to become good attorneys. The emotional burden of possibly disappointing their parents in some capacity affects how Asian American women and Latinas consider their future careers in connection with what is deemed appropriate by their parents. These women then embody Denise Segura's (1992) assertion that Chicanas' gender and race not only intersect – they interact. Chicanas in white-collar professions are expected to be primary caregivers to their children, which is not always expected of their Chicano peers. According to the parents, a Chicana's appropriate gender role is to ensure cultural survival. In other words, to be good cultural ambassadors, these women must perform appropriate gender roles as primary caregivers. Pursuing a professional goal then becomes fraught with racial-ethnic, or cultural politics. In the office, the conjoined ethnic-gender negotiations leave Chicanas feeling as if they have a more difficult time securing work or getting promoted, when compared with their counterparts who are men or white women. As Chicana professionals, they feel as though they have to "prove" themselves more at work and at home.

Asian American women and Latinas negotiate professional and familial expectations, and assumptions based on their race and gender. Ethnicity and gender interact to influence how these women conceptualize their ambitions and capabilities. They not only recognize how they are perceived among white peers, but also know that Asian

American and Latino men do not experience the same pressures to appease their parents. Established scholarship in education speaks to the numerous expectations of, and rules for, women, compared with their male counterparts (Flores-González 2002, Gibson 1988; Lopez 2003, Louie 2004). Familial expectations add another layer of obstacles for these women to overcome. This additional demand becomes a part of Asian American women and Latinas' socialization into the legal profession. They perform for their families and also for their peers, professors, and future colleagues.

As demonstrated in this section, Asian American women and Latina law students appear resigned to the fact that professional and familial expectations will impact their long-term career goals. They are expected to "become gentlemen," yet are also assumed to embody the "angry women of color" image. Moreover, their families demand them to "get married and have children." In general, they foresee initially working long hours, and may alter their career plans in the future as they anticipate starting families. Although they have yet to earn their JDs, thinking about how to balance work and family troubles Asian Americans women and Latinas as they progress in their legal education.

Overall, while Asian American and Latina law students in this study shared similar apprehensions, those from lower-ranked MT4 expressed hints of optimism. One difference is how the minority-minorities at MT4 rationalize raced interactions in law school. For example, Farrah, a third-year South Asian American student shares,

> So, when for example, we do the assignments in class and we go up and talk in front of people, and we pretty much do the same thing, and I felt like maybe I did better than someone or maybe that other person was just awful. But, they get this great feedback [from professors]! And then you think, "Wait, but why?" It could just be that I suck, but then sometimes I do think with race and with issues like that, sometimes they're not as blatant. They're really subtle. And, people often do not realize that they're doing something like that.

Farrah describes how she rarely receives feedback from her professors. For a moment during our conversation, she contemplates that it is perhaps due to her race, or that her professors may not be invested in her professional future. But, she quickly adds that even if her professors do not provide feedback, it is not necessarily malicious, as "... people often do not realize that they're doing something like that."

Similarly, Leah, a second-year Chinese American MT4 student relays that her professors rarely call on her to answer questions. She surmises that perhaps her Chinese last name is difficult for professors to pronounce. Nevertheless, she says, "[S]o, I'm rarely called on, which I find surprising. Before coming to law school, it was like [you learn that] the Socratic method [means] you get called on, you get cold called on very often. But, I find myself, in some classes, I'm never called on, especially in bigger classes... I'm not sure if that has anything to do with me being Asian though." We see here that Leah is surprised she is not called on in classes. While she speculates that aside from difficulty pronouncing names, some professors may harbor assumptions about Asian ethnics (i.e., reluctance to participate in class), she also expresses uncertainty as to whether her being Asian actually affects the way professors treat her.

So, why do these particular Asian American women and Latinas express optimism when their tier-one counterparts do not? For one, these women attend MT4. Lower ranked law schools emphasize teaching students how to *become* lawyers. These types of institutions attract law students who do not fit the tier-one law school prototype, as explained by Clydesdale (2004). The Asian American women and Latina students at MT4 focus on cultivating a professional demeanor, and emphasize the importance of not only learning the law, but also how to effectively practice it. When asked about their law school experiences, these students often express that their minority-minority identities are beneficial for their professional development. For example, Jenna, a third-year Japanese American student says,

> There's always that feeling when you walk into a room full of students, you do notice that you are the minority. And, that's an interesting feeling. It's not necessarily bad per se, but it can make you feel a little bit uncomfortable by virtue of being the *other* in the room. Being a woman of color, it's interesting because I've heard it go both ways. I've heard people say that's great because that's an advantage for you, because you're like a *minority* minority. You're not just a person of color – you're a *woman* of color.

Jenna relays that being a woman of color could benefit her career, yet she also recognizes that being a woman of color could mean that she may encounter some difficulties with employers. But, she chooses to be positive, much like Beatriz, a third-year Salvadoran American student, also from MT4,

Racially [sic], I think speaking Spanish and being Latino is a good thing, but I could see how it might be a negative, especially if you go into a place or you end up working somewhere where there's absolutely no diversity. It's kind of like a little bit of an isolating experience... I guess the way I see it is, I know my own personal worth and if others feel uncomfortable about it or have issues with it, that's their problem. I'm going to move forward and this is something I've always wanted my whole life. So, I'm not going to just step aside and give it up because other people don't like it.

While Beatriz recognizes that it can be isolating as the only person of color in a work environment, she remains optimistic by not letting other people's "issues" come between her and her goal to practice law.

Although Asian American women and Latinas from MT4 contend with expectations about their professional, raced *and* gendered roles, they seemingly possess a positive career outlook. These sentiments may not be surprising, especially since prior research finds that women students at lower-ranked institutions are generally happier, and experience less stress (Fischer 1996). In part, students from lower-ranked institutions interact with professors who support them, experience more diversity, are more confident, and have more available role models.[7]

Discussion, conclusion, and recommendations

As demonstrated thus far, Asian American women and Latina law students contend with multiple demands as they are typecast into the legal profession. These students are no doubt anxious about joining a profession that requires them to "become gentlemen" while also negotiating an ethnic-gender identity reflecting familial demands. How these particular women law students learn to become lawyers is an exercise in typecasting. Although these students must perform the associated roles for their careers and families, women law students from each institution seem to respond differently to their expectations. I will discuss next how law school rank seemingly affects the way these law students think about their career trajectories.

Although the law school itself has some impact on how Asian American women and Latina law students think about their careers,

[7] Fischer's field site – Chapman University Law School – is a lower-tired law school that provides students with a unique law school experience that seems to be unparalleled by larger, highly ranked institutions.

it does not appear to be the dominant factor. Instead, the circumstances leading one to attend a particularly ranked law school affect how a law student internalizes her experience. While I find the students at WT1 experience *negative* internalization where they lack role models and supportive outcomes, at MT4, the students undergo *positive* internalization where they possess a more optimistic outlook toward their careers due to the availability of mentors and role models. The real difference, however, seems to be in the individual women's training and experiences before and during law school.

Because women from WT1 tend to transition to law school directly from college, they lack "real world" experience compared to their MT4 counterparts. Women of color from WT1 develop an anticipatory vision of their careers based on stories from alumni and peers. Their more pessimistic outlook is not surprising in light of a recent *Forbes* survey identifying big law firm associates as the least happy professionals (Smith 2013). Given the strong tier-one law school-to-law firm trajectory for most students, those at WT1 anticipate a career, at least initially, filled with misery and angst.

Akin to Epstein's (1983) "tough" women mentioned earlier, women of color law students anticipate that their peers will perceive them as prioritizing family over career. Additionally, they fear that identifying as "angry women of color" would alienate future colleagues, and, they anticipate peers will expect them to be less serious about their careers because they may plan to have children in the future. Many Asian American women and Latinas in this study report beginning law school regularly expressing their opinions in the classroom about gender inequality or sexism, but became more reserved as they progressed. They notice that their comments in classrooms were often received poorly, or resulted in particular assumptions made about them. Some of the respondents felt their simple remarks to be misinterpreted, which resulted in an unwillingness or hesitance to share subsequent opinions.

It is not surprising for the Asian American women and Latina law students to feel as though their opinions are unwelcomed. Prior research on women law students convey that women, and especially women of color, are resigned to not actively contribute in the classroom. Guinier et al. (1997) observes, "women's enfeebled participation within the formal structure of legal education occurs simultaneously with their less successful performance on the anonymously graded examinations from which law school grades are derived. In other words, low levels of class participation in the formal, structured pedagogy correlate with weak performance within the formal, structured evaluation system" (p. 58). It should not be surprising then that Asian American women and Latina law students from WT1 self-report lower average grades when compared with their male counterparts, or white students, more generally. This negative internalization of expectations in and out of the classroom has real consequences for how these women perform in law school, which in turn may affect their careers (Flores-González 2002; Lopez 2003; Steele 1997).

Why the difference between how MT4 and WT1 students internalize professional and familial expectations? One reason could simply be the demographics of the students in my sample (Refer to Table 5.4). Looking at Table 5.4, we see that the average age of respondents from WT1 was 25 while the average age of respondents from MT4 was 28. Disaggregating the sample, we see that while the average age of first-year students was the same (24) for both institutions, the real differences surface by years two and three. Second-year Asian American women and Latinas from MT4 are on average 26 years old, while third-year Asian American women and Latinas from MT4 are on average 31 years old. This is a two and four year difference, respectively, from their peers at WT1. The women at MT4 already experienced gender and racial inequality in the "real world," which is qualitatively different from the experiences of the respondents from WT1.

Asian American women and Latina law students at both law schools interact with agents of socialization that affect how they prepare to enter the legal profession. Messages from alumni, and the unspoken understanding of legal culture gleaned from films, books, word of mouth, and parental/cultural expectations build the initial framework of socialization for these students. But, the students at MT4 cite a contributing third agent: the impact of "real world" expertise. The

TABLE 5.4   Average Age of Asian American Women and Latina Respondents

Average Age	WT1	MT4
1L	24	24
2L	24	26
3L	27	31
Combined	25	28

function of law school socialization depends on the triangulation of, and communication with, these three agents.

Epstein's (1983) observation that "for women going into the legal profession, law school was the first place where they would learn what it meant to be a minority in an inhospitable work world" (p. 61) does not resonate for the Asian American women and Latinas at MT4. They know that the legal culture is less than hospitable for women, but they hear of alumni or their own professors who seemingly "manage it all." Take for example, Andréa's comment about one of her role models: "My Art and Law professor herself is a woman of color, not exactly sure what her origin is, but she seems to be doing fine. So, I figure it can't be that bad for me." Andréa's professor then serves as a role model for her to pursue an interest in art and entertainment law. And, Anjali, a third-year South Asian American student who holds a part-time job at a tech startup company while attending school full time, says of her place of work: "There are a lot of women. I think over half the legal department at this point. There are a lot of women. All the companies and firms I've seen – there are a lot of women. I think a lot of women end up contracting when they have kids. But, I don't see that as a negative. I'd love to do that at some point." From their role models, these women at MT4 learn about options in their chosen profession – they can, if they desire, transition into less demanding specialties if and when they have children, such as contracting.

Asian American women and Latinas at MT4 look to seasoned attorneys who have learned how to balance work/family, and recognize that being successful may not be out of reach for them. Compared to their peers at WT1, they possess a more positive outlook about their careers and career options in part because they have access to women professors, alumni, or other attorneys who serve as mentors (Fischer 1996; Mertz 2007). Jenna, the third-year Japanese American student we met earlier shares how she met the co-founder of the small, non-profit where she interned:

> And the woman who is the co-founder of the organization, she's an attorney, and she went to Harvard Law. She's extremely smart – has her master's in criminology and all this kind of stuff. It's just amazing! I feel like I'm so lucky to have worked there kind of on a whim... I feel like I was incredibly lucky to have met her. It all started organically.

For Jenna, being able to meet an inspirational woman attorney gave her hope that she would find happiness in her chosen profession. Moreover, she now has a mentor to guide her through the challenges of completing law school and securing a job. The availability of mentors who are not only supportive, but also manage to balance work and family successfully, offers hope to these women law students.

Women from WT1 also turn to attorney role models. But, unlike their MT4 counterparts, women law students from WT1 look up to corporate attorneys who must meet billable hour demands by regularly working over 60 hours per week. In their minds, Asian American women and Latina attorneys are under constant pressures in an effort to keep their jobs. These types of messages affect women of color law students as they think about their future careers. Although women at WT1, regardless of race, overwhelmingly expressed these concerns, it should be noted that women of color contend with this fear in addition to other expectations described previously. Interactions with attorney role models paint a bleak picture for these students, unlike their MT4 peers.

"REAL WORLD"

What is the real world? Simply, it just means having worked either before or during law school. Women of color at MT4 spoke of "real world" experience as an asset to them. As referenced earlier, many of the Asian American women and Latina law students from this lower-ranked institution returned to school after a hiatus working in the "real world," and many continue paid or unpaid work while in law school. Having already experienced raced or gendered inequalities in work environments, these women speak as veterans of inequality. For example, Helen, a third-year, Chinese-Vietnamese American law student who was a scientist at a biotech company expresses: "Just being a female because there's just not a lot of females in science, in that field of science. I think there's more women in law actually than there are in science...." And, when asked whether she is apprehensive about entering a male-dominated profession, she continues: "No, because I'm already accustomed to that. That breakdown. And, I'm actually quite comfortable with it." While Helen anticipates similar gendered discrepancies in law as she witnessed in biotech, she maintains that her "real world" experience prepared her well to take on possible obstacles.

The aforementioned agents (legal culture, law school, alumni, and "real world") impact how Asian American women and Latina students perceive their socialization (See Figure 5.1). Although all four agents affect these students' experiences, available alumni, and the "real

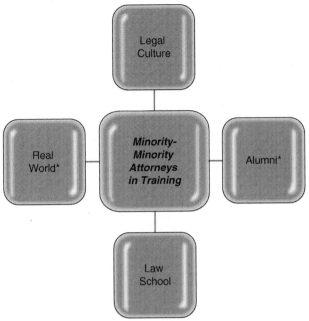

* Agents affecting optimistic outlook at MT4

Figure 5.1 Agents of Typecast Socialization

world" serve as agents that positively influence Asian American women and Latina law students from MT4. These students appreciate the opportunities they have to embark on a career path that provides not only a chance for upward mobility, but also the ability to develop professional skills. While aware of possible obstacles in their career advancement, these women are optimistic, and look toward a career ripe with opportunities.

Role models expressing frustrations and difficulties of work/life balance color Asian American women and Latina law students' career outlooks. Although these women are typecast into particular professional and familial roles, they nevertheless experience socialization differently, based not only on demographic variables, such as race or class, but importantly, exposure to particular agents of socialization at each law school. The Asian American women and Latinas from WT1 anticipate a difficult career balancing work and family. Those at MT4 are quite optimistic about their careers largely because their role models are women professors and alumni who seem to have achieved a successful work/life balance – recall Andréa who speaks highly of her Art and Law professor. These role models, who are often adjuncts, work in small firms, or in government, demonstrate to these women students that they too can "manage it all."

Aside from role models and expectations, age at start of law school also seems to affect how these women internalize their roles. Many of the women from MT4 returned to law school after experiencing other careers, or continue to work while in law school and have already been initiated into the world of gendered professional expectations. They appear to feel comfortable navigating professional and familial expectations, despite typecasting.

Asian American women and Latinas learn to become lawyers by adapting to multiple expectations. This process is filled with anxiety, and typecasts them as budding attorneys, "angry women of color," "mommies," and potential wives. I examined in this chapter how and why Asian American women and Latinas experience competing role expectations as they embark on their legal careers. While all women law students must contend with gendered professional expectations, Asian American women and Latinas negotiate the interaction of ethnicity, gender, immigrant background, and race. They fear that their passionate commentary about particular communities or issues may discourage their peers from taking seriously their contributions in class, and that they will be known as "angry women of color." But, the Asian American women and Latinas at MT4 tend to be older in age, and treat law school as an exercise in professional development. They speak positively of available role models, and also relay that they are familiar with gender inequality in the workplace because of their previous (and/ or current) work experiences.

Agents of socialization shape the ways these women think about becoming successful. Taken together, legal culture, law school, alumni and the "real world" act as agents of socialization. Parental expectations also contribute to these women's notions of success. Some parents do not understand why their daughters would pursue higher education, and others are fearful that with a law degree, their daughters will be less attractive to prospective significant others as their resumes become "too intimidating." Parental stressors further contribute to the multitude of expectations that create anxiety as Asian American women and Latinas cogitate their career trajectories.

Asian American women and Latinas' experiences leave unresolved how to successfully integrate them into the fabric of law school and the profession as a whole. While one cannot expect the gendered and raced culture of law school to alter over night, I provide some recommendations to law schools and to the profession, in an effort to create an inviting and supportive environment for these new initiates.

RECOMMENDATION 1: INSTITUTIONALLY SUPPORTED WOMEN OF COLOR STUDENT GROUPS

Law schools could sponsor women of color student organizations. A quick Internet search yields disappointing results among the nation's highly ranked law schools: most institutions do not provide safe spaces designated for women of color.[8] This recommendation needs to be property explained and contextualized. The purpose of this group is not only to serve as a space to "vent" about frustrations in law school, but more so for students to co-mentor one another. The mission of this organization could be as simple as providing academic, professional, and social support, which would be useful for women of color law students.

The women of color organization could host guest speakers and major events each academic year, bringing to campus alumni and notable women of color leaders in the field to speak about their experiences in law. This effort demonstrates to the women of color law students that the legal institutions they attend are invested in them – not only their schooling, but also their future careers. Some professors and administrators reading this recommendation may respond with minor enthusiasm since most law schools already sponsor women's associations, and race or ethnicity-based affinity groups. From conversations with women of color law students, however, it is apparent that the currently available groups do not represent their needs. The desire and need for groups dedicated to women of color is not a new phenomenon. This practice dates back to the Civil Rights era, when women of color felt that they neither belonged in white women's groups, nor race-based associations devoid of close attention to the intersection of gender *and* race (Ancheta 1998; Giddings 1984; Shah 1997). Institutionally sponsored women of color organizations would also include dedicated faculty mentors who commit the students' success in law school.

---

[8] The only law schools with identifiable women of color organizations are: NYU, Yale, University of Virginia, Stanford, and University of California, Berkeley.

RECOMMENDATION 2: FOSTERING DYNAMIC CLASSROOMS

In an effort to lessen the burdens on women of color being typecast as "angry," professors could foster dynamic classrooms that encourage dialogue from diverse perspectives. Rather than relying on women of color to "angrily" (i.e., passionately) bring to the table issues that are important to disenfranchised communities, professors could focus on different social issues as topics for each course. In other words, professors could weave into their lesson plans topics especially pertinent to women of color law students. This is not meant to take the place of substantive course material, but brief lessons spent on racial profiling and criminality, urban poverty, or domestic violence would become topics of discussion initiated by professors without regard to skin color or gender. In this way, the onus of focusing on social issues would not be limited to one group that is perceived to be "angry" in the classroom.

Given that the landscape of law schools continues to change, it is important for professors and administrators to determine how to minimize alienation on the part of their student body. Minor adjustments, such as institutionally sponsored women of color groups, or for professors to include topics that interest disenfranchised communities, would lessen the burden on this particular set of students. A holistic effort on the part of law schools to not only educate the basics of the law, but to also include their students (and issues that are important to these students) in this endeavor demonstrates the evolution of this profession.

REFERENCES

ABA Commission on Women in the Profession. 2012. "Visible Invisibility: Women of Color in Fortune 500 Legal Departments." American Bar Association.

Abel, Richard. 1989. *American Lawyers*. New York: Oxford University Press.

Alba, Richard, and Victor Nee. 2003. *Remaking the American Mainstream: Assimilation and Contemporary Immigration*. Cambridge, MA: Harvard University Press.

American Bar Association. 2009. *Legal Education Statistics*. www.abanet.org/legaled/statistics/stats.html. Accessed September 2, 2009.

——— 2011. "A Current Glance at Women and the Law (2000–2011). Prepared by the Commission on Women in the Profession. www.americanbar.org/groups/women/resources/statistics.html. Accessed March 2, 2012.

Ancheta, Angelo N. 1998. *Race, Rights, and the Asian American Experience.* New Brunswick, New Jersey: Rutgers University Press.

Anderson, Karen. 1997. *Changing Women: A History of Racial Ethnic Women in Modern America.* New York: Oxford University Press.

Banks, Taunya Lovell. 1988. "Gender Bias in the Classroom." *Journal of Legal Education* 38: 137–146.

Blair-Loy, Mary. 2003. *Competing Devotions: Career and Family among Women Executives.* Cambridge, MA: Harvard University Press.

Blair-Loy, Mary and Gretchen DeHart. 2003. "Family and Career Trajectories among African American Female Attorneys." *Journal of Family Issues* 24: 908–933.

Bolton, Sharon C. and Daniel Muzio. 2007. "Can't Live with 'Em; Can't Live without 'Em: Gendered Segmentation in the Legal Profession." *Sociology* 41: 47–64.

Bonilla-Silva, Eduardo and David R. Dietrich. 2009. "The Latin Americanization of U.S. Race Relations: A New Pigmentocracy." In *Shades of Difference: Why Skin Color Matters* (ed.) Evelyn Nakano Glenn. Stanford, CA: Stanford University Press: 40–60.

Brettell, Caroline B. 2005. "Voluntary Organizations, Social Capital, and the Social Incorporation of Asian Indian Immigrants in the Dallas-Fort Worth Metroplex." *Anthropological Quarterly* 78: 853–883.

Carbado, Devon W. and Mitu Gulati. 2004. "Race to the Top of the Corporate Ladder: What Minorities Do When They Get There." *Washington and Lee Law Review* 61: 1645–1693.

Cech, Erin, Brian Rubineau, Susan Silbey, and Carroll Seron. 2011. "Professional Role Confidence and Gendered Persistence in Engineering." *American Sociological Review* 76: 641–666.

Clydesdale, Timothy T. 2004. "A Forked River Runs Through Law School: Toward Understanding Race, Gender, Age and Related Gaps in Law School Performance and Bar Passage." *Law and Social Inquiry* 29: 711–769.

Costello, Carrie Yang. 2005. *Professional Identity Crisis: Race, Class, Gender, and Success at Professional Schools.* Nashville, TN: Vanderbilt University Press.

Epstein, Cynthia Fuchs. 1983. *Women in Law.* New York: Basic Books, Inc.

— 1992. "Tinkerbells and Pinups: The Construction and Reconstruction of Gender Boundaries at Work." In *Cultivating Differences: Symbolic Boundaries and the Making of Inequality*, Michèle Lamont and Marcel Fournier (eds). Chicago, IL: The University of Chicago Press: 232–256.

Feagin, Joe R. 2013. *The White Racial Frame: Centuries of Racial Framing and Counter-Framing.* New York: Routledge.

Fischer, Judith D. 1996. "Portia Unbound: The Effects of a Supportive Law School Environment on Women and Minority Students." *UCLA Women's Law Journal* 7: 1–56.

Flores-González, Nilda. 2002. *School Kids/Street Kids: Identity Development in Latino Students*. New York: Teachers College Press.

Frank, Reanne, Ilana Redstone Akresh and Bo Lu. 2010. "Latino Immigrants and the U.S. Racial Order: How and Where Do They Fit In?" *American Sociological Review* 75: 378–401.

Gibson, Margaret A. 1988. *Accommodation without Assimilation: Sikh Immigrants in an American High School*. Ithaca, NY: Cornell University Press.

Giddings, Paula. 1984. *When and Where I Enter: The Impact of Black Women on Race and Sex in America*. New York: Bantam Books.

Gilkes, Cheryl Townsend. 1982. "Successful Rebellious Professionals: The Black Women's Professional Identity and Community Commitment." *Psychology of Women Quarterly* 6: 289–311.

Goffman, Erving. 1959. *The Presentation of Self in Everyday Life*. New York: Anchor Books.

Golash-Boza, Tanya. 2006. "Dropping the Hyphen? Becoming Latino(a)-American through Racialized Assimilation." *Social Forces* 85: 27–55.

Granfield, Robert. 1992. *Making Elite Lawyers: Visions of Law at Harvard and Beyond*. New York: Routledge, Chapman and Hall, Inc.

Green Melanie C. and Timothy C. Brock. 2005. "Organizational Membership versus Informal Interaction: Contributions to Skills and Perceptions that Build Social Capital." *Political Psychology* 26: 1–25.

Guinier, Lani, Michelle Fine, and Jane Balin. 1997. *Becoming Gentlemen: Women, Law School, and Institutional Change*. Boston, MA: Beacon Press.

Haney-López, Ian. 1997 (2006). *White by Law: The Legal Construction of Race*. New York: New York University Press.

Kanter, Rosabeth Moss. 1977. *Men and Women of the Corporation*. New York: Basic Books, Inc.

Kay, Fiona M. and Jean E. Wallace. 2009. "Mentors as Social Capital: Gender, Mentors, and Career Rewards in Law Practice." *Sociological Inquiry* 79: 418–452.

Keith, Verna M. 2009. "A Colorstruck World: Skin Tone, Achievement, and Self-Esteem Among African American women." In *Shades of Difference: Why Skin Color Matters* (ed.) Evelyn Nakano Glenn. Stanford, CA: Stanford University Press: 25–39.

Lee, Jennifer and Frank D. Bean. 2004. "America's Changing Color Lines: Race/Ethnicity, Immigration, and Multiracial Identification." *Annual Review of Sociology* 30: 221–242.

2007. "Reinventing the Color Line: Immigration and America's New Racial/Ethnic Divide." *Social Forces* 86: 561–586.

Lopez, Nancy. 2003. *Hopeful Girls, Troubled Boys: Race and Gender Disparity in Urban Education*. New York: Routledge.

Louie, Vivian S. 2004. *Compelled to Excel: Immigration, Education, and Opportunity among Chinese Americans*. Stanford, CA: Stanford University Press.

Mertz, Elizabeth. 2007. *The Language of Law School: Learning to "Think Like a Lawyer."* New York: Oxford University Press.

Moore, Wendy Leo. 2008. *Reproducing Racism: White Space, Elite Law Schools, and Racial Inequality.* Boulder, CO: Rowman and Littlefield Publishers, Inc.

Omi, Michael and Howard Winant. 2015. *Racial Formation in the United States from the 1960s to the 1990s* (Third Edition). New York: Routledge.

Payne-Pikus, Monique R., John Hagan, and Robert L. Nelson. 2010. "Experiencing Discrimination: Race and Retention in America's Largest Law Firms." *Law and Society Review* 44: 553–584.

Portes, Alejandro and Rubén G. Rumbaut. 2001. *Legacies: The Story of the Immigrant Second Generation.* Berkeley: University of California Press.

2006. *Immigrant America: A Portrait.* Berkeley: University of California Press.

Sander, Richard H. 2004. "A Systematic Analysis of Affirmative Action in American Law Schools." *Stanford Law Review* 57: 367–483.

Schleef, Debra J. 2006. *Managing Elites: Professional Socialization in Law and Business Schools.* Boulder, CO: Rowman & Littlefield Publishers, Inc.

Segura, Denise A. 1992. "Chicanas in White-Collar Jobs: You Have to Prove Yourself More." *Sociological Perspectives* 35: 163–182.

Shah, Sonia. 1997. *Dragon Ladies: Asian American Women Breathe Fire.* Cambridge, MA: South End Press.

Smith, Jacquelyn. 2013. "The Happiest and Unhappiest Jobs in America." *Forbes.* Retrieved April 2, 2013 (www.forbes.com/sites/jacquelynsmith/2013/03/22/the-happiest-and-unhappiest-jobs-in-america/).

Smith, Ryan A. and James R. Elliott. 2002. "Does Ethnic Concentration Influence Employee's Access to Authority? An Examination of Contemporary Urban Labor Markets." *Social Forces* 81: 255–279.

Steele, Claude M. 1997. "A Threat in the Air: How Stereotypes Shape Intellectual Identity and Performance." *American Psychologist* 52: 613–629.

Tomlinson, Jennifer, Daniel Muzio, Hilary Sommerlad, Lisa Webley, and Liz Duff. 2013. "Structure, Agency, and the Career Strategies of White Women and BME Individuals in the Legal Profession." *Human Relations* 66: 245–269.

Wallace, Jean E. and Fiona M. Kay. 2012. "Tokenism, Organizational Segregation, and Coworker Relations in Law Firms." *Social Problems* 59: 389–410.

Waters, Mary C. 1999. *Black Identities: West Indian Immigrant Dreams and American Realities.* Cambridge, MA: Harvard University Press.

Watkins-Hayes, Celeste. 2009. "Race-ing the Bootstrap Climb: Black and Latino Bureaucrats in Post-Reform Welfare Offices." *Social Problems* 56: 285–310.

Wilkins, David B. 1997. "Two Paths to the Mountain Top? The Role of Legal Education in Shaping the Values of Black Corporate Lawyers." In *Lawyers: A Critical Reader.* Richard L. Abel (ed). New York: The New Press.

Wilkins, David B. and G. Mitu Gulati. 1996. "Why Are There so Few Black Lawyers in Corporate Law Firms? An Institutional Analysis." *California Law Review* 84: 493–625.

Yoder, Janice D. 1994. "Looking Beyond Numbers: The Effects of Gender Status, Job Prestige, and Occupational Gender-Typing on Tokenism Processes." *Social Psychology Quarterly* 57: 150–159.

RETHINKING THE INTERSECTIONALITY OF RACE, GENDER, AND CLASS IDENTITY
Educating underrepresented minority women for elite careers in science, technology, math, and engineering

CARROLL SERON*

INTRODUCTION

Ashley, an African-American woman, completed her undergraduate degree at MIT in Chemical Engineering. Today, she is a project manager at a major pharmaceutical company where she works with a team of engineers to develop innovative medical devices. Beginning in elementary school, Ashley was identified as "smart" and was selected for various programs to encourage talented and gifted girls to pursue math and science. Ashley grew up in a college community known for its liberal values and politics. She was encouraged by her parents, who are professionals, and particularly by her mother who earned a doctorate in Public Health. In high school, Ashley toyed with the idea of becoming a gynecologist and her mother arranged for her to shadow a friend to see what it is like.[1] Once she started taking classes at MIT, however,

* I appreciate the comments of Erin Cech on an earlier draft of this article. I also thank Anna Raup-Kounovsky for editorial assistance. Data collection for the research findings reported here was supported by a grant to Carroll Seron and Susan Silbey from the National Science Foundation (Grant #0609628).

[1] The findings reported here complement those discussed by Lareau (2011) in her longitudinal ethnography, *Unequal Families: Class, Race, and Family Life*. Echoing Ashley's experience, Lareau writes of Alexander, the son of middle class African-Americans, who she first met in elementary school; when she meets up with him ten years later, he is now in medical school at Columbia. Lareau notes that in high school, "his mother arranged for him to be in an intern in a medical office in order to build his resume for his premed college application" (p. 280). In their study of minority solicitors and barristers in the UK and Wales, Webley et al. (2016) also

Ashley found that she preferred the idea of developing innovative medical devices and opted for engineering. Ashley reported that she enjoyed the engineering classes and, also, felt that she could have a bigger impact on society through research and development of new medical devices. Asked how she was treated by her peers and teachers, Ashley remarked that racism created some background noise but it by no means derailed her; on the other hand, she found gender stereotyping by her peers – being relegated to the "secretary" role of a team project for example – far more troubling and annoying. Nonetheless, Ashley developed various strategies to gain support through extracurricular and other activities that contributed, she elaborated, to her persistence in her degree program and her job placement at career launch.

Ashley's experience is quite similar to a group of underrepresented minority (URM) women from elite schools and part of a larger study of professional socialization in engineering. There are a number of shared patterns that emerge among these URM women. First, and quite strikingly, community membership in an upper-middle class, professional background matters; not only does Ashley have the opportunity to observe what being a doctor might be like, but as we shall see in greater detail, she, like others, may deploy these advantages to navigate experiences of racial and ethnic stereotyping that she and her peers encounter. In addition, being singled out as "smart" in math and science at a young age is a confidence booster with a surprisingly long half-life; rituals of being selected for gifted programs are often described as singularly important experiences that allow these talented women to find safe havens to pursue their curiosities. Once in elite college programs in science, technology, engineering, and math (STEM) fields, we find that these URM women deploy various strategies to stay the course; for example, building social support networks through racial or ethnic identity groups. Importantly, many describe a strong commitment to using their work in science or engineering to make a difference in society or, put differently, they know *why* they want to be scientists and engineers and what they hope to accomplish. Finally, these narratives suggest that resilience, bouncing back from a difficult experience, is particularly important in explaining the decision to stay the course.

find that respondents recognize that parents' cultivation of their children's life chances begin in childhood.

A review of research on URM women in STEM fields supports several of the themes that emerge from the interviews for this study, including the "double-bind" of coping with sexism and racism, and the strategies used by minority women to realize their goals. Perhaps not surprisingly, a number of studies, reviewed by Ong et al., show that successful URM women in STEM fields bring "agency" and "drive" to their undergraduate education; this work suggests that "despite marginalization, women of color often use their status as a member of two underrepresented groups – as a woman and as a person of color – to empower themselves" to reach their goals (2011:188). Complementing this work, scholars have demonstrated that URM women live, and often experience discrimination, at the intersection of race *and* gender (also see Best et al. 2011; Crenshaw 1989). Building on this theme as well as social constructionist framing of race and ethnicity, Saperstein and Penner (2012; also see Penner & Saperstein 2013) have added class to the intersectional mix, demonstrating that *perceptions* of racial categorization, or how others slot a particular individual into a racial or ethnic group, vary with social context; categorization of race or ethnicity may be "whitened" as an individual climbs the social ladder, their findings provocatively show.

Framing intersectionality along three axes – race, gender, *and* class – I explore the experiences of URM women in STEM fields. Here intersectionality is examined through the lens of identity, or the ways in which one constructs "community membership" (Penner & Saperstein 2013: 680) and then uses that membership to navigate life course transitions. URM women in engineering are "off diagonal" to the extent that they do not "represent the prototypical images embedded in cultural stereotypes" (Ridgeway & Kricheli-Katz 2013: 295) of engineers (Faulkner 2009). Engineering and STEM fields more generally unfold in a rhetorical space that is deeply and uncritically committed to scientific positivism, individualism, and meritocracy or what has been described as a culture that recognizes "no culture." A large body of research has shown, however, that the practices of engineering culture more often than not tilt toward sexist, homophobic, and racialized assumptions and values.

This article explores the question, what patterns are discerned among URM women who take on the challenge of a STEM field? Like many studies of URM women in STEM fields, the sample here is very small. The findings from these interviews are, then, exploratory, and designed to tease out themes, questions, and hypotheses around the experiences of URM women that will require further research with larger, more robust samples. But, as I explain next, the interview data reported on here are part of a much larger, systematic study of professional socialization in engineering; thus, the themes discussed here may be weighed in a broader context and set of findings.

In the next section, I review the literature on minorities in STEM fields, and, more specifically, professional socialization. Following this, (Section 2) I describe the Method and Context of this study. I then present the key findings. Finally, I conclude with a discussion of the ways in which the findings reported here present a research agenda for explaining the successes and challenges faced by URM women in STEM fields and related professions.

THE CHALLENGE FACED BY UNDERREPRESENTED MINORITY WOMEN IN ENGINEERING

Underrepresented minority women are as motivated to enter STEM fields, including engineering, as their minority and white male and white female counterparts; URM women, like their white counterparts, are significantly more likely to depart from STEM fields, including engineering, though their academic performance, on average, is stronger than their URM male counterparts (Ong et al. 2011: 181). For those who remain in engineering, URM women are gendered and racial/ethnic "tokens" (Kanter 1977) in a profession that claims to be "a culture of no culture" (Traweek 1988).

Engineering negotiates its legitimacy around a tenacious and unwavering commitment to objective, value-neutral, universal, and meritocratic principles of scientific analysis. An anchoring point of engineering's "folk wisdom" (Freidson 1986) is that individuals who work hard and have the appropriate skills in math and science will be well-positioned to enter the engineering academy and, building on this foundation, to acquire the technical knowledge, skill set, and habits of mind required for success in the labor market. Meritocracies claim to operate objectively and without bias toward one or another group (e.g., women, racial/ethnic minorities, or lesbian, gay and bisexual individuals [LGBT]), rendering them sites that are culturally apolitical. The "color-blind" world of engineering valorizes what Bonilla-Silva has described as an "abstracted liberalism" organized around "equality of opportunity," "individualism," and "choice" (2003: 28). The apolitical space of engineering defers to objectivity and value-neutrality that, moreover, complements core values of scientific positivism (Cech & Waidzunas 2011; Faulkner 2000). Those who do not "cut the mustard" or who fail to "make it" only have themselves to blame, either because of a lack of ability, commitment, or fit (Seron et al. 2011). To walk the corridors of engineering is, then, to inhabit a world that denies cultural markers of, or historical legacies embedded in, class, race, gender, sexual orientation, political orientation – or, any other set of values and beliefs that might question the role of science, and its most fundamental claims.

Complementing a culture that valorizes "no culture," observational studies of engineering worksites show high levels of "male homosociality" (Mellstrom 1995). Whether in the form of shoptalk, humor, gossip, or banter, the worksites of engineering, including its educational training and workforce preparation, remains a male-centered world that creates a decidedly "chilly climate" for all women (Crawford & MacLeod 1990). Or, as a review of the literature concludes: engineering worksites continue to embrace a "hostile macho culture" that isolates and marginalizes all women (Bilimoria & Liang 2012: 17).

Among those who persist with an engineering education, all women, but particularly URMs, are a small proportion of every classroom, assigned team project, internship, or informal study group; findings suggest that it is not unusual for them to be the "lone woman on a team" (Bilimoria & Liang 2012: 17). Their token status creates what Kanter (1977) described as a "contrast effect;" "ironically, [tokens are] both highly visible as people, who are different and yet not permitted the individuality of their own unique non-stereotypical characteristics" (Kanter 1977: 211). Elaborating on this theme, Faulkner finds an "in/visibility" paradox whereby "women engineers are simultaneously highly visible as women yet invisible as engineers" (Faulkner 2009: 5). Bonilla-Silva's (2003) research suggests that URM women also navigate paradoxes of "color-blind racism," where we might expect that they are visible as minorities if invisible as engineers (also see Ong 2005).

URM women in the halls of engineering are "in/visible" both because of their gender and race. In their speculations on the ways in which class, gender, and race unfold for these "off-diagonal" individuals, Ridgeway and Kricheli-Katz suggest, however, that while stereotypes of racism and sexism will create "'binds'" of invisibility, it is also quite possible that, depending on context, "off-diagonal" groups, particularly Black women, may enjoy "freedoms [that] result from being unprototypical of disadvantaging statuses" (2013: 307). "Binds" may take various forms from, as we've noted, invisibility to, perhaps ironically, being seen and heard as too forceful and domineering (also see Pan 2016). Ong's study of Black women in physics found that they self-consciously adopted a "'loud Black girl' persona as a means of breaking through their intersectional invisibility to demonstrate their competence as scientists" (as cited in Ridgeway & Kricheli-Katz 2013: 310). On the other hand, in settings that value "agentic behavior and leadership" such as business and professions, once Black women have gained access, itself a challenging task, they may take advantage of stereotypes of Black women as "domineering" to, ironically, create space to act authoritatively. On balance, "binds" outnumber "freedoms" for URM women, but the opportunity to leverage those "freedoms" should not be ignored, particularly when URM women may also embody nonprotoypical class identities.

What then is required of URM women to stay the course in engineering? Prior research suggests that persistence is not just a matter of having confidence in and mastery of one's scientific and related expertise. Equally, if not more importantly, neophytes must cultivate "career-fit confidence" that allows them to envision themselves as doing the work of an engineer (Cech et al. 2011); students must become comfortable with the core values, orientations, habits of mind, and ways of being an engineer – they must adopt those values as their own. At career launch, those who stay the course must find a "cultural match" (Dimaggio 1992: 127 as cited in Rivera [2012]) between their personal values, goals, beliefs, and aspirations and the field's commitment to problem solving through scientific analysis and design. Finding that "cultural match" for URM women in engineering requires, then, a degree of comfort with the "color-blind" and de-gendered norms and values at the core of this profession. Additionally, findings suggest that URM women develop peer networks of support; draw encouragement from family, particularly mothers; display confidence, self-efficacy, and "inner drive;" and leverage the "double-bind" of their status as women and minorities to "empower themselves" (Ong et al. 2011: 185–189).

Intersectional frameworks introduce the importance of factoring in "community membership" around one's gender, race, *and* class identity. Knitting together community membership around one's gender, race, and class identity begins early in the life course and unfolds through parents' selection of place of residence, including schools, as well as the ways in which parents engage with their children's day-to-day activities with friends, lessons, extended kin, or other extracurricular activities. For example, Lareau (2011) shows that upper-middle class African-American professional parents, like their white counterparts, invest significant energy, time, and commitment in the "concerted cultivation" of their children's talents and skills with the expectation that they too will bring the habits of mind and appropriate capital to reproduce the life style of their family of origin.

The stories reported here build on these findings to ask: What kind of patterns can we discern among URM women who have successfully made it through STEM majors and, in many instances, launched a career in the field? Before turning to these findings, however, I place this study in context and briefly describe the methodology.

CONTEXT AND METHOD

Context: The findings presented here are based on in-depth interviews with URM women who are part of a much larger longitudinal study of professional socialization of engineers. The broader research project seeks to explain the social psychological, structural, and cultural factors that explain women's departure from engineering, focusing on the critical transition from college to career launch, and with a specific focus on how women perform at more elite institutions in these fields (also see McEllwee & Robinson 1992; Valian 1999). Data collection for this longitudinal, panel study included yearly surveys to the entire cohort (n=737) at four sites, in-depth interviews with a sub-sample of students across the four sites in year 1 (freshmen) and year 4 (senior) of the study (n=64), and bi-monthly diaries from a sub-sample at the four sites (n=40). Of the sixty-four cases where we have both year 1 and year 4 interviewees, nine are URM women. It is this group that is analyzed here. But to place this group in context, 39% percent of the survey respondents in year 1 were URM women (n=146), including Asian, and planned to major in engineering or another STEM field; if Asian women are removed, 12% were URM women. Eighty percent of URM women graduated with an engineering or other STEM degree; among Asian women 67% earned a STEM degree. For graduates of these elite programs, the nine in-depth profiles are not, then, atypical of persistence patterns.

Because the work reported here is part of a much larger study, all interviews and diaries have been read and coded. Analyses of these interviews and diaries are reported in various working papers (Seron et al. 2011; Seron et al., 2012). I note this point to make clear that I "read" the interviews reported in this article in the context of a much more in-depth analysis of men and women in engineering.

Method: All surveys were read and coded using ATLAS.ti. Based on a close reading of interviews and diaries, codes were developed by Seron and Silbey. At the conclusion of this phase of data analysis, research assistants reread the year 1 and year 4 interviews and prepared memos highlighting significant changes or consistencies in respondents' views about engineering, future plans, and related questions. The findings reported here are based on analysis of a close reading of the interviews in conjunction with key themes that emerge from memos.

When we interviewed this small group of URM women in their first year of college we had no idea where they would end up in year 4. In contrast to college students in most industrialized countries, Americans students can change their minds about their major – and, they do with surprising regularity (Ma 2009). The fact that eight of the nine students stayed in a STEM major at a highly selective college or university is important to bear in mind as we consider the findings that follow. Drawn from longitudinal, qualitative interviews, in this article I elaborate the patterned experiences of these URM women as they "try on" (Ibarra 1999) the roles of being a scientist or engineer, and how the majority finds congruence between personal values and the profession's culture and norms.

FINDINGS

The nine interviewees who are the focus of this analysis are graduates of some of the most competitive, elite programs in the country. Four of the graduates are Black (three African-American, one from Africa), one is Hispanic (born in Latin America), and four are Asian-American (including Chinese and Pakistani, educated in the United States if born overseas).[2] Of the nine students, I am able to trace where eight

---

[2] While Asian and Asian-American women do show educational persistence and success early in their careers, like other women of color they tend to become "outsiders" at later stages in career trajectories (Ong et al. 2011: 180–181; also see Burrelli 2009; Wu & Jing 2009).

landed post-graduation. Four went directly to graduate school in an engineering field; one is Asian, one is Hispanic, one is African-American, and one is from Africa and is pursuing a combined program in engineering and education. Of this group, Cecilia, a Latina from Columbia, has already completed her PhD and is currently an assistant professor. Four are working, three in engineering-related fields. Katy, an Asian-American, worked at a sustainable design firm before earning her MBA at Harvard;[3] and, just as she described her plans in our interviews with her during her freshman year, she is now the founder and developer of her own firm in sustainable energy. Like Ashley's career path described earlier, Nina, who is African-American, is also a project manager at a large engineering firm in the United States. Fatima, whose family is from Pakistan and grew up in Miami, is working as an assistant at a research institute in Washington, D.C.; after earning a degree in Brain and Cognitive Science, she is the only subject who is not directly engaged in a STEM field. By any measure, this is a group of highly accomplished graduates. This is not surprising in light of the schools they attended, but the proportion that stayed the course in a STEM field does not fit the pattern of what we know about URM women's persistence patterns. What factors then explain their relative success?

Community membership and social class matter: Corroborating Ashley's story most of these young women are the children of upper-middle class professionals. Six are the children of doctors, engineers, professors, economists, biostatisticians, or in one case a diplomat; five report that both parents are full-time professionals. They attended elite, private schools, or their parents moved to suburbs known for exceptionally strong public schools. While Americans like to think that each generation begins life on an equal playing field, the reality is that "class does matter. In real life, the educational and work outcomes of young people (including those from URM backgrounds) are closely tied to the class position of their parents" (Lareau 2011: 305).

Jennifer, who is African-American and the daughter of a pediatrician, grew up in a comfortable suburb outside of Chicago; she began her education at an elite private school in Chicago, but then her parents moved to a suburb known for its excellent school system; the transition was a bit of a challenge, she recalls. Nonetheless, Jennifer continued to

---

[3] An MBA is considered a logical graduate degree for engineering graduates.

cultivate the cultural capital her parents thought important – listening to Mozart on her headset – despite what the other kids might think.[4] Cai is the daughter of two PhD engineers from China who now live in Pittsburgh; of course, they expected her to follow in their footsteps to pursue a career in engineering, but she also loved math and science so it all fell into place.

They all describe their families as close knit and supportive; their parents took time and thought to cultivate their children's sense of security to be their own person; importantly, this is the case for the three women whose parents were not professionals. In contrast to findings reported by Ong et al. (2011), these women describe equally involved and supportive fathers and mothers (also see Lareau 2011: 277–286); a number of the Asian students joked about the stereotype of the over-involved Asian father. Katy's parents are from Hong Kong; her father is an electrician and her mother is a homemaker; at the time we met Katy, her older sister was in law school; her parents are very proud of both of their daughters and, particularly, her pursuit of science and math. Fatima's father works on the assembly line in a light factory and her mother is a substitute teacher; she notes that her father discouraged her from playing sports or an instrument because, she muses, in her family "academics is everything." In focusing on his daughter's academic performance to the exclusion of other activities, Fatima's father may inadvertently have missed those key cultural factors that are critical for success, particularly at elite institutions.

Math and science high school programs: All of these young women describe experiences where they were singled out for their talent in math and science, often beginning in elementary school. Katy describes how she did "Continental Math, which was a special math program where you go in early in the mornings and study special math problems then you take tests;" in high school Katy was selected for another special program at Columbia; encouraged by her "awesome" biology teacher, she also participated in a nationwide competition to build a robot, an experience that, even after four years of college engineering,

---

[4] The minority lawyers and solicitors interviewed by Webley et al. (2016) clearly recognize the importance of culture and learning the right cues. As one of their respondents notes, minority lawyers, especially those who are the children of new immigrants, "just don't have the culture at home which socializes you and educates you into the world of 'race' horses, for example" (p. 216).

remained the event that "really turned me onto engineering." Fatima participated in math and science programs beginning at a young age where she too spoke of her father's encouragement; her younger brother, who Fatima describes as a math wiz, always works with her on her various math and science projects, including her first year assignments in college.

For the remainder of these young women who came from more upper middle-class families, many described how their parents sought out appropriate programs (also see Lareau 2011). Jennifer's parents enrolled her in two engineering program for minorities and one women engineering program which "encouraged me to go into engineering. And I think those programs are very good and they're actually helping people consider that engineering is a field they might want to do." Cecilia's parents sent her to an all-girls summer camp for math, science, and engineering; at first, she said that she was reluctant to go to an all-girls camp, but it turned out that she loved the work – and her team won a robot competition. Fia described how her parents put her in a special math program in elementary school that no doubt played a role in her selection for the Gates Scholars Program in high school. Cai's parents took advantage of their proximity to Carnegie Melon, where she attended summer school while in high school; "you take like five classes and a few electives and do P-sets. It was awesome." Angela, who is African-American and the daughter of a civil engineer (father) and a biostatistician (mother), grew up in the suburbs of Washington, DC; her parents enrolled her in multiple programs affiliated with universities in the area; she was also selected for a special program at Xavier University in New Orleans. Jennifer, who is now earning a PhD in Electrical Engineering, was a Science Olympian throughout high school; that, she acknowledged, made an enormous difference – even as she tried "not to stand out" (also see Lareau 2011: 288).

Most of these young women grew up in families where their parents' community membership in the upper middle class included an understanding of the ingredients required for their daughter's success. For Cai, April, and Fatima, whose parents had fewer resources or access to social networks, teachers played a pivotal role in directing their talents. Not surprisingly, they all reported being admitted to the top schools to which they applied. Only Fatima described feeling intimidated as she transitioned from high school to college. While they in fact had some rude awakenings, describing how they were working really hard for the first time in their short lives, all, again except Fatima, tended to take it in stride, a ritual of transition that they expected.[5] For example, Angela, who was in a gifted program in high school, simply described working harder in Physics and Calculus when the course hit a point that went beyond what she had learned in high school; she reports that she heard the "horror stories," but she felt prepared to learn the more challenging material. And, she noted if she had a question, "she raised her hand and asked it." One might speculate that, like her counterparts here, her class trumped her race and gender identities to feel entitled to learn the answer to a problem – and, take action. Among these nine stars, only Fatima had a very rocky start to her college career and, even at graduation regretted her decision to attend a technical school. The remainder transitioned to college with the same class pedigrees as many of their white counterparts.

STEM and Social Responsibility: Whether we speak to these URM women in years 1 or 4, the eight who stayed the course share a commitment to engineering and science as a vehicle for improving society. The consistency of this theme among these eight URM women stands in contrast to our broader findings for this project, particularly compared to white men. This is not to be confused with an interest in politics; many of them describe themselves as ill-informed and uninterested in politics, if opposed to the Iraq war – a theme that is shared with their white counterparts, male and female. These URM women embody the typical norms and values of engineers who tend to pride themselves on being apolitical (Seron et al. 2011). There is, however, a consensus that they would not work on war related contracts, preferring to leave that kind of work to someone else.

But, the opening vignette of this article that describes Ashley's decision to study chemical engineering, going into research and development so that she can do something like "build tissue … to make things better for people" is typical of her peers. Sylvia, who grew up in Uganda, remains committed to sustainable development; as she notes, "I know I would never be in engineering like just to make money or just to build skyscrapers in New York; it has to be something that's helping

[5] Again, we see how these findings echo Lareau's: "As the first edition of the book notes, the middle-class parents appeared to see organized activities as filled with 'teachable moments' that helped cultivate their children's talents. As young adults, most of the middle-=class kids articulated a similar perspective, readily linking their past activities to enduring life benefits" (2011: 282).

people." April, a classmate, who is Asian-American, explains that her training in Chemical Engineering will allow her to do something like "monitoring water in Africa ... and I can make a difference that way." As she goes on to note, this is more effective than "being a student activist when all you're doing is ... well ... holding up signs and stuff." Cecilia is, in many respects, an engineer's engineer; she has little interest in politics, but notes that she would like "to do something for my country; I would rather do it for my country than anywhere else." Katy, who is now developing her own firm in sustainable energy, makes it clear that she will never become a "CAD monkey."

In addition to the solid foundation that they bring to their decision to study a STEM discipline, usually engineering, these URM women also express a strong rationale for that decision that goes beyond their shared love of math problems and scientific puzzles. Typical of many engineers, they are very practical young women (McIlwee & Robinson 1992), but they plan to leverage that practical bent to make a difference in the world around them – which does distinguish them. At the stage of credential acquisition, these findings show that they bring the requisite training and preparation to succeed at very competitive programs – and, they know *why* they want to succeed. Whether their sense of social responsibility will continue to sustain them as they move into the labor force remains an open question. Pan's (2016) study of the socialization of Latina and Asian women at a more elite law school, comparable in status to the schools studied here, suggests that exposure to the realities of the labor market and engineering culture may leave them somewhat more pessimistic about whether they will continue to enjoy a sense of "career-fit" confidence in engineering (Cech et al. 2011).

Managing gender and racial stereotypes: With one exception, these young women do not question whether they should be at these powerhouse institutions. Fatima failed a number of courses in her first year; she was able to make things up so that she graduated in the appropriate year; had she the option, she would have transferred to Harvard, where she had also been admitted as a freshman. In discussing her profound disappointment with her decision to attend a technical school, she does not attribute this to either her gender or ethnicity, but rather to the ways in which an institute model of education did not allow her to explore other paths.

Turning to the subject at hand, there is a consensus among these URM women that the "intersectional" challenge of race and gender will not derail them from achieving their goals. When interviewed in her fourth year, and on her way to graduate school on the West Coast, Cecilia recognizes that she may be "advantaged" because she is a Hispanic woman; as she notes, "that's what I've been told." It's not all that important to her one way or another, which may say more about her upper-middle class Latin background than her gender or ethnicity. Katy notes, "I don't believe in affirmative action; and, that's about all I have to say." She does add, however, "I've encountered very male-dominated workplaces. But, I've always felt comfortable with that because during high school I had mostly male friends because those who were in my math and science classes, which is sad but true." When asked if there is anything special about being an Asian-American woman in engineering, in her fourth year interview April describes herself as not being a "very girly girl;" as she elaborates, her work takes her into marshes, noting that some of her classmates would avoid it: "oh my god! It's a spider and they would freak out . . . I'm more rough!" That said, when she finds herself the only woman on a conservation team working on a hydrology project, she does take note, "so, yes I guess I do think about that a lot."

April's concern about gender imbalance is shared. As we learned earlier, Ashley is very clear about her experience of sexism: "I experience that more from my peers here than I do anywhere else. Like the males could be really, really condescending sometimes." Jennifer shares Ashley's experience: "Like I see a lot of women in teams taking on kind of the leadership and administrative positions in teams, while the male students will do the kind of grunt work, the calculations, the coding – that sort of thing; those are the roles they are familiar with from high school."[6]

This is not to suggest that these bright, observant young women do not play with gender (Ong 2005) or engage in what Goffman (1963) described as "impression management." Echoing Ong's "loud, Black girl," Sylvia is quite clear that she has, at times, "gone in a hard-ass direction rather than the super feminine because, you know, you're fighting;" she recognizes that it will be a "struggle because of that

[6] There is a pronounced hierarchy within engineering; "everyone knows" that Electrical Engineering and Computer Science are male and Bio, and Brain and Cognitive Science are female.

stereotype," a theme that is shared by women of color as they confront the hurdles of professionalization in law school (Pan 2016)[7] Or, Cai describes how she can use her gender as an "advantage; if I am ever stuck with homework, I can just ask a guy and he'll be like 'oh, of course!'" The same "guy" might not be so readily available to assist his male counterpart, she elaborates. But, she also shares Ashley's and April's experience: "I show up to the lab and they look at me and they just treat me like I am *so* dumb!" Cai explains that she would never ask for help in a lab because "then people are like, 'you are just a dumb girl!'" So, context matters.[8]

How do these women describe racial and ethnic stereotyping? Cai, for example, is very conscious of the ways in which Asians are stereotyped as "smart and you should know this and you should know that!" April doesn't know what to make of her demographic designation: "I'm always weirded out when people say I'm a 'woman of color' because I just don't really see myself as a woman of color." Among the African-American woman, this ambivalence around racial and ethnic categorization is equally pronounced: there is a general consensus that they are uncomfortable with affirmative action (Seron et al. 2012). Jennifer describes racialized questions in high school, but is clear that she has not experienced that in college. Ashley expects to deal with racism, especially in a city like Boston, but it does not appear to give her great pause. Angela notes that her parents prepared her for racism so she feels ready to deal with it should the situation arise, which she claims it had not.

A close reading of these interviews with URM women at highly selective institutions suggests that sexism gives them greater cause for concern than racial or ethnic stereotyping and categorization. We might speculate that they were less prepared for the macho, sexist culture of engineering than for racial and ethnic categorizing. The majority of them, moreover, do not have the added burden of dealing with their class identity as they navigate these elite halls of education

---

[7] In contrast to the cultural space of legal education where there is room to express political claims, including those of racism and sexism, the sites of engineering education bracket such discussion. Nonetheless, Pan finds that women of color in law school do worry about being stereotyped as "angry Black women" if they raise questions of racism or sexism (Pan 2016).

[8] And, there are certainly stereotypes about the men, particularly those in Electrical Engineering and Computer Science, who show up "dirty and smelly."

(Lareau 2011: 285). All of this may change as they transition from what many describe as the "bubble" of college to the world of work or graduate education. But, at this point in their young lives, they do not describe racialized encounters that affect their sense of confidence or lead them to question their chosen career path, a STEM discipline. Certainly, their behavior, as measured by their persistence and plans post graduation provides corroborating evidence. As we have seen most of these URM women enjoy "community membership" that has given them large endowments of human, social, and cultural capital. What the findings to this point underscore is the importance of factoring social class into an analysis of the experiences of URM women – and, men.

Cultivating social capital through social networks: Those who are "stigmatized" often cope with that label by finding "those who share the stigma" and using this group as a way to learn the "tricks of the trade" as well as to have a "circle of lament to which they can withdraw for moral support and for the comfort of feeling at home, at ease, accepted as a person who really is like any other normal person" (Goffman 1963: 20). A review of the literature on URM women in STEM demonstrates that this Goffmanian theme remains alive and well (Ong et al. 2011). While we just observed that, for the most part, these URM women do *not* describe themselves as "special" or "different" because of their racial or gender status in the white, male dominated fields of STEM, they nonetheless tend to join racially/ethnically identified clubs and associations.

Ashley reports that she is active in the Black Student Association (BSA); she is also a member of a sorority that gives her the opportunity to meet African-Americans at the many campuses in the Boston area. In contrast to her hometown, she finds Boston to be a more "polarized" city; this is the first time, she comments, that she finds herself with a "racially exclusive" group of friends. Like Ashley, Sylvia is also active in the BSA on her campus, as well as the International Student Association where, she has been particularly successful at finding kindred spirits. In keeping with this theme of identity associations, Fatima is active in the Muslim Student Association, and her Asian-American counterparts also join Asian identity clubs. But, to leave it at this is somewhat misleading. All of them report that their friendship networks extend beyond their own backgrounds. For example, Fatima went to high school with a large population of Hispanics; in college she participates in social activities with Hispanics as well: "they consider me half Hispanic or something," she explains. Angela, the star athlete in this group, is a varsity volleyball player; throughout her college experience, sports, and the support from her teammates have been, in her view, integral to her academic success in applied math. Cecelia also describes herself as a serious athlete, though she misses the opportunity to play as many sports as she did in high school.

Overall, and perhaps not at all surprisingly, the URM women interviewed for this project report that they engage support networks that include an ethnic/racial component that provides an important backbone for their academic success. While this is certainly one ingredient that is foundational for their success, the broader context of these findings also makes clear that their parents' membership community is equally important in understanding their success. As Jennifer notes, she takes her minority status as a "given"; after all, her parents took pains to prepare her for this. And, when asked to weigh the relative influence of the support she receives from her participation in clubs on campus versus her parents' counsel, she is quite clear that her family is the critical ingredient. On balance, these URM women at elite institutions tend to come from families who enjoy the means to cultivate their daughter's agency and confidence to launch a career in a traditionally White, male-dominated field. The point should not be lost that most of them come from families where their parents are themselves role models for navigating success in a white professional world.

Resilience: In addition to the class identity they enjoy through their community membership, many demonstrate a resilience to simply move on after a challenging event. Cecilia's story is revealing. When we met Cecilia in her first year, she was absolutely miserable. All the other colleges she applied to were liberal arts programs and she was seriously thinking of transferring; she took some liberal arts courses and it was the "only thing that was keeping me sane." But, along the way she had a course where she (re)discovered her love of math and engineering. Despite her serious doubts that she had made a mistake in attending a technical college she not only stayed the course, but is now a college professor of engineering – a career path she flatly rejected when interviewed in college.

Others display resilience as they learn to navigate the inevitable conflicts of team-based project design. By the time they graduate, all of them have weathered the challenges of working in teams, a peda-gogical foundation of engineering education and a core ingredient of engineering culture (Seron & Silbey 2009). We have already observed that team-based projects are a site of sexist stereotyping by their male peers, though we also saw that it does not derail them. Echoing her peers, Sylvia comments "I don't think I can think of an engineering class where we haven't done teamwork. [There are] good points and bad points. But, at this point I think I can work with absolutely anybody! Like you can throw whoever you want at me – I can handle it and I think that's a wonderful thing."

By contrast, Seron et al. (2012) show that for many white women the conflicts of teams as well as the gender stereotyping by their male peers tend to blunt the cultivation of career-fit confidence, or the process of imagining themselves as engineers in the future. These findings also show that all women have a relatively easier time navigating gender stereotyp-ing on teams at school than they do in the workplace (Seron et al. 2012). For many, it is the repetition of the gender stereotyping at worksites that leads to more fundamental questioning of whether they can find that special ingredient of "career-fit" confidence. The big difference between teams at school and teams in an internship or summer job is social isolation: at school they have back up and support from others, both classmates and teachers; at worksites they are on their own. The findings reported here suggest that by the point of career launch, these more isolating experiences at worksites do not disrupt the plans of these URM women. Findings from a study by Payne-Pinkus et al. (2013), however, put the issue of social isolation at worksites in a broader context; their findings show that social isolation differentially affects the career paths of minority lawyers. Whereas social isolation is a significant factor in the decision of African-American women to leave law, it is insignificant for Asian women. Speculating about the future career paths of these accom-plished URM women we might imagine that social isolation, particularly for African-American women, will become a more prominent factor in shaping their decision to stay the course in the engineering profession.

The experience of one student, Fatima, puts the issue of resilience in wider perspective. When we interviewed Fatima in her first year, she told us that the biggest change from high school to college was physics; she was fine with living on her own or doing laundry, but, she said, "I've never had such a block with learning something; it was the one traumatic moment of my life!" When we met up with her in her last year, it was clear that she had some very rocky moments, and she was quite bitter, finding many of her professors unnecessarily "arrogant." She was required to repeat many of her first year courses, but managed to graduate with her cohort. She is the one student, moreover, who, at least to this date, has exited a STEM field. Nonetheless, Fatima's story reveals an important, and underappreciated, theme of the impressive quotients of resilience she drew upon to complete her college education.

DISCUSSION AND CONCLUSION

Reviewing studies of URM women in STEM disciplines, Ong et al. (2011) show that multiple factors derail their success; in addition to the inevitable struggle of a demanding discipline, findings show that, among other factors, a "chilly" climate toward all women but particularly minority women, the difficulty in gaining "recognition" from an "external audience" that is "mostly White males" (p. 182), and negative classroom interactions with faculty combine to push URM women out the door. How, then, do we begin to explain the very different portrait gleaned from the interviews with the URM women in this study? With one exception, they successfully stayed the course, graduating with a STEM degree and robust career-fit confidence to take the next step in STEM, either entering the labor market or continuing their education in engineering.

I would suggest that three themes are revealed in this snapshot that previous research has not adequately explored or weighed: (1) community membership and social class identity, (2) social responsibility, and (3) resilience.

Community membership and social class identity: Beginning with her transition from high school to college, Fatima struggled to stay the course. While she came from a supportive family, they were also struggling to make ends meet, adapt to a new country, and did not have access to or tacit knowledge of the intangible cultural capital that, these findings suggest, are so important when navigating elite institutions of education. The transmission of cultural capital begins early and is shaped by children's exposure to extracurricular activities that middle class parents carefully and thoughtfully select and cultivate. Findings by Webley et al. (2016) suggest that these more intangible markers of cultural capital are an equally powerful barrier to the integration of first and second-generation minority barristers and solicitors in the UK and Wales.

Most of the women in this study, in contrast, enjoyed community membership in the upper middle class, including intact, dual-career, professional parents who, as they described, doted and nurtured their development. The social class backgrounds of many of these URM women are very much of a piece with the elite colleges and universities they attended (Bailey & Dynaski 2011; Blau & Duncan 1967; Hout 2012; Hout & Janus 2011; Mare 1981; Lucas 2001). If community membership is composed of the intersectional dynamics of race, gender, and class, most of these URM women enjoyed the luxury of bracketing class identity while leveraging the very tangible advantages that are conferred on those with upper middle-class, professional status.

Speculating from these findings suggests that future research on the professional paths of URM women (and by implication URM men) must factor community membership, taking into consideration race, gender, *and* class into the equation – a theme that is remarkably muted in the existent literature (but see Sanders and Taylor, discussed next). The majority of these young women are the children of highly success-ful URM parents who themselves have navigated predominantly white professional hierarchies; as they follow in their parents' footsteps, they bring robust endowments of cultural capital that provide a framework to reflect on their experience – and stay the course. Their parents also nurtured this cultural capital through special programs for women and minorities gifted in math and science; these experiences strengthened their confidence and provided camaraderie among peers, including men (Lareau 2011: 305).

The findings reported here certainly raise the possibility that an upper-middle social class background mitigates the effects of man-aging racial bias and gender stereotyping. This is not necessarily to suggest that URM women do not encounter the intersectional binds of sexism and racism; rather, their community membership includes the tools – and the freedom – to manage one's impression, including the assertion of an authoritative voice. Speculation suggests that their class background may allow them to bracket structural biases in a presumably meritocratic space, such that they share with their white, upper middle class counterparts a greater adherence to colorblind racism compared to less advantaged URMs. Alternatively, we might speculate that their class background, including their parents' success, gives them a firsthand understanding of how to "buckle down, pay whatever tax is required, and disprove the damn stereotype" (Steele 2003: 121).

Sanders and Taylor begin their recent book, *Mismatch*, with the claim "the largest, most aggressive preferences [by elite colleges and universities] are usually conferred on upper-middle-class minorities on whom they inflict significant academic harm" (2012:3). They go on to argue how this misguided practice hurts more than it helps ameliorate a history of racial bias and exclusion in American society (but see Alon & Tienda 2005; Bowen & Bok 1998; Small & Winship 2007). To be sure, one cannot draw conclusions from the very small sample of interviews of this article; that is not my intention. This snapshot of URM women does, however, challenge many of the claims of Sanders and Taylor, and at the very least suggests an alternative hypothesis: middle and upper middle class URM students enjoy the benefits of community membership at the intersection of race, gender, and class identity that gives them the tools to navigate the challenges of elite institutions.

Social responsibility: The stereotype of an engineer is that she is practical, careerist, and decidedly apolitical (Seymour & Hewitt 1997). In many respects, the portrait painted of this small group of URM women fits that image. Yet, it is striking that, as a group, they also share a commitment to directing that practical energy in ways that serves the public interest. We might speculate that the emphasis they place on doing engineering to leave the world better than they found it gives purpose and focus to their decision to stay the course in a STEM field. Further speculation suggests that this commitment distinguishes them from their white, particularly male, counterparts. Whether this shared set of values cushions the challenges of navigating STEM programs (or any professional program for that matter) certainly warrants further research. And, whether these values and orientations will sustain them as they transition to the labor market also remains an open question.

Resilience: How do we factor in the experience of Fatima, who failed her science courses during her first year, yet graduated in four years, if in a field that is considered "soft" at her university? We have very little understanding of the social, cultural, and social psychological factors that explain why the "Fatimas" persist despite challenges. She enjoyed a stellar high school record; she performed at the very top of the nation on standardized tests; this was the first time in her short life that she experienced any kind of failure. Why didn't she walk away? Why didn't she return to her state university and take what might have been an expedient route to an undergraduate degree? Fatima's resilience – and that of others with similar experiences – suggests that we need to understand better how URM women and men, or all professionals in the making, learn from failure. At the very least, her story suggests that we may have an overly simplistic understanding of how a failure shapes aspirations.

Of necessity the findings discussed here are only exploratory, but it is my hope that they raise subtle questions that point toward a more robust understanding of the ingredients that will transform the complexion of the professions in the United States.

REFERENCES

Alon, Sigal & Marta Tienda. 2005. "Assessing the 'Mismatch' Hypothesis: Differences in College Graduation Rates by College Selectivity." *Sociology of Education*. 78:294–315.

Bailey MJ, Dynarski SM. 2011. "Inequality in postsecondary education." In *Whither Opportunity? Rising Inequality, Schools, and Children's Life Chances*, ed. GJ Duncan, R Murnane, pp. 117–32. New York: Russell Sage Found.

Best, Rachel, Lauren Edelman, Linda Hamilton Kreiger & Scott Eliason. 2011. "Multiple Disadvantages: Intersectionality in EEO Litigation." *Law & Society Review*. 45:991–1025.

Bilimoria, Diana & Xiangfen Liang. 2012. *Gender Equity in Science and Engineering: Advancing Change in Higher Education*. New York: Routledge.

Blau Peter M., & Duncan Otis D. 1967. *The American Occupational Structure*. New York: Wiley.

Bonilla-Silva, Eduardo. 2003. *Racism without Racists: Color-Blind Racism and the Persistence of Racial Inequality in the United States*. Lanham: Towman & Littlefield Publishers, Inc.

Bowen, William & Derek Bok. 1998. *The Shape of the River: Long Term Consequences of Considering Race in College and University Admissions*. Princeton: Princeton University Press.

Burrelli, J. 2009. "Women of Color in STEM Education and Employment." Paper presented at the Mini-Symposium on Women of Color in STEM, Arlington, VA.

Cech, Erin & Mary Blair-Loy. 2010. "Perceiving Glass Ceilings? Meritocratic versus Structural Explanations of Gender Inequality among Women in Science and Technology." *Social Problems*. 57(3):371–397.

Cech, Erin & Tom J. Waidzumas. 2011. "Navigating the Heteronormativity of Engineering: The Experiences of Lesbian, Gay, and Bisexual Students." *Engineering Studies*. 3(1):1–25.

Cech, Erin, Brian Rubineau, Susan Silbey & Carroll Seron. 2012. "Professional Role Confidence and Gendered Persistence in Engineering." *American Sociological Review*. 76(5) 641–666.

Crawford M., & M. Macleod. 1990. "Gender in the College Classroom: An Assessment of the 'Chilly Climate' for Women." *Sex Roles*. 23(3/4):101–122.

Crenshaw, K. 1989. "Demarginalizing the Intersection of Race and Sex: A black Feminist Critique of Antidiscrimination Doctrine, Feminist Theory and Antiracist Politics." *University of Chicago Legal Forum*, 139: 57–80.

DiMaggio, Paul. 1992. "Nadel's Paradox Revisited: Relational and Cultural Aspects of Social Structure." pp. 118–42 in *Networks and Organizations: Structure, Form and Action*, eds. N. Nohria & R. Eccles. Boston, MA: HBS Press.

Faulkner, Wendy. 2000. "Dualism, Hierarchies and Gender in Engineering." *Social Studies of Science*. 30: 759–79.

2009. "Doing Gender in Engineering Workplace Cultures. II. Gender In/authenticity and the In/visibility Paradox." *Engineering Studies* 1 (3):169–190.

Freidson, Eliot. 1986. *Professional Powers*. Chicago: University of Chicago Press.

Goffman, Erving. 1963. *Stigma: Notes on the Management of Spoiled Identity*. Englewood Cliffs, NJ: Prentice Hall.

Hout, Michael. 2012. "Social and Economic Returns to College Education in the United States." *Annual Review of Sociology*. 38:379–400.

Hout M., & Janus A. 2011. "Educational Mobility in the United States since the 1930s." In *Whither Opportunity? Rising Inequality, Schools, and Children's Life Chances*, ed. GJ Duncan, R Murnane, pp. 165–86. New York: Russell Sage Found.

Ibarra, Herminia. 1999. "Provisional Selves: Experimenting with Image and Identity in Professional Adaptation." *Administrative Science Quarterly*. 44:764–91.

Kanter, Rosabeth Moss. 1977. *Men and Women of the Corporation*. New York: Basic Books.

Lareau, Annette. 2011 (2nd edn). *Unequal Childhoods: Class, Race, and Family Life*. California: University of California Press.

Lucas SR. 2001. "Effectively Maintained Inequality: Education Transitions, Track Mobility, and Social Background Effects." *American Journal of Sociology*. 106:1642–90.

Ma, Yingyi. 2009. "Family Socioeconomic Status, Parental Involvement, and College Major Choices—Gender, Race/Ethnic, and Nativity Patterns." *Sociological Perspectives*. 52(2):211–234.

Mare RD. 1981. "Change and Stability in Educational Stratification." *American Sociological Review*. 46:72–87.

McIlwee, Judith S., & J. Gregg Robinson. 1992. *Women in Engineering: Gender, Power, and Workplace Culture*. Albany, NY: State University of New York Press.

Mellstrom, Ulf. 1995. *Engineering Lives: Technology, Time and Space in a Male-Centred World*. Linköping, Sweden: Linköping University.

—— 2004. "Machines and Masculine Subjectivity Technology as an Integral Part of Men's Life Experiences." *Men and Masculinities*. 6(4):368–382.

Ong, Maria. 2005. "Body Projects of Young Women of Color in Physics: Intersections of Gender, Race, and Science." *Social Problems*. 52 (4):593–617.

Ong, Maria, Carol Wright, Lorelle L. Espinosa & Gary Orfield. 2011. "Inside the Double Bind: A Synthesis of Empirical Research on Undergraduate and Graduate Women of Color in Science, Technology, Engineering and Mathematics." *Harvard Educational Review*. 81(2):172–208.

Pan, Yung-Yi Diana. 2016. "Typecast Socialization: Race, Gender, and Competing Expectations in Law School." In *Diversity in Practice: Race, Gender, and Class in Legal and Professional Careers*, ed. S. Headworth, R. L. Nelson, R. Dinovitzer, D. B. Wilkins, pp. 141–172. Cambridge: Cambridge University Press.

Payne-Pikus, Monique R., Robert L. Nelson & John Hagan. 2013. "The Intersectionality of Race, Gender, and Social Isolation in the Retention of American Lawyers in Private Law Firms." Paper presented at the 2013 Conference of the Research Group on Legal Diversity, Chicago, IL.

Penner, Andrew & Aliya Sapterstein. 2013. "Engendering Racial Perceptions." *Gender & Society*. 27:1–26.

Ridgeway, Cecilia L., & Tamar Kricheli-Katz. 2013. "Intersecting Cultural Beliefs and Social Relations: Gender, Race and Class Binds and Freedoms." *Gender & Society*. 27:294–318.

Rivera, Lauren A. 2012. "Hiring as Cultural Matching: The Case of Elite Professional Service Firms." *American Sociological Review*. 77(6): 999–1022.

Rubineau, Brian, Erin Cech, Carroll Seron & Susan Silbey. 2013. "The Gendered Value of an Engineering Degree." Working Paper.

Sanders, Richard & Stuart Taylor, Jr. 2012. *Mismatch: How Affirmative Action Hurts Students It's Intended to Help and Why Universities Won't Admit It*. New York: Basic Books.

Saperstein, Aliya & Andrew Penner. 2012. "Racial Fluidity and Inequality in the United States." *American Journal of Sociology*. 118:676–727.

Seron, Carroll & Susan Silbey. 2009. "The Dialectic between Expertise Knowledge and Professional Discretion: Accreditation, Social Control and the Limits of Instrumental Logic." *Engineering Studies*. 1:101–129.

Seron, Carroll, Eric Cech, Susan Silbey & Brian Rubineau. 2011. "I Am Not a Feminist, but. . . :" Making Meanings of Being a Woman in Engineering.

American Society of Engineering Education (ASEE) National Conference, Panel: Liberal Education Division Session, Vancouver, Canada.

2012. "Persistence Is Cultural: Testing Prominent Explanations of Why
Engineering Students Leave the Profession." Working paper.

Seymour, Elaine, Nancy M., & Hewett N. 1997. *Talking About Leaving: Why
Undergraduates Leave the Sciences*. Boulder, CO: Westview Press.

Small, Mario & Christopher Winship. 2007. "Black Students' Graduation
from Elite Colleges: Institutional Characteristics and between-institution
Differences." *Social Science Research*. 36(3):1257–1275.

Steele, Claude. 2003. "Stereotype Threat and African-American Student
Achievement" in Perry, Theresa, Claude Steele & Asa G. Hilliard III,
eds. *Young, Gifted, and Black: Promoting High Achievement among African-
American Students*. Boston: Beacon Press, pp. 109–131.

Traweek, Sharon. 1988. *Beamtimes and Lifetimes: The World of High Energy
Physicists*. Cambridge, MA: Harvard University Press.

Valian, Virginia. 1999. *Why So Slow? The Advancement of Women*. Cambridge,
MA: MIT Press.

Webley, Lisa, Jennifer Tomlinson, Daniel Muzio, Liz Duff & Hilary Sommer-
lad. 2016. "Access to a Career in the Legal Profession in England and
Wales: 'Race', Class and the Role of Educational Background." In *Diversity
in Practice: Race, Gender, and Class in Legal and Professional Careers*, ed.
S. Headworth, R. L. Nelson, R. Dinovitzer, D. B. Wilkins, pp. 198–225.
Cambridge: Cambridge University Press.

Wu, L., & W. Jing. 2009. "Asian Women in STEM Careers: A Forgotten
Minority with a Glass Ceiling?" Paper presented at the Mini-Symposium
on Women of Color in STEM. Arlington, VA.

Xie, Yu & Kimberlee Shauman. 2003. *Women in Science*. Cambridge: Harvard
University Press.

ACCESS TO A CAREER IN THE LEGAL PROFESSION IN ENGLAND AND WALES

Race, class, and the role of educational background

LISA WEBLEY, JENNIFER TOMLINSON, DANIEL MUZIO,
HILARY SOMMERLAD, AND LIZ DUFF

INTRODUCTION

Much attention is currently focused on equality and diversity within the legal profession in England and Wales, not least because the profile of law graduates has markedly diversified over the past 20 years, although senior levels of the profession have yet to reflect the increasing number of women and Black, Asian and Minority Ethnic (BAME) entrants over that period (See the Law Society and Bar Council statistical reviews 2013). There is a strong body of research in the UK that establishes social stratification on grounds of class (see e.g. Goldthorpe, 2000; Skeggs, 1997) and there is also a pronounced link between class and race in British society (Archer, 2011; Loury et al. 2005). The results of this stratification include unequal distribution of resources (Marx and Engels, 1969; Marx, 2010), unequal life chances (see further Breen, 2005; Weber, 1956) and unequal access to occupations and thus to status (Durkheim, 1964: 371). Previous studies indicate that social and educational background have a major role to play in the extent to which aspiring lawyers gain entry into, progress and succeed within the legal profession (Nicolson, 2005; Shiner, 1994; Shiner et al., 1999; Shiner, 2000; Sommerlad, 2008; Thomas, 2000; Tomlinson et al., 2013). Further, the Milburn 'Fair Access to the Professions' Report (2009, 2012) has recognized that this stratification has a real impact on entry into professions, particularly into old professions such as law. We suggest in this chapter that the professional entry barriers experienced by BAME and lower socio-economic group law graduates would be greatly reduced were legal employers to focus on proxies for excellence more closely associated with measures of lawyer competence than of social background.

Framed using a Bourdieusian analysis, this chapter examines the extent to which background pre-university and the university at which one studies has a substantial impact on one's access to a legal career, as compared with attainment at university or legal competence. Bourdieu provides three 'thinking tools' that afford a means to analyse social practices and the stratification of access to opportunities and reward: *habitus*, practice and the social field (Bourdieu, 1986; Jenkins, 2002), and we draw upon these in this chapter. The *habitus*, the habitual ways of thinking, the dispositions of those involved in the field, are developed via subliminal inculcation within familial, social and educational contexts (Bourdieu, 1986). Practice is the expression of the habitus, of the individual's and group's dispositions enacted to further (often subconscious) interests through strategies that aim to maintain or improve positions within a social field. Practice occurs within the generative environment of social interaction and is a product of and reproduces the habitus of individuals and groups (Bourdieu, 1996: 272–273). It occurs to those within it as an objective reality, the *doxa* (Bourdieu, 1990a: 60), rather than a subjective, constructed space of power relations. The social field (in our study, the legal profession in England and Wales) is any site of contestation in which individuals seek to gain and maintain their positions viz-a-viz others with reference to the value placed on different forms of capital as understood by insiders (Skeggs, 2004: 145; Wacquant, 1989: 37–41). Capital comes in a variety of forms, principally: economic (in the form of money); social (in the form of social networks and connections), symbolic (the prestige conferred on one by others as a result of the legitimated capital one is deemed to have) and cultural capital (legitimated knowledge expressed in embodied, objectified and institutionalised forms)[1] (Bourdieu, 1986: 47; 1990a: 88). We argue that in a British legal professional

---

[1] Embodied forms of cultural capital are those relating to attitudes, manners and behaviours that are taken as markers of class/power difference. Objectified forms occur in the form of social goods and activities and experiences linked to a hierarchy of culture. Institutional forms relate to acquired 'assets' such as educational qualifications and the power that they bring within a field; cultural capital is field/context specific. For a discussion see Cook et al., 2012: 1748; McPhail et al., 2010; Willis, 1977; Waters, 2006 and 2007.

context, hiring practices occur within a neo-liberal market that is viewed as rational, equal and justified, but as they are heavily reliant on constructed notions of talent and merit they reproduce the dominant group's position within the profession (see Sommerlad, 2011: 76, 78–82). As Jenkins notes, 'privilege becomes translated into "merit"' in the eyes of those who dominate the field (Jenkins, 2002: 111). Selection practices, while applied in the same way to everyone, subtlety reproduce privilege by means of the hierarchy of value placed on key legitimated goods (Bourdieu, 1973: 97–99; Bourdieu and Passeron, 1979). Our findings suggest a particular focus on symbolic and certain forms of cultural capital for entry level hiring decisions and we suggest that these discriminate against BAME and lower socio-economic group law graduates.[2]

This chapter is informed by data collected for a study of diversity in the legal profession in England and Wales that was commissioned by the Legal Services Board (LSB) (Sommerlad et al., 2013). We used a socio-biographical interview method (n 77) to explore the choices and challenges that faced women and BAME lawyers and would-be lawyers (Rustin and Chamberlayne, 2002). The study examined the practices which produce differential opportunities and career patterns in the solicitors' profession and at the Bar. It was designed to capture the meanings that lawyers and would-be lawyers, diversity managers, and others attached to their choices, and the experiences that informed them, rather than to be a statistical description of the consequences of career choices. In-depth qualitative studies have the potential to generate 'rich sources of data which provide access to how people account for both their troubles and their good fortune' (Silverman, 1993: 4). These accounts are, by their very nature, retrospective, partial, self-reflective and egocentric, as are all personal accounts; conclusions must be reached in this context (Cicourel, 1964; Dingwall, 1997; Silverman, 1993). However, given that the Macpherson Report in the UK identified racist incidents as 'any incident which is perceived to be racist by the victim or by any other person', and while this definition remains contested and contentious, the perception of experience remains a powerful corrective to the equally problematic view that discrimination can only occur where

---

[2] See Tomlinson et al., 2013 for the effect of capital as regards promotion in a UK context and Gorman and Kay 2014 for a US context. For a discussion of Bourdieu's theories in the context of gender and the legal profession see Kay and Hagan, 1995; 1998, for example.

there is an intention to discriminate (MacPherson, 1999: 74). Themes that emerged from these data include the importance placed on aspiring law students' school and social backgrounds, their university choice, and their participation in particular forms of extra curricula and prestigious unpaid work opportunities. Socio-economic background intersected with race influenced the extent to which law graduates were deemed to have the attributes valorised by the legal profession. Our findings illustrate a number of structural factors which inhibit the development and utilization of talent within the profession in Britain, which contradict the legal profession's contention that it competes for talent on an objective basis (see Ashley and Empson, 2013; Sommerland, 2011: 79–82). The legal profession's claim of equality is challenged by the reality experienced by many of those who participated in our study.

We begin by examining the demographics of the two major branches of the legal profession in England and Wales – solicitors and barristers – to contextualise discussion of the field principally with reference to BAME law graduates'. We then turn to our findings, which draw upon the demographic data[3], the sociology of education and our analysis of the LSB study interview transcripts situated within the context of Bourdieu's conceptions of the field and habitus, and the role of social, symbolic and cultural capital.[4] The chapter then briefly addresses recent diversity initiatives and explores how these may alleviate or solidify current inequality, before reaching conclusions about how the legal profession may develop its selection practices so as to minimize continued patterned inequality.

THE DEMOGRAPHICS OF THE SOCIAL FIELD

Much of the data that we collected appeared to suggest that race and class discrimination, where present, were a function of the doxa, a consequence of stereotypes, use of proxies and a lack of reflection about the competencies inherent in good lawyering. On this same basis, our chapter could rightly be criticised for its essentialist treatment of BAME

---

[3] Data is extant on BAME status but not as regards socio-economic group. Although this data is now being collected for those who enter the profession, the data collection is still in its infancy and it is unlikely to be possible to link this to similar data at the pre-professional stage so as to permit comparison.

[4] For a discussion of our findings with regard to progression within the profession see Tomlinson et al., 2013; and for the role of the different forms of capital in senior level hiring in boardrooms see Krawiec et al. and within the legal profession in the United States (Gorman and Kay), both in this collection.

lawyers and aspiring lawyers and their class credentials (see Combahee River Collection, 1994; Harris, 1997). We recognise that the catch-all category of BAME masks tremendous heterogeneity and those individuals are drawn from a wide range of backgrounds and will self-define in sophisticated and nuanced ways.[5] This is as true for class/ socio-economic background as it is for race (Barnard and Turner, 2010). Class plays an important role in access to the professions, we have explored it here in the context of BAME status so as to demonstrate the patterned inequality that results from the intersection between being non-white and being perceived to be a member of a lower socio-economic group (Crow and Pope, 2008, 1045). Given the legal profession's historic white and elitist roots (Sommerlad, 2007), and given the data on the demographics of the senior levels of the legal profession and the experiences of our participants, the individualised nature of BAME law graduates and lawyers' backgrounds may be misrecognised by (would be) employers in their application of proxies of merit that flow from their valuation of different types of human capital. As Fox et al (2012) explain,

> Race' in this sense is not an essential trait ... but rather the socially constructed contingent outcome of processes and practices of exclusion. It is the valorised language through which structured inequalities (meas-ured in labour market position, differential access to scarce resources, legal status, and cultural stereotypes) are expressed, maintained and reproduced ... We opt for a single racialization optique that accommo-dates both its colourful and cultural dimensions.
>
> (Kushner, 2005: 208–209)

Although alive to the risk of compounding an already essentialist dialogue within the profession, our use of strategic essentialism, advocated by Spivak (1988; Spivak and Rooney, 1994), is intended to give voice to our participants' experiences of the legal profession rather than to com-pound the stereotypes that they often face (Conaghan, 2000; Fuss, 1994). Indeed, the fact that there are BAME lawyers within a range of class categories in the UK, and within different sectors and at different levels of the profession assists to reproduce the status quo, as it lends legitimacy to the contention that social stratification is associated with objective rather than constructed modes of classification (Bourdieu, 1996:

---

[5] For a discussion of the heterogeneous nature of BAME participation at HE level, and in law in particular see Connor et al., 2004.

272–273; Bourdieu, 1973: 97–99).[6] There are, of course, also White law graduates who face barriers to entry on the basis of class and perceived socio-economic status and we do not seek to minimise the existence of those barriers. However, strategic essentialism may be required so as to bring to the fore the subconscious biases that allow discrimination to persist, strategic essentialism may allow a disruption of the doxa.

The demographics of the legal profession indicate that BAME lawyers are concentrated within the less prestigious parts of the legal profession (see The Ouseley Report, 2008: 7; further Law Society, 2010: 4) and they have greater attrition from the legal profession, relative to their White counterparts. BAME solicitors and barristers are proportionately more likely to be in sole practice than are White solicitors (Bar Barometer Report, 2013: 32); this may be due, in part, to the greater difficulties they face as regards entry into and progression within the more lucrative and established parts of the profession (Webley: 2013a). The relative absence of senior BAME lawyers in medium and large law firms and in barristers' chambers may have an impact on the value attached to particular forms of human capital with a resultant impact on hiring and promotion decisions. Table 7.1 demonstrates these attrition trends.

The UK BAME population is recorded as 14% (UK Census Data 2011; it has increased from 9% in 2001 and 6% in 1991); however, the proportion of law graduates who self-define as BAME is about 32% of the graduating population. Thus, law is a strong choice for BAME aspiring professionals.[7] In most instances, upon completion of the professionally recognised LLB law degree[8] a law graduate must

---

[6] Ashley and Empson's chapter in this collection provides a detailed discussion of the intersecting roles of class and race and their role in social stratification within the UK context.

[7] Law Society data indicates that approximately 12% of law students reading for qualifying law degrees are overseas students, some of which will self-define as BAME although it is unclear the extent to which this affects the figures presented previously. Further, not all LPC/BPTC and training contract/pupillage applicants will have undertaken an undergraduate LLB degree. Approximately 5,000 students a year undertake the Graduate Diploma in Law course, which is an intensive graduate programme that one may take following successful completion of a non-law undergraduate degree. For a discussion of this route see Webley, 2010b.

[8] The LLB is a three-year undergraduate law degree, similar to the JD qualification. All LLB degree programmes must be approved by the Joint Academic Stages Board, which has a similar function to ABA accreditation. LLB degrees are classed as qualifying law degrees, meaning that once a student has successfully attained an LLB (Hons) degree, s/he may continue on to the one year vocational qualification

TABLE 7.1[9,10]   Diversity Profile in England and Wales by
Professional Stage

Solicitors Stage	% BAME	Total	Barristers Stage	% BAME	Total
Qualifying law degree	32%	c. 15,500	Qualifying law degree	32%	c. 15,500
Legal practice course	31%*	6,067*	Bar professional training course	42%*	1,732
			Call to the bar	43%	1,469
Training contract	23%	5,302	Pupillages	22% 21%	438 475 913
Admission to the roll	24%	6,758	Tenancy/full admission with a position	11%	335
Partnership	11%**	37,331**	QCs	5.5% (total 4%)	85 (total 1,559)
Overall	13%	127,676	Overall	11%	15,585

undertake a one year educational vocational course (the Legal Practice
Course (LPC) to aspire to be a solicitor, the Bar Professional Training
Course (BPTC) to aspire to be a barrister) prior to beginning a period

required to train to be a solicitor (the Legal Practice Course) or a barrister (Bar
Professional Training Course). After that a would-be solicitor would need to
secure a two-year training contract in a law firm or equivalent and undertake
some final examinations, and a would-be barrister would need to secure two six-
month pupillages. Training contracts and pupillages are forms of heavily supervised paid practise that operate similar to apprenticeships. Post completion of a
training contract or the pupillages the solicitor or barrister is fully qualified, but is
still required to work within a supervised context for an additional three years
before they have full practice rights or the opportunity to practice solo.

9   2012 figures, the Law Society, Trends in the Solicitors' Profession Annual Statistical
Report 2013 (The Law Society). Figures marked * are tentative as they have been
derived from a Law Society database that does not record part-time enrolments in
the same way as full-time enrolments. Figures marked ** are from Solicitors Regulation Authority 2013 data.

10   2011–12 figures, the General Council of the Bar, Bar Barometer Trends in the
Profile of the Bar 2013. Figures marked * are 2010–11 figures, which are the most
recent available. The figures for pupillages include both the first and the second 6-
month pupillages.

of compulsory work-based training (a two-year supervised training contract to become a qualified solicitor; two six-month supervised pupillages to become a fully qualified barrister). At each stage there is a selection process, with progressively fewer places available. As regards would-be solicitors, the point of attrition is evident at the work-based training contract stage, when the BAME population drops from over 30% at the educational vocational stage of training to 22% at the in-firm phase of training; this point is controlled, in the main, by law firms through their selection practices. In most instances it is not possible to become a fully qualified solicitor unless one has successfully completed a training contract in a law firm or similar organisation.

The picture is more nuanced with regard to would-be barristers. A large number of overseas Commonwealth nations' law graduates undertake the British BPTC as a qualification pathway to legal practice in their home jurisdiction; thus, the BAME population swells from over 30% at law degree graduation stage to over 40% at the educational vocational stage with the inclusion of overseas law graduates from India, Pakistan and Hong Kong, for example. This trend is also reflected in the 'call to the Bar' qualification point which occurs for barristers straight after successful completion of the BPTC, as opposed to at the end of the training contract for solicitors, although in truth this is not full qualification as one is not able to practice alone until post pupillage and on receipt of a tenancy. There is a stark reduction in BAME representation within the Bar at the pupillage level, from around 32% of the graduating law population down to 22% of those with pupillages, then down again to only 11% gaining a tenancy[11]. This stage is largely controlled by barristers' chambers through their selection practices. In 2011–12, over a quarter (28%) of pupillages were awarded to elite educated Oxbridge graduates, and a further 36% from other Russell Group universities (2010–11 35%; 2009–10 23.7% were Oxbridge educated 2013). Further, there is evidence that the Bar is drawing its pupils from an increasingly privileged class background (see further Zimdars, 2010). The solicitor's profession is not immune from this

---

[11] Securing a 'tenancy' means that a barrister has successfully completed their training phase (pupillage) and has been accepted as a permanent member of a set of chambers.

charge, either, as a recent Law Society study of BAME solicitors and prospective solicitors concluded:

> Having completed the Legal Practise Course, B[A]ME candidates believed that they would be on a 'level playing field' with all other LPC graduates and that, irrespective of their gender, ethnicity or social background, they would have the same chance to succeed. However, this had not been the case and the dawning reality of the actual situation had hit many B[A]ME participants hard. .... It was clear to participants that firms judged capability by academic qualifications and attendance at particular institutions. A misguided view, by firms, of what constitutes excellence meant that, for many participants, good, able solicitors are being passed over because of their social background.
>
> (2010: 4)

Although the two main legal professional bodies (equivalent to the American Bar Association in the USA) have noted these concerns, they have been more inclined to encourage measures that aim to raise the aspirations of BAME school pupils to attend elite law schools rather than to challenge the prevailing view amongst legal employers that elite schooling necessarily indicates lawyer excellence. The newly established legal profession oversight regulator, the LSB, which sits above the legal professional bodies, has been given a statutory obligation to encourage an independent, strong, diverse and effective legal profession, and further to support the constitutional principle of the rule of law (sections 1(1)(f) and 1(1)(b)Legal Services Act 2007). It has interpreted the relevant provisions in the Legal Services Act 2007 to encompass the need for the legal profession to demonstrate that it is not unlawfully discriminating against those seeking to enter and progress within the profession, given that adherence to the rule of law is fundamental to its legitimacy, and the rule of law embodies equal treatment by the law.[12] The non-discrimination requirement is also an ethical precept of regulated legal professionals and is contained within professional conduct rules. The LSB has indicated that if the legal professional bodies do not improve the profession's diversity statistics it may be minded to intervene to require reforms to the way in which lawyers are trained and/or accredited so as to force more equal representation within the profession (Edmonds, 2010). This would have a profound impact on the legal professional bodies, as it

---

[12] For a discussion of professionalism and requirements linked to the ability to maintain professional autonomy see Larson, 1977 and more specifically Abel, 1979.

would remove an even greater proportion of their self-regulatory powers than had previously been removed through the enactment of the Legal Services Act 2007. As threats go, it is a very powerful one.

SOCIAL, SYMBOLIC AND CULTURAL CAPITAL: REPRODUCTION AND EXCLUSION

Our analysis of the LSB data reveals a range of hiring proxies are used to determine suitability to practice, which are not clearly connected to the key skills and knowledge that are the mark of legal competence. For large firm recruitment, symbolic, objectified and institutionalised cultural capital is prioritized through the use of application forms that rely heavily on open questions that target extra curricula activities such as: experiences undertaken during gap years between school and university; membership of clubs and societies; school and university attended; participation in unpaid internships (which are offered competitively on a similar basis to entry level positions); with some but not particularly strong reliance on grades attained at UK law schools (Sommerlad, 2011: 79–82; Webley, 2013b). Institutionalised cultural capital is important: grades attained at school level are often considered to be objective measures of ability, but university grades are seemingly not prioritised over school grades. This may, in part, stem from the fact that the standard model of grade classification for UK undergraduate degrees is a four category scale of third, lower second, upper second and first class awards rather than a GPA score that has a greater degree of granularity, or an assessment of class rank. Having said that, each student will have a percentage grade for each module that they have studied, and were firms so minded they could request the graduate's transcript that displays all the grades (this is very rarely requested by the profession in Britain). Some smaller law firms and barristers' chambers, still make use of resumes, which are asked to address many of the proxies mentioned earlier. What is clear is that few organisations employ selection mechanisms that specifically target the accepted 'day one outcomes' that have been nationally agreed by the legal profession as the competencies expected of solicitors and barristers on the first day as a fully qualified practitioner.[13]

---

[13] See Legal Services Board (2011) *Qualified Lawyers Transfer Scheme: Map of England and Wales Solicitor Day One Outcomes against a Barrister of England & Wales on*

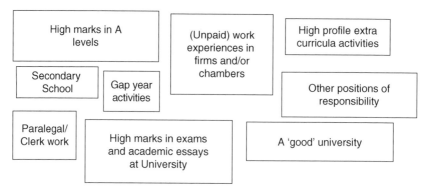

Figure 7.1 Symbolic and Cultural Capital Proxies for Excellence

As part of our analysis of the interview transcripts, we noted both the frequency with which and the weight attributed to particular proxies for merit. We cannot claim that we have developed a quantitatively robust measure of their importance, but in impressionistic terms we have attempted to represent their importance through the size of the type face used in the Figure 7.1.

The discussion that follows addresses these proxies with reference to their capital value.

Social and family background and cultural capital

There was some evidence that the value placed on embodied cultural capital is mediated through the lens of race and class. A few of our participants provided evidence of racial or social stereotyping, suggestive of employer misrecognition of their talent due to sub-conscious yet powerful notions of merit associated with preconceptions about what it is to be non-white and what it is to be from a more disadvantaged socio-economic class. Figure 7.1 depicts some of the pieces of symbolic and cultural capital that employers use as proxies for merit.

> Another example was a solicitors [firm] that was trying to go into schools to motivate Black and Asian children to think about law and someone said to me that there was no point and they would be better suited to bus

Completion of Pupillage www.legalservicesboard.org.uk/what_we_do/regulation/pdf/3.pdf for details.

driving or being plumbers. He said that there would be no way that they would make it in a career in law ... The same man identified a colleague as the exception, who was Asian, and said he was the exception and had made it out of the ghetto and into the profession. The greatest irony was that the person he referred to wouldn't even know how to get to the ghetto! He is certainly not from the ghetto! So even though they have worked together and are both equity partners together he was still making statements like that. He just thought that everyone's roots were the same and he actually was happy to say that to my face. I was sitting there as a Black woman with my jaw on the floor and I couldn't believe he would actually say that to me. There was no inkling that he had said the wrong thing ... He just carried on talking and didn't even register that that was an unacceptable thing to say.

(Female BAME Asian solicitor, North of England)

I can't say, you know, that I've felt discriminated against openly. If anything, I think, it helps that ... I'm both female and my [mixed race] background some people actually say, well, gosh that's really good and sort of, not to be cynical but you know, that helps, I think, it ticks a couple of extra boxes, which helps. So I can't really say that, but ... when I was applying for my training contracts because I've got a Greek surname, ... every time I applied with the Greek one I didn't get a single interview. And then I decided let me try with my [other] last name, and then all of them, I got interviews for. ... my uncle's had trouble with having a foreign surname. And so that's why he said just try with the American one and nobody can tell where you're from.

(Female BAME (Black & White) Assistant Solicitor In-house London).

In these recounted experiences, it appears that the value placed on the embodied capital of some BAME would-be lawyers may rule them out as legitimate professionals in the context of localised conceptions of habitus; those that succeed may have had to compensate for their lack of embodied cultural capital with higher levels of other forms of capital, such as objectified or institutionalised capital. The second excerpt is suggestive that there is misrecognition of talent via the attribution of low value to the embodied cultural capital of seemingly 'foreign' prospective lawyers; when her last name changed so did her stock of capital. This may be a reproduction of past practice which draws upon the profession's raced and classed roots. And the fact that some non-White lawyers have been successful within the profession seemingly legitimises the doxa as an objective meritocracy (Bourdieu, 1973: 97–99), when the second extract would suggest that it is anything but. Subjective attribution of merit appears to indicate that value is accorded very differently to those perceived to be within the dominant group than to those without. The Law Society in England and Wales has, at the insistence of its Equality and Diversity Committee, been required to undertake selection for its internal positions with the name of the applicant redacted, such is its concern about potential misattribution of value. This remains subject to lively debate within the Law Society and has yet to be rolled out to the profession as a whole.

Embodied capital is not only assessed within firms and chambers but by recruitment agencies too.

> I went to a recruitment agent and she said I was too common to be put forward . . . for a stand-alone role, which was on a specific case and it was for six months .. . . And she said, oh you have to appreciate the way you speak is very common, and these are very educated people, and so you may not fit in.
>
> (Female BAME Solicitor)

Accent, as a marker of class and thus of status, will not be evident at the initial stages of a selection process if conducted by a firm or a set of chambers, but it will be obvious at a first sift telephone interview carried out by a recruitment agency. Here accent, as embodied cultural capital, is conceptualised as an indicator of merit based on assumptions about suitability and knowledge. The important role of recruitment agencies in filtering out inappropriate applicants has been previously recognised (Duff and Webley, 2004). But their role in the reproduction of the field does not appear to have been examined. We have relatively little data upon which to draw in this instance, but it is a site of contestation that deserves further study.

Forms of objectified cultural and symbolic capital also appear to play an important role in hiring decisions:

> The Head of Chambers said: 'I want him, he comes hunting and shooting with us . . . my clients like him, my Greek shipping clients like him because he has everything that they are looking for, he's been to a certain public school and then to Oxbridge and he presents the right image.' These were the criteria. He hadn't actually, at that point, passed his Bar exam. So it was not the quality of his work that was important, it was the fact that he fitted.
>
> (Female White barrister North of England)

This interview extract may be read as a privileging of the social capital of the applicant, but on closer examination it appears to be an assessment of symbolic capital (prestige related to attendance at an elite school and university) and objectified cultural capital (via pursuits accorded high status on the cultural hierarchy) as the pupil barrister does not appear to be relying on his network, nor introducing a network, but instead is deemed to be someone who will fit well within an established network and who will bring with him prestige.[14] But social capital does have a role to play, and within certain sections of the profession, such as the Bar: the previous participant was asked in her first week as a pupil in London who her father was and recalling this conversation said, 'I just sort of looked at them as if to say, why would you know who my father is!? They expected to have heard of my school!' There is an expectation that people will be socially connected or know of each other via mutual contact, although there is limited evidence in our study that social capital for its own sake plays a particularly strong role in selection for initial roles within the legal profession (it is more pronounced as regards promotion: see Tomlinson et al., 2013: 249–251).

Cultural capital may also be a product of one's social capital as the next extract demonstrates. There is some evidence here that the respondent considered social capital to be important so as to allow a would-be lawyer to accrue experiences to build their embodied and objectified cultural capital pre-university and then to use that capital to realise their goal to attain a place at an elite university so as to increase their symbolic capital to assist with entry to the profession:

> Because you make networks at a very early stage and you grow up with these people. This is a school which is ... you know, it's very expensive, you have to be of a certain class background to be able to send your children there. In the summer times, you know, you're going to the houses of MPs [Members of Parliament] and whatever else and ... they can pull strings for you and open doors for you ... when you went to an exceptional school ... you are destined for great things and ... it's easier for doors to be opened for you because you're now sitting in front of someone in the City who may have gone to the same school as you and ... or gone to the same school as your father so as a result, the fact that you got a Third [class degree], we can ignore that. ...

---

[14] These are defined in note 1.

> The main goal posts were I guess, working very hard at school from 11 onwards, choosing the right GCSEs, in particular ... and then choosing the right A levels. And obviously working hard at university. Though, to be honest with you, by the time you got to my university, Cambridge, you know you were in a very good position to do very well in a legal career.
>
> (Male BAME Assistant Solicitor)

Early opportunities provide a means by which one's stock of capital can be augmented, as attendance at the right kind of school changes one's embodied capital and may in some circumstances add symbolic capital if the school is very well regarded by those in the field. This may raise social capital, which in turn provides access to experiences which increases one's ledger of embodied capital as a result of learned behaviours and manners associated with the dominant group in the field. The interviewee is clear that good grades at school are very important so as to gain entry into the right kind of university, but he suggests that the grades achieved at an elite university may be of secondary importance in hiring decisions given the existence of high levels of other forms of capital.

It could easily be argued that educational attainment in national standardised exams is a relatively objective measure of 'merit' for a knowledge based profession. But, the complex relationship between educational attainment and social class, race and sex with regard to national GCSE and A level examinations[15] has been demonstrated, and thus attainment needs to be contextualised before conclusions about a student's ability can reliably be drawn (see e.g. Connolly, 2006; Khattab, 2009).[16] As a result of competition for law degree places in elite institutions, relatively small variations in A level grades, attributable in part to school attended (Kirkup et al, 2010) and to social class (Hirsch, 2007), contribute to a reproduction of the existing social hierarchy, with BAME law students concentrated within the less prestigious universities (Connor et al., 2004). A key recent large-scale study by Kirkup et al. (2010) observed that the link between social background and educational attainment does not remain constant, and

---

[15] In England and Wales, the vast majority of school children study for standardised national exams. GCSE exams are usually undertaken at around 16 years old; A Levels are usually undertaken at around 18 years old. A Levels grades are the one most usually used by universities when making decisions as to which students will be offered places to study law.

[16] For a discussion of the connections between capital, class, race and education see further Modood, 2004; Nash, 1990; Rothon, 2007.

thus snapshots of attainment at different stages of educational progress will give very different insights into a student's academic ability and competence.[17] Snapshots of attainment at school are more heavily influenced by background, than are snapshots taken on graduation. Yet legal employers revert to school attainment, without reference to context, as if definitive evidence of merit. Worse still, elite universities also select largely on the basis of school attainment without reference to context, which reproduces rather than disrupts social stratification:

> The sociology of educational institutions and, in particular, of higher education institutions, may make a decisive contribution to the frequently neglected aspect of the sociology of power which consists in the science of the dynamics of class relations. Indeed ... probably none have been better dissimulated and, consequently, better adapted to societies which tend to reject the most patent forms of hereditary transmission of power and privileges, than that provided by the educational system in contributing to the reproduction of the structure of class relations and in dissimulating the fact that it fulfils this function under the appearance of neutrality.
>
> (Centre for European Sociology, 1972: 11–12)

Unlike some other jurisdictions such as the USA (Wilkins and Gulati, 1996), the UK does not operate positive discrimination/affirmative action programs within universities, and the one attempt to do so became so mired in controversy (and may have been unlawful, given the UK legislative framework) that it was swiftly terminated. As the next section demonstrates, elite university selection decisions became instantiated as badges of symbolic prestige by legal employers, although

---

[17] A level examinations are national examinations that are undertaken by the vast majority of students in England and Wales who intend to go to University. They are usually sat in the academic year in which students reach 18 years old, and students usually study for two years leading up to the examinations, which are broadly subject specific. In most instances students will study at least three A level subjects and university offers have historically related to grades to be attained from three A level subjects. Grades range from A* (highest) to E the lowest passing grade. Selective universities often require students to achieve grades in the A–B range across all three subjects. The Sutton Trust research (Kirkup et al., 2010) indicates that state school pupils apparently under perform in national examinations (A levels) as compared with public/private school pupils, but then achieve similar grades as their privately education peers at University. Pupils from state schools who achieved grades of ABB, from fee-paying schools who achieved grades of AAB and from elite fee paying schools who got AAA achieved similar marks on the same course at the same institutions on undergraduate degree graduation.

they occur to them as markers of greater ability and competence as a lawyer. With school attainment accorded similar weight to university attainment, and yet influenced in more pronounced terms by class, those with lower capital reserves on entry into university struggle to make up any ground as against their more privileged peers.

University attended and cultural capital

There is now incontrovertible evidence that many large law firms and barristers' chambers have a limited list of preferred universities from which they shortlist applicants. Some firms' lists have been published via the legal press; others are not in the public domain, some firms hold 'milk round'[18] hiring events at specific universities so as to actively pursue law students from particular universities and to exclude others. There are firms with online application systems that make it very difficult to apply if you cannot select your institution from a drop-down menu of recognised universities held within their database. Some human resources professionals within law firms indicate anecdotally that applications from some sectors of the university market are filtered out at the first sift. This is not true of all firms and chambers, but we did come across this practice in our study.

> Firms in the City will do the milk round at these various institutions. They wouldn't necessarily go to what was a former polytechnic and is now a City university or whatever they want to call themselves. So, if I am Clifford Chance and I have to do the milk round why am I going to go to hundreds of institutions when I can go for the top ten and get the clone that I want?
>
> (Female BAME Equity Partner)

Given the importance accorded to the university that one attends within the calculation of symbolic capital, BAME law students concentrated within the less prestigious 'new' universities – former polytechnics – face a palpable barrier to entry to the profession regardless of their level of attainment at university, a barrier which is heightened due to the intersection of class and race (see Archer, 2011; Ashley, 2010; Tomlinson et al., 2013). We have coded university attended as symbolic rather than institutionalised cultural capital as it has less to do

---

[18] The Milk Round occurs annually and it is the process by which elite law firms visit the law schools of elite universities so as to try to recruit their students. Usually law firms target second year law students with a view to employing them post-graduation.

with an assessment of legitimated knowledge in the form of the award of an educational qualification (given the discussion earlier) than it has to do with an assessment of prestige and honour. Even attendance at a high ranked and well respected institution may not be sufficient against the symbolic cachet associated with Oxford and Cambridge Universities, but a degree from a Russell Group institution (similar to the Ivy League) is likely to provide a range of job opportunities:

> I also went [for an interview] to Leeds University, where I got on extremely well with the woman there. She gave me an offer of three Cs. She just absolutely loved me ... But she did say to me, do you have any relations in the law? I said, no. She said, well then I think it's going to be extremely difficult for you to get articles [a training contract], and that was the view, and that was why the [name of law firm] articles were great, because you know, in those days, people from UCL [the university she eventually attended] didn't get to Magic Circle firms[19]. I mean, it wasn't called Magic Circle, but you didn't go to [top 10 law firm A] and [top 10 law firm B] unless you'd been to Oxbridge, pretty much, and it was our year that produced ... I think five people found themselves a combination of [UK top 10 law firm B] and [UK top 10 law firm C] and [UK top 10 law firm A] and this was regarded as a huge strive for [a] Redbrick University[20].
>
> (Female, Solicitor Salaried Partner)

The institutionalised capital associated with educational qualifications from the elite universities is far greater than for others. Some may argue this to be a function of the greater ability of their students, although the UK's external examining practices, which require independent academic oversight of all university grading, would suggest that differences in attainment within the university sector are not so marked as to justify the exclusion of some universities from consideration. And further, given race and class stratification within the UK higher education sector, and the aforementioned research evidence, it would be unwise to conclude that attendance at an elite university necessarily presupposes that a

---

[19] Magic Circle law firms are the top ten elite and large law firms that operate in the City of London.

[20] Redbrick universities are the universities established in large cities around England in the late 1800s and early 1900s. They often form part of the Russell Group (similar to the Ivy League in the United States), but are distinguished from Oxford and Cambridge universities by their relative youth.

student is educationally more gifted than those in the less prestigious parts of the higher education sector.

We found some evidence that it may be possible to overcome an apparent lack of embodied and objectified cultural capital by attending the right kind of university but it should be noted that these examples were relatively unusual and associated with studying at very highly ranked institutions,

> I think a barrier for ethnic minority lawyers may have been a cultural aspect ... especially if they're the first, second generation from parents who have emigrated to this country; they just don't have the culture at home which socialises you and educates you into the world of the race horses, for example, ... And also, not being given guidance; you just don't get the guidance at home, which is a given from educated middle class white, to use that phrase, background. I used to think it was a barrier, but I think in the age of the internet, if you're smart and you can get your three As at A level, and you can get yourself into university, I do think that there's so much information out there; maybe that's different to the cultural aspect ... Though, to be honest with you, by the time you got to my university, Cambridge, you know you were in a very good position to do very well in a legal career.
>
> (Male BAME Solicitor)

University attended is a powerful indicator of a law graduate's chances of successful entry into the legal profession, whereas university attainment, institutionalised capital, appears to become relevant only once the applicant has been awarded a threshold of symbolic capital due to attending an elite institution. High marks in a law degree from the wrong kind of university will rarely ease a graduate's passage into the profession; the greater institutionalised capital does not often make-up for the lack of symbolic capital in this regard.

Other instances of cultural and symbolic capital
We also found evidence that objectified cultural capital is acquired through participation in certain forms of extra-curricular activities, those mostly associated with middle and upper middle class backgrounds. It was difficult for working class law graduates to have acquired some of these forms of cultural capital, as the opportunities were not available through their state school experience (unlike in many fee-paying schools) and so had to be sought outside of the school environment (and paid for by the family).

216

> I think I've always done things to enhance my CV; so things like, I studied abroad, and I think that ... sometimes just helps my CV to stand out off the page; and just done things like travelling, and being a prefect, being a house captain, and different things like that. And also I studied Japanese at A-level, so I just think it's just the different extra things that have helped. Also just general work experience, I think, has helped
>
> (Female BAME Trainee Solicitor)

Some of our participants worked hard at university to augment their stock of extra curricula activities ahead of applying to firms or chambers. Internships, clerking opportunities and other forms of unpaid legal and quasi-legal work experience also counted towards applicants' reserves of cultural capital and sometimes also their symbolic capital if the internship was considered to be prestigious. Our participants appeared to consider these more appropriate forms of assessment for suitability, given that they were more closely associated with legal practice. However, there was a perception that it was easier to get this kind of work if one had good social capital, although many internships are now awarded on more transparent terms, albeit with reference to assessments of cultural capital.

> I did get asked, why haven't you been a paralegal already, why haven't you done more work experience. And I'd already done quite a lot compared to other people I knew, whereas mooting, yes, it's available at university, I never did it, but I never got asked why I didn't do it; I was continually asked, why don't you have more work experience on your CV. And the expectation is often that you should have done unpaid work experience, because that's often what you [do]; there are lots of paralegal positions that are going now, for even nothing, with a view to maybe turning into a training contract, or they are going for like, £14,000 a year
>
> (Female White Trainee Solicitor London)

Long-term unpaid internships were more difficult to undertake for those who needed to work in paid employment alongside their studies than for self- or family-supported students.[21] Thus, the proxies used and the way they are used to select would-be solicitors and barristers by law firms and chambers disproportionately affect those from lower

---

[21] It is for this reason that The Gateways to the Professions Collaborative Forum Common Best Practice Code for High-Quality Internships indicates that internships should be remunerated, at 13.

economic groups and thus, given the correlation between class and race in the UK, those from non-White British backgrounds. Unless the work experience is sufficiently meaningful such that it provides a genuine and relevant training opportunity that produces a candidate much more qualified for a role, the need to have undertaken multiple and long-term work placements acts as a form of indirect discrimination contrary to section 19 of the Equality Act 2010. There are others ways of reaching hiring decisions that are less likely to discriminate unlawfully against those from lower socio-economic groups and those from non-white backgrounds. For example, in Germany, greater weight is placed on academic attainment at university in the subject for which one is seeking professional qualification. Less weight is placed on pre-university experiences and attainment and on open questions that seek information about background and social status (see Ashley and Empson, 2013). Enacting such policies in the UK would require solicitors and barristers to be willing to consider that university and school attended are not markers of excellence in themselves, nor are periods of work experience or participation in cultural and social activities, but a function of a complex web of factors linked to class background.

CONCLUSIONS: CHALLENGES FOR THE LEGAL PROFESSION IN ENGLAND AND WALES

Following our LSB commissioned research, and a LSB consultation, the LSB now requires that all legal organisations collect diversity data from their members and return results to their professional bodies, who in turn must publish aggregated diversity data. This appears to have accelerated the growth of diversity schemes within the legal profession. Many of these initiatives aim to raise the aspirations of BAME school pupils so as to encourage them to consider law as a career (see e.g. the *Prime* scheme[22]). Universities have also adopted the 'widening participation' agenda, given the incentives (or rather the disincentives) set out in this regard by government. Diversity schemes in universities and law firms are seeking to address BAME underrepresentation;

---

[22] This is a scheme that has been championed by the elite law firms to encourage talented young people from state schools (US public schools) to consider a career in the law. Law firm visits are offered, as our short periods of work experience. For more information see: www.primecommitment.org/home

however, there is little progress at the elite ends of either and this, in part, misses the causal problem.

There is no reliable evidence to suggest that law graduates with excellent grades from non-elite institutions are any less lacking in merit as would-be lawyers than their counterparts from elite institutions, even if they may have lesser cultural or symbolic capital. And there is some evidence to suggest that the relatively minor school level grade differences between students within the elite and the middle tiers of law schools, reveal more about the students background than educational ability An ability to row, shoot, play rugby or a musical instrument provide little insight into a prospective lawyer's ability to convey a house, draft a will, cross examine a witness or mediate, unless the student is able to use those experiences as a means through which to explain the attributes and competencies s/he has that are suggestive of drafting, advocacy or mediation skills. While we continue to focus on raising BAME participation in elite schools (positive though that may be), the habitus reproduces to the benefit of those already privileged by the field. Definitions of merit and the contention that merit is objectivity defined remains unchallenged. Internships are now being advertised and offered on a more systematic and transparent basis, due to the efforts of the Law Society and the Bar, and this is a real step forward. This reduces the chance of social capital playing a key role in obtaining those opportunities. But if university attended and pre-university attainment remain potent drivers for hiring decisions, the ability to secure such a placement is likely to remain marginal to job prospects, unless it acts as a catalyst for firms and chambers to reassess their perceptions of 'outsiders' who attend non-elite law schools. More likely lawyers from minority groups who succeed in the profession will be used as evidence that merit will triumph regardless of background. Real change is unlikely until the current proxies are recognised as subjective constructions of merit, ill-designed to provide a meaningful assessment of legal ability and skill, until they are replaced with a more sophisticated competencies-based method of assessing potential lawyering ability. Job descriptions and person specifications are standard practice in most other professions, even old professions. Application forms that prompt applicants to reflect on key competencies could limit the crude application of proxies and may inject a degree of reflection within the profession's habitus. In time this may disrupt the status quo. Only then is it likely that the profession's rhetoric about equality and the search for talent can hope to be realised.

REFERENCES

Abel, R. (1979) 'The Rise of Professionalism' 6 *British Journal of Law and Society* 82.

Archer, L. (2011) 'Constructing Minority Ethnic Middle Class Identity: An Exploratory Study with Parents, Pupils and Young Professionals' 4 (11) *Sociology* 134–51.

Ashley, L. (2010) 'Making a Difference? The Use (and Abuse) of Diversity Management in the UK's Elite Law Firms' 24 (4) *Work, Employment and Society* 711–727.

Ashley, L. and Empson, L. (2013) 'Differentiation and Discrimination: Understanding Social Class and Social Exclusion in Leading Law Firms' 66(2) *Human Relations* 219–244.

Bar Council Research Department (2011) *Bar Barometer Trends in the Profile of the Bar Pilot Statistical Report March 2011*, London: The General Council of the Bar of England and Wales.

(2012) *Second Bar Barometer Trends in the Profile of the Bar Pilot Statistical Report* London: The General Council of the Bar of England and Wales.

(2013) *Third Bar Barometer Trends in the Profile of the Bar Pilot Statistical Report* London: The General Council of the Bar of England and Wales.

Barnard, H. and Turner, C. (2011) *Poverty and Ethnicity: A Review of Evidence* York, UK: Joseph Rowntree Trust.

Bottero, W. and Irwin, S. (2003) 'Locating Difference; Class, "Race" and Gender, and the Shaping of Social Inequalities' 51(4) *The Sociological Review* 453–483.

Bourdieu, P. (1973) 'Cultural Reproduction and Social Reproduction' in Brown, R. (ed.) *Knowledge, Education and Cultural Change* London: Tavistock.

(1977) Outline of a Theory of Practice. Cambridge: Cambridge University Press.

(1984) *Distinction: A Social Critique of the Judgement of Taste*. London: Routledge and Keagan Paul.

(1986) 'The Forms of Capital' in Richardson, J. (ed.) *Handbook of Theory and Research for the Sociology of Education*. New York: Greenwood, 241–258.

(1990a) *In Other Words: Essays Towards a Reflexive Sociology*. Cambridge: Polity.

(1990b) *The Logic of Practice*. Cambridge: Polity.

(1991) *Language and Symbolic Power* Thompson, J.B. (ed.) Cambridge: Polity.

(1996) *The State Nobility* Cambridge: Polity Press.

Bourdieu, P. and Passeron, J. (1979) *The Inheritors: French Students and their Relation to Culture*. Chicago: University of Chicago Press.

(1990) *Reproduction in Education, Society and Culture*. 2nd edn. London: Sage Publications.

Bourdieu, P. and Wacquant, L. (1992) *An Invitation to Reflexive Sociology*. Cambridge: Polity Press.

Breen, Richard (2005) '2 Foundations of a Neo-Weberian Class Analysis' in Wright, Erik Olin (ed.) *Approaches to Class Analysis*. Cambridge: Cambridge University Press.

Broome, L., J. Conley and K. Krawiec, Diversity and Talent at the Top: Lessons from the Boardroom, in S. Headworth, R. Nelson, R. Dinovitzer and D. Wilkins (eds.), Diversity in Practice: Race, Class, and Gender in Legal and Professional Careers (Cambridge Univ. Press, forthcoming).

Centre for European Sociology (1972) *Current Research*. Paris: Ecole Pratiques des Hautes Etudes.

Cicourel, A.V. (1964) *Method and Measurement in Sociology*. New York: Free Press.

Combahee River Collection (1994) 'A black Feminist Statement' in Eisenstein, Z. (ed.), *Capitalist Patriarchy and the Case for Socialist Feminism* Monthly Press Review.

Conaghan, J. (2000) 'Reassessing the Feminist Theoretical Project in Law' 27 (3)*Journal of Law and Society* 351–385.

Connolly, P. (2006) 'The Effects of Social Class and Ethnicity on Gender Differences in GCSE Attainment: A Secondary Analysis of the Youth Cohort Study of England and Wales 1997–2001' 32(1) *British Educational Research Journal* 3–21.

Connor, H., Tyers, C., Modood, T. and Hillage, J. (2004) *Why the Difference? A Closer Look at Higher Education Minority Ethnic Students and Graduates*. Department for Education and Skills Research Report RR552.

Cook, A., Faulconbridge, J., Muzio D. (2012) 'London's Legal Elite: Recruitment through Cultural Capital and the Reproduction of Social Exclusivity in City Professional Service Fields' 44 *Environment and Planning* 1744–1762.

Crow, G. and Pope, C. (2008) 'Editorial Foreword: The Importance of Class' 42(6) *Sociology* 1045.

Dingwall, R. (1997) 'Accounts, Interviews and Observations' in Miller, G. and Dingwall, R. (eds) *Context and Method in Qualitative Research* London: Sage Publishing 51.

Duff, L. and Webley, L. (2004) *Equality and Diversity: Women Solicitors Research Study 48 Volume II Law Society Research Study Series*. London: The Law Society.

Durkheim, E. (1964) *The Division of Labor* [Originally pub. 1893] New York, Free Press of Glencoe.

Edmonds, D. (2010) 'Training the Lawyers of the Future – A Regulator's View' *Lord Upjohn Lecture 19 November 2010* available at: www.legalservicesboard.org.uk/news_publications/speeches_presentations/2010/de_lord_upjohn_lec.pdf

Fox, J.E., Morosanu, L. and Szilassy, E. (2012) 'The Racialization of the New European Migration to the UK' Vol 46 (4) *Sociology* 680.

Fuss, D. (1994) 'Reading Like a Feminist' in Schor, N. and Weed, E. (eds.), *The Essential Difference*, Indiana University Press.

Gateways to the Profession Collaborative Forum (2013) Common Best Practice Code for High-Quality Internships, Trade Union's Congress.

Goldthorpe, J. (2000) 'Rent, Class Conflict, and Class Structure: Commentary on Sørensen' Vol. 105 No. 6 *The American Journal of Sociology* 1572–1582.

Gorman, Elizabeth H. and Fiona M. Kay. [In press 2015]. "Which Kinds of Law Firms Have the Most Minority Lawyers? Organizational Context and the Representation of African-Americans, Latinos, and Asian-Americans." in Spencer Headworth, Robert Nelson, Ronit Dinovitzer, and David Wilkins (eds.), *Racial Diversity in the Legal Profession*. Cambridge, UK: Cambridge University Press.

Graham Crow and Catherine Pope (2008) 'Editorial Foreword: The Importance of Class' 42(6) *Sociology* 1045–1048.

Harris, A. (1997) 'Race and Essentialism in Feminist Legal Theory' in Wing, A.K. (ed.), *Critical Race Feminism: A Reader New York*, New York University Press, 7–17.

Hirsch, D. (2007) *Experiences of Poverty and Educational Disadvantage*, Joseph Rowntree Trust. Available at; www.jrf.org.uk/publications/experiences-poverty-and-educational-disadvantage.

Jenkins, R. (2002) *Pierre Bourdieu*. Abingdon and New York: Routledge.

Kay, F. and Hagan, J. (1995) 'The Persistent Glass Ceiling: Gendered Inequalities in the Earnings of Lawyers' 46 (2) *British Journal of Sociology* 279.

(1998) 'Raising the Bar: The Gender Stratification of Law-Firm Capital' 93 (5) *American Sociological Review* 728.

Khattab, N. (2009) 'Ethno-religious Background as a Determinant of Educational and Occupational Attainment in Britain' 43 *Sociology* 304–322.

Kirkup, C. et al. (2010) *Use an Aptitude Test in University Entrance: A Validity Study, National Foundation for Educational Research*.

Kusher, T. (2005) Racialisation and 'White European' Immigration' in Murji, K. and Solomos, J. (eds.) *Racialisation: Studies in Theory and Practice*. Oxford: Oxford University Press 207.

Larson, M. (1977) 'The Rise of Professionalism: A Sociological Analysis. Berkley: University of California Press and more specifically Abel, R.L. 'The Rise of Professionalism' (1979) Vol. 6 *British Journal of Law and Society* 82.

Law Society (2010) *Ethnic Diversity in Law Firms Understanding the Barriers*. London: the Law Society.

Law Society Research Unit (2014) *Trends in the Solicitors' Profession: Annual Statistical Report 2013*. London: Law Society.

Legal Services Board (2011) *Qualified Lawyers Transfer Scheme: Map of England and Wales Solicitor Day One Outcomes against a Barrister of England & Wales on Completion of Pupillage*. www.legalservicesboard .org.uk/what_we_do/regulation/pdf/3.pdf.

Loury, G., Modood, T. and Teles, S. (eds.) (2005) *Ethnicity, Social Mobility and Public Policy: A Comparison of the USA and UK*. Cambridge: Cambridge University Press.

McPhail, K., Paisey, C., and Paisey, N. J. (2010) 'Class, Social Deprivation and Accounting Education in Scottish Schools: Implications for the Reproduction of the Accounting Profession and Practice' 21 *Critical Perspectives on Accounting* 31–50.

Macpherson, Sir William (1999) *The Stephen Lawrence Inquiry Report*. London: The Stationery Office.

Marx, K. (1867; trans. 2010) *Capital: A Critique of Political Economy Volume 1* Engels, F. (ed.) Moore, S. and Aveling, E. (trans.) Moscow: Progress Publishers.

Marx, K. and Engels, F. (1848; trans. 1969) *Manifesto of the Communist Party Marx/ Engels Selected Works Volume 1*. Moscow: Progress Publishers.

Milburn, A. (2009) Unleashing Aspiration: The Final Report of the Panel on Fair Access to the Professions available at: http://webarchive.nationa larchives.gov.uk/+/http:/www.cabinetoffice.gov.uk/media/227102/fair-access.pdf.

Milburn, A. (2012) Fair Access to Professional Careers A progress report by the Independent Reviewer on Social Mobility and Child Poverty London: National Archives available at: http://webarchive.nationa larchives.gov.uk/+/http:/www.cabinetoffice.gov.uk/media/227102/fair-access .pdf.

Modood, T. (2004) 'Capitals, Ethnic Identity and Educational Qualifications' 13(2) *Cultural Trends* 87–105.

Nash, R. (1990) 'Bourdieu on Education and Social and Cultural Reproduction' 11(4) *British Journal of Sociology of Education* 431.

Nelson R. (1988) *Partners with Power: The Social Transformation of the Large Law Firm* Berkley, CA: University of California Press.

Nicolson, D. (2005) 'Demography, Discrimination and Diversity: A New Dawn for the British Legal Profession.' 12 *International Journal of the Legal Profession* 201.

Office for National Statistics (2011) *Ethnicity and National Identity in England and Wales 2011 Part of 2011 Census, Key Statistics for Local Authorities in England and Wales Release* available at: www.ons.gov.uk/ons/rel/census/2011-census/key-statistics-for-local-authorities-in-england-and-wales/rpt-ethnicity.html

Rothon, C. (2007) 'Can Achievement Differentials be Explained by Social Class Alone.' 7 *Ethnicities* 306–322.

Rustin, M. and Chamberlayne, P. (2002) 'Introduction: From Biography to Social Policy'. In Chamberlayne, P., Rustin, M. and Wengraf, T. (eds.) *Biography and Social Exclusion in Europe*. Bristol: The Polity Press.

Sherr, A. (1991) *Solicitors and Their Skills: A Study of the Viability of Different Research Methods for Collating and Categorising the Skills Solicitors Utilise in their Professional Work*. London: The Law Society.

Shiner, M. (1994) *Entry into the Legal Professions: The Law Student Cohort Study*. London: The Law Society.

(1999) *Entry into the Legal Professions: The Law Student Cohort Study. Year 5* London: The Law Society.

(2000) 'Young, Gifted and Blocked! Entry to the Solicitors' Profession' in Thomas, P. (ed.) *Discriminating Lawyers*. London: Cavendish 87.

Silverman, D. (1993) *Interpreting Qualitative Data*. Aldershot: Gower.

Skeggs, B. (1997) *Formations of Class and Gender*. Sage Publications.

(2004) *Class, Self, Culture*. London: Routledge.

Sommerlad, H. (2007) 'Researching and Theorizing the Processes of Professional Identity Formation' 34(2) *Journal of Law and Society* 190.

(2008) '"What are you doing here? You should be working in a hair salon or something": outsider status and professional socialization in the solicitors' profession' 2 *Web JCLI* http://webjcli.ncl.ac.uk/2008/issue2/sommerlad2.html

(2011) 'The Commercialisation of Law and Enterprising Legal Practitioner: Continuity and Change' 18 (1/2) *International Journal of the Legal Profession* 73.

Sommerlad, H. and Webley, L., Duff, L., Muzio, D. and Tomlinson, J. (2013) *Diversity in the Legal Profession in England and Wales: A Qualitative Study of Barriers and Individual Choices*. London: University of Westminster Law Press.

Spivak, G. (1998) 'Subaltern Studies: Deconstructing Historiography' in Guha, R. and Spivak, G. (eds), *Selected Subaltern Studies*, Oxford University Press.

Spivak, G. with Rooney,E. (1994) 'In a Word: Interview with Gayatri Chakravorty Spivak with Ellen Rooney' in Naomi Schor and Elizabeth Weed (eds.), *The Essential Difference*, Indiana University Press at 98–115.

The Equality Act 2010.

The Legal Services Act 2007.

The Ouseley Report (2008) *Independent Review Into Disproportionate Regulatory Outcomes For Black And Minority Ethnic Solicitors* available at: www.sra .org.uk/ouseley/

Thomas, P. (2000) (ed.) *Discriminating Lawyers*. London: Cavendish Publishing.

Tomlinson, J., Muzio, D., Sommerlad, H., Webley, L. and Duff, L. (2013) 'Structure, Agency and Career Strategies of White Women and Black and Minority Ethnic Individuals in the Legal Profession' 66(2) *Human Relations* 245–269.

Tramonte, L. and Douglas Willms, J. (2010) Cultural Capital and Its Effects on Education Outcomes' 29 *Economics of Education Review* 200–213.

Wacquant, L.D. (1989) 'Towards a Reflexive Sociology: A Workshop with Pierre Bourdieu' 7 *Sociological Theory* 36.

Waters, J. (2006) 'Geographies of Cultural Capital: Education, International Migration and Family Strategies between Hong Kong and Canada' 31 *Transactions of the Institute of British Geographers New Series* 179.

Waters (2007) 'Roundabout Routes and Sanctuary Schools: The Role of Situated Educational Practices and Habitus in the Creation of Transnational Professionals' 7 *Global Networks* 477.

Weber, M. (1956) 'Wirtschaft und Gesellschaft' in Runciman, W.G. (ed.) and Matthews, E. (trans.) (1978) *Max Weber Selections in Translation*. Cambridge: Cambridge University Press.

Webley, L. (2013a) 'United Kingdom: What Robinson v Solicitors Regulation Authority Tells Us about the Contested Terrain of Race and Disciplinary Processes' 16 (1) *Legal Ethics* 236–241.

(2013b) "What Empirical Legal Studies Tell Us About The Legal Profession" Professorial Inaugural Lecture 20th March 2013 University of Westminster, London UK available at: www.youtube.com/watch? v=ixai0rliaRw

Wilkins, D. and Gulati. M. (1996) 'Why Are There So Few Black Lawyers in Corporate Law Firms?: An Institutional Analysis' 84 *California Law Review* 493.

(1998a) 'Fragmenting Professionalism: Racial Identity and the Ideology of "Bleached Out" Lawyering' 5 *International Journal of the Legal Profession* 141.

(1998b) 'Identities and Roles: Race, Recognition, and Professional Responsibility' 57 *Maryland Law Review* 1502.

Willis, P. (1977) *Learning to Labour: How Working Class Kids get Working Class Jobs*. Hants: Saxon House.

Zimdars, A. (2010) 'The Profile of Pupil Barristers and the Bar of England and Wales 2004–2008' 17 (2) *International Journal of the Legal Profession* 117–134.

THE NEW "PROFESSIONALISM" IN ENGLAND AND WALES

Talent, diversity, and a legal precariat

HILARY SOMMERLAD

The last ten to twenty years have seen the gradual adoption of diversity initiatives and merit-based human resource management (HRM) practices by the solicitors' profession in England and Wales.[1] Yet, over the course of roughly the same period, social differences have been reinforced: the significance of class, ethnicity, and gender in what the profession recognizes as "talent"[2] has not only persisted but actually strengthened, despite the ubiquity of discourses that announce the irrelevance of social category and the agentic power of individuals (Ashley et al. 2015). As a result, "non-normative" solicitors have disproportionately experienced the routinization of labor processes

---

[1] The United Kingdom (UK) is made up of separate legal systems and consequently professions. This chapter is concerned with the legal system of England and Wales, where, traditionally, the legal profession was divided into two main branches with different functions and routes to qualification: barristers, who were the legal specialists, had exclusive rights of advocacy in the higher courts but no direct access to clients, and solicitors, who enjoyed monopolies over certain practice areas such as transactions in land (conveyancing), had direct contact with clients, and were more likely to be general practitioners. Today the term legal professional also encompasses legal executives and paralegals; this last group comprises a growing number of fee-earners that includes those whose conditions of employment are extremely disadvantageous, which I therefore describe as a precariat (see fn. 4)

[2] The discourse of talent, which complements that of merit, characterizes it as a finite resource currently in very short supply (Michaels et al 2001). Talent is rarely defined (again like merit), and this indefinability is not explained by reference to its contextual nature; instead, talent is simply portrayed as eluding description, and the claim is made that "you simply know it when you see it" (op. cit.: xii)

and progressive technical proletarianization (Derber 1982) that has also taken place in recent years. This chapter will explore a new development in this racialized, classed, and gendered stratification of the profession. Drawing on two qualitative studies of aspiring solicitors in England and Wales, it will discuss the emergence of a group of para-legals[3] whose highly insecure working conditions and negligible prospects of a future professional career warrant the description legal precariat.[4]

The implicit comparison of credentialed para-professionals with the casualized workers who, across the world, perform low-skill, often dangerous and dirty jobs in conditions of "advanced marginality" (Wacquant 2009b) may appear overblown. Nevertheless, the labor market position and working conditions of these paralegals both resemble some of those suffered by other casualized workers and share many causal factors. These factors largely derive from the processes of macro-social change that have taken place over the course of the last three decades, and the particular impact these have had on the profession. These changes have been extensively documented elsewhere,[5] and

---

[3] There is no commonly understood definition of the term paralegal or of the range of activities that paralegal work entails (Sidaway and Punt 1997). This vagueness is central to the story of those who have completed the academic stage of qualifying to be a solicitor (the Legal Practice Course (LPC)) or a barrister (the Bar Vocational Course (BVC)), but whose difficulties in obtaining the apprenticeships with firms (training contracts) or with barristers' chambers (pupillages) lead them to take low-paid and insecure legal work, generally in the hope that this will lead to the offer of a training contract. Therefore, although the term paralegal is sometimes also used to refer to Legal Executives and paid legal clerks, here I use it to denote LPC or BVC graduates without training contracts or pupillages, working in the solicitors' profession. Firms sometimes also use the term support worker to describe people engaging in such work.

[4] The term precariat has been deployed by a number of authors (e.g., Standing 2011) to describe the growing social class of people who suffer fragmented, discontinuous, and poorly paid working conditions characteristic of neo-liberal, de-regulated economies; see, e.g., Wacquant 2009a: 5, 11–13; Ross 2009; essays in Fudge and Owens 2006; Harvey 2007: 112.

[5] For commentaries on neo-liberalism generally, see, e.g., Brown 2005: ch. 3; Harvey 2007; Hall 2011: in particular 10–11; Crouch 2011; Stedman Jones 2012. In terms of the development of the precariat, Ross (2009) relates this to the shift in economies from industry to information, the erosion of the benefits and securities of the Keynesian era and the switch in focus in the West away from sustainable employment. For discussion of the impact of neoliberalism on the English legal profession see, e.g., Lee 1992; Flood 1996; Hanlon 1999; Sommerlad 2011, 2012; Muzio et al. 2013.

I will, therefore, confine myself to a brief mention of those most relevant to the research.

Generally summarized by the term neoliberal, the macro-level social changes that are driving the emergence of a legal precariat include a discourse that sets up the autonomous possessive individual/oppressive state dichotomy, which derides interventions designed to ameliorate the inequalities created by "free" markets[6] and legitimizes the displacement of an equitable "civic culture" by a "business culture" (Marquand 1988). As Wacquant notes, these "symbolic frames" are fundamental to the actualization of neoliberalism's economic core (2009a: 306): thus, the privileging of business above all other values legitimizes the liberation of capitalism from the fetters imposed by Keynesian welfarism including employment protection law (see, e.g., Fudge and Owens 2006; Bell 2012).[7] At the same time, globalization has entailed a move to post-Fordist strategies of capital accumulation further undermining the power of labor (Harvey 1989). A range of critical scholars have documented the consequent eclipse of egalitarian movements (e.g., Fraser 2013) and growing disparities between privileged and underprivileged groups (see, e.g., Bradley 1996: 210; Ehrenreich 2002) as flexible production regimes have proliferated. Ross notes that these regimes are no longer confined to the less skilled end of work: "we have seen the steady advance of contingency into the lower and middle levels of the professional and high-wage service" (2009: 5). However, the relentless discursive mobilization of the autonomous, entrepreneurial individual (see, e.g., Pink 2001) enables the pervasive chronic insecurity to be presented as liberatory: "in attacking rigid bureaucracy and emphasizing

---

[6] My use of the inverted commas here refers to the point articulated long ago by Durkheim that the concept of a "free market" and the linked concept of the autonomous individual are ideological constructs of modernity, which only exist as a result of a vast infrastructure of social and juridical relations (Durkheim 1957: 57–64). More recently, Harcourt (2011) has traced the origins of the contemporary myth of the free market to the idea of natural order, which was fundamental to eighteenth-century economic thought.

[7] For instance, the economic liberalization and deregulation initiated by the Thatcher government (1979) has encompassed a progressive dismantlement of the protective measures enshrined in employment and equality laws and pension entitlements on the grounds that these represent barriers to growth, and the current government is engaged in a further review of this legislation in what it terms The Red Tape Challenge. See www.redtapechallenge.cabinetoffice.gov.uk/?s=employment+protection.

risk, it is claimed, flexibility gives people more freedom to shape their lives" (Sennett 1999: 9–10; and see Du Gay 2004: 41; Ross 2009: 4–5).

This extension of unprotected, temporary working conditions to certain sectors and populations of the legal profession while other sectors and their populations have become vastly enriched is part of the transformation wrought by neoliberal globalization – and the interconnections between the various dimensions of the transformation underline both the synergy and historical contingency of the profession's traditional traits. For instance, such other consequences of economic liberalization as the removal of the profession's traditional market shelters, the development of commodities with embedded expert knowledge, and the stock exchange listing of firms (see, e.g., Hanlon 1997, 1999; Kritzer 1999; Abel 2003; Empson 2007)[8] are linked to the corrosive impact of discourses of possessive individualism and a "lean" state on collectivist conceptions of public values (Yeatman 1996) and the profession's moral purpose and responsibility (Walzer 1984; Arthurs 2001). All of these developments are related to the emergence of a legal precariat, but some are more obviously relevant than others, and in the following section, I will outline these, focusing first on the corporate sector and, second, on the private client and, in particular, the legal aid sectors.

THE TRANSFORMATION OF THE PROFESSION AND THE LEGAL PRECARIAT

One of the most significant changes to the profession has been the fragmentation of its close-knit, collegial character - the product of its self-governing professional association its organization into partnerships and the apprenticeship system. Arguably, the displacement of this particularistic method of recruitment by graduate entry was particularly influential in undermining the profession's "guild" character (Krause 1999), which depended on the characterization of its members as detached experts with specialist knowledge, selected "not by the open market but by the judgement of similarly educated experts"

---

[8] In England and Wales these developments have been bolstered by the Legal Services Act 2007, which provided for a set of reforms designed to "increase competition in the legal services market and place the consumer at the heart of the regulatory system," following which many law practices describe themselves as professional service firms, and which makes possible their reorganization as multidisciplinary "alternative business structures" (ABSs).

(Perkin 1989: xiii). Professional control over its supply base was further constrained by the expansion of university education from the mid-1980s onward, the popularity of a career in law as a social mobility project, and the resulting dramatic increase in the numbers and diversity[9] of English lawyers. As a consequence, ultimate control over the numbers and social identity of new solicitors shifted to individual firms, since qualification as a solicitor in England and Wales currently requires not only the successful completion of an academic stage (the Legal Practice Course (LPC)) but also a two-year apprenticeship period with a firm (the training contract).

The expansion and diversification of the profession's supply side supported other changes, including the dramatic accentuation of the division between the profession's corporate and private client sectors as a consequence of the explosive growth of corporate legal business.[10] The resulting reconfiguration of corporate firms as (multinational) capitalist organizations – their loss of distinctiveness signaled by the switch to the appellation Professional Service Firms (PSFs) – and move to an industrial mode of production entailed both the decomposition and reconstitution of legal work[11] and the elongation of professional structures, so that standardized, specialized part work could be assigned to

[9] The expansion of higher education (HE), which was fundamental to the project to raise UK global competitiveness through the knowledge economy, led to dramatic increases in the numbers of female and black Asian, and minority ethnic (BAME) students (Dustmann and Theodoropoulos 2006: 20–24). Law was, and remains, a particularly popular degree choice, illustrating the appeal of professionalism as a potential route to social mobility and an occupational value; for instance, whereas in 2011 the proportion of BAME students in higher education generally was 18.6% (HESA www.hesa.ac.uk/content/view/2705/278/#eth), the proportions in 2011-12 for law were as follows: over one-third of students accepted into a law degree, 28% of students enrolled to do the LPC and nearly a quarter of trainee registrations (Law Society 2013: 34, 38, 43). Further, the legitimating function of law made it especially important that the profession become more socially representative, especially at its higher levels (DCA 2005; see too Cabinet Office, 2009).

[10] The growth of corporate legal business began in the late 1960s, but significantly increased in the "roaring 1980s" and thereafter, generating the legal entrepreneur who was central to the elaboration of the new international economic order (see, e.g., essays in Dezalay and Sugarman 1995; Flood 1996).

[11] Susskind's analysis of the changes focus on "disruptive legal technologies," which are "redefining the legal market and legal business, producing standardized, systematized, packaged commodities," that is, "online solutions made available for direct use by the end user, often on a DIY basis" (2010: 32). Susskind asserts that "any legal job or category of legal work can be decomposed, that is, broken down, into constituent tasks, processes and activities" (id.). Similar conclusions were reached

different hierarchies of legal workers (Sandefur 2007; Susskind 2010; Faulconbridge and Muzio 2009). The influx of outsiders[12] represented the resource who could be utilized to carry out this routine work, and who could have no expectation of ever being partners and hence full members of "the fraternity of peers" (Wilkins and Gulati 1996: 565 and see Galanter and Palay 1999). Originally predominantly female (Hagan and Kay 1995; Sommerlad and Sanderson 1998), as a result of the subsequent expansion of higher education these sub-professionals were increasingly composed of outsiders more generally – those whose race, class, and/or gender makes them unintelligible as lawyers and who therefore have the potential to undermine the profession's claims to elite status.[13] Nevertheless, the nomination of these workers as professionals serves to discipline them and confer status on their legal product (Fournier 1999), while also giving a firm the appearance of diversity – an increasingly important business asset for today's multinational firms.

The huge profitability and size of corporate firms is thus in large part attributable to their engagement in these practices – which Ross (2009) terms flexploitation[14] – of subcontracting and outsourcing, and reliance

as a result of research conducted for the Legal Services Board: "the value chain for law firms is disintegrating. This possibility had existed for some time, with new ICT technology. Much of legal knowledge can be standardized, systematized, and packaged for delivery using self-service and smart systems. Moreover, the billable hour, which developed as a common way of charging clients, has come under severe attack, as the notion of professional autonomy and self-regulation came into conflict with the notion of business efficiency and consumer interest. Combined with the availability of new locations as sources of supply of talent, ICT has pushed global corporations in the direction of offshoring" (Sako 2010: 21).

[12] Finding a term for individuals who belong to "lower status" groups which does not either essentialize or pathologize them is problematic. Some authors use the term "non-normative"; Matsuda (1989: 2320) and Carbado and Gulati (2000) speak of outsiders, which captures the closure tactics used by "insiders"; I use both terms as seems appropriate to the context.

[13] If the ascribed characteristics of individual professionals are "incongruous," they can expose a profession to "attributive judgments" (Bourdieu 1986: 473–475), thereby affecting its status.

[14] Ross (2009) argues that economic liberalization has opened up a frenetic global traffic in jobs and migrants, increasing the quantity of people available to exploit, and that the rigid social hierarchies and reservoir of unpaid domestic labor of the Fordist era has given way to the "flexploitation" of short-term contracts: "the last three decades of deregulation and privatization have re-shaped the geography of livelihoods for almost everyone in the industrialized world.... No one, not even those in the traditional professions, can any longer expect a fixed pattern of employment in the course of their lifetime, and they are under more and more

on a transient workforce of salaried solicitors, paralegals, and interns, including increasing numbers of LPC and Bar Vocation Course (BVC) graduates on temporary contracts (Hanlon and Shapland 1997), and, more recently, unpaid interns.[15] However, a further function of the allocation of routine legal work to these "lesser professionals" – described by Krause (1999) as mid-level capitalist employees, and who fall within the category that Julia Evetts (2012) terms organizational professionals[16] – is that it allows the partnership and those marked out for partnership to focus on high-level deals and relational work, and thus deliver a service to their important clients which retains bespoke elements. However, this privileged sector is, of course, itself subject to the logic of finance capital: whereas partnership was once, in accordance with the norms of traditional professionalism, a brotherhood, today relationships are deeply competitive, shaped by the "eat what you kill" ethos, formalized in the introduction of Profits per Equity Partner (PEP) league tables (Faulconbridge and Muzio 2009). The capacity of the corporate client, as an expert buyer of legal services, to negotiate prices down continually threatens these profits (LSB 2012: 46),[17] which in turn drives partners to exert increasing pressure on workers to maintain fee income.

pressure to anticipate, and prepare for, a future in which they still will be able to compete in a changing marketplace. The rise in the percentage of contingent employment, both in low-end service sectors and in high-wage occupations, has been steady and shows no sign of leveling off. It has been accompanied by an explosion of atypical work arrangements far removed from the world of social welfare systems, union contracts, and long-term tenure with a single employer" (2009: 2–3). Commentators on the specific impact of this on the legal profession include Faulconbridge and Muzio (2009), who argue that one effect of the profession's financialization has been the shift to a predominantly employed occupation and pressure on salaried lawyers to generate greater profits.

[15] Of course, the profession also increasingly outsources work to qualified lawyers in, for instance, South Africa.

[16] Both Krause and Evetts discuss the ongoing decline in power in relation to the state experienced by professional occupations over the past three to four decades in a range of countries, and the concomitant shift from a guild like structure toward capitalist control. Both note the resulting reduction of the status and autonomy of many professionals. Evetts' term for this development is "organizational professionalism"; distinguishing it from classical, occupational professionalism; she argues that in the process of change an important normative value has been lost – as evidenced by, for instance, the replacement of professional trust and collegiality by audit and targets.

[17] Corporate clients also directly fuel the growth in contingent legal labor by seeking cheaper alternatives to law firm services (Strategic Legal Advisor 2009, www.strategi

At the other end of the professional spectrum, the private client sector remained for a long time committed to traditional practices. However, the impact on profitability of the loss of its traditional market shelters (conveyancing and probate[18]) and the managerialization of legally aided work gradually generated changes. As in the corporate sector, individual professionals began to experience a dramatic decline in their autonomy, as intense cost pressures and new discourses drove practice managers to become "business-like" and, particularly in legal aid practices, to engage in micromanagement (Sommerlad1995; 1999; 2004; Sommerlad and Sanderson 2011; 2013). As a result, firms throughout this sector have closed, replaced, on the one hand, by increased numbers of solo practices and, on the other hand, by firms that have merged and transformed themselves into capitalist factories, rationalizing and simplifying work processes. The decline of this sector is also evidenced by the diminution in training places it offers; instead, it employs an increasing number of paralegals and interns to provide cheap, off-the-shelf services to clients. These processes of impoverishment, de-professionalization, and commercialization have entered a new phase with the development of "Tesco Law,"[19] and, in the legal aid sector, the Legal Aid, Sentencing, and Punishment of Offenders Act 2012 (LASPO), which the Ministry of Justice (MOJ) anticipates will save £450 million per annum with over 60 percent (£270 million) of these savings arising from changes to the scope of legal aid.[20]

clegaladvisor.com/news-features/General-counsel-look-for-alternatives-as-law-firm-fees-continue-to-soar/).

[18] Conveyancing is the technical term for legal transactions in land, probate for handling wills and estates. The solicitors' profession traditionally enjoyed monopolies in these areas of work, but these shelters were abolished in Courts and Legal Services Act 1990, which also capped the legal aid budget.

[19] Tesco is a UK supermarket, and the term Tesco Law was coined to refer to the changes to legal services made possible by Part 5 of the Legal Services Act 2007 – specifically the establishment of, first, Legal Disciplinary Partnerships and then ABSs. The stated objective of the legislation was to improve access to justice by opening up the market for the provision of legal services, packaged as "off the shelf" commodities. The Co-operative is another large UK retailer, which also provides a range of other consumer services from insurance to travel, and which was one of the first to establish a Legal Services wing. Self-evidently, the provision of such services entails routinization of legal work under sub-professional conditions.

[20] These deep cuts in legal aid have dramatically eroded the finances of legal aid firms and not-for-profit agencies: the MOJ estimated that agencies might lose up to 75% of that part of their income that is derived from legal aid: 75, www.official-docu ments.gov.uk/document/cm80/8072/8072.pdf. A report commissioned by the Law

The topography of the contemporary profession is thus highly complex; nevertheless, all sectors have shared in the impact of the corrosion of its traditional traits, which, as discussed earlier, includes the capitalization of firms, the displacement of a claimed ideology of altruism by an explicitly calculative rationality, the decline in the importance of expert legal knowledge, the routinization of work, and the loss of individual discretion.[21] All these features have generated multiple hierarchies, or labor markets, which for the majority of workers do not connect to the next market up, and quantitative and qualitative studies of the English solicitors' profession indicate that these processes have sustained and reinforced endemic, deep-rooted patterns of racial, gender, and class division.[22] It is commonplace that these developments have affected legal professions across the world; for instance, Arthurs and Kreklewich (1996) have discussed the new economy's exacerbation of the profession's preexisting tendencies toward stratification and marginalization. However, an added complexity in the United Kingdom is that they are taking place in a society that failed to complete its bourgeois revolution (Anderson 1964), with the result that the aristocratic order of property, privilege, and hierarchy remains fundamentally intact.[23] The division of labor characteristic of the contemporary English profession, therefore, not only forms part of a general devaluation of human capital (Brown and Lauder 2011; 2012)[24] but also rationalizes the revitalization and commodification

Society prior to the enactment of LASPO to consider the impact on firms franchised to deliver legal aid services found that the proposed cuts to fees and removal of work from scope would "have a catastrophic impact" on a supplier base, which was already very impoverished (Otterburn 2011: 6); and see Sommerlad and Sanderson 2013.

[21] See Pleasence et al. (2012) for an overview of the dramatic changes the English legal profession is undergoing.

[22] See, e.g., Shiner (1999; 2000); Vignaendra (2001); Thomas and Rees (2000); Collier (2005); and Sommerlad et al. (2011). See too Rider et al. in this volume on evidence of impact of ethnicity on career mobility in US law firms.

[23] Rustin (2011: 48–9). Martin Loughlin uses Walter Bagehot's phrase "club government" to capture the resilience of pre-modern aristocratic type characteristics of the upper reaches of UK society and in particular the legal profession (2000: 70–73).

[24] Numerous studies of Professional Service Firms (PSFs) indicate that qualifications and knowledge are now taken for granted (e.g., Kumra and Vinnicombe 2008); and a review of graduate early career experiences concluded that traditional academic skills were the least used by recent graduate entrants to the workplace (Purcell et al. 1999). Further, my data revealed how the meaning of skill and knowledge has expanded to encompass personal characteristics and psychological traits (Keep and

of traditional status markers such as attendance at elite schools and universities.[25] Whereas for a brief moment (stretching from roughly the 1970s to the early 1990s), it was possible in the United Kingdom to enter the profession from an "ordinary" background, today, as the discussion by Webley et al. (this volume) indicates, success is predicated on having both cultural and social capital (Ashley 2010; Ashley and Empson 2013; Sommerlad 2011; 2012). As a result, partnerships, especially in the corporate sector, are dominated by a small minority of overwhelmingly white, upper-class males (Rolfe and Anderson 2002; Sutton Trust 2009; Law Society 2013)[26]. Hence, not only did the capitalization of the corporate sector flow ineluctably from its marketization, it also stimulated internal closure, consolidating authority and revenue in the (equity) partnership, renewing its collective, symbolic capital, and reinforcing its position as the power base of the profession as a whole. Today, as the extent to which education was once perceived as a public good is replaced by its construction as a positional good – and hence the private property of the individual – we have seen a re-florescence of aristocratic ideas of merit and archaic status signifiers, repackaged as commodities. As a result, despite the new legal order, there remains a group of elite lawyers whose working conditions

Mayhew 1999), echoing the findings of a study of accountancy that "ways of conducting oneself" are more important (Grey 1998; and see Ashley et. al 2015)

[25] See Bourdieu and Passeron (1977) on education as a source of cultural capital and an engine of social reproduction, and Jewel's application of Bourdieusian theory to the reproduction of class within the US legal profession through the ranking of law schools (2008).

[26] Law Society statistics reveal that in 2012, 23.8% of BAME private practitioners were partners; however, this apparently high percentage must be contextualized by the fact that they were twice as likely to be sole practitioners as were white Europeans (Law Society 2013: 28), and, conversely, were significantly underrepresented in the higher echelons: in 2006, Legal Week reported that just 3% of partners in the top 100 firms were "from ethnic minority groups," 8 June; see too Hoare (2006). The Black Solicitors' Network has reported that the average percentage of BAME partners in firms remains flat at 5.1% (Hall, K. 2013 "Diversity League Table Shows Promotion Gap," Law Society Gazette, 11 November, www.lawgazette.co.uk/5038711.article?utm_source=dispatch&utm_medium=email &utm_campaign=GAZ121113). The average percentage of female associates in firms is 56%, but the average percentage of females who are partners is just 20.4%, whereas 46.1% of men are partners (Law Society 2013: 26). Again, the percentage drops in the elite firms: women make up less than 10% of equity partners in the top 100 firms, and in the top 30 are only 5% of equity (Lawyer Diversity Report 2012; and see Hall, K. 2013 "Glass Ceiling Most Apparent in Magic Circle," Law Society Gazette 7).

continue to be characterized by some of the core features of traditional occupational professionalism such as autonomy (Evetts 2012), though this inner circle of professionals is more impenetrable than ever.

This leads me to the final point I would like to make as a background to the research discussed later. Freeman sums up his critique of the "crony capitalism," which he argues is characteristic of neoliberalism, as "economic feudalism ... in which a small set of wealthy masters dominate markets and the state and subvert or outsmart efforts to regulate their behavior or rein them in."[27] Other writers have similarly conceptualized the commodification and privatization of public goods as a "new feudalism." Shearing's (1983; 2001) primary focus is on the mass privatization of what was previously public property, producing a proliferation of communities governed by contract, and entailing the exclusion of those not privy to that contract. However, my deployment of the term is designed to convey the relationship between the marginalization of some forms of legal labor and the consecration of others, and the reinvigoration of both patron-client relations and archaic status symbols. This in turn leads to the creation of spaces in which an exclusive, particularistic order comes to be defined and enforced, thereby supporting a privatization of the property rights in elite professional jobs. This elite sector depends on the labor of the growing numbers of "technicians" whose aspirations to belong to the professional community and commitment to its ideology make them ideal workers. Thus, the influx of new, diverse professionals can be understood as central to the profession's transformation, even though they exist on its margins.

THE RESEARCH: RECRUITING, MAKING, AND DRIVING THE NEW LEGAL PROFESSIONAL

The first qualitative study that I draw upon investigated what the corporate sector requires of work experience students, trainees, and junior solicitors,[28] and the impact of these requirements on aspiring solicitors from the "wrong background." In my discussion of this study,

[27] From summary of talk to London School of Economics (LSE) 2012, www.lse.ac.uk/publicEvents/miliband/201112LectureSeries.aspx#DynamicJumpMenuManager_1_Anchor_5).

[28] This study was funded by the UK Centre for Legal Education (UKCLE) and directed by Andrew Francis (University of Keele); methods comprised two samples:

I cite partners and representatives of HRM from 10 multinational firms based in London, drawn from practices belonging to what are designated as the top thirty firms.[29] I then draw on research into the intern and paralegal market, focusing particularly on the situation in the most impoverished sector of the profession: legal aid.[30]

The insights generated by the first study into employers' requirements of their employees illustrate how the corporate sector's marketization has resulted in the displacement of the traditional discourse of legal professionalism by the language of business; for instance, "the commercial element is something we look for more and more ... our role as lawyers in the commercial environment has changed" (white male partner; cited in Sommerlad 2011: 87); "assessment exercises are designed to reveal the extent to which an applicant has a business sense and is enterprising" (white female HRM, cited id.). HRM strategy in these firms is premised on a view of employees as resources, components of corporate strategy, reshaped by the logics of finance capitalism. A key characteristic of the entrepreneurial employee (termed by Pongratz and Voss (2003) an "entreployee") is the ability to function as a self-regulating and self-maximizing productive unit from very early on in their careers. An equity partner admitted that these expectations, which are linked to the significance of PEP metrics, places extreme pressure on salaried solicitors; his comments reveal the decline in collegiality and support for junior colleagues that were once defining

first, employers (graduate recruitment officers, diversity officers, and senior partners), and, second, LPC students at two universities, one of which belonged to the elite group of universities termed Russell Group (see www.russellgroup.ac.uk/our-univer sities/), the other which was one of the lower status new universities (which had been polytechnics and are commonly referred to as post-1992 institutions or new universities). The methods comprised questionnaires followed by in-depth interviews and focus groups. For full details see Francis and Sommerlad (2009; 2010), www.ukcle.ac.uk/research/projects/francis.html; and Sommerlad (2011). Much of the data and discussion drawn on here is from Sommerlad (2011).

[29] The Lawyer Diversity Report (2010), www.google.co.uk/search?q=The+Lawyer+Diver sity+Report+2010&oq=The+Lawyer+Diversity+Report+2010&aqs=chrome..69i57 .1334j0j4&sourceid=chrome&espv=210&es_sm=122&ie=UTF-8.

[30] This second study used in-depth interviews and a questionnaire survey that was distributed through the Junior Lawyers Group and Young Legal Aid Lawyers. The data presented in this chapter is drawn from eight interviews and also from a separate survey conducted by the Young Legal Aid Lawyers (YLAL) 2008, the trade press, and Law Society and Legal Services Board (LSB) data.

characteristics of professional relations (Evetts 2012): "this sounds incredibly harsh, but it's in the interest of the firms to maximize the hours that are being delivered, because in a professional service firm ... your product is the hours they charge out" (Asian male equity partner, cited in Sommerlad 2011: 83).[31]

Residues of "gentlemanly" professionalism do persist, however. Even while respondents later on in interviews stated that commercial sense and interpersonal skills were more important than academic qualifications, the first requirement of all corporate law firms is that their trainees have strong academic qualifications. The function of this requirement as a class barrier is underlined by a concern not just with degree classification but also with preuniversity academic performance including GCSEs;[32] thus several firms only considered candidates who had achieved A stars in all their GCSEs, which is effectively a proxy for a public school education.[33] Similarly, applicants needed to be from elite universities: "we target 10 universities – Oxford and Cambridge" and "we go for traditionally the better universities" (white female HRM officers, cited in Sommerlad 2011: 80). Implicit in this preference is a view of new universities as inauthentic (Archer 2007: 641). Although it is in the new university sector that the greatest rationalization of legal education has occurred with the result that the skills acquired by graduates from this sector are explicitly tailored to the needs of legal practice, they are nevertheless devalued. Instead, archaic symbols of power, such as having received a traditional "aristocratic" education (Dorling 2010; Ashley and Empson 2013) and displaying an upper

---

[31] Magic Circle is an informal term for those elite commercial law firms whose headquarters are in the City of London, which consistently have the highest earnings per partner and earnings per lawyer and which are among the largest law firms in the world measured by revenue.

[32] GCSE stands for General Certificate of Secondary Education, an academic qualification awarded in a specified subject, taken in a number of subjects by students aged 14–16 years. Generally only those from public (i.e., fee-paying) schools, which focus on consistently high attainment in exams from early on, and have the resources to support this, tend to achieve top grades at this stage in their education. Therefore, going back to this early stage in an applicant's education (rather than simply focusing on their higher education record) acts as a barrier to those who have not attended elite schools.

[33] The term public school refers to exclusive fee-paying private independent schools in the United Kingdom, which cater primarily for 13 to 18 year olds. Their nomination "public" indicates that, when founded, access to them was not restricted on the basis of religion, occupation, or home location.

middle-class aesthetic, have been reconstructed as commercial and meritocratic artefacts.[34] Some firms are explicit about the value of upper-class Englishness as a commodity that they sell their clientele; for instance, one "Silver Circle"[35] firm described themselves as *consiglieri* to their primary client group of rich Saudi Arabians, and employed Oxbridge[36] graduates who would fulfil the stereotype they sought.

Students' accounts testified to the importance of having the "right" background: "the first thing partners ask you is what university you're from"; and "they wanted to know if our parents were lawyers or worked in the City[37]; my mother is a single parent, a cleaner" (students, cited in Sommerlad 2011). These experiences were echoed in those depicted in messages posted on *The Lawyer 2B* website in response to a City firm Social Mobility Moot launched in 2011. The significance of class was underscored in an agenda item for the moot that a work experience scheme be created to "encourage young people from nontraditional backgrounds to consider support roles – within law firms."[38] Not surprisingly, this provoked outrage on the part of many of the posters; the following comments are exemplary: "SUPPORT ROLES? This is exactly where they think people from the lowest socioeconomic backgrounds belong! They think this would be a great achievement for

---

[34] Thus, the profession's increasingly complex occupational hierarchies, segmented and stratified on the basis of sex, ethnicity, and class, are justified on meritocratic grounds by the corresponding stratification of UK higher education (HE) institutions (Shattock 2003). The implicit equation of outsiders' qualities with demerit and the devaluation of their capital make them appropriate for particular (low grade) parts of legal labor process; at the same time, it also justifies the privileging of normative professionalism: the professional identity of the insider professional is consequently constructed in opposition to the lesser professionalism (or commitment) of the outsider.

[35] The Silver Circle is a group of corporate law firms headquartered in London, which are outside of the Magic Circle, but which have an average profit per equity partner (PEP) and average revenue per lawyer considerably above that of most other UK law firms.

[36] The term Oxbridge, an amalgam of Oxford and Cambridge, is a shorthand term for the universities of Oxford and Cambridge.

[37] The City refers to the traditional financial center of London; the C is always capitalized.

[38] Swift and Manning (2011) "Magic Circle Moots Joint Social Mobility Strategy," 4 April, http://l2b.thelawyer.com/magic-circle-moots-joint-social-mobility-strategy/1007521.article?PageNo=2&SortOrder=dateadded&PageSize=10#comments.

them. Makes me sick." "It would probably never cross their minds that people from nontraditional backgrounds (whatever "nontraditional" means – foreign, poor, or perhaps a combination of both?) could ever make good lawyers." Other responses included accounts of encountering blatant class prejudice, and were overwhelmingly characterized by the view that the profession is stratified on class and race lines: for example, "at least the Magic Circle firms are clear about their intentions. People from less privileged backgrounds/ethnic minorities should remain in support roles and the lawyer roles should be reserved for the white middle classes."[39]

Nevertheless, by the time of the moot, the growth in support roles had for some time been a theme in the trade press. The following comment cited in an article reporting on a survey of the future of the corporate law sector supports Brown and Lauder's argument (2012) that one aspect of global restructuring is the reluctance of employers to invest in human capital: "law firms will shy away from fixed overheads. Partners will be performance paid and will draft in associates and niche experts from a pool" (Hardman 2010: 11). The article's author proceeded to argue that flexibility was needed to operate in a fluctuating economy and, further, that the drive to reduce costs and raise profits would be enhanced as firms became Alternative Business Structures (ABS), fuelling legal process outsourcing to both offshore legal centers and specialist low-cost centers and an increase in "the growing proportion of paralegals" (op. cit. 10–11). Furthermore, the research suggests that these paralegal positions are disproportionately filled by individuals drawn from BAME[40] groups, graduates of new universities, and older

[39] http://l2b.thelawyer.com/magic-circle-moots-joint-social-mobility-strategy/1007521.article?PageNo=3&SortOrder=dateadded&PageSize=10#comments.
[40] Of course, the acronym BAME – meaning black, Asian, and minority ethnic – is deeply problematic: not only does it deny the fluidity of the process of racialization, but it also homogenizes subjects. The longstanding problematization of concepts of race (and class) has been further complicated by the rise of identity politics. As a result, the increasingly complex classifications that are required in order to capture the contemporary multiplicity and fluidity of identity have undermined the validity of any synoptic analysis of social life (Carrier, 2012) and this problem is exemplified by the portmanteau term BAME, which is commonly used in statistical surveys of the professions and yet encompasses the entire range of "non-white ethnicities," as well, of course, as other intersecting forms of identity. As a result, all social commentators on diversity are locked into a number of contradictions related to the simultaneous continuing salience of category and fluidity of contemporary identities.

individuals (Shiner, 2000; Fletcher 2006: 9; Law Society: 2010).[41] Thus, as discussed earlier, the radical restructuring of the legal labor market in both the corporate and private client sectors mirrors the wider socioeconomic polarization resulting from neoliberalism, as the valorization of archaic signs of privilege is matched in the concentration of certain groups within a contingent, casualized labor force, thereby producing a cultural consolidation of inequality (Wacquant: 2009b) that is raced, classed, and gendered.

A brief scan of the Law Society and recruitment agency websites indicates the sorts of conditions that firms throughout the profession are offering paralegals; the following examples illustrate the use that the corporate sector is making of this form of labor:[42]

- An exciting opportunity has arisen for a paralegal based in Central London in a business services company: French native speaker is essential; banking and finance legal, essential; a team player; must be immediately available to begin. Salary: £14 per hour; location: London (05/04/2012).

Position: Paralegal Location: London

- An opportunity has arisen to join a young, dynamic law firm as a paralegal. The firm is a commercial practice, including current practice areas: property, litigation, wills, and probate and immigration.

---

[41] Fletcher's analysis of the Law Society's Regis Survey Data for 1993-2003 led her to conclude that "even when age, LPC results, and LPC course type were controlled for, associations between ethnicity and success in terms of training contract registrations and admissions were apparent" (2006: 9). Since then it has become far harder to obtain a training contract (fuelling the paralegal population), though, as Wilson has noted "reliable data on the scale and make-up of the paralegal workforce, both within and outside regulated legal activities are ... in short supply. Estimates vary wildly, from around 30,000 to 250,000. Official statistics suggest a figure nearer the lower end of the scale" (2012: 9). Wilson proceeded to cite the UK Commission for Employment and Skills (UKCES) study of 2010, which reported that the number of paralegals had risen from 24,509 in 2001 to 51,250 in 2010 and predicted that the commoditization of legal work and increased competition, which would result from the introduction of ABS, would fuel further increases. According to the Solicitors' Regulatory Authority (SRA) in 2009/10, around 40% of fee earners in firms regulated by the SRA are not solicitors, and for legal aid solicitor firms, diversity surveys consistently show around two out of five fee earners are non-solicitors (LSB 2012: 85, and see LSRC surveys, www.justice.gov.uk/publications/research-and-analysis/lsrc/research-publications).

[42] www.lawcareers.net/MyLCN/MyLibrary/Default.aspx?o=add&ti=Paralegal&r=2944 &u=London&ReturnUrl=%2fImmediateVacancies.aspx%3f%26utm_source% 3dTwi%23immvac2944. Since 2012, the use of paralegals and unpaid interns has increased and the conditions further deteriorated.

- You will be assisting the team of fee-earners potentially in all areas as well as the partners with various caseloads and tasks.
- The role will suit a hardworking and conscientious graduate who is mature and autonomous, and who respects the space they are given.
- Candidates will have: strong academics and ideally completed the LPC, excellent personal and communication skills, and be highly IT literate.
- Salary: £15,000 pro-rata (05/04/2012).

Generally the incentive that firms offer for these low-waged and unpaid positions is the promise of either a training contract or a move up into the next hierarchy (YLAL 2008); for instance, one respondent in my second study, who had originally wanted to be a barrister, recounted how he had taken a paralegal position at £12,000 a year in a large corporate firm because he was promised that this would constitute the 2 years' work experience (QLTS)[43] he needed to become a solicitor, after which he was also promised that he would be given a job however:

> After I had started working there I found out that everyone in the department (around 10 people) had been made similar promises – some of training contracts., some of a job (because the majority were law graduates and had passed the LPC) – but that these had never materialised.

Others had suffered a similar deception; for instance, "I have had experience of working as a paralegal in 3 firms, two of which promised training contracts when there was no real intention of giving one"; and "after 12 months at the firm (as a paralegal) I may be eligible to 'be considered' for a training contract" (responses to YLAL Survey 2008: 14). Some respondents stated that they had worked for more than four years in the hope of getting a contract.

These accounts echo those cited in research into ethnic diversity in firms (Law Society 2010), which included several of people working for nothing: "a remarkable fact that came up in nearly every focus group was that some BME solicitors were working for no pay whatsoever. Participants could relate their own experiences or experiences of friends

---

[43] The acronym QLTS stands for the Qualified Lawyers Transfers Scheme, which is the route by which lawyers from other jurisdictions (and barristers of England and Wales) can be admitted by the Solicitors' Regulation Authority (SRA) as solicitors of England and Wales (see www.sra.org.uk/qlts/).

and colleagues who had become so desperate to secure a training contract that they offered to work for free."[44]

Paralegals are further disadvantaged by the fact that the work itself rarely offers any potential for skill development, since it generally consists of basic, repetitive tasks that may have very little to do with legal practice, such as document management. The dead end nature of the work featured in many accounts; for instance, a paralegal in the banking sector said, "The work was very routinized and specialized and effectively scripted by the computer – you'd just click buttons according the stage of the case, pull out certain court forms." He went on to explain that the advocacy work (which once would have been a source of training for young solicitors) was now similarly routinized, discrete piece work outsourced to a "specialist low-cost center":[45]

> The actual advocacy was outsourced to a firm called LPC, which has offices in all major cities and which uses unqualified people who've done the BVC for mass production work, like lender re-possession hearings – you might do 30 in a day.

A British Chinese LPC graduate described her work as "monkey tasks . . . and it's so repetitive you can't learn anything . . . it's basically just a data entry job." Her subsequent comments clarify the significance of the ways in which these outsider professionals are being incorporated into the profession, namely, as the other against which the true profession defines itself: "hierarchy is fantastically important and we are just conveyancing clerks" – an utterly devalued status from which there was "no escape" because she was the wrong class, gender, and ethnicity: "I don't fit any of the boxes . . . I feel like I'm slave labor. I'm an ethnic minority and this is what it was like for my ancestors." She went on to describe how she strove to overcome this disadvantage through what Carbado (2005) has termed "surplus compliance" in her performance, which entails observing the "racial etiquette" and sig-naling happiness in menial work. This understanding of her situation chimes with the findings of the Law Society research cited earlier, that BAME solicitors felt they were expected to be "grateful" for any

---

[44] Interestingly the author of this Law Society report went on to present this situation as one of free choice: "In today's society with wrangles over minimum wage and government guidelines about the minimum amount people need to live on, it seems incredible that individuals are still prepared to work without remuneration in order to fulfill their passion to break into the legal profession" (Law Society 2010:. 62).

[45] Hardman (2010): 10.

position or salary offered to them (2010: 78), and also the accounts of some of my respondents; for instance, "I witnessed one colleague being told (by an embarrassed supervisor) that she wasn't from the right socio-economic background to be given a training contract – or words to that effect – not the right sort," and "one of my colleagues complained about her treatment, and said she felt it was racist – she was dismissed." The comments of some explicitly suggest a dual labor market (Doeringer and Piore 1971): "we were in a completely different labor market to the trainees and solicitors"; and "we had the feeling that we were kept out of sight because we didn't fit with the presentation of the firm [i.e., glossy]. Queries to the main offices were not encouraged."

The multilayered nature of the segregation of paralegal positions from the mainstream professional community means that they generally cannot offer prospects of inclusion:

> ... the promotion track was admin. worker, junior casehandler, senior casehandler – after that you might be considered for a managerial position. In other words there was no ladder out of being a paralegal – so the only escape was via a training contract – which no one got while I was there.

One way in which an intern or paralegal might be able to move on would, of course, be through training, However, the extreme working hours demanded of interns and paralegals generally left no time for this; for instance, a paralegal with a Magic Circle firm said that he "would start at 9.30 and very rarely leave before 11/12 p.m., would generally work weekends too, and there would be at least two all-nighters once a month." This man (a law graduate) wanted to do the LPC by distance learning, and was eventually forced to give up his job because it left him no time to do the course. Further, there was little evidence of firms offering support: "the only training people received was for the work they were doing – that is, there was no staff development that would assist them in moving out of that sort of low-level paralegal work. It was really just a brief induction." The YLAL survey of paralegals and interns made the same finding: "I have not come across anyone that has received any structured training" (2008: 10).

In the rare cases where training was offered, workers had to fund it themselves: "if they [the paralegals] themselves pay to sit the very expensive Law Society Immigration and Asylum Accreditation exams [and also pay themselves for the training and manual to pass the test], they may be promoted to the position of Level 1 caseworker."[46] This self-funding requirement needs to be contextualized by the extremely low levels of pay most paralegals were receiving; the following account by a respondent to the YLAL survey was not untypical:

> I started by outdoor clerking for two firms. This was very hard and felt like I was literally scratching a living, picking up half days (£30 plus travel) here and there, and occasionally the odd trial which would tide me over. Considering the rents in London I was literally living hand to mouth . . . and getting myself into debt.

Moreover, by this stage in their careers, in the words of another respondent, "most people have already accrued so much debt, they're really stuck."[47]

Complaint or redress is therefore very difficult, as a result of the combination of debt: "you just get on and do it. The financial pressure means you can't complain to anyone"; the insecurity of their conditions: "I don't know if there will be a job the next morning because my employment arrangement depends on the volume of work the firm is engaged in"; and the desperate need for a training contract: "part of the problem is that these exploited individuals are all too often loyal to the firm in the belief that it will eventually get them somewhere." As a result, respondents are highly vulnerable to bullying: "I was told by HR that if I asked about it (promises of training contracts and jobs), it would be a disciplinary offence."

The evidence (for instance LSB 2012) indicates that the use of unpaid interns extends throughout the profession.[48] The account given by one solicitor of the practices of a small High Street practice[49] in London where he briefly worked is exemplary:

> This 2 partner firm had an open policy of advertising for interns (i.e., unpaid workers) who would work with them for 3 months for the

---

[46] A level 1 caseworker signifies the lowest level of worker who is assigned her own cases to work on.

[47] In 2011 Full-time LPC fees ranged from £7,500 for the cheapest course to £13,550 at the top end. In 2015 the range was from £9000 to £14000: http://www.chambers student.co.uk/law-schools/legal-practice-course.

[48] Welsh and Aitchison (2012) predicted an 18% growth in paralegal employment over the next five years.

[49] High street practice is the term used to describe generalist law firms, usually located in the center of towns, whose work was primarily generated by the private client and local small businesses.

experience, and whom they would then replace with other unpaid short term interns. In this way they got people from the College of Law – who were all therefore either doing or had done the LPC – on the basis that this would be a 3 month probationary period and that after that, if they were good, they would get a job as a secretary – but they never did. The partner who ran the scheme was quite open that these people would be ditched after 3 months.

As a result of the dramatic impoverishment of many legal aid firms, the use of paralegals and unpaid labor is particularly common in this sector; further, it appears that their working conditions may be worse than they are in other parts of the profession (YLAL Survey 2008; Janes 2008; Davin and Navarrete 2008):

> [Name of firm] has been hiring unpaid work experience people for some time now, maybe a matter of several years. These poor work experience people have mostly already got their LPC and generally seem to work full time for nothing, for anything between 3 and 6 months before being made a "paralegal" where they mostly do admin work on a salary of £14k.

Despite these very poor working conditions and the lack of training, not all paralegals and interns in the legal aid sector were restricted to routine tasks, and, as noted earlier, some could become caseworkers. Such a promotion can, however, be a mixed blessing, since "they have to work a lot harder as they have their own caseload and targets," and it did not necessarily mean more money: "they do not actually start getting paid at the caseworker salary of £17k until they have passed their 5 month probation period, and even then, only if they are meeting the 7 chargeable hours a day target."

Others recounted being employed to do work that greatly exceeded their training and levels of expertise. For instance, some paralegals explained that they were expected to do work which is essentially that of a solicitor, and in some cases to carry the same caseloads: "I was expected to do work close to the standard of a qualified solicitor and often the same as a qualified solicitor." Yet, not only did this paralegal not have the same training and experience as a solicitor, she was also not provided with basic "resources such as a Dictaphone or work mobile phone or even a desk...." She was, nevertheless, expected to work the same hours as a solicitor and to bring in fees.

This use of large numbers of paralegals in the legal aid sector is, however, officially condoned, having been recommended in a report on the profession (Carter 2006)[50] as the model way to run a profitable legal aid firm. Yet, as respondents to the YLAL survey argued, it is questionable whether "such a large number of paralegals can be adequately supervised by one partner"; and "I have worked in a place comparable to the model envisaged by Carter ... the quality of the work was definitely substandard in that the staff were untrained, unvalued, and fairly unregulated" (YLAL Survey 2008: 18). One of my respondents described her experience at one of these "model" firms "[name of firm] is a factory, it's terrible. It's the firm which the LSC based their fixed fee system on, and which the LSC[51] cite as having helped x number of clients at the same cost as another firm might have helped far fewer clients." She went on to reflect on what this type of lawyering meant, first, for access to justice in general: "they routinely cherry pick 'negative advice cases', opening new matters to tell people their case has no merit and then closing them and claiming the fixed fee, when often the case might well have merit but be complex." Her powerlessness to exercise her discretionary judgment to act "professionally" is implicit in her subsequent reflections on the impact on the individual client: "they have huge numbers of untrained and poorly paid paralegal workers. I did unpaid work experience there in 2006, they cannot deliver a good service."

These experiences highlight the impact of these working conditions on what were once regarded as two core features of professionalism: the fiduciary duty to the client, which entails acting in her best interest; and the duty to the administration of justice, which entails abiding by legal processes and procedures. The following accounts (given by different respondents) are cited at length since they set out in some detail how both these duties may be transgressed by the conditions under which paralegals are employed:

---

[50] The Carter Review's recommendation to contain and reduce the legal aid budget through creating a competitive legal services market followed earlier moves to deregulate the legal services sector, and aimed to produce "procurement driven restructuring" in the hope that it would lead to mergers and rationalization (i.e., industrialization) of the sector (2006: 3) and the greater use of non-legally qualified fee earners. Its recommendations were enthusiastically endorsed by the New Labour government that began their implementation with the imposition of fixed and graduated fees.

[51] LSC stands for the Legal Services Commission, the executive nondepartmental body of the Ministry of Justice (MOJ), which administered the legal aid scheme. It was abolished in 2012 by LASPO and replaced by an executive agency of the MOJ.

[Working like this] is impossible without cutting corners, and from some of the files I have seen, this all too often results in the delivery a poor quality of service to the clients. One of the paralegals told me last week that our latest unpaid work experience girl who has only been at the firm for a month was last week given asylum representations to draft by my "supervisor" - supervisor in name only - with no precedent to work from and no direction as to where to look up the relevant law or country of origin information. Never having done any legal representations before, she could not finish this in the one day at work she was given and ended up taking it home and working on the representations over the weekend as she was so afraid of otherwise being dismissed from this exploitative role!

There is a culture at my firm of cutting and pasting legal advice letters, representations and even attendance notes. People will often cut and paste from precedent letters, rather than look up the law, particularly because as a general rule time spent carrying out legal research is not chargeable under legal aid, and as practitioners we are under enormous pressure to meet high chargeable hour targets that do not allow for time spent doing non-chargeable work during the day. I think precedents are useful and have their place but only if they are used in combination with legal research, because, if as legal practitioners we only work from precedents, we may be missing important issues that are relevant to our client's case but not to that of the precedent we are working from. It is not a good way to work or learn. I will not work like that – I do spend time looking up statute, case law and policy and considering how the legal research I have carried out applies to and can assist with my case, and I consider the individual facts of and try to fight every case in my caseload giving each the time they really require to progress them.

CONCLUSION

A primary preoccupation of the sociology of the professions has been with the strategies deployed to exclude individuals drawn from non-normative groups; less attention has been paid to patterns of inclusion. Yet, the transformation of the solicitors' profession in England and Wales is both a story of the general impact of neoliberalism, and also of its specific response to outsiders' usurpationary projects and the way this can be related to the United Kingdom's aristocratic heritage. The data discussed earlier illustrates how the capitalization and industrialization of firms has led to the increasing routinization of work, and its shifting into ever more poorly rewarded and spatially segregated sectors of the workforce (Brown and Lauder 2012). In the corporate sector, this downgrading of legal expertise forms part of a countervailing stress on entrepreneurialism, and commodification of upper middle-class Englishness. As a result, those who embody gentlemanly professionalism are likely both to obtain training contracts and to be fast-tracked. By contrast, the human capital of those of the "wrong" ethnicity, class, and gender is unlikely to compensate for their lack of cultural capital, but instead rationalizes their allocation to the routine, standardized legal work that the professional factory requires, either as paralegals or lower status solicitors. As Dixon noted in a 2011 report for the Law Society, "it is likely that the delegation to unqualified staff of work that solicitors have done traditionally will continue and gather pace" (2011: 6); his subsequent comments exemplify the traditional professional closure strategy: "there is nothing wrong with an oversupply of candidates for training contracts. It is in the best interests of the profession that many people aspire to join it but it is not necessarily in the best interests of the profession that all of them should become solicitors. If anyone who wants to could become a solicitor, the profession would lose much of its prestige" (Dixon 2011: 15)

Thus the varying degrees of exclusion/inclusion in the professional community discussed here exemplify the disjuncture between the neoliberal discourse of choice and agency and the reality of a profession that continues to practise social closure. They also illustrate the notion underpinning Agamben's (1998) conception of bare life, namely, that inclusion can be a social mechanism for exclusion (Carbado 2005: 639). Or, to put it another way, the insecure and marginalized terms on which some professionals are included locks them into a parallel socio-spatial reality thereby simultaneously positioning them as lesser or inauthentic professionals while reconstituting the core or elite of the profession as the property of upper-class white males.

The impoverishment of the other end of the professional spectrum has institutionalized the use of LPC graduates as cheap and even free labor, and means that they are particularly disposable (Elliott and Lemert 2009. The fact that in the legal aid sector this extreme marginality is due in large part to government retreat from anything other than a nominal commitment to access to justice for the poor[52]

---

[52] Indeed, the state is retreating from responsibility for civil law altogether, as witnessed by the degradation of court facilities, growing pressure on people to use ADR (Genn 2012) and massive hikes in court fees.

underlines the specificity of the profession, that is, as discussed in my introduction, the need to understand its current configuration as a product of the contemporary socio-historical matrix. Hence the possibility that appeared briefly to exist from the late 1960s to around the early 1980s of a democratic justice system and a legal profession genuinely committed to representing a diverse citizenry and according people from all parts of society access to justice and dignity – and likewise, the contemporary obverse of this possibility: a polarized profession in a polarized society, a professional precariat serving a precariat (Crouch 2011).

Considering the character of the contemporary profession through the lens of young professionals and their working conditions also highlights the material ways in which the ideal of law and hence of the profession has been corroded in a time shaped by the increasing reliance on market mechanisms and the rhetorical assault on justice as a public good. Autonomy and expertise, once considered core traits of professionalism, are largely precluded by the strict cost pressures, time constraints, and routinized practices, which characterize young legal aid professionals' working conditions. As a result, my data, that of other studies (YLAL 2008), and the results of peer review[53] clearly suggest that young lawyers in this sector are routinely obliged to give a service that is barely competent, thereby transgressing the fundamental legitimating principles of the profession and the justice system – fidelity to the law and to the client. In the corporate sector, the problem is, in a way, the reverse: here the elite of the profession, as a privileged group saturated in class, masculinity, and whiteness, survives both materially and symbolically, still able to act as the engine room of capital and express the idea of a universal form of law. Yet in practice its autonomy has similarly been eroded, but here it is because clients' power is such that it has taken precedence over lawyers' duty to the law and to the administration of justice (Markovits 2008;[54] Simon 2010; Douglas

---

[53] 52% of legal aid firms were found to be only at threshold competence, 11% below and 1% failed. Only 34% were competence plus (LSB 2012: 57, https://research.legalservicesboard.org.uk/wp-content/media/Impacts-of-the-LSA-2012-Final-baseline-report.pdf).

[54] Markovits argues that "adversary advocacy" requires lawyers to "lie" (deceive in various ways) and "cheat" (take advantage of rules in ways not intended by their drafters) on the grounds of "the principles of lawyer loyalty and client control that ... establish the center of adversary advocacy" (2008: 88); Simon attacks this position, and evokes the lawyer ethic implied by purposivism, which strives to

Scott 2013) – as Linklaters' recent subservience to Lehman Brothers vividly demonstrated (Kershaw and Moorhead 2011)[55]. And as in the legal aid sector, the capacity of young lawyers to withstand pressure to act unethically is severely weakened by their precarious position.

Thus, the dramatic increase in law graduates over the course of the last 20 years is a central part of the story both of what we might term the pseudo-modernization of the United Kingdom and the profession's transformation. While this increase has been underpinned by the neoliberal discourse of agency and aspiration, in practice it has produced a pool of people whose capacity to refuse the marginalized positions they are being slotted into is fettered by both this very discourse and their indebtedness. At the same time, as Wacquant argues, the story is also part of the wider consequences of neoliberal capitalism: "with the onset of desocialized wage labor, employment no longer supplies a common temporal and social framework because the terms of the labor contract are increasingly volatile and individualized, job tenures are shorter and unstable, and a growing number of positions do not entail a collective mechanism of protection against material deprivation illness or joblessness, not to mention adequate retirement" (2008: 267).

Evidently, there exists a tension between this extension of the logic of flexible capitalism to legal professionalism and many of those features that were once held to be its distinguishing marks, such as its special ethicality and collegiality. Further, the highly exploitative relationships my respondents recounted run counter to claims the profession might seek to make to represent equity and justice – and possibly legalism as well. On the other hand, research into the profession and diversity has frequently suggested that in practice the profession has a cavalier

---

directly connect the lawyer's service to individual clients to the values that underlie applicable legal norms (2010).

[55] Kershaw and Moorhead (2011) highlight the tension between the public interest duty and the duty to the client for corporate lawyers, giving as an instance of a failure in ethical duty the legal opinion given by Linklaters, a Magic Circle firm, which facilitated transactions that, according to Lehman's Bankruptcy Examiner, were solely designed to give the appearance that Lehman was de-leveraging. A newspaper editorial illustrates the damage this practice does to the profession's ethical reputation: "Linklaters and Ernst and Young will say they were only following the rules but auditors and lawyers are professionals and they gave Lehmans' highly questionable practices a sheen of respectability. Lehman's Advisers were Guard Dogs that didn't Bark," The Observer, 14 March 2010.

attitude toward legalities in its own workplace.[56] The result for these outsider professionals is an existence which, to paraphrase Fanon (1963),[57] entails passing like shadows on the edge of professional experience, enserfed by their precariousness which, as Bourdieu has observed, is the new mode of domination.

REFERENCES

Abel, R. (2003) *English Lawyers between Market and State*, Oxford University Press.

Agamben, G. (1998) *Homo Sacer: Sovereign Power and Bare Life*, Stanford, Stanford University Press.

Anderson, P. (1964) "Origins of the Present Crisis," *New Left Review*, 1 (23):26–53.

Archer, L. (2007) "Diversity, Equality and Higher Education: A Critical Reflection on the Ab/uses of Equity Discourse within Widening Participation," *Teaching in Higher Education*, 12 (5/6):635–653.

Arthurs, H. W. and Kreklewich, R. (1996) "Law, Legal Institutions and the Legal Profession in the New Economy," *Osgoode Hall Law Journal*, 34:1–60

Arthurs, H. W. (2001) "The State We're In: Legal Education in Canada's New Political Economy," 20*Windsor Year Book Access Just.*:35–54.

Ashley, L (2010) "Making a Difference? The Use (and Abuse) of Diversity Management at the UK's Elite Law Firms," *Work, Employment and Society*, 24(4):711–727.

Ashley, L., and Empson, L. (2013) "Differentiation and Discrimination: Understanding Social Class and Social Exclusion in Leading Law Firms," *Human Relations*, 66(2):219–244.

Ashley, L., Duberley, J., Sommerlad, H. and Scholarios, D. (2015) *A Qualitative Evaluation of Non-Educational Barriers to the Elite Professions*, London: Social Mobility and Child Poverty Commission.

Barmes, L. (2012) "Learning from Case Law Accounts of Marginalized Working," in J. Fudge, S. McCrystal and K. Sankaran (eds.), *Regulating*

[56] Consonant with my earlier discussion of the persistence of pre-modern, patron client relationships within the profession, despite the supposed erasure of the traditional kinship culture of law firms, we might therefore suggest that legal employers, like other business people, tend to favor the personalist, non-legal over formal, legal practices (Macaulay 1963); see Law Society (2010) generally, and particularly pages 78–78, for law firms' poor employment practices.

[57] Fanon's conceptualization of the notion of race is as a tightly woven web that awaits the arrival of individuals and incorporates them into the framework (Fanon, 1967: 134), operating as a straitjacket on individuals' agency: "the meaning . . . was already there, pre-existing, [and] waiting" (id.).

Legal Work: Challenging Legal Boundaries, Onati International Series in Law and Society Oxford: Hart.

Bell, M. (2012) "Between Flexicurity and Fundamental Social Rights: The EU Directives on Atypical Work," *European Law Review*, 37:31–48.

Bourdieu, P. (1986) *Distinction*, London: Routledge.

(1996) *Rules of Art*, Cambridge: Polity Press.

(1998) *Acts of Resistance: Against the Tyranny of the Market*, Cambridge: Polity Press.

Bourdieu, P. and Passeron (1977) *Reproduction in Education, Society and Culture*, London: Sage Publications.

Bradley, H. (1996) *Fractured Identities: Changing Patterns of Inequality*, Cambridge: Polity Press.

Brown, P. and Lauder, H. (2011) *The Global Auction*, Oxford: Oxford University Press.

(2012) "The Great Transformation in the Global Labour Market," *Soundings*, 51 (Summer):41–53.

Brown, W. (2005) "Neoliberalism and the End of Liberal Democracy," in *Edgework: Critical Essays on Knowledge and Politics*, Princeton, NJ:Princeton University Press.

Burton, L. (2012) "Revealed: Females Make up Less Than 10 Per Cent of Top 100's Equity Partner Ranks," *Legal Week*, 24 October, www.thelawyer.com/revealed-females-make-up-less-than-10-per-cent-of-top-100s-equity-partner-ranks/1015190.article.

Cabinet Office (2009). *Unleashing Aspirations: The Final Report of the Panel on Fair Access to the Professions*. London: Cabinet Office http://webarchive.nationalarchives.gov.uk/+/http:/www.cabinetoffice.gov.uk/media/227102/fair-access.pdf, accessed 1/8/12.

Carbado, D. and Gulati, G. (2000) "Working Identity," *Cornell Law Review*, 85:1259–1308.

Carbado, D. W. (2005) "Racial Naturalization," *American Quarterly*, 57 (3):633–658.

Carrier, J. (2012) "The Trouble with Class," *European Journal of Sociology*, 53 (3):263–284.

Carter, L. (2006) *Legal Aid: A Market Based Approach to Reform Lord Carter's Review of Legal Aid Procurement*, London: MOJ, www.lccsa.org.uk/assets/documents/consultation/carter%20review%2013072006.pdf, accessed 1/8/12.

Collier, R. (2005) "'Be Smart, Be Successful, Be Yourself . . .'?: Representations of the Training Contract and Trainee Solicitor in Advertising by Large Law Firms," *International Journal of the Legal Profession*, 12 (1):51–92.

Crouch, C. (2011) *The Strange Non-death of Neo-liberalism*, Cambridge: Polity Press.

Davin, S. and Navarrete, M. (2008) "YLAL Survey Reveals Unfair Treatment of Paralegals," *Legal Action*, March 2008:8–9.

DCA (2005) *Increasing Diversity in the Legal Profession – A report on Government Proposals*, Department of Constitutional Affairs: London.

Derber, C. (1982) *Professionals as Workers: Mental Labor in Advanced Capitalism*, Boston, MA: GK Hall & Company.

Dezalay, Y. and Sugarman, D. (1995) *Professional Competition and Professional Power: Lawyers, Accountants and the Social Construction of Markets*, London: Routledge.

Dixon, D. (2011) *Entry to the Solicitors' Profession 1980–2010*, London: Law Society.

Doeringer, P. B., and Piore, M. J. (1971) *Internal Labor Markets and Manpower Analysis*, London: ME Sharpe.

Douglas-Scott, S. (2013) *Law after Modernity*, Oxford: Hart.

Dorling, D. (2010) "The Return to Elitism in Education," *Soundings*, 44 (Spring):35–46.

Du Gay, P. (1996) *Consumption and Identity at Work*, London: Sage.

(2004) "Against 'Enterprise' (but not against enterprise, for that would make no sense)," *Organization*, 11(1):37–57.

Durkheim, E. (1957) *Professional Ethics and Civic Morals*, London: Routledge.

Dustmann, C. and Theodoropoulos, N. (2006) *Ethnic Immigrants Miss Out in UK Job Market Despite Higher Educational Qualifications*, UCL Centre for Research and Analysis of Migration (CReAM) bulletin.

Ehrenreich, B. (2002) *Nickel and Dimed: Undercover in Low-Wage America*, London: Granta Books.

Elliott, A. and Lemert, C. (2009) *The New Individualism*, London: Routledge.

Empson, L. (2007) *Managing the Modern Law Firm: New Challenges, New Perspectives*, Oxford: Oxford University Press.

Evetts, J. (2012) "Professionalism in Turbulent Times: Changes, Challenges and Opportunities," delivered at Propel Inaugural Conference: Professions and Professional Learning in Turbulent Times: Emergent Practices and Transgressive Knowledges, Stirling University, 11 May, www.propel.stir.ac.uk/downloads/JuliaEvetts-FullPaper.pdf, accessed 5/5/13.

Fanon, F. (1963) *Wretched of the Earth*, New York: Grove Press.

(1967) *Black Skins, White Masks*, New York: Grove Press.

Faulconbridge, J. and Muzio, D. (2009) "The Financialization of Large Law Firms: Situated Discourses and Practices of Reorganization," *Journal of Economic Geography*, 9(5): 641–661.

Fletcher, Nina (2006) *Paralegals Study – Analysis of REGIS Data August 2006* [Unpublished], The Law Society.

Flood, J. (1996) "Megalawyering in the Global Order: The Cultural, Social and Economic Transformation of Global Legal Practice," *International Journal of the Legal Profession*, 3:169–214.

Fournier, V. (1999) "The Appeal to 'Professionalism' as a Disciplinary Mechanism," *The Sociological Review*, 47:280–307.

Francis, A. and Sommerlad, H. (2009) "Access to Legal Work Experience and Its Role in the (Re)production of Legal Professional Identity," *International Journal of the Legal Profession*, 16 (1):63–86.

(2010) "Access to Legal Work Experience and Its Role in the (Re) production of Legal Professional identity," www.ukcle.ac.uk/research/ projects/francis.html, accessed 5/5/13.

Fraser, N. (2013) *Fortunes of Feminism: From State-Managed Capitalism to Neoliberal Crisis*, London: Verso.

Freeman, R. (2011) "Drivers and Consequences of Growing Inequalities," *OECD Ministerial Meeting on Social Policy Forum*, Paris, 2 May, www .ukcle.ac.uk/research/projects/francis.html.

(2012) "Public Lecture: Toward Economic Feudalism? Inequality, Financialization and Democracy," *Ralph Miliband Programme: The Future of the Left*, LSE, www.lse.ac.uk/publicEvents/miliband/201112Lecture Series.aspx#DynamicJumpMenuManager_1_Anchor_5, accessed 5/5/13.

Fudge, J. and Owens, R. (2006) "Precarious Work, Women and the New Economy: The Challenge to Legal Norms," in J. Fudge and R. Owens (eds.) *Precarious Work, Women and the New Economy: The Challenge to Legal Norms*, Onati International Series in Law and Society, Oxford: Hart: 3–28.

Galanter, M. S., and Palay, T. M. (1999) "Large Law Firm Misery: It's the Tournament, Not the Money," *Vand. L. Rev.*52:953–971.

Genn, H. (2012) "Why the Privatisation of Civil Justice Is a Rule of Law Issue," 36th FA Mann Lecture, Lincolns Inn, London, 19 November, www.ucl.ac.uk/laws/academics/profiles/docs/Hazel/36th%20F%20A% 20Mann%20Lecture%20Website.pdf.

Grey, C. (1998) "On Being a Professional in a 'Big Six' firm." Accounting, *Organizations and Society*, 23(5):569–587.

Hagan, J. and Kay, F. (1995) *Gender in Practice: A Study of Lawyers' Lives*, Oxford: Oxford University Press.

Hall, K. (2013) "Diversity League Table Shows Promotion Gap," *Law Society Gazette*, 11 November, www.lawgazette.co.uk/5038711.article? utm_source=dispatch&utm_medium=email&utm_campaign=GAZ121113).

(2013) "Glass Ceiling Most Apparent in Magic Circle," *Law Society Gazette*, 7 November, www.lawgazette.co.uk/practice/glass-ceiling-most-apparent-in-magic-circle/5038631.article.

Hall, S. (2011) "The Neoliberal Revolution," *Soundings* 48:9–27.

Hanlon, G. (1999) *Lawyers, the State and the Market: Professionalism Revisited*, Basingstoke: Macmillan.

Hanlon, G. and Shapland, J. (1997) "Professional Disintegration. The Case of Law," in J. Broadbent, M. Deitrich and J. Roberts (eds.) *The End of the Professions?*, London: Routledge: 45.

Harcourt, B. (2011) *The Illusion of Free Markets: Punishment and the Myth of Natural Order*, Boston, M.A: Harvard University Press.

Hardman, L. (2010) "Are You Prepared for the Future?" *Legal Week Bench-marker*, 10–11 April: www.legalweek.com/digital_assets/3861/Future_Lawyers_Benchmarker_Report_April_2010_with_new_logo.pdf.

Harris, J. (2013) "Diversity Efforts Fail to Pay Off at Top End of Profession," *The Lawyer*, 5 August, www.thelawyer.com/analysis/the-lawyer-management/management-news/diversity-efforts-fail-to-pay-off-at-top-end-of-profession/3008182.article.

Harvey, D. (1989) *The Condition of Postmodernity*, Oxford: Basil Blackwell.

(2007) *A Brief History of Neo-liberalism*, Oxford: Oxford University Press.

(2011) *The Enigma of Capital: And the Crises of Capitalism*, London: Profile Books.

Hoare, S. (2006) "Ethnic Minorities Make Up Only 3 Per Cent of UK 100 Partners," *The Lawyer*, 3 April.

Janes, L. (2008) "Paralegals in Legal Aid: A Growing and Unhealthy Dependency?" *Socialist Lawyer*, www.younglegalaidlawyers.org/node/203, accessed 5/5/13.

Jewel, L. (2008) "Bourdieu and American Legal Education: How Law Schools Reproduce Social Stratification and Class Hierarchy," 56*Buff. L. Rev.*:1155–1224.

Keep, E. and Mayhew, K. (1999) "The Assessment: Knowledge, Skills, and Competitiveness," *Oxford Review of Economic Policy*, 15 (1): 1–15.

Kershaw, D. and Moorhead, R. (2011) "High Risk and Hard Cases: Does the Collapse of Lehman Brothers Tell Us Anything about Regulation of the Legal Profession," Paper Submitted to SLS Conference, Cambridge, September.

Krause, E. (1999) *Death of the Guilds: Professions, States, and the Advance of Capitalism, 1930 to the Present*, New Haven, Conneticut: Yale University Press.

Kritzer, H. M. (1999) "The Professions Are Dead, Long Live the Professions: Legal Practice in a Postprofessional World," *Law and Society Review*, 33 (3):713–759.

Kumra, S. and Vinnicombe, S. (2008) "A Study of the Promotion to Partner Process in a Professional Service Firm: How Women are Disadvantaged," *British Journal of Management*, 51 (19):65–74.

The Law Society (2010) "Ethnic Diversity in Law Firms – Understanding the Barriers," May, www.lawsociety.org.uk/representation/research-trends/research-publications/documents/ethnic-diversity-in-law-firms—understanding-the-barriers/.

(2013) *Annual Statistical Report*, London: Law Society.

The Lawyer (2011) "Magic Circle Moots Joint Social Mobility Strategy," 4 April, www.thelawyer.com/04-april-2011/1966.issue, accessed 1/8/11.

The Lawyer Diversity Report (2010) www.google.co.uk/search?q=The+Lawyer+Diversity+Report+2010&oq=The+Lawyer+Diversity+Report

+2010&aqs=chrome..69i57.1334j0j4&sourceid=chrome&espv=210&es_
sm=122&ie=UTF-8.

Lee, R. (1992) "From Profession to Business: The Rise and Rise of the City
Law Firm," *Journal of Law & Society*, 19:31–48.

Legal Services Board (LSB) (2012) *Market Impacts of the Legal Services
Act – Interim Baseline Report April 2012*, London: Legal Services Board,
https://research.legalservicesboard.org.uk/wp-content/media/Impacts-
of-the-LSA-2012-Interim-baseline-report.pdf.

Legal Week (2012) "Employment, Equal Opportunities and Diversity:
More Equal Than Others," www.legalweek.com/legal-week/news/
1159976/employment-equal-opportunities-diversity-more-equal-than-
others.

Loughlin, M. (2000) *Sword and Scales: An Examination of the Relationship
Between Law and Politics*, Oxford: Hart Publishing.

Macaulay, S. (1963) "Non-Contractual Relations in Business. A Preliminary
Study," *American Sociological Review*, 28:55–67.

Markovits, D. (2008) *A Modern Legal Ethics: Adversary Advocacy in a Democratic Age*, Princeton, NJ: Princeton University Press.

Marquand, D. (1988) *The Unprincipled Society: New Demands and Old Politics*,
London: J. Cape.

Matsuda, M. (1989) "Public Response to Racist Speech: Considering the
Victim's Story," *Michigan Law Review*, 87:2320–2381.

Mayhew, K., and Keep, E. (1999) "The Assessment: Knowledge, Skills, and
Competitiveness," *Oxford Review of Economic Policy*, 15(1):1–15.

Michaels, E., Handfield-Jones, H., and Axelrod, B. (2001) *The War for Talent*,
Boston, MA: Harvard Business School Press.

Ministry of Justice (2010) *Proposal for the Reform of Legal Aid in England and
Wales: Ministry of Justice, Consultation Paper CP12/10*, Ministry of Justice,
London: The Stationery Office.

    (2011) *Legal Aid Reform in England and Wales: The Government Response*
Cmn 8072. London: Stationary Office. www.official-documents.gov.uk/
document/cm80/8072/8072.pdf.

Muzio, D., Brock, D. M., and Suddaby, R. (2013) "Professions and Institutional Change: Towards an Institutionalist Sociology of the Professions." *Journal of Management Studies*, 50(5):699–721.

Milburn, A. (2012) "Fair Access to Professional Careers: [Progress Report]"
(Cabinet Office) (Web address: https://update.cabinetoffice.gov.uk/sites/
default/files/resources/IR_FairAccess_acc2.pdf)

Otterburn Legal Consulting (2011) *The Law Society: Impact of the MOJ Green
Paper Proposals on Legal Aid Firms, February*, London: The Law Society,
www.otterburn.co.uk/legalaidreport.pdf.

Perkin, H. (1989) *The Rise of Professional Society: England Since 1880*, London:
Routledge.

Pleasence, P., Balmer, N., and Moorhead, R. (2012) *Time of Change: Solicitors' Firms in England and Wales*, London: The Law Society, Legal Services Board, Ministry of Justice.

Pink, D. (2001) *Free Agent Nation: How America's New Independent Workers Are Transforming the Way We Live*, New York: Warner Books.

Pongratz, H., and Voss, G. (2003) "From Employee to 'Entreployee': Towards a 'Self Entrepreneurial' Workforce?," *Concepts and Transformation* 8 (3):239–254.

Purcell, K., Pitcher, J., and Simm, C. (1999) *Working Out: Graduates' Early Experiences of the Labour Market*, Manchester: Careers Service Unit.

Rolfe, H. and Anderson, T. (2002) *A Firm Decision: The Recruitment of Trainee Solicitors*, London: The Law Society, Research Study 42.

Ross, A. (2009) *Nice Work If You Can Get It: Life and Labor in Precarious Times*, New York and London: NYU Press.

Rustin, M. (2011) "The Crisis of a Social System," *Soundings*, 48 (Summer): 40–53.

Sako, M. (2010) *Possible Futures for International Law Firms in the Future of Legal Services: Emerging Thinking*, London: Legal Services Board, 20–22.

Sandefur, R. (2007) "Staying Power: The Persistence of Social Inequality in Shaping Lawyer Stratification and Lawyers' Persistence in the Profession," *Sw. U. L. Rev*, 36(3):539–556.

Sennett, R. (1999) *The Corrosion of Character*, New York: Norton.

Shattock, M. (2003) *Managing Successful Universities*, Milton Keynes: Society for Research into Higher Education and Open University Press.

Shearing, C. D. (1983) "Private Security: Implications for Social Control." *Social Problems*, 30(5):493–506.

Shearing, C. (2001) "Punishment and the Changing Face of the Governance." *Punishment & Society*, 3(2):203–220.

Shiner, M. (1999), *Entry into the Legal Professions: The Law Student Cohort Study*, Year 5, London: The Law Society.

(2000) "Young, Gifted and Blocked! Entry to the Solicitor's Profession," in P. Thomas (ed.) *Discriminating Lawyers*, London: Cavendish.

Sidaway, J. and Punt, T. (1997) *Paralegal Staff in Solicitors' Firms*, RPPU Law Society, London, Research Study No. 23.

Simon, W. (2010) "Role Differentiation and Lawyers' Ethics: A Critique of Some Academic Perspectives," *The Georgetown Journal of Legal Ethics*, 23 (4):987–1010.

Sommerlad, H. (1995) "Managerialism and the Legal Professional: A New Professional Paradigm," *International Journal of the Legal Profession* 2(2/3):159–185.

(1999) "The Implementation of Quality Initiatives and the New Public Management in the Legal Aid Sector in England and Wales:

Bureaucratisation, Stratification and Surveillance," *International Journal of the Legal Profession* 6:311–343.

(2004) "Some Reflections on the Relationship between Citizenship, Access to Justice and the Reform of Legal Aid," *Journal of Law & Society*, 31 (3):345–368.

(2007) "Researching and Theorizing the Processes of Professional Identity Formation," *Journal of Law & Society*, 34 (2):190–217.

(2011) "The Commercialisation of Law and the Enterprising Legal Practitioner: Continuity and Change," *International Journal of the Legal Profession*, 18 (1–2):73–108.

(2012) "Minorities, Merit, and Misrecognition in the Globalized Profession," *Fordham Law Review*, 80:2482–2512.

Sommerlad, H. and Sanderson, P. (1998) *Gender, Choice and Commitment*, Aldershot: Ashgate.

(2011) *Training and Regulating Those Providing Publicly Funded Legal Advice Services: A Case Study of Civil Provision*, London: Ministry of Justice, www.justice.gov.uk/latest-updates/training-regulating-legal-advice.htm.

(2013) "Social justice on the Margins: The Future of the Not for Profit Sector as Providers of Legal Advice in England and Wales," *Journal of Social Welfare & Family Law*, 35 (3): 305–327.

Sommerlad, H., Webley, L., Muzio, D., Tomlinson, J., and Duff, L. (2010) *Diversity in the Legal Profession in England and Wales: A Qualitative Study of Barriers and Individual Choices*, London: Legal Services Board, www.legalservicesboard.org.uk/what_we_do/Research/Publications/pdf/lsb_diversity_in_the_legal_profession_final_rev.pdf.

Standing, G (2011) *The Precariat: The New Dangerous Class*, London: Bloomsbury Academic.

Stedman Jones, D. (2012) *Masters of the Universe: Hayek, Friedman, and the Birth of Neoliberal Politics*, Princeton, NJ: Princeton University Press.

Sutton Trust (2009) "The Educational Backgrounds of Leading Lawyers, Journalists, Vice-Chancellors, Politicians, Medics and Chief Executives," www.suttontrust.com/research/educational-backgrounds-for-submission/ST MilburnSubmission.pdf.

Susskind, R. (2010) *The End of Lawyers?: Rethinking the Nature of Legal Services*, Oxford: Oxford University Press.

Swift, J. and Manning, L. (2011) "Magic Circle Moots Joint Social Mobility Strategy," *Lawyer 2B*, 4 April, http://l2b.thelawyer.com/magic-circle-moots-joint-social-mobility-strategy/1007521.article?PageNo=2&SortOrder=dateadded&PageSize=10#comments.

Thomas, P. and Rees, A. (2000) Law Students – Getting in and Getting on, in P. Thomas (ed.) *Discriminating Lawyers*, London: Cavendish Publishing: 19–40.

Vignaendra, S. (2001) *Social Class and Entry into the Solicitor's Profession*, Research Study 41, London: The Law Society.

Wacquant, L. (2008) *Urban Outcasts: A Comparative Sociology of Advanced Marginality*, Cambridge: Polity Press.

(2009a) *Punishing the Poor: The Neo-liberal Government of Social Insecurity*, Durham and London: Duke University Press.

(2009b) "Sustaining the City in the Face of Advanced Marginality." in Mohsen Mostafavi (ed.) *Ecological Urbanism: Sustaining the City*, Cambridge: MIT Press : 354–357.

Walzer, M. (1984) *Spheres of Justice: A defence of Pluralism and Equality*, Oxford: Martin Robertson.

Welsh, C. and Aitchinson, G. (2012) *Findings from Research of 'Paralegals' Employed in the Legal Sector and Related Employer Apprenticeship Ambition*, Sheffield: Skills for Justice.

Wilkins, D. and Gulati, M. (1996) "Why Are There So Few Black Lawyers in Corporate Law Firm? An Institutional Analysis," *Calif Law Review*, 84:493–625.

Wilson, A. (2012) "Future Workforce Demand in the Legal Services Briefing Paper for Legal Education and Training Review 2/2012," Warwick Institute for Employment Research, 25 September, http://letr.org.uk/wp-content/uploads/The-Changing-Demand-for-Skills-in-the-Legal-Services-Sector-Full-v2-2.pdf.

Witz, A. (1992) *Professions and Patriarchy*, London: Routledge.

Yeatman, A. (1996) "The New Contractualism: Management Reform or a New Approach to Governance?" in G. Davis and P. Weller (eds.) *New Ideas, Better Government*, St. Leonards, Australia: Allen and Unwin.

Young Legal Aid Lawyers (2008) "Paralegals Working In Legal Aid: An Unhealthy Dependency?" A Report by Young Legal Aid Lawyers, www.younglegalaidlawyers.org/sites/default/files/Releases_Responses/YLAL%20Paralegal%20Survey%20Report_280208.pdf.

3

INEQUALITY AND OPPORTUNITY IN THE
CAREERS OF DIVERSE ATTORNEYS

WHICH KINDS OF LAW FIRMS HAVE THE MOST MINORITY LAWYERS?

*Organizational context and the representation of African-Americans, Latinos, and Asian-Americans**

FIONA M. KAY AND ELIZABETH H. GORMAN

Over the last fifty years, large law firms have grown to employ hundreds or even thousands of lawyers in multiple offices across the United States and abroad. To what extent have these dramatic changes in law firm size and structure been matched by changes in the hiring and retention of ethnic and racial minorities? Although large US firms have opened their doors to lawyers from diverse racial and cultural backgrounds, including both women and men, the pace of change in such firms has been slow. Since the late 1980s, the percentage of minority law school graduates has more than doubled, from 10% to 24%, but as of 2012 minorities still constituted only 12.9% of major firm lawyers. Furthermore, minority representation steadily declines with increasing hierarchical rank within major firms. In 2012, minorities accounted for 29.5% of summer associates, 20.3% of regular associates, and a mere

* The authors acknowledge that the data analyzed in this study were licensed to them by the National Association for Law Placement (NALP). The views and conclusions stated herein are those of the authors and do not necessarily reflect the views of NALP or of any individuals associated with NALP. This research was supported by a grant from the Law School Admissions Council. The authors thank Emerald Group Publishing Ltd. for permission to incorporate into this chapter materials that previously appeared in "Racial and Ethnic Minority Representation in Large U.S. Law Firms," *Studies in Law, Politics and Society* 52: 211–238 (2010). The authors also acknowledge that portions of this chapter draw on their previously published article, "Developmental Practices, Organizational Culture, and Minority Representation in Organizational Leadership: The Case of Partners in Large U.S. Law Firms," *The Annals of the American Academy of Political and Social Science* 639: 91–113 (2012).

263

6.7% of partners in such firms (National Association for Law Place-ment 2012). Despite the importance of this continuing underrepresen-tation, research attention to the issue has been surprisingly sparse. Whereas gender inequality in law firms has generated an extensive research literature (see, e.g., Beckman and Phillips 2005; Epstein, Sauté, Oglensky, and Gever 1995; Gorman 2005, 2006; Gorman and Kmec 2009; Hagan and Kay 1995; Kay and Hagan 2003; Noonan, Corcoran and Courant 2007), we were able to locate only a handful of studies of the presence and success of racial and ethnic minorities (reviewed below).

To begin to address this knowledge gap, we ask which kinds of firms have higher or lower proportions of minorities among their lawyers. We begin by exploring the relationship between minority presence and organizational size, organizational economic resources, and aspects of firm structure. Organizational size is usually associated with more bureaucratic structure and with greater visibility and susceptibility to external pres-sures, both of which may push firms toward racial equality. Organizational resources may enable firms to pursue diversity even if it is financially costly, or they may spark fierce competition among lawyers that aggra-vates disadvantage for minorities. Elements of organizational structure may affect minority associates' partnership prospects as well as their inclination to remain with their firms. With respect to each dimension, we pose three central questions. First, does variation on this characteristic correspond to variation in the overall presence of minority lawyers? Second, how is this characteristic associated with minority presence at different levels of the law firm hierarchy? Third, does this organizational characteristic affect African-Americans, Latinos, and Asian-Americans in similar ways, or does it operate differently for different minority groups?

After this initial inquiry, we focus our attention on firms' formal and informal practices relating to the professional development of associates in general – not those targeted specifically at minorities – and ask whether such practices are associated with minority representa-tion among partners. Research in a variety of professional and corporate workplaces suggests that minorities typically experience a disadvantage in access to developmental experiences such as mentoring and challen-ging assignments. Formal developmental practices can potentially offset this disadvantage and narrow any resulting racial differences in skills and knowledge. Informal practices and norms can lead senior lawyers to offer mentoring and developmental assignments widely, rather than only to junior lawyers with whom they are comfortable or whom they perceive as future stars. We explore these questions using a national sample of more than 1,300 offices of corporate law firms across the United States.

PREVIOUS RESEARCH ON MINORITIES IN LAW FIRMS

Explanations for minorities' low rates of persistence and success in major US law firms have largely focused on the behavior of individuals. On the one hand, there could be racial differences in individual lawyers' preferences and qualifications. On the other hand, decision-makers acting on behalf of the firm – partners responsible for hiring, assignment, or promotion decisions – could harbor conscious or unconscious racial preferences.

One possible explanation for the underrepresentation of racial minorities in law firms is that minority lawyers are simply less interested in working in corporate law firms. However, the existing evidence tends to undermine that argument. Analyzing data from several sources, Sander (2006) found that similar proportions of white and minority law students have aspirations to work in large corporate law firms. Another study found that, after controlling for constraints like academic grades and educational loans, black graduates of elite law schools were *more* likely to take jobs at corporate law firms than were their white counterparts (Kornhauser and Revesz 1995). It is also possible that minorities enter large law firms with lower levels of relevant abilities and skills than their white counterparts, which would place them at a disadvantage when they come under consideration for challenging work assignments or promotions.[1] There is some evidence for this view. On average, minority law students' grades are lower than those of white law students (Clydesdale 2004; Sander 2004, 2006), and large law firms seem to be willing to accept somewhat lower grades when hiring minorities than when hiring whites (Sander 2006). However, large law firms tend to hire minorities only from a small number of elite law schools (Wilkins and Gulati 1996), and firms' grade cut-offs for such schools are usually lower than for lesser-ranked schools.[2]

---

[1] Importantly, this explanation does not necessarily blame minorities for any such deficits, which could be the result of inadequate educational, cultural, and social opportunities during youth and early adulthood.

[2] Wilkins and Gulati (1996) report that 70% of all the black partners listed in the *Minority Partners Handbook* in 1995 graduated from one of eleven elite schools – a

On the other side of the employment relationship, partners involved in selection decisions may favor whites, intentionally or unintentionally.[3] For one thing, decision-makers are likely to feel a conscious or unconscious "in-group preference" for their own racial or ethnic group (see Hewstone, Rubin, and Willis 2002; Hogg 2003). Consistent with this argument, when a minority group is better represented among firm partners, more members of that group are subsequently hired as associates (Chambliss and Uggen 2000). For another, racial stereotypes may distort partners' impressions and evaluations of minority associates regardless of whether the partners consciously endorse those stereotypes (see Fiske 1998; Fiske et al. 2002). As an example, in García-López's (2008) qualitative study, female Mexican-American lawyers perceived that their contributions and competence were undervalued within their firms.

As a result of processes on both sides of the employment relationship, minority lawyers' experience in large law firms is often different from that of their white peers. Minority associates are less likely to receive the mentoring and challenging assignments that are essential for developing skills needed for success (Sander 2006; Wilkins and Gulati 1996). Minority lawyers' earnings are lower (Ornstein 2001, 2004). Compared to their white peers, they are less likely to be promoted to partnership and more likely to be made non-equity partners (Chambliss and Uggen 2000; Wilkins 1999). Those who do attain partnership face barriers in recruiting new clients, obtaining referrals from their partners for work from existing firm clients, and securing the services of adept associates (Wilkins 1999). It is not surprising, then, that the rate of minority attrition is "devastatingly high" (Sander 2006; see also Wilkins 1999; Wilkins and Gulati 1996).

Yet the pattern of minority underrepresentation is not uniform across law firms. In general, it is well established that gender and racial workplace inequality vary with organizations' employment practices and structural characteristics (see, Reskin 2003; Stainback, Tomaskovic-Devey and Skaggs 2010). We were able to identify only one previous study that examined racial variation in law firms, however (Chambliss

---

considerably higher percentage than the corresponding figure for white partners in most firms.

[3] Extensive research in cognitive social psychology has established that most people's thought processes are affected by unconscious or "implicit" cognitive biases (see Banaji and Greenwald 2013).

1997). Analyzing data on ninety-seven large firms between 1980 and 1990, Chambliss found higher proportions of minority lawyers in firms with more branch offices and more international offices. She also found that minority representation varied with firms' mix of practice areas.

RESEARCH STRATEGY

To address our research questions, we analyzed data on more than 1,200 law firm offices across the United States in 2005. Our data were obtained from the 2005–2006 edition of the *National Directory of Legal Employers* (the "*NALP Directory*") compiled by the National Association for Law Placement (NALP), a nonprofit organization established to provide information about legal employment to law schools and their students. The NALP conducts an annual survey of all law firms that conduct on-campus recruiting at law schools, asking for quantitative and qualitative information, and compiles the results in annual editions of the *NALP Directory*. Our unit of analysis is the office, not the entire firm.[4] The final sample includes 1,394 offices. Because the *NALP Directory* does not provide data on revenues, profits, or (in most cases) total firm size, we merged the *NALP Directory* data with measures from the 2005 *AmLaw 200* rankings published in the *American Lawyer* magazine. Similar to the *Fortune 500* for corporations, this data source ranks the top 200 US law firms by their gross revenues. Nearly two-thirds of the offices in our sample are part of *AmLaw 200* firms (N = 835). Analyses involving firm size and profits are restricted to this subsample.

For each salient organizational dimension, we first examined its association with all minorities together, then with African-Americans, Latinos, and Asian-Americans considered separately. We also examined how minority presence varies at different ranks in the standard firm hierarchy: summer associate, regular associate, senior non-partner positions such as "counsel" or "senior attorney," and partner.[5] We

---

[4] In most cases, law firms with multiple offices provide information pertaining to each office separately; the few firms that did not provide office-specific information were eliminated from the sample.

[5] The title "counsel" (and variants such as "special counsel," "senior counsel," and so on) can refer to a variety of statuses, such as former associates who have not been made partners but have been retained as senior employees, and externally recruited senior lawyers who may eventually be made partners. As measured by the NALP, this category may also include former partners who continue to work for their firms on a

defined the *partner–summer associate ratio* as the ratio of the proportion of minorities among partners to the proportion of minorities
among summer associates. This ratio gives us some purchase, albeit
imperfect, on the extent of minority attrition and persistence between
initial entry and partnership. Summer associate positions serve as
"ports of entry" to law firms: many large firms make permanent offers
to almost all of their summer associates, and a high proportion of
those who receive such offers eventually return. Indeed, in their
narrative statements in the *NALP Directory*, many establishments
describe their summer associate program as their primary source of
new associates. The partner–summer associate ratio should be interpreted with caution as a measure of persistence, however, because
with cross-sectional data, minority summer associates and minority
partners are not the same lawyers. Moreover, the proportion of
minorities among partners is a weighted average of the corresponding
proportions in each annual cohort of partners, and low proportions in
the older cohorts are likely due to low minority entry rates when they
were associates as well as to minority attrition after entry. This caveat
carries particular force in the case of Asian-Americans, whose
numbers in the legal profession as a whole increased dramatically in
the two decades prior to 2005.[6]

In the second phase of our research, we used multivariate regression
analysis to model an office's proportion of partners who belong to any
of the three racial or ethnic minority groups as a function of the
office's formal and informal professional development practices, along
with several control variables. Our measures are described in more
detail in the Appendix. We also used regression to model the proportions of African-Americans, Latinos, and Asian-Americans separately. Space considerations preclude us from reporting all these
results in tabular form, but salient differences are highlighted in
the text.

---

non-partnership compensation basis prior to retirement, who are traditionally said to
be "of counsel" to their firms.

[6] Asian-American law school enrollment increased fivefold between 1984–1985 and
2004–2005, according to statistics compiled by the American Bar Association (see
www.americanbar.org/groups/legal_education/resources/statistics.html, last visited on
December 23, 2013). During the same period, Latino enrollment increased by 130%,
and African-American enrollment rose by only 73%.

TABLE 9.1.   Average Minority Representation in Major US Law Firm Offices, 2005

	All Minorities	African-Americans	Latinos	Asian-Americans
All lawyers[a]	8.9%	2.5%	2.3%	4.1%
By rank:				
Summer associates	17.8	6.5	3.4	7.6
Associates	13.7	3.9	3.2	6.7
Counsel/Sr. attorneys	5.1	1.7	1.5	1.8
Partners	4.9	1.6	1.6	1.7
Partner–summer associate ratio	28%	25%	47%	22%

[a] Excluding summer associates.
Note: N = 1,394.
© Emerald Group Publishing. Reprinted with permission.

CORE ORGANIZATIONAL FACTORS ASSOCIATED WITH MINORITY REPRESENTATION

Overall, as of 2005, minorities represented 8.9% of lawyers in the average major law firm office (Table 9.1). When rank is considered, minority representation declines noticeably and steadily from summer associates (17.8%) to partners (4.9%). Examining ethnic groups separately, we see that 2.5% of lawyers were African-American, 2.3% were Latino, and 4.1% were Asian-American. The steady decrease with increasing rank is observable for each of the three groups. Interestingly, all three groups have a similar presence among partners (1.6% to 1.7%), although they begin at different places: Asian-Americans are the best represented among summer associates at 7.6%, followed by African-Americans at 6.5% and Latinos at 3.4%.[7] As a result, the

---

[7] In comparison, during the 2004–2005 academic year, among enrolled law students, Asian-Americans represented 7.3%, African-Americans represented 6.4%, and Latinos represented 5.4%, respectively (see www.americanbar.org/groups/legal_educa tion/resources/statistics.html, last visited on December 23, 2013). Thus, Asian-Americans and African-Americans are represented among large-firm summer associates at levels slightly above their representation among law students, but Latinos are noticeably less conspicuous among summer associates than they are among law students.

partner–summer associate ratio is noticeably higher for Latinos (47%) than for African-Americans (25%) or Asian-Americans (22%). How do these numbers differ when organizational characteristics are taken into account?

Firm size

It is well established that organizational size, measured by number of workers, can affect minority representation. Because it is closely associated with bureaucratization, size can help disadvantaged groups by establishing objective standards and procedures for employee evaluation (Baron et al. 2007; Reskin and McBrier 2000) – but it can also hurt them by constraining them in rigid roles or segregated job ladders (Kalev 2009; Smith-Doerr 2004). Larger, more visible organizations are also more susceptible to pressures to conform to institutionalized practices (Edelman 1990), which should operate to promote diversity.

We focused on the size of the entire *law firm* in Table 9.2, where the categories represent quartiles of the distribution of firm size.[8] (In other analyses, we also looked at the size of the particular *office*, but found little variation in minority presence.) There is a clear positive association between minority presence and firm size. Minority lawyers represent 7.9% of lawyers in offices affiliated with the smallest firms and 13.2% of lawyers in offices affiliated with the largest firms. The minority presence among summer associates increases with firm size. Minority representation increases even more rapidly among partners, so that the minority partner–summer associate ratio tends to increase with firm size.[9]

Considering the three ethnic groups separately, a pattern of increasing representation with firm size is evident for both Latinos and Asian-Americans. Latinos make up 2% of lawyers in offices linked to the smallest firms, and 3.4% of lawyers in offices linked to the largest firms. Asian-Americans constitute 3.3% of lawyers in offices affiliated with the smallest firms, and 6.7% of lawyers in offices affiliated with the largest firms. Interestingly, the same pattern does not appear for African-Americans, who represent 2.7% of lawyers in offices of both the smallest and the largest firms. They are best represented in firms in the third quartile (506 to 823 lawyers). Offices of firms in the third quartile also attract and retain the most African-Americans among

[8] This analysis is restricted to offices of firms in the 2005 *AmLaw 200*.
[9] In contrast, minority representation among partners does *not* increase with *office* size (results not shown).

TABLE 9.2. Average Minority Representation in Major US Law Firm Offices, by Firm Size, 2005

	All Minorities	African-Americans	Latinos	Asian-Americans
All office lawyers[a]				
138 to 332 lawyers	7.9%	2.7%	2.0%	3.3%
333 to 505 lawyers	7.7	2.6	2.1	3.1
506 to 823 lawyers	11.9	3.3	2.4	6.2
824 to 2,984 lawyers	13.2	2.7	3.4	6.7
By rank:				
138 to 332 lawyers				
Summer associates	19.3%	6.4%	3.5%	9.4%
Associates	13.3	4.0	3.0	6.3
Counsel/Sr. Attorneys	5.1	2.5	1.2	1.4
Partners	3.5	1.4	1.2	0.9
Partner–summer associate ratio	18%	22%	34%	10%
333 to 505 lawyers				
Summer associates	13.8%	6.3%	2.1%	5.4%
Associates	11.1	3.5	2.5	5.0
Counsel/Sr. Attorneys	6.5	2.5	1.9	2.1
Partners	4.2	1.4	1.7	1.1
Partner–summer associate ratio	30%	22%	81%	20%
506 to 823 lawyers				
Summer associates	21.8%	8.4%	3.7%	9.7%
Associates	17.2	4.5	3.2	9.4
Counsel/Sr. Attorneys	7.0	1.8	2.0	3.1
Partners	5.5	1.8	1.4	2.3
Partner–summer associate ratio	25%	21%	38%	24%
824 to 2,984 lawyers				
Summer associates	23.7%	6.0%	5.0%	12.8%
Associates	19.3	3.9	5.2	10.1
Counsel/Sr. Attorneys	6.7	1.3	2.4	3.0
Partners	6.4	1.5	2.4	2.5
Partner–summer associate ratio	27%	25%	48%	20%

[a] Excluding summer associates.

Note: N = 835 (analysis is restricted to the subsample of offices affiliated with *AmLaw* 200 firms).

© Emerald Group Publishing. Reprinted with permission.

summer associates (8.4%), associates (4.5%), and partners (1.8%), compared with other firm size ranges. For Latinos and Asian-Americans, the strongest presence at all three of those levels occurs in the largest firms. Once again, partner–summer associate ratios are relatively high for Latinos compared with the other two groups, ranging as high as 81% in the second quartile. In contrast, the partner–summer associate ratio for Asian-Americans in the smallest major law firms is only 10%.

Firm profits

Are the financial resources at a firm's disposal a benefit or an obstacle for minorities? On the one hand, wealthier firms may be more able to afford to pursue diversity as a goal. On the other hand, wealthier firms typically offer higher levels of compensation, which in turn may attract larger numbers of qualified white applicants and reduce incentives to overcome bias in hiring and promotion. In Table 9.3, we analyzed how minority presence varies with firm profits per partner, a clear indicator of the financial rewards that firms offer to their successful lawyers. In this table, office categories represent quartiles of the distribution of firm profits per partner.[10] Overall minority representation increases steadily with firm profits per partner. Disaggregating by rank, it is interesting to note that the minority presence among partners increases sharply from the lowest quartile (3.3%) to the second quartile (5.2%) and only slightly in the third and fourth quartiles (5.4% and 5.7%, respectively).

The pattern of a steadily increasing presence with firm profits per partner holds across all three ethnic groups. When rank is taken into account, an interesting difference emerges, however. Among partners, both Latinos and Asian-Americans have their weakest presence in the lowest profit bracket (1.2% and 0.6%, respectively) and their strongest presence in the highest profit bracket (2.0% and 2.6%, respectively). In contrast, African-Americans have their strongest presence among partners in the second profit quartile (1.9%) and their weakest presence in the top quartile (1.1%). While this difference between Latinos and Asian-Americans, on the one hand, and African-Americans, on the other, is noteworthy, minority group presence in the partnership ranks remains very small across all profit quartiles. We note that, once again, Latinos have the highest partner–summer associate ratios, ranging

---

[10] This analysis is restricted to offices of firms in the 2005 *AmLaw 200*.

TABLE 9.3.   Average Minority Representation in Major US Law Firm Offices, by Firm Profits per Partner, 2005

	All Minorities	African-Americans	Latinos	Asian-Americans
All office lawyers[a]				
$335,000 to $515,000	5.8%	2.3%	1.6%	1.9%
$515,000 to $720,000	10.3	3.3	2.8	4.2
$720,000 to $1,065,000	11.4	2.9	2.8	5.8
$1,065,000 to $3,790,000	13.3	2.8	2.9	7.5
By rank:				
$335,000 to $515,000				
Summer associates	15.8%	6.9%	2.5%	6.4%
Associates	10.1	3.4	2.4	4.2
Counsel/Sr. attorneys	4.5	1.6	1.6	1.3
Partners	3.3	1.5	1.2	0.6
Partner–summer associate ratio	21%	22%	48%	9%
$515,000 to $720,000				
Summer associates	17.8%	7.2%	4.1%	6.5%
Associates	15.5	4.4	4.1	7.0
Counsel/Sr. attorneys	8.7	3.8	2.0	2.8
Partners	5.2	1.9	1.8	1.6
Partner–summer associate ratio	29%	26%	44%	25%
$720,000 to $1,065,000				
Summer associates	24.9%	8.1%	3.9%	12.8%
Associates	17.0	4.2	3.8	8.9
Counsel/Sr. attorneys	6.2	1.0	1.6	3.6
Partners	5.4	1.5	1.8	2.2
Partner–summer associate ratio	22%	19%	46%	17%
$1,065,000 to $3,790,000				
Summer associates	20.6%	5.0%	3.8%	11.8%
Associates	18.3	3.9	3.6	10.8
Counsel/Sr. attorneys	5.8	1.6	2.3	1.9
Partners	5.7	1.1	2.0	2.6
Partner–summer associate ratio	28%	22%	53%	22%

[a] Excluding summer associates.

Note: N = 835 (analysis is restricted to the subsample of offices affiliated with *AmLaw 200* firms).

© Emerald Group Publishing. Reprinted with permission.

between 44% in the second profit quartile and 53% in the top profit quartile. African-American and Asian-American partner–summer associate ratios are similar across quartiles.

Organizational structure

Studies have repeatedly shown that organizational structure can play an important role in generating or perpetuating workplace inequality. Here we consider three aspects of organizational structure that bear on lawyers' mobility prospects and overall job quality: an office's "leverage" (the ratio of its number of associates to its number of partners), whether an office has a "two-tier" partnership (with an upper tier of equity partners and a lower tier of senior salaried lawyers who hold the title of "partner" but do not own equity stakes in the firm), and whether an office is a branch office (rather than its firm's principal office). All three characteristics tend to make lawyers' jobs less attractive. Higher leverage is associated with lower chances of making partner and, for those who do become partners, greater pressure to generate business to keep associates employed. In two-tier partnerships, the lower tier of non-equity partners may find themselves in dead-end positions, blocked from advancing to equity partner status. Lawyers in branch offices may have difficulty gaining visibility and access to important information, clients, and political allies. If minorities tend to be relegated to less attractive jobs, we might expect that all these features are linked to a greater minority presence.

Overall, minority representation increases in a straightforward manner as leverage increases (Table 9.4). Office categories here represent quartiles of the distribution of leverage. It is noteworthy that more than half of sample offices exhibit leverage values under unity, indicating that the number of partners exceeds the number of associates. (However, leverage values do range up to a maximum of 11.5.) Minorities constitute 6.4% of lawyers, on average, among offices in the bottom leverage quartile and 11.9% of lawyers among offices in the top leverage quartile. By definition, leverage has different implications for associates and partners. We might expect to see more minorities in the lower ranks within firms and fewer minorities among partners as leverage increases. When we consider all minorities together, in the left-hand column, we see that minority representation among summer associates does indeed increase steadily with leverage. However, the minority presence among partners does not follow a clear pattern.

TABLE 9.4. Average Minority Representation in Major US Law Firm Offices, by Associate-partner Leverage, 2005

	All Minorities	African-Americans	Latinos	Asian-Americans
All office lawyers[a]				
0 to 0.63	6.4%	2.0%	1.9%	2.5%
0.64 to 0.94	7.8	2.7	2.1	3.0
0.95 to 1.41	9.5	2.7	2.3	4.6
1.42 to 11.50	11.9	2.7	2.7	6.5
By rank:				
0 to 0.63				
Summer associates	15.7%	6.4%	3.2%	6.1%
Associates	12.4	4.3	3.3	4.8
Counsel/Sr. attorneys	3.6	1.6	1.1	0.9
Partners	5.3	2.1	1.5	1.7
Partner–summer associate ratio	34%	33%	47%	28%
0.64 to 0.94				
Summer associates	16.7%	7.2%	3.8%	5.7%
Associates	13.1	4.6	3.2	5.3
Counsel/Sr. attorneys	4.3	1.5	1.1	1.6
Partners	4.2	1.4	1.4	1.4
Partner–summer associate ratio	25%	19%	37%	25%
0.95 to 1.41				
Summer associates	19.1%	6.7%	3.5%	8.9%
Associates	13.6	3.6	2.8	7.2
Counsel/Sr. attorneys	6.9	1.9	2.2	2.8
Partners	5.2	1.7	1.7	1.9
Partner–summer associate ratio	27%	25%	49%	21%
1.42 to 11.50				
Summer associates	19.6%	5.8%	2.9%	10.9%
Associates	16.0	3.3	3.4	9.2
Counsel/Sr. attorneys	5.6	1.9	1.7	2.0
Partners	4.8	1.1	1.8	2.0
Partner–summer associate ratio	25%	19%	62%	18%

[a] Excluding summer associates.
Note: N = 1,394.
© Emerald Group Publishing. Reprinted with permission.

Looking at the three ethnic groups separately in the top panel, we see an increasing pattern among Latinos and Asian-Americans across leverage quartiles. In contrast, African-American presence remains stable at 2.7% across the top three leverage quartiles. When we look at representation by rank in the three groups, interesting differences appear. The African-American presence among partners is weakest in the top leverage quartile, as we might expect. For Latinos and Asian-Americans, the strongest representation among associates is in the top leverage quartile (3.4% and 9.2%, respectively), again as we might expect, but their strongest representation among *partners* is also in that quartile (1.8% and 2.0%, respectively). Despite these similarities between Latinos and Asian-Americans, we see very different partner–summer associate ratios for the two groups in this top quartile (62% for Latinos and 18% for Asian-Americans) due to Asian-Americans' much greater presence among summer associates.

Two-tier partnerships are not strongly linked to overall minority presence (Table 9.5). Minorities represent 9.0% of lawyers in both single-tier and two-tier offices. Taking rank into account in the left-hand column, however, reveals that minorities are more prevalent at every level in two-tier firms. Then again, the partner–summer associate ratio is higher in single-tier firms. When the three groups are considered separately, we see that African-Americans and Latinos are better represented in two-tier offices, while Asian-Americans actually have a stronger presence in offices with single-tier partnerships. The same pattern holds when we look at specific hierarchical ranks.

Minority lawyers are more often located in branch offices, where they constitute 9.9% of lawyers, rather than firms' principal offices, where they represent 7.5% of lawyers (Table 9.6). Moreover, minority representation in branch offices is greater at every hierarchical rank. The partner–summer associate ratio is the same in the two types of offices. Looking at the three ethnic groups separately, Latinos and Asian-Americans are more prevalent in branch offices. We observe a distinctive pattern for African-Americans: although the differences are slight, African-Americans are better represented in *principal* offices than in branch offices at all levels except counsel/senior attorneys. Partner–summer associate ratios for African-Americans are similar in the two settings. For Latinos, the partner–summer associate ratio is higher in branch offices, while for Asian-Americans it is higher in principal offices.

TABLE 9.5.   Average Minority Representation in Major US Law
Firm Offices, by Partnership Structure, 2005

	All Minorities	African-Americans	Latinos	Asian-Americans
All office lawyers[a]				
Single-tier partnership	9.0%	2.3%	2.0%	4.7%
Two-tier partnership	9.0	2.7	2.6	3.6
By rank:				
Single-tier partnership				
Summer associates	16.5%	5.6%	2.8%	8.2%
Associates	13.7	3.8	2.8	7.1
Counsel/Sr. attorneys	4.5	1.0	1.7	1.8
Partners	4.8	1.5	1.3	2.0
Partner–summer associate ratio	29%	27%	46%	24%
Two-tier partnership				
Summer associates	19.2%	7.5%	3.9%	7.8%
Associates	13.8	4.1	3.5	6.2
Counsel/Sr. attorneys	5.7	2.5	1.4	1.8
Partners	5.0	1.6	1.8	1.5
Partner–summer associate ratio	26%	21%	46%	19%

[a] Excluding summer associates.
Note: N = 1,394.
© Emerald Group Publishing. Reprinted with permission.

Discussion

Several key findings emerge from these analyses. First, total minority
representation declines noticeably and steadily across ascending ranks
of the typical law firm hierarchy, from summer associates at the bottom
to partners at the top. Larger and wealthier firms are more able or more
inclined to pursue lawyer diversity: minority presence tends to increase
with firm size and firm profits per partner. Yet, minority lawyers are also
more prevalent in offices with structural features that accentuate workplace inequality, such as high associate-partner leverage, two-tier partnership, and branch offices. Somewhat paradoxically, these findings
suggest that minorities are most welcomed in firms and offices that
offer both richer potential rewards and lower chances of success.

Considered separately, the three minority groups examined here
present somewhat different profiles. African-American lawyers are best

TABLE 9.6.   Average Minority Representation in Major US Law Firm Offices, by Principal Versus Branch Office, 2005

	All Minorities	African-Americans	Latinos	Asian-Americans
All office lawyers[a]				
Principal office	7.5%	2.3%	1.6%	3.6%
Branch office	9.9	2.6	2.7	4.6
By rank:				
Principal office				
Summer associates	16.4%	6.6%	3.1%	6.6%
Associates	12.4	4.1	2.5	5.8
Counsel/Sr. attorneys	3.9	1.7	0.9	1.4
Partners	4.4	1.6	1.1	1.7
Partner–summer associate ratio	27%	24%	35%	26%
Branch office				
Summer associates	19.0%	6.5%	3.5%	9.0%
Associates	14.8	3.8	3.6	7.3
Counsel/Sr. attorneys	6.0	1.8	2.1	2.2
Partners	5.2	1.5	1.9	1.8
Partner–summer associate ratio	27%	23%	54%	20%

[a] Excluding summer associates.

Note: **N = 1,394.**

© Emerald Group Publishing. Reprinted with permission.

represented in the middle ranges of firm size and firm profits per partner. African-Americans are more likely to be found in branch offices and offices with higher leverage and two-tier partnerships. Yet, higher partner–summer associate ratios among African-Americans – which suggest greater persistence and lower attrition – are associated with low leverage and single-tier partnerships. Our findings thus hint that the contexts where African-Americans are most numerous are not the ones where they experience the best chances of success.

Latinos are more numerous in the biggest firms and in firms with higher profits per partner. Like African-Americans, Latino lawyers are more prevalent in branch offices, offices with higher leverage, and offices with two-tier partnerships. Interestingly, Latino partner–summer associate ratios tend to be strikingly higher than those of the other two groups, both overall and within most of the categories specified by various organizational characteristics. These higher partner–summer associate ratios stem primarily from markedly lower representation among summer associates rather than from higher representation among partners. There is some evidence that Latinos are disproportionately likely to attend less-prestigious local and evening law schools (Heinz et al. 2005, p. 65), which may help to explain their low entry rates into elite corporate firms. The highest Latino partner–summer associate ratios are associated with the middle range of firm size, higher profits per partner, higher leverage, and branch offices.

Asian-American representation increases markedly and steadily with firm size and firm profits per partner. Like the other two groups, Asian-American lawyers are more likely to be found in offices with high associate-partner leverage and in branch offices; unlike the other two groups, they are better represented in offices with single-tier partnerships. In contrast to Latinos, Asian-Americans exhibit the lowest partner–summer associate ratios, stemming from their unusually high representation among summer associates. Clearly, large numbers of Asian-Americans enter big firms, but few remain to become partners. Moreover, like African-Americans, Asian-Americans tend to experience higher partner–summer associate ratios in contexts where they are less prevalent. Thus, these ratios are higher in the middle range of firm size, in firms with lower profits and leverage, and in principal offices.

To sum up, many of the organizational characteristics linked to the transformation of modern corporate law firms – such as larger firm size, higher profits, greater leverage, two-tier partnerships, and branch offices – are also associated with a greater minority presence. As a result, minorities tend to be better represented in offices and firms with greater resources and rewards but lower chances of success. Indeed, all three groups experience increasing attrition at successively higher hierarchical levels, and all three groups arrive at similarly low representation levels among law firm partners. Yet differences among the groups are intriguing and present puzzles for future research.

PROFESSIONAL DEVELOPMENT PRACTICES AND MINORITY REPRESENTATION AMONG PARTNERS

In the second phase of our research, we investigate the consequences of law firms' professional development practices for the representation of minorities at the partner level. One possible explanation for the underrepresentation of minorities in law firms, particularly at the higher ranks, is that minority and white employees enter organizations with relatively similar levels of skills and resources, but whites pull ahead *during the course of employment* as a result of greater access to mentoring, "stretch" assignments, and other developmental opportunities (Kay et al. 2009). In the absence of firm intervention, whites may be more likely than minorities to receive the attention and coaching that enable them to develop the skills needed to function as a partner (Wilkins and Gulati 1996). Organizational practices could alter this pattern in ways that reduce the developmental gap, help minorities become more competitive partnership candidates, and decrease their likelihood of dissatisfaction and attrition. We emphasize that we are *not* concerned here with practices that explicitly target minorities, but rather with policies and practices that tend to make developmental guidance more broadly available to all associates.

Formal developmental practices. To a certain extent, some formal developmental practices can substitute for spontaneously occurring developmental experiences by providing an alternative vehicle for learning. We examined two such practices: formal training programs and formal mentoring programs. Formal training programs, which aim to ensure that all associates have the same baseline level of knowledge and skill, can improve employee performance, job satisfaction, and organizational commitment and increase promotion chances (Saks 1996; Tharenou and Conroy 1994; Wholey 1990).[11] We suspect that formal training programs are most successful at building technical and analytical skills and are less effective at other developmental functions, such as teaching "soft skills" or helping lawyers build social networks and navigate office politics. Still, to the extent that formal programs make training accessible to all junior employees, they should serve to reduce any skill and productivity gap that may emerge between minorities and whites and improve minorities' chances for promotion.

Firms may also offer formal mentoring programs that match associates to more senior colleagues. A formal mentoring program ensures

---

[11] Law firms offer training in a variety of forms. We focus on relatively intensive and sustained programs consisting of multiple classroom-style sessions in which senior lawyers present information and impart skills, and not brief orientation sessions or occasional workshops.

that each junior lawyer is assigned to a mentor and has a contact for guidance. Of course, the benefits of formal mentoring are weaker than those of informal mentoring relationships, which develop spontaneously and typically have longer durations than formal relationships (Underhill 2006). Nonetheless, formal mentoring programs have generally been found to be satisfying to employees and offer such benefits as learning new skills, organizational understanding, psychosocial support (Allen, Eby, and Lentz 2006; Weinberg and Lankau 2011), developing self-confidence and professional direction (Wanberg, Kammeyer-Mueller and Marchese 2006), and realizing opportunities for career progress (Kay, Hagan, and Parker 2009). Research suggests that formal mentoring programs have extensive benefits for racial minorities (Ortiz-Walters and Gilson 2005), and diversity-targeted formal mentoring programs are positively associated with the representation of African-Americans among corporate managers (Kalev, Dobbin and Kelly 2006).

A different kind of formal developmental practice is the length of the expected or typical "partnership track" period leading up to consideration for promotion. The duration of the partnership track could have either positive or negative consequences for minorities. On the one hand, a longer partnership track could aid minorities by giving them time to overcome conscious or unconscious employer bias through repeated strong performances.[12] On the other hand, if partners disproportionately select whites for informal mentoring and challenging assignments, then whites are likely to gain greater skills and resources, further solidifying the impression that they are more competent and better suited for positions of responsibility and increasing their advantage in the next round of selection. A longer partnership track could worsen minorities' disadvantage by allowing more repetitions of this cycle.

Informal developmental practices. Informal practices and organizational culture represent two sides of the same coin. Informal practices give rise to cultural values and norms, as "what is" comes to be seen as "what should be" (Barker 1993). Conversely, organizational culture can shape employee behavior in important ways (Wallace and Leicht

---

[12] Research in corporate settings reveals that minority managers who attain the executive level often take longer to achieve promotion than their white colleagues (Thomas and Gabarro 1999).

2004). Three of these practices/values may be especially important for minority success in law firms: commitment to professional development, early delegation of responsibility, and collegiality.

For some firms, commitment to the professional development of associates is a central tenet of organizational culture. In some of these organizations, developmental efforts are understood as a professional and ethical obligation (Barnhizer 2003; McManus 2005). Others accept the "business case" argument that professional development efforts increase productivity and reduce costs (Montgomery 2008). Either way, senior lawyers are expected to take responsibility for the formation of less experienced juniors, as a service to the firm or the profession rather than for the purpose of enhancing their own status or clout. And senior employees are more likely to engage in mentoring when they see their organizations encouraging it (Allen, Poteet, and Burroughs 1997).

Like a longer partnership track, a commitment to professional development could be either beneficial or detrimental to minority success. It could be beneficial if it leads senior lawyers to offer informal mentoring and challenging assignments more inclusively and consistently to associates of all races and ethnicities. If so, developmental commitment would make it more likely that whites and minorities receive similar developmental experiences, and that in turn should lessen the disparity in their attrition and prospects of promotion to partnership.[13] In contrast, developmental commitment could be detrimental to minorities if partners and other senior lawyers respond by intensifying the attention they pay to associates who are socially similar to themselves. In that case, given that most senior lawyers are white, developmental commitment would only aggravate the disadvantage that minorities face in gaining access to developmental experiences.

The impact of developmental commitment may depend on organizational size. In smaller firms with relatively few associates, it may be easier for potential mentors to justify their choice of socially similar protégés by pointing to their individual strengths and apparently greater promise. In larger organizations, which are usually both more bureaucratic and more visible to external audiences than smaller

---

[13] In the corporate setting, an organizational emphasis on the internal development of employees is positively associated with the presence of African-Americans among managers (Fields, Goodman and Blum 2005).

organizations, lawyers may more consciously accept that a commitment to professional development should extend to all associates.

The effect of developmental commitment could also depend on the representation of minorities among associates. It may be easier for potential mentors, who are predominantly white in most organizations, to maintain an inclusive, even-handed commitment to the professional growth of all junior lawyers when the numbers of minorities among them are relatively few. As the minority presence among associates grows, white senior lawyers may feel increasingly uncomfortable, and may – consciously or unconsciously – gravitate more strongly toward white protégés.

A second important informal practice is the extent to which senior lawyers delegate responsibility to associates at early stages of their careers, rather than keeping them under close supervision for long periods of time. Once again, it is possible to foresee both advantages and disadvantages for minorities. On the one hand, early responsibility for strategy formulation and relationships with major clients is highly desirable to the career advancement of associates who are aiming for partnership. Because minority employees may be more likely to find themselves confined to support roles and "back office" tasks than their white counterparts (Sander 2006), a norm of early responsibility may give them greater access to challenging developmental assignments than they would otherwise receive. On the other hand, early responsibility can operate as a screening device, selecting those who already have the necessary skills – or are able to acquire them quickly on their own – and weeding out the rest. In that case, early delegation of responsibility could intensify the disadvantage of minorities, whose early missteps are likely to be perceived as evidence of weaker abilities (Coleman and Gulati 2006).

A third significant informal practice, or norm, is the extent to which interactions and relationships among lawyers within the firm are collegial in nature. In law firms, the idea of collegiality encompasses both a social atmosphere of openness and trust and a relatively nonhierarchical way of organizing work in which authority is based on expertise rather than formal role (Greenwood and Empson 2003; Lazega 2001; Waters 1989). Whereas the formal differentiation of roles can reinforce racial divides, the blurring of roles and collective self-management can benefit minorities (Kalev 2009). An emphasis on collegiality could tend to reduce the salience of racial group boundaries, which could in turn increase access to developmental opportunities for minority lawyers.

Results

Table 9.7 presents the equations modeling the proportion of partners who belong to any of the three minority groups. Model 1 is a baseline model including only control variables. As expected, the proportion of minorities among associates has a strong positive effect on minority presence among partners. Surprisingly, office size has a negative effect. The coefficient on a firm's membership in the *AmLaw 200* is also negative, but the effect does not reach statistical significance. Also unexpected is the negative impact of departmentalization. As we anticipated, minority presence among partners is positively associated with leverage and with status as a branch office, but a two-tier partnership has no significant effect. Geographically, minority representation is especially high in the West and South, and lowest in the Northeast. These control variable effects do not change substantially across models.

Model 2 introduces the professional development variables. Neither formal training programs nor formal mentoring programs are significantly associated with overall minority presence. Longer partnership tracks reduce minority representation among partners, however, consistent with our second alternative conjecture. Interestingly, a commitment to fostering the professional development of associates has a significant negative effect, in line with our second alternative conjecture about the role of this variable. A norm of early responsibility is also negatively linked to minority presence among partners, again consistent with our second alternative argument. Collegiality is not associated with the proportion of minority partners.

In Model 3, we added an interaction between developmental commitment and office size. Model 4 substitutes an interaction between developmental commitment and minority presence among associates.[14] In Model 3, as we anticipated, the interaction with office size is positive and statistically significant, indicating that the negative effect of developmental commitment is weaker in larger offices.[15] Conversely, the negative effect of size is only half as strong in offices with a commitment to professional development as it is in those

---

[14] Because both continuous variables were centered before the multiplicative interaction terms were created, the coefficients on the cultural value variable reflect its effect when office size (in Model 3) and proportion of minorities among associates (in Model 4) are at their means.

[15] The effect does not actually become positive until office size reaches 174, nearly the 90th percentile of the office size distribution in our sample.

TABLE 9.7. Regressions of Log-odds of Proportion of Minorities among Partners on Selected Organizational Characteristics

Variable	Model 1	Model 2	Model 3	Model 4
Professional development practices				
Formal training program		.008	.012	−.001
		(.058)	(.058)	(.055)
Formal mentoring program		−.079	−.081†	−.066
		(.057)	(.056)	(.056)
Partnership track length		−.076**	−.076**	−.074**
		(.033)	(.033)	(.032)
Cultural values and norms				
Cultural value on professional development		−.089*	−.092*	−.079*
		(.049)	(.049)	(.047)
Cultural value on professional development × office size			.001*	
			(.001)	
Cultural value on professional development × group presence among associates				−1.059*
				(.508)
Cultural norm of early responsibility		−.089*	−.091*	−.092*
		(.046)	(.046)	(.045)
Cultural value on collegiality		.050	.051	.050
		(.046)	(.046)	(.046)
Control variables				
Group presence among associates:				
Proportion of minority associates	2.632***	2.703***	2.716***	2.639***
	(.456)	(.453)	(.452)	(.408)
Establishment size	−.002***	−.002***	−.002***	−.002***
	(.000)	(.000)	(.000)	(.000)
AmLaw 200	−.059	−.032	−.032†	−.023†
	(.063)	(.061)	(.061)	(.060)
Departments	−.167**	−.141**	−.136**	−.151**
	(.058)	(.055)	(.055)	(.055)
Starting salary (difference from city mean)	.000	.000	.000	.000
	(.000)	(.000)	(.000)	(.000)
Two-tier partnership	−.010	−.005	−.001	−.002
	(.049)	(.053)	(.053)	(.053)
Leverage	.266***	.278***	.279***	.276***
	(.028)	(.030)	(.030)	(.029)
Branch	.250***	.290***	.287***	.295***
	(.071)	(.072)	(.073)	(.071)
Region Midwest[a]	.215**	.195**	.194**	.196**
	(.068)	(.069)	(.069)	(.068)

TABLE 9.7. (*cont.*)

Variable	Model 1	Model 2	Model 3	Model 4
Region South	.391***	.337***	.339***	.339***
	(.059)	(.056)	(.056)	(.056)
Region West	.380***	.344***	.346***	.351***
	(.060)	(.060)	(.060)	(.060)
Constant	−3.681***	−3.113***	−3.307***	−2.784***
	(.100)	(.268)	(.267)	(.261)
R^2	.328	.358	.360	.362
N	1,384	1,353	1,353	1,353

[a] Comparison category is the Northeast region.
Note: Standard errors appear in parentheses;
   † $p < .10$;
  * $p < .05$;
 ** $p < .01$;
*** $p < .001$.

without such a commitment. Interestingly, the effect of a formal mentoring program also becomes marginally significant ($p < .10$) and *negative* in this model.

In Model 4, also as expected, the interaction with minority group presence among associates is negative, indicating that the negative impact of developmental commitment is especially strong when minorities hold a greater share of associate positions. At the same time, the positive effect of high representation of minorities among the associate ranks is diminished when an office places emphasis on professional development.

Specific minority groups. In separate analyses not shown here (see Kay and Gorman 2012), we found that while the pattern of results is similar for each of the three minority groups, a few differences are worth noting. For example, partnership track length is not significantly associated with African-American presence among partners, whereas it has a negative effect for minorities overall. Developmental commitment has a more negative impact, and a norm of early responsibility has a less negative impact, for African-Americans than they do for all minorities combined.[16] In contrast to the results for all minorities together, formal mentoring programs are negatively associated with Latino representation among partners, and a norm of early responsibility has no significant effect.

[16] Early responsibility is only marginally statistically significant for African-Americans.

Asian-Americans are distinctive in that the presence of a formal training program is negatively associated with their representation among partners. Intriguingly, an office's developmental commitment has no significant impact for Asian-Americans. Finally, Asian-Americans experience the greatest negative impact from a norm of early responsibility.[17]

Discussion

Law firms that hope to fill their partnership ranks through internal promotion have an interest in the growth and development of their associates. Such firms often maintain both formal and informal practices intended to bolster associates' technical skills, interpersonal competencies, and social connections. Although these practices are not specifically aimed at fostering diversity, the idea that minority lawyers might derive particular benefit from them is intuitively appealing. Whites are likely to have better access to spontaneously occurring developmental opportunities, so organizational efforts to make developmental experiences more uniformly available should help to "level the playing field."

Our findings suggest that this intuitive expectation is misguided, however. Strikingly, none of the practices or cultural characteristics considered was positively associated with the presence of minorities among partners. All of them had either negative effects or no effects.

Perhaps the most notable finding is that an organizational culture of fostering and taking responsibility for employees' professional development works to *decrease* the proportions of minorities among partners. Senior lawyers who receive encouragement to nurture the progress of associates may simply direct their attention even more vigorously to protégés who are socially similar to themselves. If this interpretation is correct, it may help to explain the unanticipated finding that the negative effect of an office's developmental commitment is strongest for African-Americans, weaker for Latinos, and nonsignificant for Asian-Americans. It is possible that white senior managers feel the least social dissimilarity and discomfort with Asian-American protégés,

---

[17] There is notable consistency across the different racial groups when we examine the control variables. The proportions of all three groups among partners increase with their group's current representation among associates. Larger offices and establishments with departments both have negative effects on the proportions of all three racial groups among firm partners. Leverage and status as a branch office are both positively associated with presence among partners for all three racial groups. Only the role of a two-tier partnership varies: it is negatively linked to representation among partners for Asian-Americans, but not for the other two groups.

somewhat more with Latinos, and considerably more with African-Americans. Our findings suggest that altering longstanding patterns of minority underrepresentation will require firms to move beyond well-intended cultural values and informal practices such as developmental commitment and collegiality.

Our findings also imply that firms should pay careful attention to how office size and the representation of minorities among associates moderate the impact of developmental commitment. In the case of office size, the interaction is positive, so that the negative effect of a cultural emphasis on professional development becomes weaker as organizational size increases. Although additional research is needed, it is possible that larger organizations are better able to translate their cultural values into actual behavior on the part of senior managers. Furthermore, in larger organizations, mentors and sponsors may be more aware of the organizational context surrounding them and more likely to understand themselves as enacting organizational roles, rather than merely forming personal bonds with protégés.

The interaction between developmental commitment and group presence among associates is negative, so that the negative effect becomes stronger as a greater share of associate positions are filled by minorities. Again, more research is needed, but it seems that, as minority group presence at the associate level increases, firms find it increasingly difficult to implement their professional development efforts in an even-handed way. Sociologists have long argued that racial and ethnic prejudice and discrimination increase as a minority group increases in size and is perceived to pose a greater threat to the dominant group (Blalock 1967). Consistent with this idea, it may be that, as minority presence among non-management employees grows, white senior lawyers increasingly respond to their firm's developmental mandate by concentrating their mentoring and sponsorship efforts toward white protégés.

Some research suggests that racial minorities are disadvantaged by a lack of opportunity to take on significant responsibility early in their careers (Sander 2006). Because they are asked to prove their competence repeatedly before being trusted with challenging tasks, they have fewer opportunities to gain visibility and take longer to advance than their white counterparts (Thomas and Gabarro 1999). However, early responsibility can be a two-edged sword for minority associates: if they are given responsibility and make mistakes, those mistakes are likely to be viewed much more negatively – and more conclusively attributed to weak ability – than the comparable missteps of whites. Our finding that a norm of early responsibility is negatively associated with minority representation at the partner level suggests that the second process outweighs the first.

Formal practices intended to help associates build skills and resources also fail to benefit minorities. One might expect that formal training and mentoring programs would help by offsetting minorities' likely disadvantage in access to informal developmental opportunities. Yet, neither type of program has a positive effect on minority representation among partners. Although formal training programs may provide certain important information and limited opportunities to practice new skills, they likely fall far short of imparting the full range of technical and interpersonal skills that are vital to being perceived as having managerial potential – let alone the social connections and alliances that are essential for success. Formal mentoring programs, as well, are likely too limited in their effects to make a real difference. Research suggests that formal mentoring arrangements tend to be shorter in duration, less close, and focused primarily on technical skills and procedures rather than on career planning, advice on office politics, emotional support, and reputation building (Kay et al. 2009; Ragins and Cotton 1999). Because matches are assigned rather than arising from interpersonal compatibility, mentors may lack motivation to help their protégés.[18] Thus, while formal training and mentoring programs may be better than nothing, they typically yield more modest career outcomes than informal arrangements (Underhill 2006). More difficult to understand are the unanticipated *negative* effects of formal training programs for Asian-Americans and of formal mentoring programs for Latinos.

Another noteworthy finding is that longer partnership tracks are negatively linked to racial minorities' representation among partners. Longer "probationary" periods are sometimes thought to be beneficial to employees who face a disadvantage of some kind. For example, "mommy tracks" in corporations and paused tenure clocks in universities are meant to allow parents additional time to establish a strong record of performance. However, our findings suggest that if the same lengthened period is made available to employees who are *not* disadvantaged – in this case, whites – then the extended period may actually

---

[18] Studies have documented the challenges of formal mentoring programs, including associates' unmet expectations, lack of interpersonal attraction or identification, scheduling difficulties, mentor neglect, mentors' feelings of personal inadequacy, and difficulty forging a post-program relationship (Blake-Beard 2001; Wanberg et al. 2006).

289

worsen minorities' promotion prospects by allowing repeated cycles of cumulative advantage for whites and cumulative disadvantage for minorities. As a result, by the end of the partnership track, minority associates may (on average) have acquired fewer important skills than their white counterparts, thus limiting their prospects even if the promotion process is entirely fair. Minority associates, recognizing the compounding effects of being repeatedly passed over for career development experiences, are less likely than whites to feel committed to a future with the firm and more likely to leave in search of better opportunities elsewhere (Payne-Pikus, Hagan, and Nelson 2010).

Broadly speaking, our findings align with the view that the formalization of human resources policies furthers workplace diversity by checking bias and introducing procedural fairness (Reskin 2001). Although formal developmental practices do little to help minorities, informal, cultural approaches to professional development seem to actively hurt them. No matter how well intentioned such approaches may be, day-to-day behavior in organizations is only loosely coupled to organizational ideals, and policies that are intended to be even-handed may not be implemented in that same fashion. Hearing organizational encouragement to provide mentoring and support, senior managers may simply direct their efforts more vigorously to aiding protégés who are socially similar to themselves.

CONCLUSION

To return to our point of departure, which kinds of firms have the most minority lawyers? Many of the organizational characteristics associated with the dramatic transformation of the large law firm in recent decades are also associated with a greater minority presence. Minority representation tends to be greater in larger firms and firms with higher revenues and profits. Minorities are also better represented in branch offices, offices with higher associate-to-partner leverage, and offices with two-tier partnerships. These are some of the same changes that commentators have pointed to when lamenting the legal profession's loss of autonomy, challenge, and status (e.g., Kronman 1993). Unfortunately, minority representation may be greatest in environments offering the fewest chances for advancement. Nonetheless, increasing the proportion of minorities among law firm associates is an important foundation for building diversity in law firms and for making possible minorities' accent to the partnership ranks.

When it comes to professional development, neither old nor new approaches seem to work. Many law firm practices that are intended – or at least might be expected – to support associate professional development do not increase minority presence among partners or even actively decrease it. Old-fashioned developmental commitment, early responsibility, and collegiality have no effect or only accentuate white lawyers' advantages. Newer practices like formal mentoring and training programs do not compensate minorities for reduced access to informal developmental experiences, and longer partnership tracks do not offer minorities more time to succeed, but instead allow them to fall further behind. It is vital to note that the formal mentoring and training programs we explored are not specifically aimed at supporting racial minorities in law. Such diversity-targeted programs may be needed to raise awareness of cognitive biases against minorities and to provide minorities with the sponsorship and professional guidance needed to succeed. Similarly, old-style collegiality and a commitment to early responsibility may simply reinforce existing inequalities by fostering a workplace culture that extends help more often to associates who are socially similar to law firm partners. Minorities may find themselves left to take on new challenges without the generous mentoring of senior lawyers committed to their advancement in the firm.

Our findings also show that minority representation is generally strong at the entry level across dimensions of organizational variation. It is evident that minority underrepresentation in large firms is driven primarily by the steep fall-off in their numbers with greater seniority and higher rank. As firms have increasingly ceased to resemble the gentlemen's clubs documented in Smigel's classic, *The Wall Street Lawyer* (1969), both economic interests and institutional pressures have pushed law firms to open the front door and invite minority lawyers over the threshold; the key question is whether they stay and move up or find themselves heading out the back door. Future research should focus specifically on the organizational characteristics and processes that influence minority attrition. Two areas may prove fruitful. First, innovative studies are needed to collect detailed information on corporate cultures to help better understand which cultures are attentive to social norms of equal opportunity and embracing of diversity programs (Dobbin, Kim and Kalev 2011). Second, research is required to directly assess the efficacy of both formal mentoring programs and informal mentoring arrangements in promoting the retention, professional growth, and career advancement of minority lawyers in law firms.

APPENDIX: MEASURES EMPLOYED IN THE REGRESSION ANALYSIS

Dependent variables. We modeled the proportion of partners who belong to any of three racial or ethnic minority groups – African-Americans, Latinos, and Asian-Americans – as well as the proportions of partners who are members of each group separately. We followed previous research (Gorman 2005; Kalev 2009; Reskin and McBrier 2000) in transforming these proportions to their log-odds, in order to avoid predicted proportions below 0 and above 1, and because the functional form is likely to provide a better fit to the data.

Independent variables. Offices' *partnership track length* is measured in years (ranging from four to nine and half years). Other variables were coded from the narrative statements included in offices' responses to the NALP questionnaire. Four other independent variables were coded from the narrative statements that offices provided as part of their responses to the NALP questionnaire. An initial subsample of fifty cases was coded by three graduate-student research assistants, resulting in high inter-coder reliabilities. Discrepancies in coding this subsample were discussed and resolved before the research assistants proceeded to code remaining subsamples individually. Coded variables include two binary (0–1) variables indicating whether or not an office offers a *formal training program* or a *formal mentoring program*, and three binary (0–1) variables measuring whether or not the office's culture includes *a commitment to professional development*, a norm of *early responsibility*, and an emphasis on *collegiality*.

Control variables. The rate at which minorities are promoted to partnership depends on their presence among associates. *Minority group presence among associates* is measured by the proportion of associates who belong to the relevant group.

Various aspects of jobs and workplaces are also likely to influence the representation of minorities in partnership positions. Organizational size is a perennial subject of interest because it is closely associated with so many organizational processes. It is tapped here by two measures: *office size* (the number of lawyers in the establishment as reported in the 2005 *NALP Directory*) and whether the establishment's firm was included the 2005 *AmLaw 200* rankings published by the *American Lawyer* magazine. Similar to the *Fortune 500* for corporations, this data source ranks the top 200 US law firms by their gross revenues; because revenues are generated by lawyers' billable hours, revenues are highly correlated with firm size. To capture bureaucratization more directly, we also included a measure of whether an office is divided by *departments* (0 if no, 1 if yes).

If employers tend to place whites ahead of minorities in their "labor queues" for hiring and promotion (Alon 2004; Reskin and Roos 1990), then minorities' prospects depend on the number of available positions relative to the number of white candidates interested in filling them. Thus, characteristics that make jobs more attractive are likely to be negatively associated with the representation of minorities, presumably because they then face greater competition from whites (and, conversely, characteristics that make jobs less attractive are likely to be positively linked to minority presence). Although we did not have data for all cases on partner compensation, we did have a measure of the *starting salary* paid to associates. Associate and partner compensation are likely to be at least loosely linked. Because starting salaries vary across cities, we used the difference between an office's starting salary and the city mean.

We also included four structural characteristics that are likely to limit lawyers' opportunities for advancement, recognition, and self-actualization, thus making jobs less appealing to white competitors: leverage, a two-tier partnership, and branch office status (see Gorman and Kay 2010). *Leverage* is measured as the ratio of non-partner lawyers to partners within the office. Higher leverage is associated with lower chances of making partner and, for those who do become partner, greater pressure to generate business to keep associates employed (but also greater profits in the event of success).[19] A dichotomous (0–1) variable indicates the presence of a *two-tier partnership* including both traditional, equity-holding partners and salaried lawyers who bear the title of "partner" without its traditional ownership rights. Another binary variable indicates whether the office is a *branch office* (0 if headquarters, 1 if branch office); lawyers

---

[19] Leverage could also have a negative influence on minority presence among managers, because it is associated with a steeper hierarchical structure and fewer managerial positions to fill. Thus, leverage could mean that employers find it easier to meet their staffing needs with whites and are not pushed to go deeper into their "labor queues."

TABLE 9.8. Descriptive Statistics for Variables Used in the Regression Analysis

Variable	Mean	SD	Min.	Max.
Group presence among partners:				
Proportion of minority partners	.049	.089	0	1
Proportion of African-American partners	.016	.055	0	1
Proportion of Latino partners	.016	.045	0	.455
Proportion of Asian-American partners	.017	.049	0	.583
Formal training program	.391	.488	0	1
Formal mentoring program	.205	.404	0	1
Partnership track length	7.66	.821	4	9.5
Cultural value on professional development	.406	.491	0	1
Cultural norm of early responsibility	.406	.491	0	1
Cultural value on collegiality	.450	.498	0	1
Group presence among associates:				
Proportion of minority associates	.138	.129	0	1
Proportion of African-American associates	.040	.062	0	1
Proportion of Latino associates	.032	.064	0	.833
Proportion of Asian-American associates	.067	.093	0	1
Establishment size	81.604	86.042	5	809
AmLaw 200	.600	.490	0	1
Departments	.713	.453	0	1
Starting salary (difference from city mean)	−14.99	8704.761	0	1
Two-tier partnership	.500	.500	0	1
Leverage	1.427	1.055	.133	12.333
Branch	.559	.497	0	1
Region Midwest	.149	.356	0	1
Region Northeast	.306	.461	0	1
Region South	.271	.445	0	1
Region West	.274	.446	0	1

in a firm's principal office are likely to have better prospects and perform more interesting work.

Finally, three dichotomous variables indicating *regions of the United States* (Midwest, South, and West, with Northeast as the reference category) were included to tap geographical variation in racial and ethnic presence.

Table 9.8 reports means, standard deviations, and ranges for the variables used in the analysis. In the average establishment, minorities represented 14% of associates and just 5% of partners. When we consider minority groups separately, we find African-Americans made up 4% of associates and 1.6% of partners; Latinos, 3% of associates and 1.6% of partners; and Asian-Americans, 7% of associates and 1.7% of partners. Thus, all three minority groups start out at different levels of representation in the lower ranks of firms, but end up at with a similar presence (1.6% to 1.7%) among partners. Formal training programs were more common (present in 39% of offices) than formal mentoring programs (less than 21% of offices offered these). A sizable share of establishments (41%) encouraged junior employees to take on significant responsibilities early, and the same percentage maintained a cultural value of fostering professional development of junior employees. An emphasis on collegiality was present in only 22% of establishments.

REFERENCES

Allen, Tammy D., Lillian T. Eby, and Elizabeth Lentz. 2006. "The Relationship between Formal Mentoring Program Characteristics and Perceived Program Effectiveness." *Personnel Psychology* 59:125–139.

Allen, Tammy D., M. L. Poteet, and S. M. Burroughs. 1997. "The Mentor's Perspective: A Qualitative Inquiry and Future Research Agenda." *Journal of Vocational Behavior* 51:70–89.

Alon, Sigal. 2004. "The Gender Stratification of Employment Hardship: Queuing, Opportunity Structure and Economic Cycles." *Research in Social Stratification and Mobility* 20:115–143.

American Bar Association. 1994. *The Burdens of Both, the Privileges of Neither: A Report of the Multicultural Women Attorneys' Network*. Chicago, Ill.: ABA.

Banaji, Mahzarin R. and Anthony G. Greenwald. 2013. *Blindspot: Hidden Biases of Good People*. New York, NY: Random House.

Barker, James R. 1993. "Tightening the Iron Cage: Concertive Control in Self-Managing Teams." *Administrative Science Quarterly* 38:408–437.

Barnhizer, Daniel. 2003. "Mentoring as Duty and Privilege." *Michigan Bar Journal* 82:46–47.

Baron, James N., Michael T. Hannan, Greta Hsu, and Ozgecan Kocak. 2007. "In the Company of Women – Gender Inequality and the Logic of Bureaucracy in Start-Up Firms." *Work and Occupations* 34:35–66.

Beckman, Christine M. and Damon J. Phillips. 2005. "Interorganizational Determinants of Promotion: Client Leadership and the Attainment of Women Attorneys." *American Sociological Review* 70:678–701.

Blake-Beard, Stacy D. 2001. "Taking a Hard Look at Formal Mentoring Programs: A Consideration of Potential Challenges Facing Women." *The Journal of Management Development* 20:331–345.

Blalock, Hubert M. 1967. *Toward a Theory of Minority-Group Relations*. New York, NY: John Wiley & Sons.

Chambliss, Elizabeth. 1997. "Organizational Determinants of Law Firm Integration." *American University Law Review* 46:669–746.

Chambliss, Elizabeth and Christopher Uggen. 2000. "Men and Women of Elite Law Firms: Reevaluating Kanter's Legacy." *Law and Social Inquiry* 25:41–68.

Clydesdale, Timothy T. 2004. "A Forked River Runs Through Law School: Toward Understanding Race, Gender, Age, and Related Gaps in Law School Performance and Bar Passage." *Law and Social Inquiry* 29:711–769.

Coleman, James E. and Mitu Gulati. 2006. "A Response to Professor Sander: Is It Really All about the Grades?" *North Carolina Law Review* 84:1823–1839.

Dobbin, Frank, Soohan Kim, and Alexandra Kalev. 2011. "You Can't Always Get What You Need: Organizational Determinants of Diversity Programs." *American Sociological Review* 76:386–411.

Edelman, Lauren B. 1990. "Legal Environments and Organizational Governance: The Expansion of Due Process in the American Workplace." *American Journal of Sociology* 95:1401–1440.

Epstein, Cynthia Fuchs, Robert Sauté, Bonnie Oglensky, and Martha Gever. 1995. "Glass Ceilings and Open Doors: Women's Advancement in the Legal Profession." *Fordham Law Review* 64:291–449.

Fields, Dail L., Jodi S. Goodman, and Terry C. Blum. 2005. "Human Resource Dependence and Organizational Demography: A Study of Minority Employment in Private Sector Companies." *Journal of Management* 31 (2):167–185.

Fiske, Susan T. 1998. "Stereotyping, Prejudice, and Discrimination." pp. 357–411 in *Handbook of Social Psychology*, edited by D. T. Gilbert, S. T. Fiske, and G. Lindzey. New York, NY: Oxford University Press.

Fiske, Susan T., Amy J.C. Cuddy, Peter Glick, and Jun Xu. 2002. "A Model of (Often Mixed) Stereotype Content: Competence and Warmth Respectively Follow from Perceived Status and Competition." *Journal of Personality and Social Psychology* 82:878–902.

Foschi, Martha. 2009. "Gender, Performance Level, and Competence Standards in Task Groups." *Social Science Research* 33:447–457.

García-López, Gladys. 2008. "'Nunca te toman en cuenta [They Never Take You into Account]': The Challenges of Inclusion and Strategies for Success of Chicana Attorneys." *Gender and Society* 22(5):590–612.

Gorman, Elizabeth H. 2005. "Gender Stereotypes, Same-Gender Preferences, and Organizational Variation in the Hiring of Women: Evidence from Law Firms." *American Sociological Review* 70:702–728.

———. 2006. "Work Uncertainty and the Promotion of Professional Women: The Case of Law Firm Partnership." *Social Forces* 85:864–890.

Gorman, Elizabeth H., and Fiona M. Kay. 2010. "Racial and Ethnic Minority Representation in Large U.S. Law Firms." *Studies in Law, Politics, and Society* 52:211–238.

Gorman, Elizabeth H. and Julie A. Kmec. 2009. "Hierarchical Rank and Women's Organizational Mobility: Glass Ceilings in Corporate Law Firms." *American Journal of Sociology* 114:1428–1474.

Greenwood, Royston, and Laura Empson. 2003. "The Professional Partnership: Relic or Exemplary Form of Governance?" *Organizational Studies* 24:909–934.

Hagan, John and Fiona Kay. 1995. *Gender in Practice: A Study of Lawyers' Lives.* Oxford, UK: Oxford University Press.

Heinz, John P., Robert Nelson, Rebecca Sandefur, and Edward O. Laumann. 2005. *Urban Lawyers: The New Social Structure of the Bar.* Chicago, IL: University of Chicago Press.

Hewstone, Miles, Mark Rubin, and Hazel Willis. 2002. "Intergroup Bias." *Annual Review of Psychology* 53:575–604.

Hogg, Michael. 2003. "Social Identity." pp. 462–479 in *Handbook of Self and Identity*, edited by M. Leary and J. Tangney. New York, NY: Guilford Press.

Kalev, Alexandra. 2009. "Cracking the Glass Cages? Restructuring and Ascriptive Inequality at Work." *American Journal of Sociology* 114:1591–1643.

Kalev, Alexandra, Frank Dobbin, and Erin Kelly. 2006. "Best Practices or Best Guesses? Assessing the Efficacy of Corporate Affirmative Action and Diversity Policies." *American Sociological Review* 71:589–617.

Kay, Fiona M. and Elizabeth H. Gorman. 2012. "Developmental Practices, Organizational Culture, and Minority Representation in Organizational Leadership: The Case of Partners in Large U.S. Law Firms." *The Annals of the American Academy of Political and Social Science* 639:91–113.

Kay, Fiona M. and John Hagan. 2003. "Building Trust: Social Capital, Distributive Justice and Loyalty to the Firm." *Law & Social Inquiry* 28:483–519.

Kay, Fiona M., John Hagan, and Patricia Parker. 2009. "Principals in Practice: The Importance of Mentorship in the Early Stages of Career Development." *Law & Policy* 31:69–110.

Kornhauser, Lewis A. and Richard L. Revesz. 1995. "Legal Education and Entry into the Legal Profession: The Role of Race, Gender, and Educational Debt." *New York University Law Review* 70: 829–964.

Kronman, Anthony T. 1993. *The Lost Lawyer: Failing Ideals in the Legal Profession.* Cambridge, MA: Belknap Press of Harvard University Press.

Lazega, Emmanuel. 2001. *The Collegial Phenomenon: The Social Mechanisms of Cooperation among Peers in a Corporate Law Partnership.* New York, NY: Oxford University Press.

McManus, Elizabeth K. 2005. "Intimidation and the Culture of Avoidance: Gender Issues and Mentoring in Law Firm Practice." *Fordham Urban Law Review* 33:217–231.

Montgomery, John E. 2008. "The Case for Law Firm Mentoring Programs." *South Carolina Lawyer* 19:40–43.

National Association for Law Placement. 2012. *Representation of Women among Associates Continues to Fall, Even as Minority Associates Make Gains.* National Institution for Law Placement, Washington, DC. www.nalp.org/2012lawfirmdiversity, accessed on June 26, 2013.

Noonan, Mary C., Mary E. Corcoran, and Paul N. Courant. 2007. "Is the Partnership Gap Closing for Women? Cohort Differences in the Sex Gap in Partnership Chances." *Social Science Research* 37:156–179.

Ornstein, Michael. 2001. *Lawyers in Ontario: Evidence from the 1996 Census,* A Report to the Law Society of Upper Canada, online: See http://rc.lsuc.on.ca/pdf/equity/lawyersinOntario1996.pdf. [accessed 10 September 2015]

2004. *The Changing Face of the Legal Profession, 1971–2001,* A Report to the Law Society of Upper Canada, online: See www.lsuc.on.ca/media/convoct04_ornstein.pdf. [accessed 10 September 2015]

Ortiz-Walters, Rowena, and Lucy L. Gilson. 2005. "Mentoring in Academia: An Examination of the Experiences of Protégés of Color." *Journal of Vocational Behavior* 67:459–475.

Payne-Pikus, Monique R., John Hagan and Robert L. Nelson. 2010. "Experiencing Discrimination: Race and Retention in America's Largest Law Firms." *Law and Society Review* 44:553–584.

Ragins, Belle Rose, and John L. Cotton. 1999. "Mentor Functions and Outcomes: A Comparison of Men and Women in Formal and Informal Mentoring Relationships." *Journal of Applied Psychology* 84:529–550.

Reichman, Nancy J., and Joyce S. Sterling. 2002. "Recasting the Brass Ring: Deconstructing and Reconstructing Workplace Opportunities for Women Lawyers." *Capital University Law Review* 29:923–977.

Reskin, Barbara F. 2001. "Rethinking Employment Discrimination and Its Remedies." pp. 218–244 in *The New Economic Sociology: Developments in an Emerging Field,* edited by M. Guillén, R. Collins, P. England, and M. Meyer. New York, NY: Russell Sage.

2003. "Including Mechanisms in Our Models of Ascriptive Inequality." *American Sociological Review* 68:1–21.

Reskin, Barbara F. and Debra B. McBrier. 2000. "Why Not Ascription? Organizations' Employment of Male and Female Managers." *American Sociological Review* 65:210–233.

Reskin, Barbara F., and Patricia Roos. 1990. *Job Queues, Gender Queues: Explaining Women's Inroads into Male Occupations.* Philadelphia, PA: Temple University Press.

Saks, Alan M. 1996. "The Relationship between the Amount and Helpfulness of Entry Training and Work Outcomes." *Human Relations* 49:429–451.

Sander, Richard. 2004. "A Systemic Analysis of Affirmative Action in American Law Schools." *Stanford Law Review* 57:367–483.

———. 2006. "The Racial Paradox of the Corporate Law Firm." *North Carolina Law Review* 84:1755–1822.

Smigel, Erwin O. 1969. *The Wall Street Lawyer: Professional Organization Man?* Bloomington, Indiana: Indiana University Press.

Smith-Doerr, Laurel. 2004. "Flexibility and Fairness: Effects of the Network Form of Organization on Gender Equity in Life Science Careers." *Sociological Perspectives* 47:25–54.

Stainback, K., D. Tomaskovic-Devey, and S. Skaggs. 2010. "Organizational Approaches to Inequality: Inertia, Relative Power, and Environments." *Annual Review of Sociology* 36:225–247.

Tharenou, Phyllis and Denise Conroy. 1994. "Men and Women Managers' Advancement: Personal or Situational Determinants." *Applied Psychology: An International Review* 43:5–31.

Thomas, David A. and John J. Gabarro. 1999. *Breaking Through: The Making of Minority Executives in Corporate America.* Boston, MA: Harvard Business School Press.

Underhill, Christina M. 2006. "The Effectiveness of Mentoring Programs in Corporate Settings: A Meta-Analytical Review of the Literature." *Journal of Vocational Behavior* 68:292–307.

Wallace, Michael, and Kevin Leicht. 2004. "Culture Wars in the Workplace?: Cultural Antecedents of Workers' Job Entitlement." *Work and Occupations* 31(1):3–37.

Wanberg, Connie R., John Kammeyer-Mueller, and Marc Marchese. 2006. "Mentor and Protégé Predictors and Outcomes of Mentoring in a Formal Mentoring Program." *Journal of Vocational Behavior* 69:410–423.

Waters, Malcolm. 1989. "Collegiality, Bureaucratization, and Professionalization: A Weberian Analysis." *American Journal of Sociology* 94:945–972.

Weinberg, Frankie J. and Melenie J. Lankau. 2011. "Formal Mentoring Programs: A Mentor-Centric and Longitudinal Analysis." *Journal of Management* 37:1527–1557.

Wholey, Douglas R. 1990. "The Effects of Formal and Informal Training on Tenure and Mobility in Manufacturing Firms." *The Sociological Quarterly* 31:37–57.

Wilkins, David. 1999. "Partners Without Power? A Preliminary Look at Black Partners in Corporate Law Firms." *Journal of the Institute for the Study of Legal Ethics* 2:15–48.

Wilkins, David and Mitu Gulati. 1996. "Why Are There So Few Black Lawyers in Corporate Law Firms? An Institutional Analysis." *California Law Review* 84:493–625.

GENDERED PATHWAYS

Choice, constraint, and women's job movements in the legal profession

JULIET R. AIKEN* AND MILTON C. REGAN, JR.**

INTRODUCTION

The career paths of men and women in the legal profession diverge with respect to advancement and job changes. This is reflected in notable differences in "career mobility, specifically with reference to partnerships in law firms, promotions in various settings, and subsequent hiring or job moves" (Kay and Gorman 2008: 323). Women lawyers not only disproportionally leave law firms and the legal profession as a whole (Kay and Gorman 2008: 323; Dinovitzer et al. 2009: 58; The National Association of Women Lawyers and the NAWL Foundation 2012) but are also more likely to want to leave their current job (Dinovitzer et al. 2004), to change jobs frequently (Dinovitzer et al. 2004: 58), and to move to a position of lower prestige when changing jobs (Reichman and Sterling 2004: 30). Moreover, over the course of their careers, women become more concentrated than men in non-law firm sectors while men become more concentrated than women in law firms (Dau-Schmidt et al. 2006: 1455; Dinovitzer et al. 2009: 63). Scholars attribute these differences primarily to the disparity between sexes in the assumption of family responsibilities, the ability to acquire clients, and access to mentoring (Reichman and Sterling 2002;

* Program Director and Clinical Assistant Professor, Master's in Professional Studies in Industrial Organizational Psychology, University of Maryland College Park.
** McDevitt Professor of Jurisprudence and Co-Director, Center for the Study of the Legal Profession, Georgetown University Law Center.

Reichman and Sterling 2004–2005). Most research on sex differences in the legal profession, however, has focused on what influences *job satisfaction* rather than on what influences *job turnover* (Kay and Gorman 2008: 320; Sterling and Reichman 2013), with one notable exception (Kay 1997). Our understanding of men's and women's job satisfaction in the legal profession, therefore, is richer than our understanding of why women and men change jobs.

Our research informs the literature on female job movement within the legal profession in two ways. First, we focus our investigation on why lawyers change jobs rather than on how satisfied they are with them. Second, we examine differences in why men and women graduates change jobs across their careers. We collected data on initial job placement after law school and subsequent career paths, including up to 12 jobs, for 1,618 lawyers who graduated from the Georgetown Law Center between 1974 and 2010. Using this dataset, we identified predictors of turnover for men and women by year of graduation, employment sector (e.g., law firm, business, government), and when a job change occurs in the course of a lawyer's career.

Our data indicate that women were more likely than men to leave jobs in all sectors to meet family responsibilities. This is the case despite the fact that women's concentration in some sectors may reflect a belief that work in these sectors enables them to balance work and family obligations. Common assumptions about the ease of balancing work and family responsibilities in some sectors, therefore, may be unfounded. In addition, with respect to possible differences between men and women in what they value at work beyond family concerns, our data reveal no significant differences once job sector is taken into account. Lawyers in different sectors, both men and women, tend to move into or out of certain sectors to seek particular types of rewards. Differences that appear to be a function of sex thus may be explained by the sectors in which men and women concentrate in over time.

FEMALE JOB MOVEMENT IN THE LEGAL PROFESSION

Women in the legal profession are more likely than men are to want to change jobs (Teitelbaum 1991: 7; Dinovitzer et al. 2004: 58), to change jobs (Dinovitzer et al. 2009: 58), to change jobs earlier in their careers (Reichman and Sterling 2004–2005: 4), and to move to less prestigious positions when changing jobs (Dinovitzer et al. 2009). In addition, men and women tend to move, over the course of their careers, into different job sectors. Women are more likely to work in government, whereas men are more likely to work in private practice (Hull and Nelson 2000; Dau-Schmidt et al. 2006: 1455; Sandefur 2007; Dinovitzer et al. 2009: 63). Sex differences are also prevalent in private practice: men are more likely to be promoted to partners (Gellis 1991; Ziewacz 1996: 973–974; Reichman and Sterling 2004–2005: 38–40; Dau-Schmidt et al. 2009: 10), whereas women are more likely to be of counsel (Dau-Schmidt et al. 2006: 1456; The National Association of Women Lawyers and the NAWL Foundation 2011: 2–3), non-equity partners (Dinovitzer et al. 2009: 63–64), and staff lawyers (The National Association of Women Lawyers and the NAWL Foundation 2011: 2).

Some researchers are now exploring why women leave law firms and the legal profession more than men. These scholars typically attribute patterns in women's job movements to a combination of four powerful ways in which women are disadvantaged at work: discrimination, differences in access to and quality of mentoring, differences in rainmaking ability, and differences in family responsibilities (Ziewacz 1996).

Considerable evidence indicates that, as Fiona Kay and Elizabeth Gorman observe, "many women lawyers face gender discrimination, including sexist behavior, harassment, demeaning comments, and a negative courtroom environment" (Kay and Gorman 2008: 305). Almost 40% of women participating in the 2004 Indiana Law School Study, for instance, reported that they experienced discrimination in pay decisions and 27% of women reported that they experienced discrimination in promotion decisions (Lopez 2008). Consistent with this perspective, women who reported experiencing sexual discrimination in the practice of law were much more likely to leave the profession than those who did not (Kay 1997).

Mentorship in the legal profession also favors men (Epstein 1995; Rhode 2011; Payne-Pikus, Nelson, and Hagan 2010). Women and minorities in corporate law firms perceive that white men have greater access to mentorship and partnership opportunities (Garth 2009: 1364). Because of these disparities in mentorship, women and minorities may not receive the same opportunities for work, or the support from both inside and outside the firm that is necessary for advancement (Kay, Fiona and Hagan 2003: 482; Kay, Fiona and Hagan 2005: 281; Garth 2009: 1364–1365).

Sex disparities in client development may also contribute to women's departure from law firms. Women lawyers may invest less time than men invest in developing clients (Gellis 1991) and have less access to client development opportunities (Reichman and Sterling 2004–2005). Women may generally struggle with client development, as it requires mentoring, a substantial time investment, access to powerful individuals both inside and outside the firm, and access to meaningful work assignments – all resources to which women lawyers may have less access than their male peers (Ziewacz 1996; French 2000).

Finally, female movement within or departure from the legal profession is frequently attributed to the heavier burden women bear in family and childcare responsibilities (Noonan and Corcoran 2004: 130; Porter 2006: 55; Kay and Gorman 2008: 307). For example, women in the legal profession are more likely than men are to work part time and be unemployed, and to report that they spend more time caring for children (Monahan and Swanson 2009). Additionally, when women in the legal profession are married, they often have spouses with equally demanding jobs (Dau-Schmidt et al. 2006; Monahan and Swanson 2009) who earn more than they do (Dau-Schmidt 2006; Monahan and Swanson 2009). Earnings differences between even high-achieving women in the legal profession and their spouses may place additional pressure on women to assume more childcare responsibilities. Consistent with this perspective, research on Indiana Law School alumni and Massachusetts lawyers reveals that women are more likely to report leaving their jobs for family reasons (Dau-Schmidt et al. 2009) and work-life balance than men are (Harrington and Hsi 2007).

Research has thus far focused on the ways in which patterns of women's job changes in the legal profession reflect the role of discrimination, differences in access to and quality of mentoring, differences in rainmaking ability, and differences in family demands. These factors result in women in law practice suffering significant tangible disadvantages compared to men. Women report lower median incomes and statuses (e.g., associate versus partner) than men report across almost all sectors (Dinovitzer et al. 2004: 58) within the legal profession (The National Association of Women Lawyers and the NAWL Foundation 2012: 5). The extensive research on sex differences in pay in the legal profession reveals that the discrepancies between men and women in pay persist even when accounting for differences in hours worked, years in practice, job sector, geography, work profiles, credentials, and other demographic and personal characteristics (Teitelbaum et al. 1991: 454–455; Gellis 1991: 945; Reichman and Sterling 2002: 10–14;

The National Association of Women Lawyers and the NAWL Foundation 2012: 5; Dinovitzer et al. 2004: 58; Reichman and Sterling 2004–2005: 37; Lopez 2008: 60; Monahan and Swanson 2009: 451–483).

It would be natural to assume that the tangible disadvantages that women in the legal profession suffer leave them less satisfied with their jobs than men. Notwithstanding these differences, however, what is known as "the paradox of the contented female lawyer" (Hull 1999) indicates that women and men in the legal profession tend to be equally satisfied with their jobs as a whole (Dau-Schmidt et al. 2006; Cantrell et al. 2007–2008). A few studies find that women in legal work are less satisfied with their jobs than are men (Hall 1995; Chiu 1998), but "most studies reveal that women and men are surprisingly similar in their levels of job satisfaction" (Chambers 1989; Mueller and Wallace 1989; Hull 1999; Kay and Hagan 2007; Kay and Gorman 2008: 316).

One possible explanation for this paradox is that women value pay less than men do (Rhode 2001). If this is the case, we would expect that their job satisfaction is less tied to their satisfaction with income than is the case with men, and more tied to other dimensions of their work. Consistent with this, research on the After the JD project concludes that women tend to rate what that project's researchers describe as law firms' "lifestyle" profiles (job characteristics such as office environment, hours expected, advancement opportunities, and training and mentorship) as more important in their choice of firms than men do (Dinovitzer et al. 2009). Similarly, Kay and Hagan found that men's intentions to leave a law firm were affected by their satisfaction with promotion opportunities, compensation, and job security, while women's plans to leave were influenced by the extent to which they enjoyed intrinsic rewards such as opportunities to demonstrate their skill and to obtain a sense of accomplishment through their practice. Other research consistent with this indicates that men are more likely than women to change jobs for prestige (Teitelbaum et al. 1991), new opportunities (Reichman and Sterling 2002: 25), and advancement (Dau-Schmidt et al. 2009), findings that are consistent with the hypothesis that men are more motivated than women are by extrinsic rewards (Dau-Schmidt et al. 2009). However, other research finds no differences between men and women in the value they place on the intrinsic and extrinsic aspects of law practice (Mueller and Wallace 1989; Hull 1999; Heinz et al. 2005).

At this point, research on the differential values theory is inconclusive. Our study seeks to contribute to the research on this question by exploring the extent to which women and men gave reasons for leaving jobs that reflect different sources of satisfaction from their work. If such differences exist, they might serve to "push" women from jobs that fail to provide the sources of satisfaction that women seek or "pull" them into new jobs that do provide these sources.

SEX DIFFERENCES IN REASONS FOR JOB CHANGES

The aim of our research was to determine if there were statistically significant differences in the reasons that women and men in our study gave for changing jobs over the course of their careers. In addition to focusing on meeting family responsibilities and accommodating one's spouse as possible reasons, we sought to identify men's and women's endorsement of reasons that would reflect differences in the importance that men and women attach to various features of their work.

First, research indicates that women still carry the brunt of the load when it comes to childcare and family responsibilities (Dinovitzer et al. 2009); women are more likely than men are to work part time, be unemployed, and spend more time on childcare than men (Dinovitzer et al. 2009; Monahan and Swanson 2009). Since women continue to take on traditional caregiver roles, and since women in the legal profession are typically married to spouses with equally or more demanding and financially rewarding jobs (Dau-Schmidt et al. 2009), research suggests that women are more likely than men to leave jobs for family reasons (Dau-Schmidt et al. 2009) and to achieve work-life balance (Harrington and Hsi 2007). While prior research has often focused on the different investments men and women make in childcare, women in the legal profession may be more likely to move to accommodate their higher-earning spouse or partner's career or financial goals since women's spouses typically have more demanding and financially rewarding jobs (Dau-Schmidt et al. 2006).Our first hypothesis, therefore, is that women are more likely than men to change to meet their family responsibilities or to accommodate their spouse or partner.

Hypothesis 1a: *Women are more likely than men to cite a desire to have more time for family responsibilities as a reason for changing jobs.*

Hypothesis 1b: *Women are more likely than men to cite moving to accommodate a spouse or partner as a reason for changing jobs.*

Women leave law firms in greater numbers than men do (Hagan and Kay 1995; Harrington and Hsi 2007). Women in the legal profession are therefore more concentrated than men are in government; men more than women are concentrated in law firms (Dau-Schmidt et al. 2006: 1455; Dinovitzer et al. 2009: 63). Our data reflect this phenomenon. While 58% of men in our sample occupied law firms in their first job, only 51.3% of women worked in law firms in their first job (χ^2 = 5.62, p < 0.05). Over time, this discrepancy increased; 46.7% of men in their 10th year post-graduation worked in law firms, whereas 33.6% of women in their 10th year post-graduation worked in law firms (χ^2 = 14.46, p < 0.05). Similarly, while men and women in our sample were more equally represented in government, public interest/education, and business in their first jobs (38.4% of women and 32.5% of men, χ^2 = 4.78, p < 0.05), by their 10th year post-graduation, women dominated work in government, public interest/education, and business (39.0% of women and 23.9% of men, χ^2 = 21.82, p < 0.01). Law firms and sectors other than law firms thus tend to be gendered to varying degrees.

Sex disparities such as these are often attributed to women's assumption of family responsibilities, as work outside law firms is perceived as offering better work-life balance than law firm work (French 2000: 196–197; Reichman and Sterling 2004–2005: 26; Harrington and Hsi 2007: 232–233). If this perception is true, we would expect that women would be more likely than men to move out of law firms, and less likely than men to move into law firms, for family responsibilities. Likewise, women would be more likely than men to move into non-law firm jobs (i.e., government, business, and public interest/education), and less likely than men to move out of non-law firm jobs, for family responsibilities. These dynamics contribute to the concentration of women in settings outside of law firms. Therefore, we hypothesize that:

Hypothesis 2a: Women are less likely than men to move out of non-law firm jobs because of family responsibilities, and are more likely than men to move into non-law firm jobs because of family responsibilities.

Hypothesis 2b: Women are more likely than men to move out of law firm jobs because of family responsibilities, and are less likely than men to move into law firm jobs because of family responsibilities.

As we have discussed, some research indicates that meaningful work may be more important to women than to men in the legal profession (Dinovitzer 2009). Furthermore, women are more motivated than men by social issues to join the legal profession (Teitelbaum 1991: 449;

Dau-Schmidt et al. 2006; Dau-Schmidt et al. 2009; Schleef 2000). Assuming that involvement in social issues is associated with meaningful work, this latter result suggests that women in the legal profession are more likely than men to seek meaningful work. We therefore hypothesize that women are more likely than men to change jobs for meaningful work.

Hypothesis 3a: Women are more likely than men to cite a desire for meaningful work as a reason for changing jobs.

Professional training and development may play a crucial – yet under-studied – role in why women decide to stay, or move to another job. Only one study to date addresses the role of training in decisions to move in the legal profession. In this study, Fortney reported that associates changed jobs for many reasons – one of which was to receive better training and supervision (cited by 8% of respondents) (Fortney 2000). However, the results of this study do not reveal how these motivators of turnover may differentially drive men and women.

Why might we expect there to be sex differences in changing jobs to attain more training and development? Unmet career expectations contribute to voluntary turnover (Houkes et al. 2001). Additionally, female job movement is often attributed to differences between men and women in access to mentorship (Reichman and Sterling 2002; Reichman and Sterling 2004–2005). To the extent that the negative experiences in law firms – including discrimination and a lack of mentorship – make it more difficult for women to attain their career aspirations, women lawyers may have more unmet career goals than men do. If women feel that their developmental needs are not being met, women may be more likely change jobs for training. Furthermore, research suggests that women typically value professional development more than men do (Reichman and Sterling 2004–2005), with developmental opportunities and personal growth more strongly predicting satisfaction (Dinovitzer et al. 2004: 58), choice of firm (Dinovitzer, 2009–2010), and even entry into the legal profession as a whole for women (Teitelbaum et al. 1991). Consistent with this perspective, we hypothesize that women are more likely than men to leave for developmental opportunities, such as training.

Hypothesis 3b: Women are more likely than men to cite a desire for more training and development as a reason for changing jobs.

While women may change jobs to accommodate family responsibilities or to obtain more training and development, men may leave jobs to satisfy different aspirations. Specifically, as previously discussed, men are slightly more likely to change jobs for prestige (Teitelbaum et al. 1991) and new opportunities (Reichman and Sterling 2004–2005), and are generally more motivated than women by extrinsic rewards such as income (Dau-Schmidt et al. 2009). One activity that is important in obtaining these rewards is building one's practice. Thus, consistent with prior research, we hypothesize that men are more likely to leave jobs to build their practice and to obtain higher pay.

Hypothesis 4a: Men are more likely than women to cite opportunities to build their practice as a reason for changing jobs.

Hypothesis 4b: Men are more likely than women to cite greater financial rewards as a reason for changing jobs.

While individual values and preferences influence turnover, research consistently shows that situational constraints exert a powerful influence over job change decisions (Hom 1987; Cohen 1999). Consequently, while there may be global differences between men and women in reasons for leaving their jobs, drivers of job movement for men and women may vary by sector, over time, and by time of entry into the legal profession.

To the extent that some motivators of job change are more predictive of leaving certain job sectors, these motivators may push lawyers into certain jobs. In contrast, if some motivators of job change are more predictive of entry into certain sectors, these motivators may be pulling lawyers into those sectors. Analysis of how job sectors relate to reasons for job change will therefore shed some light on whether certain motivators tend to push or pull lawyers out of or into their jobs, and on whether those motivators differ for women and men.

Research   Are there sex differences in motivations for changing jobs by prior
Question 1:   or subsequent job sector?

Different motivations also may drive early career movements for men and women compared to mid- and later-career movements. Moreover, men and women who entered the legal profession in the late 1970's may have had different values, motivations, and options than those who entered in the 1980's, 1990's, and 2000's. Consequently, we will also explore how men's and women's motivations for leaving jobs differ over stage of career, and time of entry into the legal profession.

Research   Are there sex differences in motivations for changing jobs for early,
Question 2:   mid-, and later-career job changes?

309

Research   *Are there sex differences in motivations for changing jobs by time of*
Question 3:   *entry into the legal profession?*

METHOD

Sample

In 2010, Georgetown Law Center graduates were surveyed on their career histories. Since surveying all Georgetown graduates would not be feasible, we reached out to alumni in the graduating classes of 1977, 1980, 1985, 1990, 1995, 2000, 2005, and 2007. We issued invitations both by mail and electronically, and made follow-up phone calls to remind alumni to take the survey. In total, 1,631 graduates of 4,973 invited responded to this survey (32.8%). Some 48.1% of respondents were female, and 81.2% were white. To assess the extent to which our sample was representative of the population of Georgetown graduates, we compared the demographic information about all JD students graduating in the targeted years who had employment within 9 months of graduation with the demographic information about our sample of JD students. Overall, our alumni sample as a whole seems to be reasonably representative of the graduates of Georgetown Law Center. The sole exception is that our sample appears to comprise of a larger proportion of white graduates than the proportion of white graduates in the population.[1]

MEASURES

Career history

On the survey, lawyers were prompted to provide information on up to twelve jobs. For each job held, respondents selected a job sector, how long they worked in that job, and indicated up to four reasons why they left that job. Job sectors included solo practice, contract lawyer, law firms (from 2 to over 1,000 lawyers), government, public interest, educational institutions, business and industry, or other organizations.

Due to the relatively small proportion of jobs occupied in several sectors (e.g., education, public interest, solo practice, contract lawyers), we condensed responses into eight categories. These eight categories were (a) solo or contract lawyers, (b) small to mid-sized law firms

---

[1] A discussion of the analyses we conducted and conclusions we reached is available from the first author.

(2 to 500 lawyers), (c) large law firms (over 500 lawyers), (d) government, (e) public interest or education, (f) law clerks, (g) business or industry, and (h) other sectors. We coded data for each category into a separate variable in our dataset. Lawyers who worked in a given sector for a given job received a "1" for that sector for that job and a "0" for all other sectors for that job. The number of jobs each lawyer held in each of these eight sectors was summed across their career to yield the total number of jobs held in each sector. In total, lawyers held between 1 (20.9%) and 12 (0.3%) jobs throughout their careers; the large majority of lawyers held 5 or fewer jobs (87.7%).

Lawyers indicated the length of time they held each job in years. We created a variable to denote when in a lawyer's career he or she changed jobs by summing the length of time a lawyer held one job with the length of time a lawyer held all prior jobs. For example, if a lawyer held his or her first job for two years, second job for five years, and third job for three years, the point in that lawyer's career that he or she changed jobs first would be two (2), second would be seven (2 + 5), and third would be 10 (2 + 5 + 3). Lawyers changed jobs between 0 and 37 years into their careers (mean = 9.17, St. Dev. = 8.16).

Lawyers could select up to four reasons for leaving each job, including having more time for family responsibilities, doing work that was more meaningful, having more opportunity to build a practice, enjoying greater financial rewards, obtaining more professional training and development, and moving to a new city because of a spouse or partner. In total, lawyers ranged in offering 0 (16.3%) to 22 (0.1%) of the above reasons for changing jobs across their careers.

Demographics

Respondents also provided information about their sex, earnings in 2008, marital status, number of dependents, and year of graduation from law school. Sex was coded with women as "0" and men as "1." Currently married lawyers and lawyers in marriage-like unions were coded as "1" and currently unmarried lawyers were coded "0." Some 70.9% of respondents were married or in marriage-like unions at the time of the survey. Lawyers' number of dependents ranged from 0 (41.7%) to 6 (0.5%), with the overwhelming majority of lawyers having 2 or fewer dependents (83.7%). Earnings in 2008 were provided in intervals; lawyers checked a box that best described their earnings in 2008. Options included "not employed in 2008," and ranged from "up to 25,000" to "$5,000,000 or more." As a small proportion of lawyers made more than $400,000 (12.5% total), we collapsed several categories to facilitate analysis. We created thirteen dummy-coded variables to compare earnings in 2008, with those lawyers who were not employed in 2008 serving as the comparison group. We do not report or interpret the coefficients associated with the effects of our control variables (i.e., earnings, marital status, and number of dependents).

ANALYSIS

Why do men and women change jobs?

Hypotheses 1, 3, and 4 suggested that men and women change jobs for different reasons. Since the outcome variables (how many times a lawyer changed his or her job for a given reason) are count variables with unequal means and variances, we conducted two negative binomial regressions predicting the number of times men and women cited each reason for changing jobs to test each hypothesis. We first regressed each reason for changing jobs onto gender, controlling for the number of jobs each lawyer had held by the time the survey was conducted. Next, we ran negative binomial regressions using additional covariates to ensure that the relationship between sex and changing jobs for family responsibilities could not be accounted for by these confounding variables. Specifically, we controlled for the number of jobs each lawyer had in different sectors (i.e., solo/contract lawyering, law firms, government, public interest/education, clerking, legal business jobs, and other), the year the lawyer graduated with a degree, marital status, number of dependents, and earnings in 2008. Results of these analyses for each hypothesis are discussed in more detail later, and a summary of support for these analyses is available in Table 10.1.

Hypotheses 1a and 1b stated that women would be more likely than men to mention family responsibilities or accommodating a spouse or partner as reasons for changing jobs. Women were significantly more likely to leave their jobs for family responsibilities ($B = -0.71$, $p < 0.05$) and to move for a spouse or partner ($B = -0.55$, $p < 0.05$). Even after we controlled for additional covariates, women were still more likely to change jobs to have more time for family responsibilities ($B = -0.58$, $p < 0.05$) and to move to a new city to accommodate a spouse or partner ($B = -0.52$, $p < 0.05$). Since the relationships between sex and leaving for family responsibilities or moving for a spouse/partner hold across both sets of negative binomial regressions, men and women are differentially changing jobs for family responsibilities

TABLE 10.1: Summary of Support from Negative Binomial Regressions of Hypotheses 1, 3, and 4 and Research Question 1

Hypothesis or Research Question	Model 1[1]	Model 2[2]
1a: Women are more likely than men to change jobs for family responsibilities	Supported	Supported
1b: Women are more likely than men to move to accommodate a spouse/partner	Supported	Supported
3a: Women are more likely than men to change jobs for meaningful work	Not supported	Not supported
3b: Women are more likely than men to change jobs for training	Supported	Not supported
4a: Men are more likely than women to change jobs to build their practice	Supported	Not supported
4b: Men are more likely than women to change jobs for financial rewards	Supported	Not supported

Note: N = 1619
[1] Controlling for total number of jobs
[2] Controlling for number of jobs in different sectors, year of graduation, marital status, number of dependents, and earnings

and accommodations in a way that cannot be accounted for by sector, years in the market, marital status, earnings, or number of dependents.

Hypotheses 3a and 3b stated that women would be more likely than men to leave jobs for meaningful work and for training. Women were not significantly more likely to leave their jobs for more meaningful work ($B = -0.12$, $p > 0.10$), but were significantly more likely to leave their jobs to obtain more training and development ($B = -0.47$, $p < 0.05$). After controlling for additional covariates, women and men still did not differ in citing meaningful work as a motivator to leave their jobs ($B = 0.00$, $p > 0.10$). Moreover, although the coefficient remains in the hypothesized direction, women and men did not significantly differ in citing a desire for more training and development as a motivation for changing jobs ($B = -0.19$, $p > 0.10$). In this last equation, the numbers of jobs lawyers previously held in different sectors significantly predicted job changes for more training. Consequently, the tendency for women to leave jobs for training and development may be related to the tendency for men and women to occupy jobs in different sectors of the legal marketplace.

Hypothesis 4 stated that men would be more likely than women to cite opportunities to build their practice, and the desire to obtain greater financial rewards as reasons for changing jobs. Men were significantly more likely than women were to leave their jobs to build their practice ($B = 0.72$, $p < 0.05$) and to enjoy greater financial rewards ($B = 0.29$, $p < 0.05$). Controlling for additional covariates, men and women did not differ significantly in citing opportunities to build their practice ($B = 0.16$, $p > 0.10$) or to gain more financial rewards ($B = 0.13$, $p > 0.05$) as reasons for a job change. However, the number of law firm, government, solo lawyer/contract lawyer, and other jobs all predicted the likelihood that a lawyer cited building his or her practice or gaining more financial rewards as reasons for changing jobs. In other words, the more jobs a lawyer held in almost any sector, the more likely he or she would be to cite advancement, building a practice, or financial rewards as reasons for changing jobs. This is simply because the more jobs a lawyer held, the more opportunities he or she had to cite any given reason for changing jobs. The sex difference we initially found in changing jobs to build a practice or gain financial rewards may be explained by other, job-related variables, or by generational differences.

Do sex differences in job changes vary by context?

Hypotheses 2a and 2b and our first, second, and third research questions addressed the extent to which there were sex differences in reasons for changing jobs by prior job sector, by subsequent job sector, by time in career, and by time of entry into the legal profession. To answer these questions, we conducted autoregressive generalized estimating equations (GEE) using SPSS software. GEE analysis is a multivariate statistical approach that accounts for dependencies in data (i.e., when data are collected from the same individual over time). Controlling for marital status, number of dependents, total number of jobs, and earnings, we estimated the main effects of sectors, year of graduation, and time in career on reasons for leaving followed by the interactive effects of job sector (both prior and subsequent), year of graduation, and time in career, by lawyer sex on reasons for leaving jobs. For these analyses, we did not interpret main effects when $p < 0.10$. However, we did interpret and discuss interactions that trended toward significance with $p < 0.10$. Tests for interaction effects are lower in power than tests of main effects; it is likely that a researcher will declare that an interaction effect does not exist even if it does exist in the population. This is especially true in nonexperimental studies, when there are unequal sample sizes of sub-groups (i.e., men and women), and when the interaction effect is small in the population (Aguinis and

Stone-Romero 1997; McClelland and Judd 1993). Table 10.2 summarizes the results of the analyses by prior job sector (research question 1), subsequent work sector (research question 1), and year of graduation/time in career (research questions 2 and 3), respectively. Note that we would find support for hypotheses 2a and 2b if sex interacted with sector to predict changing jobs for family reasons. This would occur if women were especially likely for family reasons to leave law firms (and not to leave non-law firm jobs) and to enter sectors other than law firms (and not enter law firms).

While we were able to collapse observations in different sectors down to eight groups in our prior analyses (i.e., solo or contract lawyering, small/mid-sized law firm, large law firm, government, public interest/education, clerking, business, other), there were too few observations in some of these job categories to conduct GEEs with all eight groups. We therefore collapsed some of these sectors into "other," including solo lawyering, contract lawyering, and clerking. We then effects-coded job sectors, resulting in five variables each for leaving and entering focal sectors.

In contrast to our prediction in hypothesis 2, our analysis indicates that female lawyers in all sectors were more likely than male lawyers were to change jobs for family responsibilities ($B = -0.50$, $p < 0.05$), even when controlling for prior job sector, subsequent job sector, time in career, year of graduation, and earnings. In other words, while there are some differences by sector in lawyers leaving for family reasons, women – regardless of sector – leave for family reasons more than men do. The data, therefore, do not support hypothesis 2a that women are less likely than men are to move out of jobs in non-law firm sectors because of family responsibilities. In fact, we found that women in our sample experienced more work-family conflict than men do in law firms (women = 4.43, men = 3.82, $t(491) = 3.58$, $p < 0.05$), in government (women = 3.17, men = 2.68, $t(287) = 2.85$, $p < 0.05$), in business (women = 3.24, men = 3.08, $t(228) = 0.69$, $p > 0.10$), and even in public interest (women = 3.17, men = 2.68, $t(72) = 1.06$, $p > 0.10$). Thus, while it may be especially difficult for women to balance family responsibilities while employed in law firms, it is only somewhat less difficult for them to do so when employed in other sectors in the legal profession.

Research question 1 investigated whether there were sex differences in changing jobs depending on prior or subsequent job sector. Indeed, women and men left certain sectors – and entered certain sectors – for

TABLE 10.2: Summary of Support for GEE Tests of Hypothesis 2 and Research Questions 2, 3, and 4

Hypothesis or Research Question	Summary
2a: Women are less likely than men to move out of non-law firm jobs because of family responsibilities, and are more likely than men are to move into non-law firm jobs because of family responsibilities.	Not supported
2b: Women are more likely than men are to move out of law firm jobs because of family responsibilities, and are less likely than men are to move into law firm jobs because of family responsibilities.	Not supported
R1: Are there sex differences in motivations for changing jobs by prior or subsequent job sector?	W > M leave business for family M > W leave business for training M > W leave large firms for family M > W enter large firms for meaningful work W > M leave small/mid firms for meaningful work M > W enter small/mid firms for family W > M enter pub int/ed. for meaningful work M > W enter pub int/ed. for building practice
R2: Are there sex differences in motivations for changing jobs for early, mid-, and later-career job changes?	W change jobs later rather than earlier for family M change jobs earlier rather than later for family W change jobs earlier rather than later for financial rewards M change jobs later rather than earlier for financial rewards
R3: Are there sex differences in motivations for changing jobs by time of entry into the legal profession?	W who entered job market earlier changed jobs for family > W entered later W who entered job market recently changed jobs for training > W who entered earlier M who entered job market recently changed jobs for family > W

316

different reasons. First, women left business jobs for family responsibilities, whereas men did not ($B = -0.87$, $p < 0.05$). Moreover, men were actually more likely to leave large law firms for family responsibilities than women ($B = 0.86$, $p < 0.05$), and women were less likely to move into small or mid-sized law firms for family responsibilities ($B = 0.57$, $p < 0.10$). Women were also less likely than men to move into large law firms ($B = 0.73$, $p < 0.10$), more likely than men to move into public interest/education ($B = -0.44$, $p < 0.05$), and more likely than men to leave small and mid-sized firms for meaningful work ($B = -0.35$, $p < 0.05$). Additionally, women were less likely than men to leave business jobs for training ($B = 0.80$, $p < 0.05$). Finally, women lawyers were less likely to enter public interest/education to build their practice, whereas men lawyers were more likely to enter public interest/education to do so ($B = 0.67$, $p < 0.05$).

Research question 2 investigated whether there were sex differences in changing jobs for early, mid-, and later-career job changes. Movements for family responsibilities were more common later rather than earlier in women lawyers careers ($B = -0.05$, $p < 0.05$). Additionally, women trended toward being more likely to change jobs early in their careers for financial reasons, whereas men trended toward being more likely to change jobs to do so later in their careers ($B = 0.02$, $p < 0.10$).

Finally, research question 3 investigated whether there were sex differences in changing jobs depending on when a lawyer graduated with their degree. Women lawyers who entered the job market earlier (e.g., graduates of the 1970's) were more likely to have changed jobs for family responsibilities than women lawyers who entered the job market later (e.g., graduates of the 2000's) ($B = 0.04$, $p < 0.05$). In contrast, men lawyers who entered the job market later were more likely to have changed jobs for family responsibilities than men lawyers who entered the job market later. Further, women who had entered the workforce more recently (e.g., graduates of the 2000's) changed jobs more for training and development than women who had entered the workforce earlier ($B = 0.03$, $p < 0.05$).

DISCUSSION

Women in the legal profession continue to change jobs more frequently than men do (Reichman and Sterling 2002; Dinovitzer, et al. 2009). While scholars have discussed some potential drivers of women's job movements, including discrimination, family responsibilities, access to mentoring (Reichman and Sterling 2002; Dinovitzer et al. 2009), and differences in rainmaking, the majority of research on sex differences in the legal profession has focused on job satisfaction, not job turnover. In the current study, we sought to understand why lawyers change jobs, rather than how satisfied they are with their jobs, in a sample of male and female graduates who graduated from the Georgetown Law Center between 1974 and 2010.

Our initial analyses of differences in the valuation of particular work characteristics were partially consistent with our hypotheses. Controlling for the number of jobs a lawyer previously held, women were more likely to leave jobs to obtain more training and men were more likely to leave jobs to build their practice and to enjoy greater financial rewards. However, these significant differences largely dissipated when we controlled for the number of jobs held in specific sectors, the year lawyers graduated from law school, and lawyer earnings. Thus, while men and women may leave jobs for different reasons, at least initially, these differences may be a function of the different sectors that men and women occupy and move into over the course of their careers.

As we have described, research indicates that while women increasingly occupy non-law firm sectors, men increasingly dominate law firm jobs (Dinovitzer, et al. 2004; Dau-Schmidt et al. 2009). Our findings could suggest that women and men value different aspects of work, assuming the relationship between sex and leaving for different reasons is fully explained by the different sectors men and women move into over time. That is, lawyers in general may tend to select law firm jobs for financial reasons, and men tend to seek financial rewards. More men than women therefore move into law firms. Likewise, lawyers tend to select non-law firm jobs for training and development, and women tend to seek training and development. More women than men therefore move into non-law firm jobs. Consistent with this theory, men in our sample consider compensation more important than women in staying in their current job (men = 5.42, women = 5.12, $t(1423) = -3.93, p <$ 0.05). The idea is that the differences in the extent to which women and men are concentrated in different sectors reflect their preferences for the forms of job satisfaction that those sectors provide.

This theory is at least plausible. However, it does not fully explain patterns of job movement. Specifically, our data are also consistent with literature that suggests that men and women move into different employment settings because of differences in the assumption of family responsibilities (Dinovitzer et al. 2009; Dau-Schmidt et al. 2009).

Scholars argue that women move into non-law firm jobs because these jobs are more family friendly and promote better work life-balance (French 2000: 196–197; Reichman and Sterling 2002: 26; Harrington and Hsi 2007: 232–233). If this conclusion held in our research, we would expect that the significant main effect of sex on leaving for family responsibilities would disappear after accounting for job sector. We also would expect that interaction effects would emerge whereby, for example, women left law firms more – and non-law firms less – for family responsibilities.

Instead, we found that, even when controlling for sector, women still leave their jobs more for family responsibilities than men do. In other words, sex disparities in changing jobs for family reasons are pervasive, persisting across sectors, year of graduation, and different earnings levels. While sectors may vary in the intensity of work-family conflict that women face, family responsibilities appear to push female lawyers from job to job. Indeed, family responsibilities may be a driving force not simply in job-to-job movement, but in pushing women out of the legal profession altogether (Dau-Schmidt et al. 2000). Consistent with this perspective, 78.7% of the 122 unemployed alumni in our sample were women, and 77.4% of the 106 part-time or reduced-hour employed alumni in our sample were women.

What explains the differences in men's and women's concentration in different sectors, if non-law firm sectors are not as family friendly as expected? According to the theory of attraction-selection-attrition, applicants first are attracted to an organization that they think matches their values (attraction) (Schneider 1987). Organizations then hire applicants that they perceive match their values. Naturally, not every-one who is hired will actually match an organization's values; employ-ees who do not will often leave the organization, either voluntarily or involuntarily (attrition). The attraction and selection stages of this cycle characterize what pulls lawyers from one job to the next; attrition captures what pushes lawyers out of their jobs. Lawyers may believe that practice sectors other than law firms offer a better work-life balance, and therefore may be attracted to non-law firm jobs. They subsequently may find, however, that they are still unable to meet their family responsibilities even in these sectors.

Overall, then, gendered motivations – in the aggregate – appear to drive men and women to change jobs: men place emphasis on tangible rewards such as income, while women place priority on family. The pervasive force of gender roles, however, may nonetheless constrain the choices that men and women make. Lawyers may make choices that tend to align with gendered constraints; seeking more training and development is certainly not at odds with work-family balance, whereas seeking financial rewards may be. At the same time, lawyers may seek to minimize the influence of this constraint by constructing explanations for their job movements that characterize them as the result of choices to seek particular forms of satisfaction at work.

For men, gender roles require attention to financial concerns more than training. Within this constraint, however, men may also "choose" to build their practice, since doing so contributes to their ability to earn a higher salary. Because married women lawyers tend to have spouses with equally demanding jobs (Dau-Schmidt et al. 2006; Monahan and Swanson 2009), women in the legal profession generally may feel freed from the constraint of supporting their family financially. This apparent freedom, however, is tied to a different constraint: the responsibility for physically supporting their family by caring for children (Kay and Gorman 2008; Monahan 2009). Within this constraint, women may be able to "choose" training, since they need not make obtaining financial rewards a priority. Men's and women's preferences and choices therefore may reflect adaptations to the constraints imposed by gender roles (Broadbridge 2010: 254–256).

Our study, however, provides at least some basis for thinking that these patterns may be slowly shifting. Women lawyers who recently entered the profession were less likely to have left their jobs for family responsibilities than women who have been in the legal profession longer. In addition, men lawyers who entered the legal profession more recently were more likely to have left their jobs for family responsibilities than men lawyers who have been in the profession longer, and men were more likely to leave large law firms for family responsibilities than women were. In other words, while women have traditionally shouldered family responsibilities, it appears that men may increasingly desire to prioritize family and take on these responsibilities as well.

Furthermore, the influence of gender roles on choices and constraints implicitly assumes a certain family structure – a wife and a husband with at least one dependent – and set of attitudes that may be less common in the future. With the rise of single parents, childless and/or unmarried workers, and the recognition of same-sex partnerships, the influence of gender roles on constrained choices may be disrupted at least in part. Future research should therefore focus on how gender roles and family structure shape constraints and choices in both men's and women's career paths.

What can organizations in the legal profession do to attract and retain talented women? While not a surprise, our conclusion is that the most important thing that they can do is to make it more feasible for both men and women lawyers to balance professional and family obligations. In recent years, some large law firms have made some strides toward creating a family-friendly working environment for women through flexible hour arrangements, on-site childcare, and other interventions (Working Mother 2012). However, lawyers – both men and women – still leave law firms, and choose not to enter them, when they change jobs for family responsibilities.

At this point, men appear to be more likely to leave large law firms for family responsibilities; in contrast, women are less likely to move into small and mid-sized firms for family reasons. These findings suggest that some of the initiatives that large law firms are implementing to make their work more family-friendly may have worked to some degree for women, but not, perhaps, for men (Kay 1997). Given the greater likelihood of men rather than women leaving large firms for family reasons, these firms may wish to ensure that their family-friendly work options apply equally to both men and women lawyers. On the other hand, small and mid-sized law firms may now be lagging behind in retaining women and men who wish to spend time with their families. By implementing programs similar to those of large law firms, small and mid-sized law firms may be able to better retain women lawyers. This may be a challenge, however, because the smaller workforce in such firms may make it more difficult to accommodate flexible work arrangements.

In addition, both our study and prior research indicate that women tend to work outside of law firms, while men more to work in them over the course of their careers (Dau-Schmidt et al. 2000; Dinovitzer et al. 2004). As we have discussed, one reason in addition to family responsibilities that women move out of law firms may be for better training and professional development. To the extent that this occurs, law firms that desire to retain talented women need to provide these benefits (Menkel-Meadow 1994; Diaz and Dunican, Jr. 2011). To this end, firms should foster organizational climates – or employees' shared perceptions of what an organization rewards, supports, and expects (Schneider and Reichers 1983) – for learning (Dragoni 2005) and fairness (Ehrhart 2004) to retain diverse talent (Kyrillidou et al.

2009). By fostering such climates, law firms can signal to women lawyers that they care about their development, the quality of their work, and ensuring that work is assigned impartially.

Limitations

While our research helps illuminate reasons for women's and men's movements among jobs in the legal profession, it also has some limitations. First, it focuses exclusively on graduates of a top 14 law school, and graduates of elite law schools may follow different paths than graduates of non-elite schools (Dinovitzer and Garth 2007). However, given how closely our results replicate findings on lawyers graduating from other law schools (Teitelbaum 1991; Dau-Schmidt et al. 2009) and working in specific states (Harrington and Hsi 2007), these findings may generalize across a broader population of lawyers.

In addition, we studied career histories retrospectively. Since memory is often inaccurate (Loftus 1974), and since people are more likely to remember information that is consistent with their beliefs (Nickerson 1998), lawyers may not accurately recall and report reasons for leaving prior jobs. However, if lawyers were recalling only motivations for leaving prior jobs that perfectly matched their current values, we would expect that the reasons they cited for leaving jobs would not vary by the time of each job change. Since time in career does predict motivations for changing jobs, it is unlikely that lawyers are responding to career movements in ways that perfectly align with their current values. Future research, however, may begin to resolve this issue by focusing on how motivations, desires, and goals change for lawyers prior to law school, prior to entering the legal profession, and throughout the course of their careers.

CONCLUSION

Difficulty in meeting professional and family demands is a pervasive feature of women's experience across all sectors of the legal profession. Law firms are commonly regarded as the worst sector for achieving work-family balance, while government is commonly regarded as the best; the concentration of men in law firm practices and women in government would seem to support these assumptions. Our data on reasons for job movement, however, indicate that while women in law firms experience the highest level of work-family conflict, women in government experience the next highest level of conflict. Additionally, we found that women leave all sectors of legal employment more than men to meet family responsibilities. Consequently, we believe that it is plausible to claim that men and women on average experience two very different legal professions.

Some of the literature on different sources of job satisfaction for men and women might suggest that women and men tend to move to sectors that provide different types of rewards, respectively. Once we control for certain variables, however, our data indicate no difference between women and men in the desire for several different types of rewards as a reason for job movements. The explanation for differences in men's and women's job movement that is most supported by our data is that men and women move into different sectors because of their perceptions of the relative difficulty of meeting family demands in these sectors.

REFERENCES

Aguinis, Herman and Eugene F. Stone-Romero. 1997. "Methodological Artifacts in Moderated Multiple Regression and Their Effects on Statistical Power." *Journal of Applied Psychology* 82:192–206.

Broadbridge, Adelina. 2010. "Choice or Constraint? Tensions in Female Retail Executives' Career Narratives." *Gender in Management: An International Journal* 25(3):244–260.

Cantrell, Deborah J., Elizabeth Levy Paluck, Heather Lord, and April Smith. 2007–2008. "Walking the Path of the Law: How Law Graduates Navigate Career Choices and Tolerate Jobs that Fail to Meet Expectations." *Cardozo Journal of Law and Gender* 14:267–317.

Chambers, David. 1989. "Accommodation and Satisfaction: Women and Men Lawyers and the Balance of Work and Family." *Law and Social Inquiry* 14:251–287.

Chiu, E.G. 1998. "Do Professional Women Have Lower Job Satisfaction than Professional Men? Lawyers as a Case Study." *Sex Roles* 38:521–537.

Cohen, Aaron. 1999. "Turnover among Professionals: A longitudinal study of American lawyers." *Human Resource Management* 38: 61–75.

Dau-Schmidt, Kenneth Glenn, Jeffrey Evans Stake, Kaushik Mukhopadhaya, and Timothy A. Haley. 2006. "The Pride of Indiana: An Empirical Study of the Law School Experience and Careers of Indiana University School of Law—Bloomington Alumni," *Indiana Law Journal* 81:1427–1478.

Dau-Schmidt, Kenneth Glenn, Marc Galanter, Kaushik Mukhopadhaya, and Kathleen E. Hull. 2000. "Men and Women of the Bar: The Impact of Gender on Legal Careers." *Michigan Journal of Gender and Law* 16:49–145.

2009. "Men and Women of the Bar: The Impact of Gender on Legal Careers." *Michigan Journal of Gender and Law* 16:49–145.

Dinovitzer, Ronit and Bryant G. Garth. 2007. "Lawyer Satisfaction in the Process of Structuring Legal Careers." *Law and Social Policy Review* 41:1–50.

Dinovitzer, Ronit, Bryant G. Garth, Richard Sander, Joyce Sterling, and Gita Z. Wilder. 2004. *After the JD: First Results of a National Study of Legal Careers.* The American Bar Foundation and the NALP Foundation for Law Career Research and Education.

Dinovitzer, Ronit, Nancy Reichman, and Joyce Sterling. 2009–2010. "The Differential Valuation of Women's Work: A New Look at the Gender Gap in Lawyers' Incomes." *Social Forum* 88:819–864.

Dinovitzer, Ronit, Robert L. Nelson, and Gabriele Plickert. 2009. *After the JD II: Second Results from a National Study of Legal Careers.* The American Bar Foundation and the NALP Foundation for Law Career Research and Education.

Diaz, Luis J. and Patrick D. Dunican, Jr. 2011. "Ending the Revolving Door Syndrome in Law." *Seton Hall Law Review* 41:947–1003.

Dragoni, Lisa. 2005. "Understanding the Emergence of State Goal Orientation in Organizational Work Groups: The Role of Leadership and Multilevel Climate Perceptions." *Journal of Applied Psychology* 90:1084–1095.

Ehrhart, Mark G. 2004. "Leadership and Procedural Justice Climate as Antecedents of Unit-Level Organizational Citizenship Behavior." *Personnel Psychology* 57:61–94.

Epstein, Cynthia Fuchs, Robert Sauté, Bonnie Oglensky, and Martha Gever. 1995. "Glass Ceilings and Open Doors: Women's Advancement in the Legal Profession," *Fordham Law Review* 64:200–360.

Fortney, Susan Saab. 2000. "Soul for Sale: An Empirical Study of Associate Satisfaction, Law Firm Culture, and the Effects of Billable Hour Requirements." *University of Missouri Kansas City Law Review* 69:239–299.

French, Steve. 2000. "Of Problems, Pitfalls and Possibilities: A Comprehensive Look at Female Attorneys and Law Firm Partnership." *Women's Rights Law Reporter* 21:189–216.

Garth, Bryant G. and Joyce Sterling. 2009. "Exploring Inequality in the Corporate Law Firm Apprenticeship: Doing the Time, Finding the Love." *Georgetown Journal of Legal Ethics* 22:1361–1394.

Gellis, Ann J. 1991. "Great Expectations: Women in the Legal Profession, a Commentary on State Studies." *Indiana Law Journal* 66:941–976.

Hagan, John and Fiona Kay. 1995. *Gender in Practice: A Study of Lawyer's Lives.* New York: Oxford University Press.

Hall, Donna. 1995. "Job Satisfaction among Male and Female Public Defense Attorneys." *Justice System Journal* 18:121–138.

Harrington, Mona and Helen Hsi. Spring 2007. "Women Lawyers and Obstacles to Leadership: A Report of MIT Workplace Center Surveys on Comparative Career Decisions and Attrition Rates of Women and Men in Massachusetts Law Firms." Retrieved November 21, 2013 (http://web.mit.edu/workplacecenter/docs/law-report_4-07.pdf).

Heinz, John P., Robert L. Nelson, Rebecca L. Sandefur, and Edward O. Laumann, 2005. *Urban Lawyers: The New Social Structure of the Bar*. IL, Chicago: University of Chicago Press.

Hom, Peter W. and Angelo J. Kinicki, 2001. Toward a Greater Understanding of How Dissatisfaction Drives Employee Turnover. *Academy of Management Journal* 44: 975–987.

Houkes, Inge, Peter P.M. Janssen, Jande Jonge, and Frans J.N. Nijhuis. 2001. "Work and Individual Determinants of Intrinsic Work Motivation, Emotional Exhaustion, and Turnover Intention: A Multi-Sample Analysis." *International Journal of Stress Management* 8:257–283.

Hull, Kathleen E. 1999. "The Paradox of the Contented Female Lawyer." *Law and Society Review* 33:687–702.

Hull, Katherine and Robert Nelson. 2000. "Assimilation, Choice, or Constraint? Testing Theories of Gender Differences in the Careers of Lawyers." *Social Forces* 79:229–264.

Kay, Fiona M. 1997. "Flight from Law: A Competing Risks Model of Departures from Law Firms." *Law and Society Review* 31:301–336.

Kay, Fiona and Elizabeth Gorman. 2008. "Women in the Legal Profession." *Annual Review of Law & Social Sciences* 4:299–332.

Kay, Fiona and John Hagan. 2003. "Building Trust: Social Capital, Distributive Justice, and Loyalty to the Firm." *Law and Social Inquiry* 28:483–519.

2005. "Social Mobility and Hierarchical Structure in Canadian Law Practice." *Reorganization and Resistance: Legal Professions Confront a Changing World* 281–311.

2007. "Even Lawyers Get the Blues: Gender, Depression, and Job Satisfaction in Legal Practice." *Law and Society Review* 41:51–78.

Kyrillidou, Martha, Charles Lowry, Paul Hanges, Juliet Aiken, and Kristina Justh. 2009. ClimateQUAL™: Organizational Climate and Diversity Assessment, *in Pushing the Edge: Explore, Engage, Extend* (pp. 150–164). Chicago: American Library Association.

Loftus, Elizabeth F. and JC Palmer. 1974. "Reconstruction of Automobile Destruction: An Example of the Interaction Between Language and Memory. *Journal of Verbal Learning & Verbal Behavior* 13:585–478.

Lopez, Maria Pabon. 2008. "The Future of Women in the Legal Profession: Recognizing the Challenges Ahead by Reviewing Current Trends." *Hastings Women's Law Journal* 19:53–104.

McClelland, Gary G. and Charles M. Judd. 1993. "Statistical Difficulties of Detecting Interactions and Moderator Effects." *Psychology Bulletin* 114:376–390.

Menkel-Meadow, Carrie. 1994. "Culture Clash in the Quality of Life in the Law: Changes in the Economics, Diversification and Organization of Lawyering." *Case Western Reserve Law Review* 44:621–664.

Monahan, John and Jeffrey Swanson. 2009. "Lawyers at Mid-Career: A 20-Year Longitudinal Study of Job and Life Satisfaction." *Journal of Empirical Legal Studies* 6(3):451–483.

Mueller, Charles W. and Jean E. Wallace. 1989. "Justice and the Paradox of the Contented Female Worker." *Social and Psychological Quarterly* 59:338–349.

Nickerson, Raymond S. 1998. "Confirmation Bias: A Ubiquitous Phenomenon in Many Guises." *Review of General Psychology* 2:175–220.

Noonan, Mary C. and Mary E. Corcoran. 2004. "The Mommy Track and Partnership: Temporary Delay or Dead End?"*Annals of the American Academy of Political Science* 596:130–150.

Payne-Pikus, Monique R., Robert L. Nelson and John Hagan. 2010. "Experiencing Discrimination: Race and Retention in America's Largest Law Firms." *Law & Society Review* 44(3–4):553–584.

Porter, Nicole Buonocore. 2006. "Re-Defining Superwoman: An Essay on Overcoming the 'Maternal Wall' in the Legal Workplace." *Duke Journal of Gender, Law and Policy* 13:55–84.

Reichman, Nancy and Joyce S. Sterling. 2004. "Gender Penalties Revisited." Retrieved November 21, 2013 (www.law.du.edu/documents/directory/publications/sterling/Genderpenalties10.pdf).

———. 2002. "Recasting the Brass Ring: Deconstructing and Reconstructing Workplace Opportunities for Women Lawyers." *Capital University Law Review* 29:923–977.

———. 2004–2005. "Sticky Floors, Broken Steps, and Concrete Ceilings in Legal Careers." *Texas Journal of Women and the Law* 14:27–76.

Rhode, Deborah L. 2011. "From Platitudes to Priorities: Diversity and Gender Equity in Law Firms." *Georgetown Journal of Legal Ethics* 24:1041–1078.

Sandefur, Rebecca. 2007. "Staying Power: The Persistence of Social Inequality in Shaping Lawyer Stratification and Lawyers' Persistance in the Profession." *Southwestern University Law Review* 36: 539–556.

Schleef, Deborah. 2000. "That's a Good Question: Exploring Motivations for Law and Business School Choice." *Sociological Education* 73:155–174.

Schneider, Ben. 1987. "The People Make the Place." *Personnel Psychology* 40:437–453.

Schneider, Ben and Reichers, A. E. 1983. "On the Etiology of Climates." *Personnel Psychology* 36:19–39.

Sterling, Joyce S. and Nancy J. Reichman. 2013. "Navigating the Gap: Reflections on 15 Years Researching Gender Disparities in the Legal Profession." *Florida International Law Review*, 8, 515–539.

Teitelbaum, Lee E., Antoinette Sedillo López, and Jeffrey Jenkins. 1991. "Gender, Legal Education, and Legal Careers." *Journal of Legal Education* 41:443–482.

The National Association of Women Lawyers and the NAWL Foundation. 2011. "Report of the sixth annual national survey on retention and promotion of women in law firms." Retrieved September 1, 2015. (www.nawl.org/d/do/62).

2012. "Report of the Seventh NAWL Annual National Survey on Retention and Promotion of Women in Law Firms." Retrieved November 21, 2013 (http://nawl.timberlakepublishing.com/files/NAWL%202012%20Survey%20Report%20final.pdf).

Working Mother. 2012. "2012 Working Mother & Flex-Time Lawyers Best Law Firms for Women." Retrieved November 21, 2013 (www.working mother.com/best-companies/2012-working-mother-flex-time-lawyers-best-law-firms-women).

Ziewacz, Elizabeth K. 1996. "Can the Glass Ceiling be Shattered? The Decline of Women Partners in Large Law Firms," *Ohio State Law Journal* 57: 971–997.

THE EFFECTIVENESS OF INHERITANCE VS. RAINMAKING STRATEGIES IN BUILDING BOOKS OF BUSINESS FOR FEMALE AND MINORITY PARTNERS

FORREST BRISCOE* AND ANDREW VON NORDENFLYCHT

This chapter is an adaptation of "Which Path to Power? Workplace Networks and the Relative Effectiveness of Inheritance vs. Rainmaking Strategies for Professional Partners," *Journal of Professions & Organization*, *1(1)* March 2014.

Partners in large law firms enjoy very high incomes, and these incomes have risen substantially over the last two decades (Kaplan 2008, 2009). Yet economic stratification has also been increasing in the professions at all levels (Leicht and Fennell 2001; Mouw and Kalleberg 2010) such that the highest earning law firm partners out-earn the average lawyer more and more each year (Garicano and Hubbard 2009; Heinz et al. 2005). Within this context of rising inequality, a historical pattern of lower earnings for women and minorities appears to be persisting (Baker 2002; Kay and Gorman 2008).

Since the economic rewards in law firms overwhelmingly accrue to those lawyers that become partners (Gilson and Mnookin 1985; Malos and Campion 1995), much research on demographic inequality among lawyers has focused on the careers of associates and whether they achieve the milestone of making partner – "the brass ring" of a legal career (Galanter and Palay 1991; Groysberg et al. 1999; Greenwood

* This project benefitted from comments by *Journal of Professions and Organization* editors David Brock, Huseyin Leblebici, and Daniel Muzio, and *JPO* editorial review board members Mustafa Ozbilgin, Carole Silver, and Roy Suddaby. We also received valuable feedback from participants in the American Bar Foundation's Conference of the Research Group on Legal Diversity, including Len Bierman, Jack Heinz, Bill Henderson, Carroll Seron, Bob Nelson, and David Wilkins.

et al. 2005). That research indeed shows that women and minorities do not appear to be making partner at the same rate as white men, despite decades of increasing representation in the graduating classes of law schools and the entering cohorts of law firm associates (Hagan and Kay 1995; Holder 2001; Heinz et al. 2005; Kay and Gorman 2008; Rhode 2011; Wilkins 1999; Wilkins and Gulati 1996).

But what happens after making partner? Given that lawyers typically make partner around age 35, much of their careers are still ahead of them. While there is some research on partners who move from one partnership firm to another (Rider 2012; Sherer and Lee 2002), there is little research about the careers and outcomes of partners within a given firm, which accounts for the vast majority of all partners' careers. The conventional or stylized model of the law firm partnership is that it is a group of peers, a "company of equals" (Nelson 1988). This view is perhaps reinforced by the distinctive practices that are often attributed to professional partnerships – such as lack of formal positional hierarchy or management roles that rotate among partners (Greenwood, Hinings, and Brown 1990; Malhotra, Morris, and Hinings 2006). However, as anyone who has ever spent time in a law firm can attest, it is certainly not the case that all partners are equal – instead, the partnership ranks are stratified (Wilkins 1999). In fact, Nelson (1988) pointed out that "collegial hierarchy" and inequality in authority and earnings within law firms increased steadily since at least the 1960s. We know little about how differences among partners translate into power, money, and status within firms, or how partners achieve different individual outcomes with a given level of human capital. And therefore, we also lack knowledge about the ongoing roles of gender and ethnicity after making partner and whether there are additional mechanisms that contribute to – or perhaps work against – demographic inequality in earnings and status among lawyers.

As Nelson (1988) argues persuasively, the primary source of cross-partner differences in compensation, status, and power is control over clients – that is, the partner's book of business: "power in the firm remains inextricably tied to 'control of clients'" (Nelson 1988: 5). Clients tend to have strong relationships with individual partners and so the revenue paid by clients is attributed to individual partners. In many firms, each partner's contribution to the firm's total revenue influences, to varying degrees, the distribution of the firm's annual profits among the partners (Altman Weil 2000). In fact, this "eat what you kill" model of profit distribution has been steadily increasing in prevalence and intensity (Gabarro and Burtis 2006; Regan 2004).

Even where compensation is not strongly determined by client revenues (as in the lock-step model), partners who control more client revenues, nonetheless, enjoy more power and status (Nelson 1988). Because clients tend to form relationships with individual partners, clients can – and often do – move to another firm if the partner moves. Thus, partners with larger books of business enjoy more labor market mobility, which can yield compensation increases if they actually move, but also generate corresponding power within their firm, based on the implicit threat of leaving. For instance, Somaya et al. (2008) show that when partners leave one law firm for another law firm, the original firm experiences lower performance in subsequent periods. In short, for law firm partners, client revenue is *the* source of power (Blair-Loy 2001). As Nelson writes, "the leadership of the firm is dictated by those who control the largest clients" (Nelson 1988: 27).

A key question, then, is how partners come to acquire client relationships and books of business (we use the terms "book of business," "client billings," and "client revenues" interchangeably). Given that client revenue arises from a social relationship between partner and client, the process of building a book of business necessarily involves social networks. Certainly differences across partners in law school status and years of experience (Hitt et al. 2001) may play a role in the relative strength of partners' networks. However, our primary interest in this analysis is on the strategies partners use for building such networks. In this chapter, we identify two different network strategies for building a book of business: "inheritance," which focuses on networks within the firm, and "rainmaking," which focuses on networks outside the firm. Using a database of client billings and inter-partner relationships over 10 years at a single large law firm, we examine the relative effectiveness of each for individual partners.

We then use this framework to conceptually consider and empirically assess how these networking strategies may differ based on partner gender and ethnicity. Since building client revenues involves building social networks, it raises the question of whether this process works differently for female and minority partners, given the preponderance of white males in both the internal and external networks relevant to building client revenue. We examine whether the relative effectiveness of the two network strategies differs for female versus male partners, and minority partners versus non-minority partners.

Our results contribute to research on legal careers, as well as to the sociology of networks and stratification.[1] In discussing our findings from a single US law firm, we also consider how our findings may generalize to law firms as well as other professional service settings. We close with implications for policy and practice, as well as suggestions for future research to develop more of a systematic understanding of this fundamental yet relatively unexplored aspect of the structure of law firm careers.

TWO NETWORK STRATEGIES FOR LAW FIRM PARTNERS: INHERITANCE AND RAINMAKING

In order to consider how networking strategies contribute to partner careers, we consider those basic features of professional services that generally shape work and organizational structures across law firms. Professional services are characterized by the application of complex, customized knowledge to client problems (von Nordenflycht 2010; von Nordenflycht, Malhotra, and Morris 2015). These conditions make it difficult for clients to assess the quality of a professional's service, either before or after the service has been performed (Galanter and Palay 1991; Parsons 1939; Sharma 1997). This chronic uncertainty about the nature and quality of the services being provided leads to economic transactions that are "embedded" or intertwined with ongoing social relationships (Uzzi 1996). There are two salient aspects of this embeddedness for law firm partners trying to build a book of business.

First, because clients may have difficulty assessing technical competence across lawyers and law firms, they will select a lawyer partly (or even largely) on the degree to which they feel they can trust the lawyer. Of course, that trust will be based partly on the reputation of the law firm for quality service (Galanter and Palay 1991), and related information the firm provides to clients. But trust is also rooted in the formation of a social relationship between individual decision-makers at the client organization and individual partners at the law firm. Trust also arises through personal referrals: clients will look to people they already have trusted relationships with for endorsements of new

---

[1] Note that in our chapter we follow common usage in referring to "female and minority partners," but that should not obscure the unique experience of women of color – of whom there are too few to analyze in our data – nor deny the importance of differences within and across racial and ethnic groups.

lawyers. In short, client-professional advisor relationships are deeply embedded in social relationships between individuals.

A related aspect of embeddedness that affects partner careers stems from the fact that clients will prefer to deal with those who they already trust as a result of repeated, successful past exchanges; parties even routinely make extra accommodations in order to preserve the ongoing benefits that flow from these embedded economic transactions (Uzzi and Lancaster 2004). In other words, uncertainty about quality and associated embeddedness implies a strong degree of inertia: clients will favor their current lawyer, with whom they have already been transacting.

These implications pose significant challenges to new partners in building a book of client relationships. They imply that partners must find potential clients who are very dissatisfied with their existing lawyers or have not yet established relationships with lawyers, and generate trust in the client that the partner will deliver high-quality service. The embeddedness of client-professional advisor relationships also means that social networks are a critical factor.

The inheritance strategy
In this context, perhaps the most obvious path for a partner to develop a client base is to "inherit" clients from senior partners in the same firm. While existing client-partner relationships tend to be quite stable and resilient, partners do eventually retire (or otherwise exit the profession) and thus their clients will need to find new lawyers. Barring some kind of falling out or bad outcome attributed to their current lawyer, clients will be positively disposed toward a future lawyer whom they come to trust through the strong endorsement of their current advisor.

The inheritance strategy has several benefits. As noted, the primary one is that the retiring partner can provide the focal partner with perhaps the best reference possible, as it comes from an advisor the client has trusted to perform precisely the role that the client is looking to fill. Second, the client does not have to worry about choosing a new firm, along with a new partner, thus preserving some of the inertia and embeddedness. Third, to the extent that the younger partner has worked with the retiring partner on the client's business, the client will have gained direct experience of the younger partner's technical expertise, increasing the degree of trust. Fourth, inherited clients are likely to offer a substantial (or at least known) quantity of billings revenue for the junior partner right away.

From a social network perspective, the inheritance strategy thus involves forming connections with those incumbent partners who control clients but who may be relinquishing their control sometime soon. For instance, it is common knowledge in law firm circles that a primary strategy for landing clients is "to attach yourself to an aging partner" and hope to acquire that partner's clients when he or she retires (Scheiber 2013). The investment required for this strategy is the allocation of one's time to doing work for the senior partners' clients.

It is important to note that this "inheritance" strategy is not without risks from the perspective of the partner pursuing it. For one thing, a retiring partner may have relationships with multiple junior partners, all of whom have worked with the client. Thus, even if the focal partner has invested time and energy in working with the retiring partner and his/her clients, the retiring partner may recommend a different junior partner to take over clients. Second, there is no guarantee that a client will stay with the incumbent firm upon the incumbent partner's retirement. Third, allocating time to work with partners who are closer to retirement has opportunity costs in terms of where that time might otherwise be spent. It may preclude forming closer ties to mid-career partners with practices in cutting-edge areas that offer better opportunities to build relevant expertise. For instance, in our sample, partner tenure has a convex relationship with client billings, indicating that mid-career partners may have larger books of business than retiring partners. Allocating one's time to working with retiring partners may also cut into the time required to find and develop new clients. In other words, there is no deterministic relationship between working with retiring partners' clients and subsequently building a larger book of business – rather, it is an open empirical question.

For these reasons, we view the inheritance strategy as a networking investment with some risk, and we theorize that, on balance, there will be positive returns to this inheritance strategy. Thus, we predict that pursuing this strategy by cultivating relationships with senior (retiring) partners will, on average, lead to a subsequent increase in a partner's book of billings.

Hypothesis 1: *The network strategy of working with retiring partners (i.e., the inheritance strategy) will increase a partner's subsequent book of business.*

The rainmaking strategy

A major alternative strategy for gaining control over client relationships, which we call "rainmaking" after the commonly used colloquial expression, involves building external relationships to new clients. This strategy involves drawing on one's social network outside of the firm, as well as investing one's time in both building that network through professional and community organizations and building trust with potential client contacts generated by those activities.

We argue that this strategy is harder than the inheritance strategy, primarily in that it involves more risks. First, partners pursuing this strategy cannot rely on any incumbent partner or client relationship within their firm in order to help overcome the embeddedness and inertia problems with new clients (in contrast, the inheritance strategy benefits from those advantages). Second, whereas the investment required for the inheritance strategy involves spending time on work that generates revenue (e.g., billing existing clients), soliciting new clients requires time investments for meetings and presentations that are uncompensated by any client payment. Thus, the partner risks appearing less productive and profitable to the overall partnership. Third, the partner will likely be competing for these potential clients with lawyers from many other firms – whether the potential clients are new organizations that have recently discovered the need for a lawyer, or they are established organizations that have become dissatisfied with their current lawyer.

The arguably greater risk attendant to investing time in the rainmaking strategy, relative to the inheritance strategy, raises the question of why partners would pursue it. There are at least two reasons. First, rainmaking may offer the promise of building a book of business more quickly, as it does not require waiting for senior partners to retire and relinquish their clients. Second, some partners may be constrained in pursuing the inheritance strategy, disadvantaged in the internal network competition for relationships with senior partners. Thus, both strategies are likely to be observed – and both are likely to be viable.

Ideally, one would assess the returns to the rainmaking strategy by measuring the investment of time a partner makes in building external social networks and wooing potential clients. However, as we note later in this chapter, we are not able to observe that behavior directly. Instead, we can observe the formation of relationships with new clients. As we noted earlier, one benefit of inherited clients is that they will tend to yield substantial revenue right away. By contrast, the amount of revenue that will be generated by new clients is both uncertain and likely to be smaller at the outset. Therefore, while it is reasonable to assume a positive relationship between a partner landing a new client and that partner's future total book of business, this relationship is by no means certain – again, it is at least an open empirical question worth testing. Therefore, we explicitly hypothesize that landing new clients is likely to lead to a larger book of business:

Hypothesis 2:   *The network strategy of developing new clients (i.e., the rainmaking strategy) will increase a partner's subsequent book of business.*

Diverse partners and network strategies

Although both inheritance and rainmaking strategies are likely to be viable in general, they may differ in their effectiveness for women and minorities. A common theme that emerges out of research on gender and race stratification among junior professionals involves social networks. For associates (non-partner professionals), formal and informal contact with key partners provides a potential range of benefits, including learning opportunities, sponsorship and visibility, and opportunities to demonstrate skills (Briscoe and Kellogg 2011; Chanen 2006; Wilkins and Gulati 1996). Once in the workforce, women and minorities often have more restricted access than white men to social networks that represent the informal structures of the workplace – including voluntary connections among colleagues that consequentially shape access to resources, learning, and advancement and career opportunities (e.g., Fernandez and Sosa 2005; Ibarra 1992, 1995; Thomas 1990).

In research on law firms, for instance, access to partners and mentoring have been shown to be important influences on career outcomes, and this may be especially true for minority lawyers (Dinovitzer and Garth 2007; Higgins 2000). For example, Payne-Pikus Hagan and Nelson (2010) recently analyzed the *After the JD* survey data to find that African American and Hispanic associates are dissatisfied with access to key partners and mentoring, contributing to intentions to leave their law firms. Kay and Hagan (1998) found that female lawyers scored lower than their male counterparts on measures of social capital that reflect professional network connections. Briscoe and Kellogg (2011) found that work assignments to powerful partners increased retention and performance bonuses for associates, and that this effect was even more important for those (mostly women) who later used work-family employee benefits. Gorman (2005) found that gendered preferences negatively affect the hiring and career processes of female junior lawyers.

In sum, social networks and associated social processes appear to be critical in explaining stratification outcomes for female and minority lawyers prior to becoming partners. This is likely to be the case after becoming partner, as well. Specifically, we consider the implications for the effectiveness of the two alternative network strategies.

First, consider the inheritance strategy. In this strategy, the focal partner aims to build a relationship with a senior partner nearing retirement in order to increase the chances of gaining that partner's clients. Yet this strategy only works to the extent that the retiring partner is inclined to pass the clients on to the focal partner. For this to occur, the retiring partner needs to feel a bond of trust – if not friendship – with the focal partner, greater than bonds with other junior partners within the firm with which the retiring partner has worked.

For women and minorities, building such a strong bond is likely to be a challenge. Much research has corroborated the existence of homophily in interpersonal relationships: the tendency for people to be drawn to and feel greater affinity for people who are like themselves in terms of race and gender (Brass 1985; Ibarra 1992; McPherson, Smith-Lovin, and Cook 2001). This tendency suggests that the retiring partners will more readily form bonds with other partners whose backgrounds are more similar to their own. Where senior partners are largely white males (such as in our research setting), retiring partners will more easily form bonds with other white men rather than women or minority partners, which poses a double-phased problem for female and minority partners. They will have a harder time forming network ties to senior partners in the first place (Payne-Pikus, Hagan, and Nelson 2010), and even where they are able to establish such ties, they may be less likely than white males to be chosen to inherit the retiring partners' clients. Thus we hypothesize:

Hypothesis 3A: *The inheritance strategy will be less effective for female partners compared with male partners.*

Hypothesis 3B: *The inheritance strategy will be less effective for minority partners compared with non-minority partners.*

As noted earlier, where the inheritance strategy is blocked – in this case by homophily effects for female or minority partners – then an alternative path to increasing client billings may be rainmaking. Yet homophily poses a challenge for female and minority partners in rainmaking as well. To the extent that client organizations are largely staffed by white males, homophily will again advantage white or male partners in rainmaking. For instance, Blair-Loy (2001), in a study of senior executives at financial services firms, documents that men experience rainmaking quite naturally, as easy personal, social interaction with males at potential clients, whereas female executives experience the personal interactions necessary to rainmaking with male clients as much more difficult and contrived. This mirrors earlier observations by Epstein (1981) and Hagan and Kay (1995) on greater difficulty in rainmaking for female lawyers. Hence we expect:

Hypothesis 4A: *The rainmaking strategy will be less effective for female partners compared with male partners.*

Hypothesis 4B: *The rainmaking strategy will be less effective for minority partners compared with non-minority partners.*

DATA AND METHOD

The case firm and data structure
The data for this research come from the internal records of a large US corporate law firm, and span a time period from 1993 to 2007. The firm is like many other large law firms in that its lawyers are organized into multiple departments and office locations, and nearly all lawyers are part of a conventional partnership system with a lengthy associate period followed by the possibility of promotion to partner.

We used three types of internal records from the case firm: detailed project billing records, lists of partners with responsibility for each client, and personnel records. For this analysis, panel data on individual partners are structured into partner-year observations. For each partner, our analysis includes up to 10 different partner-year observations spanning the period 1998 to 2007. Additional data from the earlier period 1993 to 1997 are used in the creation of lagged historical variables as explained in the following sections. There were 200 to 250 partners available for analysis with complete data, generating an unbalanced panel of approximately 1500 partner-year observations used for the analysis.

Dependent variable
Book of business: We operationalized each partner's book of business in a given year by aggregating lawyer/project level billings (i.e., billable hours) data up to the partner who is responsible for each client. Specifically, total client billings represent the annual sum of all partner and associate billable hours associated with the clients that are

337

controlled by a given partner. In this law firm, there is only one client responsible partner for each client, and these relationships do not change often during the study period, except when a partner nears retirement and/or leaves the firm (and those are rare events). Total client billings exhibit a skewed distribution, so we used the log of total client billings.

Independent variables

Ties to retiring partners: We defined retiring partners in a given year as those partners who were within 5 years of retirement or exit from the firm at that time. Identification of retiring partners was facilitated by the firm having a policy of mandatory retirement at a certain age. We then operationalized ties to retiring partners by aggregating the total number of hours that the focal partner had billed to the clients of retiring partners, from the start of available records in 1993 up to the present year. The final variable is divided by 1,000 to facilitate interpretation. Hence this variable represents the extent of the workplace relationships that each partner has built up with retiring partners and their clients.

New client generations: We operationalized new client generations as the count of new clients that each focal partner had generated up to the present year. We defined clients as new if the firm's lawyers had never billed them previously in the records extending back to 1993 (i.e., 5 years prior to the start of the study period). Using the client respon-sible lawyer lists, each new client was assigned to a single partner who served as the responsible lawyer for that client.

Female partner: We used personnel records to identify female partners, and coded this dummy variable 1 for female partners. As in the partnership lists of other law firms, diverse partners are relatively rare in this dataset. Note that we have suppressed the reporting of the number of female and minority partners in the firm in order to protect the anonymity of the case study firm.

Minority partner: We defined minority partners as those who are identified as black, Hispanic, or Asian in the firm's personnel records, and coded them 1 for this dummy variable.

Analysis and control variables

One common concern in analyzing performance outcomes across individuals is the need to control for differences in individual endowments. To some degree, this can be done by including controls for characteristics that can be observed (such as law school status, age, experience), but then the significant problem of unobserved differences remains. To control for unobserved differences across partners that are stable over time, we predict book of business using ordinary least squares (OLS) regressions with a fixed effect for each partner. However, by including partner fixed effects, we cannot simultaneously estimate coefficients for individual characteristics that are stable. Thus, we do not estimate direct effects of stable individual variables. Since two of our variables of interest – gender and ethnicity – fall into this category, we estimate their impact using interaction terms. Namely, we interact the strategy measures (ties to retiring partners and new clients) with two dummy variables set to 1 if the partner is a female or minority, respectively.

We do include several controls for time-varying characteristics. First, we included a lagged dependent variable (*Client revenues/Book of business (t − 1)*). In addition, to control for common influences on the book of business that are a function of the partner's time as a partner in the firm, we include controls for tenure. We also include tenure squared to capture a nonlinear effect of tenure on book of business. The independent variables and controls are all lagged one year $(t − 1)$.

Using this fixed-effect approach, our results can be interpreted as the average effect of changes in a given independent variables on changes in partner book-of-business outcomes, across all partners. For the models interacting partner gender or ethnicity, significant interaction-term results can be interpreted as the difference in the effect of a given independent variable, between one gender/ethnicity category and the other.

FINDINGS

Basic descriptive statistics are provided in Table 11.1. Figures 11.1 to 11.3 show the distribution of client revenue across partner-years. Figure 11.1 shows the percentage distribution of all partner-year units across raw measures of client revenue. For instance, approximately half of the partner-year observations generated billings of between 0 and 5000 h ($0 to $2.5 million in revenue, assuming an average rate of $500/h). Figure 11.1 shows that the distribution of client revenue is highly skewed, as expected, with a few partners with very large books and many partners with relatively small books. Figures 11.2 and 11.3 break the

TABLE 11.1:   Summary Statistics

Variable	Description	Mean	Std. Dev.
Book of business	Logged total hourly billings to clients for whom partner is the Responsible Lawyer	7.40	1.79
Tenure	Cumulative years of tenure as a partner in the firm	11.38	7.77
Tie to retiring partner (Inheritance strategy)	Cumulative hours (in thousands) billed to clients of partners who were within 5 years of mandatory retiring age or of exit from the firm	0.10	0.46
New clients landed (Rainmaking strategy)	Cumulative count of new clients generated, defined as clients that were never previously billed by the firm, for whom the partner is the responsible lawyer	15.93	28.10
Female partner	Dummy variable set to 1 if partner is female	[Suppressed]	
Minority partner	Dummy variable set to 1 if partner is Black or Hispanic	[Suppressed]	

sample into two distributions: Figure 11.2 shows the distributions for male and female partners; Figure 11.3 shows the distributions for white and minority partners. In these figures, we present the logged values of client revenue, hence the difference from Figure 11.1. Again, as expected, Figures 11.2 and 11.3 show that female and minority partners' overall distribution sits to the left of male and white partners' distribution, indicating lower levels of client revenues on average. While the visual difference between the distributions in these figures may appear slight, the logged nature of the client revenue measures means that these differences are noteworthy; on the logged scale, the female partner mean is approximately 15% lower than the male partner mean, and the minority mean is similarly approximately 15% lower than the non-minority partner mean.

Turning now to our primary analyses, Table 11.2 presents the results of our regression analyses. Our first hypothesis predicted that the inheritance strategy would increase client revenues. The first model in Table 11.2 provides support for this hypothesis. The significant

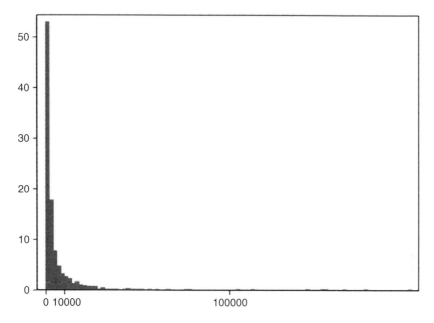

Figure 11.1: Distribution of Client Revenues: Percentage of Partner-Year Observations by Range of Client Revenue. Client Revenue Measured as Hours Billed.

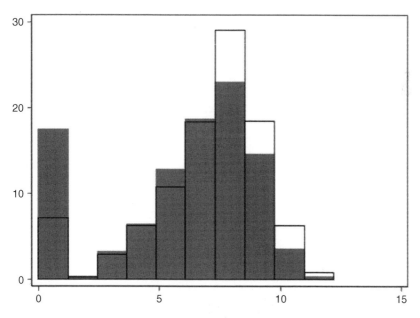

Figure 11.2: Histogram of Client Revenues: Male Partners vs. Female Partners. Client Revenue Measured as Log (Hours Billed). (Shaded gray bars represent female partners, and clear bars with black outlines represent male partners.)

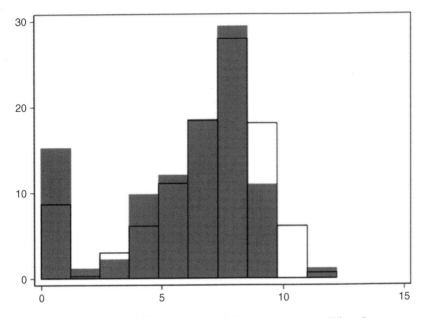

Figure 11.3: Histogram of Client Revenues: Minority Partners vs. White Partners. Client Revenue Measured as Log (Hours Billed). (Shaded gray bars represent minority partners, and clear bars with black outlines represent non-minority partners.)

coefficient on *ties to retiring partner* indicates that partners who bill more hours to the clients of retiring partners increase their own subsequent book of business.

Our second hypothesis is that the rainmaking strategy – consisting of landing more new clients – will increase client revenues. This hypothesis is also supported by the results in Model 1. The significant coefficient on *count of new clients* indicates that an increase in the number of new clients is associated with a rise in subsequent book of business.

Our third hypothesis predicts that the inheritance strategy will not be as effective for female or minority partners. Relevant results are in the second and third models in Table 11.2, reporting on regressions that interact the networking strategies with the gender (Model 2) and ethnicity (Model 3) of the partner. The interaction term on *female * ties to retiring partner* in Model 2 support Hypothesis 3 for gender, and the corresponding term on *minority * ties to retiring partner* in Model 3 support Hypothesis 3 for ethnicity. The corresponding results are plotted graphically in Figures 11.4 and 11.5, which show the different

INHERITANCE VS. RAINMAKING STRATEGIES

TABLE 11.2:   Results of OLS Individual Fixed-Effects Regressions Predicting Book of Business among Law Firm Partners

Variables	(1)	(2)	(3)
Client revenues (t − 1)	0.31**	0.28**	0.31**
	(0.03)	(0.03)	(0.03)
Tenure	0.03	0.05*	0.03
	(0.02)	(0.03)	(0.02)
Tenure squared	−0.002**	−0.003**	−0.002**
	(0.001)	(0.001)	(0.001)
Tie to retiring partner (t − 1) Inheritance strategy	0.18*	0.05	0.18*
	(0.09)	(0.08)	(0.09)
New clients landed (t − 1) Rainmaking strategy	0.04*	0.04*	0.04*
	(0.02)	(0.02)	(0.02)
Female * Tie to retiring partner (t − 1)		−1.76**	
		(0.62)	
Female * New clients landed (t − 1)		0.12*	
		(0.05)	
Minority * Tie to retiring partner (t − 1)			−1.77*
			(0.88)
Minority * New clients landed (t − 1)			0.07
			(0.06)
Constant	5.17**	5.85**	5.17**
	(0.22)	(0.28)	(0.22)
Observations	1471	1471	1471
R-squared	0.13	0.15	0.14
Number of partners	[200–250]	[200–250]	[200–250]

Note: Standard errors in parentheses
** $p < 0.01$,
* $p < 0.05$

effects of this inheritance strategy for women versus men (Figure 11.4) and for minority versus white partners (Figure 11.5). Figure 11.4 indicates that although stronger ties to retiring partners provide a small positive benefit for male partners, they actually have a strong *negative* effect on book of business for female partners. Figure 11.5 shows a similar pattern for minority partners, for whom there is a negative effect of ties to retiring partners on book of business.

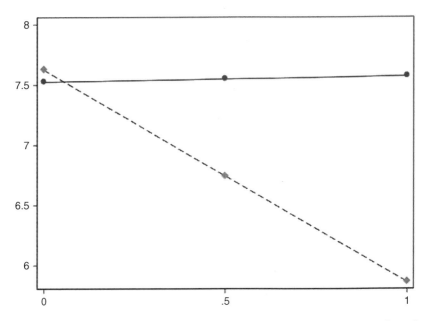

Figure 11.4: The Effect of the Inheritance Strategy on Book of Business (Annual Total Client Revenues, Logged), for Male and Female Partners. (Solid line indicates male partners, and dashed line indicates female partners.)

Hypothesis 4 predicts that the rainmaking strategy would also be less effective for female and minority partners. The results in the second and third models of Table 11.2 do not support this hypothesis. The interaction term on *female * new clients landed* in the second model is significant, but the direction of the effect is opposite Hypothesis 4 for gender. The corresponding term on *minority * new clients landed* in the third model is also in the opposition direction, but is insignificant. Figure 11.6 shows the graphic interpretation of the significant inter-action result for gender: while increases in new clients landed are associated with a rise in book of business for male partners, the steeper slope on the female line indicates that this positive effect is much *greater* for female partners.

It is also worth noting that the significant tenure squared variable is consistent with the notion that book of business has a general curvilin-ear relationship with partner tenure, initially rising at low levels of tenure and then declining at high levels of tenure.

Additional analyses. We also conducted several additional analyses. First, we confirmed that female partners and minority partners were

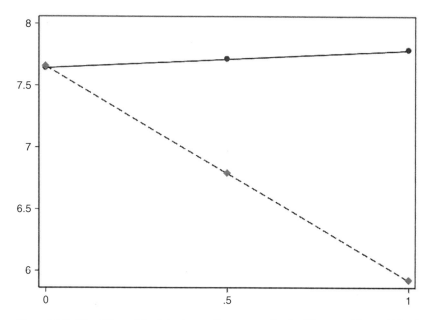

Figure 11.5: The Effect of the Inheritance Strategy on Book of Business (Annual Total Client Revenues, Logged), for Minority versus White Partners. (Solid line indicates non-minority partners, and dashed line indicates minority partners.)

associated with lower average book of business in cross-sectional OLS regressions. However, we did not report those results because we are unable to adequately control for individual differences in endowments across different partners, limiting our ability to distinguish between the effects of gender/ethnicity from other factors such as detailed differences in education or social class background.

Second, we ran regressions predicting differences among partners in ties to retiring partners and landing of new clients. Using random-effects Poisson regressions with controls to predict count of new clients, female partners were not associated with differences in new clients. Nor were minority partners associated with differences in new clients. Similar regressions predicting ties to retiring partners did not show significant differences for female or minority partners either.

Finally, in analysis not shown, we also predicted the focal partner's book of business using ties to the most powerful partners as measured by that tied partner's own book of business. Those results indicate that stronger ties to the most powerful partners are negatively associated with the focal partner's book of business, regardless of the gender or ethnicity of that focal partner.

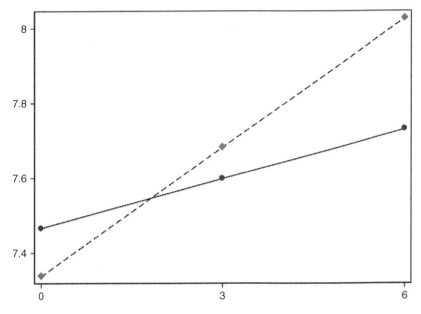

Figure 11.6: The Effect of the Rainmaking Strategy on Book of Business (Annual Total Client Revenues, Logged), for Male and Female Partners. (Solid line indicates male partners, and dashed line indicates female partners.)

DISCUSSION

This chapter examines the effects of two networking investment strategies, inheritance and rainmaking, on partners' book of business in a law firm. Consistent with our hypothesized expectations, we found that increases in both an inheritance strategy and a rainmaking strategy were associated with subsequent increases in client billings. In addition, we found that the effects of those strategies differed in several important ways for female partners and for minority partners. First, the inheritance strategy is not only less effective for female and minority partners, but it actually is associated with a decline in subsequent client billings. Second, contrary to our expectations, the rainmaking strategy is actually *more* effective for female partners than for male partners. Finally, while we did not find a significant effect of rainmaking for minority partners, as with female partners the coefficient was in the opposite direction from our expectations.

We were surprised to find that for female and minority partners, the inheritance strategy was associated not just with lower increases, but

346

actually *decreases* in client billings. We see three possible explanations for this, stemming from female and minority partners' presumed social capital disadvantages. First, female and minority partners may simply be more vulnerable to the disadvantages of the inheritance strategy – failure actually to inherit the client after foregoing investments in work that might broaden the focal partners' skills or social network – because homophily makes it less likely that these partners will inherit the retiring partner's clients. One alternative explanation is that the female and minority partners may be developing ties to retiring partners with smaller or declining books of business that limit their client inheritance potential. A third explanation, consistent with earlier research that indicates that female and minority lawyers experience disadvantaged access to social networks that may limit their human capital development, is that female and minority partners who bill many of their hours retiring partners' clients represent lawyers with lower levels of human capital who need "care and feeding" by senior partners. Once these "caretakers" retire, the junior partners' human capital disadvantages manifest in drops in client revenue.

The greater returns to rainmaking for female partners were also a surprise to us. However, several arguments suggest that rainmaking may, nonetheless, be a more effective investment for female and minority partners. For one thing, in rainmaking, the focal partner can choose which potential clients to pursue. Thus, female and minority partners may choose to pursue clients with female or minority personnel, where homophily may work to their advantage. Growing demographic diversity among corporate clients, and commitment to diversity among those clients, may also be expanding the external opportunity set for female and minority partners (Beckman and Phillips 2005). Third, in pursuing rainmaking, partners draw on their social networks outside of their law firm. These personal external social networks are likely of little use in pursuing the inheritance strategy, but of potentially great help in generating referrals to new clients. Gladwell (2000) and von Nordenflycht (2011) relate similar patterns for Jewish lawyers and advertising professionals in the 1950s and 1960s who responded to a context of predominately Protestant senior partners and clients by turning to an expanding segment of Jewish clients. In fact, research suggests that underrepresented professionals in organizations tend to develop and benefit more from external social capital than internal organizational networks (e.g., Groysberg 2008; Ibarra 1995; Kay and Hagan 1998).

Boundary conditions for generalizing our findings

Our findings from a single firm are likely to have boundary conditions that will be important to assess in future studies. Although we are limited in our ability to generalize our results, we believe that our findings regarding inheritance and rainmaking network strategies and how their effectiveness varies for women and minorities should apply most readily in professional service organizations where the following conditions are met: (1) an individual's relative stature and rewards in the organization depend to some degree on attracting and controlling client revenues; (2) organizational rules or informal norms regarding client "ownership" assign significant credit for growing client relationships to individual partners (relative to client teams or the whole organization); and (3) junior partners are more demographically diverse than their senior colleagues. Those conditions appear common not just to many law firms but also to firms in a range of other professional service industries, including accounting, advertising, medicine, investment banking, and management consulting.

In terms of conditions 1 and 2, organizations, industries, and national contexts will of course vary in the extent to which rules or norms assign client ownership to individuals. In many professional industries, so-called eat what you kill systems that richly reward client ownership tend to be associated with strong norms of individual control. In contrast, "lock step" systems that tie pay to seniority regardless of client revenues may reduce the incentive for individuals to control clients (Gilson and Mnookin 1985). "One firm" policies that emphasize shared organizational ownership over clients are intended to weaken norms of individual ownership (Maister 1985, 1993; Regan 2004). Still, individual ownership norms are likely to persist as long as decision-makers at client organizations prefer professionals whom they know personally and, therefore, feel they can trust with important matters (Nelson 1988).

Regarding condition 3, the homophily mechanism – which appears to limit the returns to the inheritance strategy for female and minority partners – should apply most readily in firms where the senior partners available for bequeathing inheritances are predominately male and white. This condition of low diversity among senior professionals is common to many professional industries and national contexts (see Leitschuh 2007 for accountants, Bolton and Muzio 2007 for UK lawyers; and U.S. Census Bureau 2011 for female and minority representation across professional occupations). It is important to underscore the point that this homophily mechanism does not imply the presence of discrimination among senior partners, but rather reflects a universal tendency for affiliations to be stronger among individuals who share similar backgrounds.

Contributions to research

Our findings contribute to research on diversity and inequality in law and in the professions more broadly by articulating and empirically assessing mechanisms that affect the relative success of individual partners' careers and thus shape the nature and degree of inequality across partners. We first articulate a framework for understanding and analyzing inequality across partners and career strategies of individual partners. Drawing on Nelson's (1988) analysis, we argue that differences in partner careers are essentially about the book of business that each partner is able to develop. We then identify and develop two strategies for investing in social networks – inheritance and rainmaking – that help build this book of business. Finally, we show that these strategies work differently for women and minorities.

Recent research has deepened our understanding of the complex processes through which organizational employment practices can contribute to differences in earnings across demographic groups (Bidwell, et al. 2013; Briscoe and Konrad 2006; Fernandez and Sosa 2005; Kay and Gorman 2012), yet many questions remain. Our findings from the current study suggest that one mechanism contributing to persisting gender and racial inequality is the relational process involving the circulation and generation of valuable client resources within professional service partnerships. Relational strategies aimed at those valuable client resources do not appear to benefit women and minority partners equally.

At the same time, our findings also offer some hope on this score, in the sense that rainmaking may provide a viable strategy for underrepresented partners to counter the challenges associated with homophily barriers to accessing resources within the organization. In fact, for several decades, the importance of rainmaking for organizational and individual success has been rising in law firms (Galanter and Palay 1991; Nelson 1988) as well as across-professional services generally (Blair-Loy 2001). Thus there may be expanding opportunities for diverse partners to counteract the adverse effects of the inheritance process.

Practical and policy implications

Our findings regarding the challenges of the inheritance and rainmaking strategies for female and minority partners suggest several practical implications for managing corporate law firms. In general, female and minority partners in these firms do not appear to be achieving the same level of stature and power as their male and non-minority colleagues. Yet because partners are highly autonomous, many organizational levers used as tools for upper-level diversity in more traditional organizations may not be appropriate or even feasible in the partnership setting (Nelson 1988).

Our findings suggest steps that might be considered by firms seeking to increase diversity in the upper echelons of the partnership ranks. First, the fact that female and minority partners appear disadvantaged in client inheritance suggests more attention to diversity in client succession. Simply tracking and summarizing patterns of client inheritance across departments and offices may precipitate changes in behavior among partners, as they become more aware of homophily tendencies and their aggregate consequences for the demographic composition of the senior partnership. Going a step further, for firms that are developing processes to broaden client relationships from individual partners toward teams of partners, attention to lawyer diversity could be built into those processes.

Second, our findings regarding the beneficial effects of rainmaking for diverse partners suggests focusing attention on diversity within the domain of new client development. In particular, as firms increasingly fund and empower rainmaking efforts, they may recognize the particular benefit of those activities for the career development of female and minority partners. Supporting diverse junior partners by enhancing their rainmaking abilities may yield a double payoff in terms of the firm's overall revenue as well as diversity goals.

These findings also raise parallel issues for professional governing bodies, such as the American Bar Association, that are interested in policy goals related to diversity within the profession. For example, the fact that rainmaking helps diverse junior partners suggests that programs to support minority lawyers might be particularly well served by focusing on the purchasing decisions of in-house counsel at client organizations.

Recommendations for future research

Our findings suggest an array of promising directions for future research. First, although our analytic strategy uses individual fixed effects to control for unobserved differences between people in their baseline human capital endowments and backgrounds, future studies should explore how differences in those baseline factors – such as status and years of experience, as suggested by Hitt et al. (2001) – may shape the networking strategies we documented. For example, do rainmaking strategies benefit individuals who can signal expertise or status with elite educational credentials? Conversely, do inheritance strategies offer more benefit for individuals who lack those signals, but can otherwise convey their expertise through collaboration? Is the payoff to the rainmaking strategy relatively better for partners whose expertise is more easily demonstrated to prospective clients?

It will also be fascinating to explore how networking strategies evolve over the career itself. Although we control for the (curvilinear) effects of partner tenure, and our findings are also robust to the inclusion of partner age, future work could explore how the payoffs to each strategy evolve over the course of a partner's career. For example, does inheritance provide a better strategy for partners earlier in their careers? Does rainmaking become more feasible later on, after partners have built up more expertise and experience? Is there an optimal sequencing of strategies over time? A related issue is the nature of specialization in these strategies, as investing in one strategy may limit a person's bandwidth to invest in alternatives. Can simultaneously pursuing both strategies pay off, or is that a recipe for losing both the internal competition for inheriting existing clients and the external competition for growing new clients?

A range of organizational factors may also influence these networking strategies. Beyond the two boundary conditions we noted earlier – the importance of client revenues to success, and norms regarding individual client ownership – there are other differences across firms that could be explored. Nelson (1988), for instance, showed that law firms vary in the nature of intrafirm networks. Some firms with more bureaucratic orientations feature more team-based work, whereas firms with more traditional (professional) orientations feature less collaboration and more isolated partner-associate dyads. These alternative configurations of intrafirm collaboration structures may affect both the degree to which clients are "owned" by individual partners and the relative effectiveness of the networking strategies for diverse partners.

As an example, the extent of inequality among partners in a law firm, or in a given office or department, may influence the relative effectiveness of the networking strategies. When rewards and stature are based on control of client revenues, greater inequality implies that a few senior partners control a larger portion of the firm's total client revenues – and thus those partners are likely to each have many junior partners working "for" them on their client accounts. In a high-inequality scenario, there will be more competition among the junior partners angling for inheritance, potentially making that strategy less attractive relative to the rainmaking strategy. Conversely, firms with lower inequality may be more conducive settings for the inheritance strategy.

Recent trends in law and other professional industries also need to be considered in future research on partner careers. For example, for several decades now, clients have become increasingly willing to part ways with law firms with whom they have had historical relationships – and at the same time, law firms themselves are increasingly competing by hiring "lateral" partners (and their clients) away from rival firms (Citi-Hildebrandt 2013; Galanter and Palay 1991; Nelson 1988). Those trends suggest intriguing implications for the inheritance and rainmaking strategies. For example, how do declining client loyalties shape opportunities for junior partners to pursue the rainmaking strategy, to attract new clients from rival firms? On the flip side, does the rise in client and partner defections increase the risk of the inheritance strategy, as senior partners decamp with their clients but leave former colleagues behind? With these questions, we hope to have indicated a few of the many enticing opportunities for further research on partner careers in law and across professional services more broadly.

REFERENCES

American Institute for Certified Public Accountants (AICPA). (2006) "A Decade of Changes in the Accounting Profession: Workforce Trends and Human Capital Practices." Report available at www.aicpa.org.

Altman Weil, Inc. (2000) "2000 Law Firm Compensation System Survey." Report available at www.altmanweil.com.

Baker, J. (2002) "The Influx of Women into Legal Professions: An Economic Analysis." *Monthly Labor Review*, 8:14–24.

Beckman, C. M. and Phillips, D. J. (2005) "Interorganizational Determinants of Promotion: Client Leadership and the Attainment of Women Attorneys," *American Sociological Review*, 70:678–701.

Bidwell, M., Briscoe, F., Fernandez-Mateo, I., and Sterling, A. (2013) 'Changing Employment Relationships and Inequality: Causes and Consequences'. *Academy of Management Annals*, 7/1:61–121.

Blair-Loy, M. (2001) "It's Not Just What You Know, It's Who You Know: Technical Knowledge, Rainmaking, and Gender Among Finance Executives," *Research in the Sociology of Work*, 10:51–83.

Bolton, S. and Muzio, D. (2007) "Can't Live with 'em, Can't Live without 'em: Gendered Segmentation in the Legal Profession," *Sociology*, 41/1:47–64.

Brass, D. (1985) "Men's and Women's Networks: A Study of Interaction Patterns and Influence in an Organization," *Academy of Management Journal*, 28:327–343.

Briscoe, F. and Kellogg, K. (2011) "The Initial Assignment Effect: Local Employer Practices and Positive Career Outcomes for Flexible-Work Program Users," *American Sociological Review*, 76:291–319.

Briscoe, F. and Konrad, T. R. (2006). "HMO Employment and African-American Physicians," *Journal of the National Medical Association*, 98(8): 1318–1325.

Briscoe, F. and Tsai, W. (2011) "Overcoming Relational Inertia: How Organizational Members Respond to Acquisition Events in a Law Firm," *Administrative Science Quarterly*, 56:408–440.

Brock, D. M., Powell, M. J., and Hinings, C. R. (1999) *The Changing Professional Organization: Accounting, Healthcare, and Law*. New York: Routledge.

Chanen, J. S. (2006) "Early Exits," *American Bar Association Journal*, 92:32–39.

Citi-Hildebrandt (2013) "2013 Client Advisory." A Report of Hidebrandt Consulting LLC and Citi Private Bank's Law Firm Group.

Dinovitzer, R. and Garth, B.G. (2007) "Lawyer Satisfaction in the Process of Structuring Legal Careers," *Law & Society Review*, 41:1–50.

Epstein, C. F. (1981) *Women in Law*. New York: Basic Books.

Fernandez, R. M. and Sosa, M. L. (2005). "Gendering the Job: Networks and Recruitment at a Call Center," *American Journal of Sociology*, 111(3): 859–904.

Gabarro, John J. and Burtis, A. (2006) Brainard, Bennis & Farrell (A). Case #495037, Harvard Business School Publishing.

Galanter, M. and Palay, T. (1991) *Tournament of Lawyers: The Transformation of the Big Law Firm*. Chicago: University of Chicago Press.

Garicano, L. and Hubbard, T. (2009) "Earning Inequality and Coordination Costs: Evidence from US Law Firms," NBER Working Paper #14741.

Gilson, R. J. and Mnookin, R. H. (1989) "Coming of Age in a Corporate Law Firm: The Economics of Associate Career Patterns," *Stanford Law Review*, 41/3:567–595.

(1985) "Sharing Among the Human Capitalists: An Economic Inquiry into the Corporate Law Firm and How Partners Split Profits," *Stanford Law Review*, 37/2:313–397.

Gladwell, M. (2000) *The Tipping Point*. New York: Little Brown.

Gorman, E. (2005) "Gender Stereotypes, Same-Gender Preferences and Organizational Variation in the Hiring of Women: Evidence from Law Firms," *American Sociological Review*, 70/4:702–728.

(1999) "Moving Away from 'Up or Out': Determinants of Permanent Employment in Law Firms," *Law and Society Review*, 33:637–666.

Greenwood, R. and Empson, L. (2003) "The Professional Partnership: Relic or Exemplary Form of Governance?," *Organization Studies*, 24/6:909–933.

Greenwood, R., Hinings, C. R., and Brown, J. (1990) "'P2-Form' Strategic Management: Corporate Practices in Professional Service Firms," *Academy of Management Journal*, 33/4:725–755.

Greenwood, R., Li, S. X., Prakash, R., and Deephouse, D. L. (2005) 'Reputation, Diversification, and Organizational Explanations of Performance in Professional Service Firms', *Organization Science*, 16/6:661–673.

Groysberg, B., Lee, L. E., and Nanda, A. (2008) "Can They Take It with Them? The Portability of Star Knowledge Workers' Performance," *Management Science*, 54/7:1213–1230.

Groysberg, B., Matthews, S., Nanda, A., and Salter, M. (1999) The Goldman Sachs IPO (A). Case 800016, Cambridge, MA: Harvard Business School Publishing.

Hagan, J. and Kay, F. (1995) *Gender in Practice: Lawyers' Lives in Transition*. New York: Oxford University Press.

Heinz, J. P., Nelson, R. L., Sandefur, R. L., and Laumann, E.O. (2005) *Urban Lawyers: The New Social Structure of the Bar*. Chicago: University of Chicago Press.

Higgins, M. C. (2000) "The More, the Merrier? Multiple Developmental Relationships and Work Satisfaction," *Journal of Management Development*, 19/4:277–296.

Hitt, M. A., Bierman, L., Shimizu, K., and Kochhar, R. (2001) "Direct and Moderating Effects of Human Capital on Strategy and Performance in Professional Service Firms: A Resource-Based Perspective," *Academy of Management Journal*, 44/1:13–28.

Holder, E. (2001) "The Importance of Diversity in the Legal Profession," *Cardozo Law Review*, 23:2241–2251.

Ibarra, H. (1992) "Homophily and Differential Returns: Sex Differences in Network Structure and Access in an Advertising Firm," *Administrative Science Quarterly*, 37/3:422–447.

(1995) "Race, Opportunity and Diversity of Social Circles in Managers' Networks," *Academy of Management Journal*, 38/3:673–703.

Kahn, C., and Huberman, G. (1988) "Two-Sided Uncertainty and 'Up-or-Out' Contracts," *Journal of Labor Economics*, 6/4:423–444.

Kaplan, S. (2008) "Are US CEOs Overpaid?," *Academy of Management Perspectives*, 22/2:5–20.

(2009) "Economist Debates: Executive Pay," Economist.com, 20 October, www.economist.com/debate/days/view/402.

Kay, F. and Hagan, J. (1998) "Raising the Bar: The Gender Stratification of Law Firm Capitalization." *American Sociological Review*, 63/5:728–743.

Kay, F. and Gorman, E. (2008) "Women in the Legal Profession," *Annual Review of Law and Social Science*, 4:299–332.

    (2012) "Developmental Practices, Organizational Culture and Minority Representation in Organizational Leadership: The Case of Partners in Large U.S. Law Firms," *Annals of the American Academy of Political and Social Science*, 639:91–113.

Leicht, K. and Fennell, M.(2001) *Professional Work: A Sociological Approach.* Malden, MA: Blackwell.

Leitschuh, C. (2007) "Women in the Accounting Profession: Status and Trends," *Tennessee CPA Journal*, October: 4–5.

Maister, D. (1985) "The 'One-Firm' Firm," *Sloan Management Review*, 27/1:3–13.

    (1993) *Managing the Professional Service Firm.* New York: The Free Press.

Malhotra, N., Morris, T., and Hinings, C. R. (2006) "Variation in Organizational Form among Professional Service Organizations." In: Greenwood, R. and Suddaby, R. (eds.) *Research in the Sociology of Organizations: Professional Service Firms* Vol. 24, pp. 171–202. Oxford: Elsevier JAI Press.

Malos, S. B. and Campion, M. A. (1995) "An Options-Based Model of Career Mobility in Professional Service Firms," *Academy of Management Review*, 20/3:611–644.

    (2000) "Human Resource Strategy and Career Mobility in Professional Service Firms: A Test of an Options-Based Model," *Academy of Management Journal*, 43/4:749–760.

McPherson, M., Smith-Lovin, L., and Cook, J. (2001) "Birds of a Feather: Homophily in Social Networks," *Annual Review of Sociology*, 27:415–444.

Mouw, T. and Kalleberg, A. (2010) "Occupations and the Structure of Wage Inequality in the United States," *American Sociological Review*, 75/3:402–431.

Nelson, Robert. (1988) *Partners with Power: The Social Transformation of the Large Law Firm.* Berkeley: University of California Press.

O'Flaherty, B. and Siow, A. (1995) "Up-or-Out Rules in the Market for Lawyers," *Journal of Labor Economics*, 13/4:709–735.

Parsons, T. (1939) "The Professions and Social Structure," *Social Forces*, 17/4:457–467.

Payne-Pikus, M., Hagan, J., and Nelson, R. 2010. "Experiencing Discrimination: Race and Retention in America's Largest Law Firms," *Law & Society*, 44:553–584.

Regan Jr. Milton C. (2004) *Eat What You Kill: The Fall of a Wall Street Lawyer.* Ann Arbor: University of Michigan Press.

Rhode, D. (2011) "From Platitudes to Priorities: Diversity and Gender Equity in Law Firms," *Georgetown Journal of Legal Ethics*, 24:1041–1077.

Rider, C. (2012) "Networks, Hiring, and Attainment: Evidence from Law Firm Dissolutions," Working Paper, Emory University.

Scheiber, N. (2013) "The Last Days of Big Law: You Can't Imagine the Terror When the Money Dries Up," *The New Republic*, July 21.

Sharma, A. (1997) "Professional as Agent: Knowledge Asymmetry in Agency Exchange," *Academy of Management Review*, 22/3:758–798.

Sherer, P. D. and Lee, K. (2002) "Institutional Change in Large Law Firms: A Resource Dependency and Institutional Perspective," *Academy of Management Journal*, 45/1:102–119.

Somaya, D., Williamson, I.O., and Lorinkova, N. (2008) "Gone But Not Lost: The Different Performance Impacts of Employee Mobility Between Cooperators versus Competitors," *Academy of Management Journal*, 51:936–953.

Thomas, D. A. (1990) 'The Impact of Race on Managers' Experiences of Developmental Relationships', *Journal of Organizational Behavior*, 2/4:479–492.

U.S. Census Bureau. (2011) "Statistical Abstract of the United States 2011." 393–396, Table 615. Available at www.census.gov/compendia/statab/2011/tables/11s0615.pdf.

Uzzi, B. (1996) "The Sources and Consequences of Embeddedness for the Economic Performance of Organizations: The Network Effect," *American Sociological Review*, 61/4:674–698.

Uzzi, B., and Lancaster, R. (2004) 'Embeddedness and Price Formation in the Corporate Law Market', *American Sociological Review*, 69/3:319–344.

von Nordenflycht, A. (2010) "What Is a Professional Service Firm? Toward a Theory and Taxonomy of Knowledge-Intensive Firms," *Academy of Management Review*, 35/1:155–174.

(2011) "Firm Size and Industry Structure under Human Capital Intensity: Insights from the Evolution of the Global Advertising Industry," *Organization Science*, 22/1:141–157.

von Nordenflycht, A., Malhotra, N., and Morris, T. (2015) "Sources of Homogeneity and Heterogeneity Across Professional Services," In: Empson, L., Muzio, D., Broschak, J., and Hinings, C.R. (eds.), *Oxford Handbook of Professional Service Firms*, Chapter 7, pp. 135-160. Oxford: Oxford University Press.

Wilkins, D. (1999) "Partners without Power? A Preliminary Look at Black Partners in Corporate Law Firms," *Journal of the Institute for Studying Legal Ethics*, 2:15–48.

Wilkins, D. and Gulati, G. M. (1996) "Why Are There So Few Black Lawyers in Corporate Law Firms? An Institutional Analysis," *California Law Review*, 84/3:496–625.

CAREER MOBILITY AND RACIAL DIVERSITY IN LAW FIRMS[*]

CHRISTOPHER I. RIDER, ADINA D. STERLING, AND DAVID TAN

Although the legal profession has become much more diverse in recent decades, observed attainment still varies with a lawyer's race (Gorman and Kay, 2010; Payne-Pikus, Hagan, and Nelson, 2010). Black lawyers, in particular, experience higher attrition rates at nearly every career stage on the path to law firm partner. The Law School Admission Council (LSAC) reports that blacks constituted approximately 25% of all attendees at Law School Forums (a pre-application event) but only 11% of all law school applicants between 2000 and 2009 (Law School Admission Council 2009). Although blacks constituted 7% of all admitted law school applicants in 2010 and 2011, they constituted a smaller percentage of law school graduates and an even smaller percentage of all practicing attorneys (EEOC report 2003).

Black lawyers also face significantly lower odds of making partner in large corporate law firms than white males, even after accounting for the racial composition of associates (EEOC report, 2003: 31). For example, the National Association for Law Placement's (NALP) *Directory of Legal Employers* (available at www.nalpdirectory.com) reports that in 2011 black lawyers represented approximately 4.3% of all law firm associates but only 2% of all law firm partners. Despite extensive efforts of law firms to address such issues (e.g., Kay and Gorman 2012), such racial disparities are a persisting reality for the legal profession.

[*] Prepared for the 2nd Annual Conference of the Research Group on Legal Diversity. Research support from the Law School Admission Council is gratefully acknowledged.

357

One prominent explanation for these racial disparities centers on social capital. Relative to white peers, blacks are generally believed to access lesser social capital, or the resources located within social networks (see Fernandez and Fernandez-Mateo 2006 for a detailed account). Wilkins argues more specifically that for black lawyers, a lack of access to elite networks reinforces their disadvantage in the profession, and that "contacts are ultimately what will allow [black lawyers] to be a successful partner" (2004: 27). This argument is consistent with sociological research that suggests that network contacts are a crucial source of job referrals and intra-organizational support (Granovetter 1974; Fernandez and Weinberg 1997; Podolny and Baron 1997) and that being admitted to elite professional circles requires access to elite networks (Useem and Karabel 1986; Payne-Pikus et al. 2010). Why might social networks be so central to our understanding of persistent racial disparities in the legal profession?

Industry patterns indicate that, as in other professions, legal careers are becoming increasingly interorganizational in nature (Bidwell and Briscoe 2010; Rider and Tan 2015). Hiring competitors' partners has long been a law firm growth strategy (McEvily, Jaffee, and Tortoriello 2012) but over the past few decades, lateral hiring has become an even more common mechanism for law firm growth and competitiveness (Henderson and Bierman 2009; Coates, Nanda, and Wilkins 2011). Figure 12.1 illustrates the trend in lateral partner hiring from 2000 to 2009. In 2000, 64% of partner hires by an American Lawyer 200 (AM Law 200) firm were from an employer outside of the AM Law 200, such as in-house legal departments of corporations, government, or smaller firms. By 2009, however, the modal partner transition was from one AM Law 200 firm to another (i.e., 59% of all partner hires). Although these particular data are limited to partners' lateral transitions, more junior lawyers also exhibit substantial mobility (e.g., Lempert, Chambers, and Adams 2000; Dinovitzer et al. 2009).

Because legal careers increasingly constitute successive employment spells at multiple employers, a race-based disadvantage in interorganizational mobility opportunities is likely to contribute substantially to race-based differences in career attainment. Social networks are often implicated in the generation of mobility opportunities. For example, in a prior study, the first author investigated the role of social capital in obtaining employment following the dissolution of one's employer and found that lawyers tended to move to subsequent employers along with former coworkers (Rider 2014). Motivated by this work, we initiated a

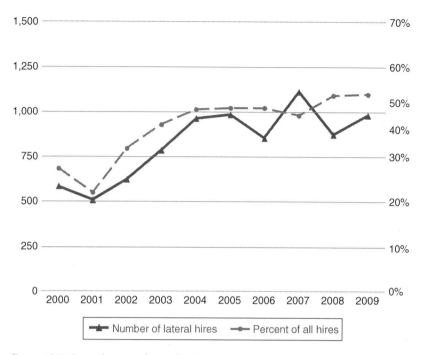

Figure 12.1. Lateral partner hiring by American Lawyer 200 firms, 2000–09.

study of race-based differences in reemployment prospects following employer dissolution and further explored the role of work relationships in aiding the post-dissolution job search process.

Our inquiry was guided by a large body of sociological work that demonstrates how socioeconomic disparities persist because workers have differential access to social capital (see Lin 2000 for a review). Differential access to network contacts that aid job searches often results from environmental constraints that affect the opportunities individuals have to interact with coworkers (Lincoln and Miller 1979; Astley and Fombrun 1983). For example, employees of large organizations tend to have more social ties than employees of small organizations presumably because of differences in the number of coworkers (McPherson and Smith-Lovin 1987; Moore 1990). If individuals of different races vary in terms of coworker relationships and mobility opportunities are often realized through such relationships, then one can reasonably expect race-based differences in career attainment. We, therefore, ask if the differences in career attainment between white lawyers and lawyers of other races can be attributed to variation in opportunities to change employers.

Our analytical approach is to first document a race-based difference in reemployment prospects following the dissolution of one's employer. We then probe the contribution of coworker relationships to our understanding of that difference. Importantly, the dissolution context enables us to obtain a large sample of lawyers who become mobile for the same reason at approximately the same time. This research design reduces the data collection burden on researchers. To obtain a sample of over 1,000 lawyers who move in a given year, one would need to track the careers of tens of thousands of lawyers. More difficult would be to account for selection into changing employers. The dissolution context provides obvious advantages in data collection and analysis.

We treat the unexpected dissolutions of six large law firms as quasi-experiments (i.e., mobility shocks). We analyze over 1,400 lawyers' post-dissolution labor market outcomes. Our empirical analyses produce three key findings that are consistent with a race-based mobility advantage in legal careers. First, following the dissolution of their employer, black lawyers were less likely to regain employment than white lawyers or lawyers who are neither white nor black. Second, white partners were most likely to regain employment and black associates were least likely to regain employment. Third, white lawyers were more likely to regain employment in the largest, highest-grossing, and most prestigious US law firms than lawyers of all other races, and black lawyers were least likely to regain employment in the most prestigious firms. White lawyers appear to have better prospects for interorganizational mobility than lawyers of other races and black lawyers seem to have the worst mobility prospects.

We then consider how coworker relationships contribute to this race-based difference in inferred mobility opportunities. We analyze summary statistics on the co-movements of displaced lawyers from the six dissolved firms. Our analyses reveal that black lawyers who regained employment were less likely to move with former coworkers than were white lawyers. Moreover, this disadvantage is almost entirely concentrated in associate lawyers; there does not appear to be any difference between white and black partners. We infer that black lawyers – primarily associates – face mobility constraints due at least in part to the intra-organizational structure of work relationships. In other words, despite increasing diversity within the legal profession there may be systematic differences in lawyers' opportunities to form valuable relationships with coworkers, especially the ones that provide access to interorganizational mobility opportunities. We note a paucity of research on the formation and maintenance of coworker relationships within law firms and, therefore, echo calls for greater practitioner attention to industry mentoring and staffing practices (e.g., Payne-Pinkus et al. 2010; Kay and Gorman 2012). We conclude by discussing the rhetoric and reality of mobility and legal diversity.

EMPIRICAL ANALYSES

We analyze the labor market outcomes of over 1,400 lawyers who lost their jobs due to the unexpected failures of six large US law firms in 2008 and 2009: Dreier LLP, Heller Ehrman LLP, Morgan & Finnegan LLP; Thacher Proffitt Wood LLP, Thelen LLP, and WolfBlock LLP. The six firms dissolved unexpectedly and fairly quickly; each firm's dissolution is detailed in *Appendix 1*. These six firms primarily represented clients in businesses most sensitive to the economic downturn during this time period: mortgage-backed securities, real estate, construction, and other financial services. All lawyers in the sample participated in the labor market for reasons largely independent of their legal ability, professional networks, or job performance. Most were simply employed by the wrong organization at the wrong time.

Dissolutions of law firms this large are fairly rare (Heinz 2009), so the dissolution of several around the same time enables us to observe many interorganizational transitions over a short time. As a reference point, in 2008 there were approximately 42,000 partners employed in the 200 highest-grossing US law firms ranked by the *American Lawyer* and approximately 2,100 lateral movements of partners into or out of those firms. Although a similar figure for non-partners is unavailable, this low partner turnover rate of approximately 5% informs our baseline assumption that absent a firm dissolution a lawyer is likely to remain with their firm in any given year. Therefore, to construct a sample of 1,400 lawyers (such as ours) one would have to follow approximately 50,000 lawyers over a given year to obtain just 1,400 employment transitions. Furthermore, credible inferences on mobility would be difficult to draw from this sample because lawyers who are not displaced by dissolution are probably not randomly drawn into the labor market (see Rider 2014).

These six firm dissolutions were also largely unexpected. Struggling firms tend to merge or to be acquired; few firms simply dissolve.

TABLE 12.1 Lawyers in Sample, by Dissolved Firm

Firm	Partners	Associates	Other	Total	Employed	% Employed
Dreier LLP	49	52	19	120	92	77%
Heller Ehrman	113	200	39	352	320	91%
Morgan Finnegan	32	32	8	72	62	86%
Thacher Proffitt & Wood	55	106	14	175	135	77%
Thelen LLP	188	152	52	392	367	94%
WolfBlock	155	111	49	315	272	86%
Totals	592	653	181	1,426	1,248	88%

Importantly, the six firms vary in terms of size, prestige, practice areas, geographic locations, and other key dimensions. The sample is probably representative of lawyers employed by large, corporate-oriented law firms (Heinz, Nelson, and Laumann 2001), as the lawyers range from first-year associates to partners with decades of legal experience.

From the six firms' websites, we identified all 1,459 lawyers employed at the time of dissolution to construct the sample summarized in Table 12.1 We collected data suitable for analysis from firm website biographies, the Martindale-Hubbell Law Directory ("Martindale-Hubbell"), the West Law Legal Directory ("West Law"), and the Internet Archive. Specifically, we obtained each lawyer's level (e.g., associate, partner), area(s) of practice, office location, law school attended, and, if available, year in which they passed the bar. We excluded thirty three lawyers (2.3%) from the analysis because we could not obtain sufficient data, so the analyzed sample includes 1,426 (97.7%) of the six firms' lawyers.

We then utilized searches of other firms' website directories, the online version of Martindale-Hubbell, individuals' LinkedIn profiles, ZoomInfo, and other Internet resources to identify post-dissolution employers for 1,248 of the 1,426 lawyers (88%). Almost 80% were employed in one of four US Metropolitan Statistical Areas centered on New York City, San Francisco, Philadelphia, or Washington, DC (see Table 12.2). The data on subsequent employment includes information on each individual's education, title, gender, race, practice area, geographic office location, and legal experience.

Importantly, the 178 lawyers who could not be located could be unemployed or, alternatively, employed but we were unable to locate them using our search methods. For analytical purposes, we treat these

TABLE 12.2   Lawyers in Sample, by Geographic Labor Market and
Legal Practice Area

City	Lawyers	% total	Practice area	Lawyers	% total
New York	567	40%	Litigation	496	35%
San Francisco	230	16%	Corporate law	414	29%
Philadelphia	179	12%	Corporate finance	316	22%
Washington, DC	96	7%	Intellectual property	249	17%
Silicon Valley	72	5%	Securities	229	16%
Northern New Jersey	69	5%	Real estate	196	14%
Los Angeles	64	4%	International	192	13%
Seattle	48	3%	Labor	191	13%
Hartford	28	2%	Government	129	9%
San Diego	25	2%	Technology	98	7%
Boston	13	1%	Emerging companies	91	6%
Harrisburg	13	1%	Energy	90	6%
Stamford	13	1%	Construction	86	6%
Wilmington	11	1%	Appellate	84	6%
Anchorage	4	0%	Antitrust	74	5%
Madison	2	0%	Bankruptcy/ restructuring	51	4%

178 lawyers as not being employed by a major legal employer and assume that there is no significant difference in terms of preferences for working for a major legal employer between the 178 lawyers we did not locate and the 1,248 we did locate. If a lawyer was not located by our search methods, then the lawyer is also unlikely to be located by potential employers or clients, which is a labor and product market disadvantage for a legal professional.

Analyses and dependent variables
We use probit models to estimate the likelihood that a lawyer obtains employment and is located by our sampling methods ("employment analyses"). In these analyses, the dependent variable is coded as 1 for the 1,248 lawyers for whom subsequent employment data was located and 0 for the 178 lawyers for whom data could not be located. In supplementary analyses of more specific employment outcomes, we model the likelihood that a lawyer is employed by an NLJ 250 firm, an American Lawyer 200 firm (AM Law 200), or a Vault 100 firm. These more restrictive dependent variables are coded as follows: 1 for

the 933 lawyers who were hired by an NLJ 250 firm and 0 for all others; or 1 for the 910 lawyers who were hired by an AM Law 200 firm and 0 for all others; or 1 for the 598 lawyers who were hired by a Vault 100 firm and 0 for all others. Of the 1,426 lawyers in the sample, 1,139 (or 78.3%) regained employment within one of these firm subsets (i.e., NLJ 250, AM Law 200, or Vault 100). We also code a dependent variable that equals 1 for the 40 lawyers who founded or joined a new organization following dissolution and 0 for all other lawyers.

Independent variables

The first author and four trained research assistants reviewed photos and biographical information like membership in the National Bar Association (an association for African-American lawyers and judges), to categorize each lawyer according to the US Census Bureau's racial and ethnic classifications. Because over 86% of the lawyers in the full sample were identified as "white" and "black" was the next most common category (3.4%) we coded two variables that equal 1 if the majority of the five coders coded an individual as "white" or "black," respectively, and 0 otherwise. The omitted category includes lawyers that were classified neither as "white" nor as "black" but instead were classified primarily as Arab, Asian, Indian, Hispanic, Latino, or Middle Eastern. There are not enough lawyer observations in the sample to employ a broader coding scheme.

Control variables

We rely primarily on fixed effect specifications to account for heterogeneity by dissolved firm, geographic location, and practice area. All models include unreported fixed effects for the six dissolved firms (i.e., Heller, Thelen, Thacher, WolfBlock, Dreier, and Morgan & Finnegan). Office location fixed effects include Los Angeles, Northern New Jersey, New York, Philadelphia (including suburban areas in Southern New Jersey), San Francisco, Seattle, Silicon Valley, Washington, and "other" (Anchorage, Boston, Harrisburg, Hartford, Madison, San Diego, Stamford, and Wilmington). Approximately 80% of the sample lawyers were employed in offices in the greater New York City area, the San Francisco Bay Area, Philadelphia, or Washington, DC. Consequently, in some specifications it was necessary to collapse office locations (e.g., Silicon Valley and San Francisco were collapsed into a Bay Area indicator variable). Practice area fixed effects include litigation, bankruptcy and restructuring, corporate law, corporate finance, intellectual property, securities, real estate, government law, international law, labor and employment, technology, and "all other." See Table 12.2 for more information on both office locations and practice areas.

Additional control variables are included in the analyses. The first author and four trained research assistants reviewed lawyer names, photos, and/or biographical information like membership in a women's bar association to code lawyer gender. The "female" variable takes a value of 1 if the majority of the five coders identified the lawyer as female and 0 otherwise; 31.0% of the 1,426 lawyers were identified as female. Similar results were obtained by using the percentage of coders who identified the lawyer as female instead. Consistent with prior research on law firms (Gorman 2005; Gorman and Kmec 2009), females constitute 42.7% of the 653 associates in the full sample but only 20.2% of the 592 partners.

The lawyers in the sample graduated from 120 law schools that vary in terms of prestige and in the geographic distribution of their alumni. To account for heterogeneity in prestige, we included the numeric rank of each lawyer's law school in the 2008 US News & World Report "Best Law School" (USN&WR) rankings (see Espeland and Sauder, 2007 or Sauder and Espeland, 2009 for studies of these rankings). Unranked law schools were assigned a rank of 120, the lowest ranked school in the rankings. To account for geographic variance in the local prevalence of specific school alumni networks, we included a variable for each lawyer that is the percentage of all NLJ 250 lawyers within the lawyer's Core-Based Statistical Area (CBSA), as defined by the U.S. Office of Management and Budget, that graduated from the focal lawyer's law school.

We coded a partner indicator variable as 1 if a lawyer was a partner at their prior (dissolved) firm and 0 if the lawyer was an associate, counsel, or another title. We computed the number of years of legal experience for each lawyer by subtracting the year in which the lawyer was first admitted to a state bar from 2008; we added one and transformed the sum by the natural logarithm to adjust for the skewness of the legal experience variable (long right tail).

Results
Summary statistics and correlations for the variables in the employment analyses are presented in Table 12.3; the key results are presented in Table 12.4. In Models 1 through 8, the dependent variable equals 1 if

TABLE 12.3 Summary Statistics and Correlations of Variables in Employment Analyzes (N = 1,426 lawyers)

	Mean	SD	(1)	(2)	(3)	(4)	(5)	(6)	(7)	(8)	(9)	(10)	(11)	(12)
(1) Lawyer employed and located (0/1)	0.88	0.33	1.00											
(2) Employed by NLJ 250 firm and located (0/1)	0.65	0.48	0.52	1.00										
(3) Employed by AM Law 200 firm and located (0/1)	0.64	0.48	0.50	0.96	1.00									
(4) Employed by Vault 100 firm and located (0/1)	0.42	0.49	0.32	0.61	0.64	1.00								
(5) Lawyer starts or joins a new firm (0/1)	0.03	0.17	0.06	−0.23	−0.23	−0.14	1.00							
(6) Female (0/1)	0.31	0.46	−0.06	−0.05	−0.05	−0.02	0.01	1.00						
(7) Partner (0/1)	0.42	0.49	0.16	0.18	0.17	0.06	−0.03	−0.20	1.00					
(8) ln (years of legal experience)	2.48	0.97	0.03	0.04	0.03	−0.05	0.02	−0.25	0.61	1.00				
(9) Rank of law school attended	40.6	37.9	0.00	−0.04	−0.06	−0.15	0.02	0.02	−0.07	−0.09	1.00			
(10) % of local attorneys from lawyer i's law school	0.08	0.06	0.18	0.12	0.13	0.00	−0.01	−0.03	0.03	0.05	−0.13	1.00		
(11) Black (0/1)	0.04	0.18	−0.11	−0.07	−0.06	−0.08	0.01	0.07	−0.01	−0.06	−0.02	0.02	1.00	
(12) White (0/1)	0.86	0.34	0.19	0.12	0.11	0.03	0.01	−0.17	0.19	0.21	0.00	0.07	−0.38	1.00

TABLE 12.4 Probit Models of the Likelihoods of Regaining Employment (Y_i = 1 if "yes" 0 if "no")

[dependent variable]	(1)	(2)	(3)	(4)	(5)	(6)	(7)	(8)
	[employed]	[employed]	[employed]	[employed]	[employed]	[employed]	[employed]	[employed]
Female (0/1)	-0.058	-0.051	-0.038	-0.067	-0.058	-0.312	-0.130	-0.636
	(0.100)	(0.103)	(0.106)	(0.103)	(0.106)	(0.250)	(0.138)	(0.311)
Partner (0/1)	0.810**	0.871**	0.931**	0.867**	0.921**			
	(0.122)	(0.123)	(0.127)	(0.125)	(0.129)			
ln (years of legal experience)	-0.246**	-0.265**	-0.290**	-0.260**	-0.289**	-1.06**	0.135	-0.579**
	(0.066)	(0.066)	(0.068)	(0.065)	(0.067)	(0.330)	(0.116)	(0.204)
Rank of law school attended	0.002*	0.004**	0.003*	0.004**	0.003*	0.001	0.001	0.011*
	(0.001)	(0.001)	(0.001)	(0.001)	(0.001)	(0.001)	(0.002)	(0.004)
% of local attorneys from lawyer's law school	5.31**	5.84**	6.88**	5.81**	6.84**	9.19**	8.37**	3.48
	(1.15)	(1.17)	(1.22)	(1.17)	(1.21)	(2.54)	(2.07)	(2.54)
Black (0/1)	-0.514*	-0.586*	-0.543*	-0.602*	-0.570*	0.181	-0.928**	1.64*
	(0.218)	(0.227)	(0.242)	(0.237)	(0.252)	(0.516)	(0.311)	(0.633)
White (0/1)	0.535**	0.520*	0.501**	0.513**	0.485**	1.00*	0.248	1.90**
	(0.125)	(0.126)	(0.129)	(0.128)	(0.131)	(0.404)	(0.163)	(0.400)
Constant	0.653**	0.658*	1.01**	0.313	0.641†	6.42**	0.466	0.075
	(0.195)	(0.264)	(0.339)	(0.317)	(0.388)	(1.20)	(0.546)	(1.20)

TABLE 12.4 (cont.)

	(1)	(2)	(3)	(4)	(5)	(6)	(7)	(8)
N (lawyers)	1,426	1,426	1,426	1,426	1,426	592	653	181
Sample	All	All	All	All	All	Partners	Associates	Other
Firm fixed effects	No	Yes	Yes	Yes	Yes	Yes	Yes	Yes
Office city fixed effects	No	No	Yes	No	Yes	Yes	Yes	Yes
Practice area fixed effects	No	No	No	Yes	Yes	Yes	Yes	Yes
Log pseudolikelihood	-467.8	-444.3	-422.2	-437.4	-415.3	-92.0	-206.7	-63.0
Wald Chi-square (d.f.)	107.71 (7)	156.8 (12)	190.6 (20)	184.1 (23)	226.5 (31)	1,166.2 (26)	80.8 (26)	80.6 (25)

Robust standard errors in parentheses.

** $p < 0.01$;

* $p < 0.05$;

† $p < 0.10$; two-tailed tests.

the focal lawyer regained employment at any organization and was located via employment searches and 0 otherwise. In Models 1 through 5, the analyzed sample is all 1,426 lawyers; partners, associates, and other lawyers are analyzed in Models 6, 7, and 8, respectively. The dependent variable is coded 1 for lawyers whose subsequent employer was located and 0 for all others.

Model 1 of Table 12.4 indicates that of the 1,426 lawyers in the full sample, partners were more likely to regain employment than associates or other lawyers (e.g., of counsel, contract attorneys). Holding level constant (i.e., partner or otherwise), the more experienced a lawyer, the less likely they regained employment. The lesser the prestige of a lawyer's law school (i.e., the greater the numeric rank), the more likely they were to regain employment, and lawyers located in labor markets with disproportionately more fellow alumni were more likely to regain employment. Evidence of a race-based mobility disadvantage is provided by the coefficients on the black and white indicator variables. White lawyers were more likely and black lawyers less likely than lawyers of other racial or ethnic categories (e.g., Asian, Indian, Hispanic/Latino) to regain employment and to be located. Because the omitted category in this specification includes all lawyers identified as members of a category other than white or black, the coefficients suggest that whites are advantaged and that blacks are disadvantaged over lawyers from all other racial categories in terms of regaining employment, post-dissolution.

Models 2 through 5 maintain the baseline specification but also include unreported firm, office location, and practice area fixed effects. Model 2 indicates that there is substantial heterogeneity across lawyers from the six dissolved firms but that the coefficient estimates on the covariates are fairly stable when firm fixed effects are included. Model 3 indicates that the likelihood that a lawyer regained employment varies with local labor market conditions, as evidenced by the improved model fit when including office fixed effects to account for each lawyer's geographic location.

Model 4 demonstrates that legal practice area also has a substantial influence on labor market outcomes, again as evidenced by the improved model fit when practice area fixed effects are included. Model 5 includes all of these controls and demonstrates that the key baseline effects of partner level, experience, and local alumni on a lawyer's reemployment prospects are robust to including firm, office, and practice fixed effects. Most importantly, the race-based employment

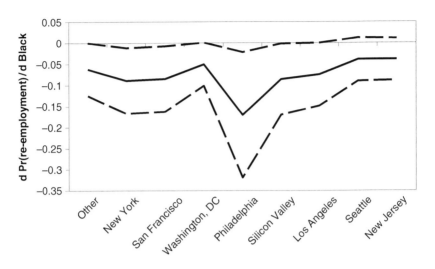

Figure 12.2. Marginal effect of race on probability of reemployment

advantages remain significant even when accounting for the possibility that lawyers systematically sort into firms, geographic areas, or practice areas based on racial differences.

Figure 12.2 shows the estimated marginal effect of being black on the likelihood of reemployment. The solid line represents the point estimate of the marginal effect. Dashed lines represent the 95% confidence interval. Estimates and confidence intervals vary across cities due to the uneven distribution of lawyers across cities. Across the entire sample, black lawyers are on average 9% less likely to regain employment. The effect is strongest for lawyers in Philadelphia, where black lawyers are 17% less likely to regain employment. Race effects on reemployment are also statistically significant in New York, San Francisco, Silicon Valley, Los Angeles, and cities in the baseline "other" category. Race effects are not significant in Washington, DC, Seattle, or New Jersey. Although these results differ from prior law firm research that documents substantial geographic variation in minority representation (i.e., Gorman and Kay 2010), one must bear in mind that our sample is very small with respect to the number of black lawyers in each geographic location. Our geography-specific results are probably not comparable to those of prior work.

In Models 6, 7, and 8, we investigate race-based differences for lawyers at different levels. Model 6 demonstrates that white partners are more likely to regain employment than are lawyers of any other

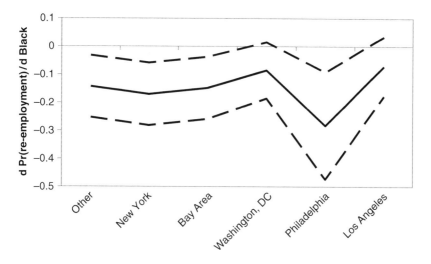

Figure 12.3. Marginal effects of race on probability of reemployment: Associates

racial category. Model 7 demonstrates that black associates are less likely to regain employment than are lawyers of any other racial category. Model 8 suggests that both black and white lawyers who are neither partners nor associates are more likely to regain employment than lawyers of other racial categories. But the sample of other lawyers is exceedingly small (especially for racial minorities) so caution is warranted in interpreting the coefficients in Model 8. We infer from these results that the greatest advantage in interorganizational mobility accrues to the most senior, white lawyers while the most junior, black lawyers are the most disadvantaged.

Figure 12.3 shows the estimated marginal effects of being black on the likelihood of reemployment for associates. Across the entire sample, black associates are 16% less likely to regain employment. The effect is strongest for associates in Philadelphia, where black associates are 28% less likely to regain employment. Race effects are also statistically significant in New York, the Bay Area, and cities in the baseline "other" category. Race effects are not significant in Washington, DC or Los Angeles. Again, one must bear in mind that our sample is very small with respect to the number of black lawyers in each geographic location.

Race-based differences in employer type
In Table 12.5, we explore race-based differences in regaining employment within specific sectors of the legal services industry by coding the

TABLE 12.5   Probit Models of the Likelihoods of Regaining
Specific Employment ($Y_i = 1$ if "yes"; 0 if "no")

	(9)	(10)	(11)	(12)
[Dependent Variable]	*[NLJ 250]*	*[AML 200]*	*[V100]*	*[Entrep.]*
Female (0/1)	−0.030	−0.037	−0.06	0.039
	(0.084)	(0.083)	(0.091)	(0.173)
Partner (0/1)	0.645 **	0.644 **	0.502 **	−0.485 *
	(0.100)	(0.099)	(0.111)	(0.196)
ln (years of legal experience)	−0.175 **	−0.189 **	−0.210 **	0.268 **
	(0.052)	(0.051)	(0.057)	(0.097)
Rank of law school attended	0.001	0.001	−0.001	0.001
	(0.001)	(0.001)	(0.001)	(0.002)
% of local attorneys from lawyer's law school	2.36 **	2.82 **	2.17 **	1.45
	(0.705)	(0.684)	(0.738)	(0.960)
Black (0/1)	−0.345	−0.289	−0.625 *	0.312
	(0.227)	(0.229)	(0.264)	(0.423)
White (0/1)	0.371 **	0.358 **	0.305 *	0.255
	(0.118)	(0.119)	(0.124)	(0.226)
Constant	0.801 **	0.378	−0.531	−7.01 **
	(0.306)	(0.307)	(0.339)	(0.511)
N (lawyers)	1,426	1,426	1,426	1,426
Sample	All	All	All	All
Firm fixed effects	Yes	Yes	Yes	Yes
Office city fixed effects	Yes	Yes	Yes	Yes
Practice area fixed effects	Yes	Yes	Yes	Yes
Log pseudolikelihood	−754.4	−767.7	−649.0	−147.7
Wald Chi-square (d.f.)	283.3 (31)	296.4 (31)	279.3 (31)	1,548.8 (29)

Robust standard errors in parentheses.
** $p < 0.01$;
 * $p < 0.05$.

dependent variable more restrictively so that the unemployed and those employed outside of the largest, highest-grossing, and most prestigious law firms are treated as observationally equivalent. In Model 9, the dependent variable equals 1 if the focal lawyer was found to be employed by a firm in the 2009 NLJ 250 and 0 otherwise (i.e., either not located, not employed, or not employed by an NLJ 250 firm). White lawyers were most likely to regain employment at an NLJ 250 firm. In Model 10, the dependent variable equals 1 if the focal lawyer was found to be employed an AM Law 200 firm and 0 otherwise. Again, white lawyers were most likely to regain employment at an AM Law 200 firm.

In Model 11, the dependent variable equals 1 if the focal lawyer was reemployed by a Vault 100 firm and 0 otherwise. White lawyers were most likely to regain employment at a Vault 100 firm and, additionally, black lawyers were least likely to regain employment in one of these highly prestigious firms. In Model 12, we find no race-based differences in the likelihood of founding or joining a new organization, post-dissolution. Importantly, if we remove the white indicator variable from the specifications of Models 9, 10, and 11, the coefficient on the black indicator variable is negative and significant. This indicates that black lawyers were less likely than lawyers of any other racial category to regain employment within the largest, highest-grossing, or most prestigious US law firms.

Mediating role of coworker relationships

In Table 12.6, we explore a potential mediating mechanism of these race-based differences: relationships with coworkers. In this exploratory analysis, we focus on the 938 lawyers who regained employment in the largest US law firms (the NLJ 250). Specifically, we compare the tendency of black lawyers versus lawyers of other racial categories to move to their first post-dissolution employer with at least one other former coworker. We consider moving with a coworker to be informative for two reasons. First, generally, coworker relationships are import-ant sources of career support (Podolny and Baron 1997). Second, more specific to the mobility context, potential employers are likely to view a coworker's endorsement of a lawyer to be a good signal of a lawyer's ability and character.

One must bear in mind that there are only twenty five black lawyers in the sub-sample of reemployed lawyers (versus 40 in the full sample). Yet, these analyses reveal two statistically significant differences between black lawyers and others. In all comparisons, we consider two lawyers to "move together" if following the dissolution of their employer they regain employment at the same firm office. Two lawyers who regain employment at the same firm but in different offices are not considered to have moved together. Comparison 1 reveals that black lawyers are less likely to regain employment with a former coworker than are lawyers of

TABLE 12.6   Percentage of Lawyers Who Move with ≥ 1 Former Coworker

1. All lawyers	N	%	t
Black	25	72%	
Non-black	915	88%	
Δ (Black − Non-black)		−16%	2.34
2. Black and white lawyers	N	%	t
Black	25	72%	
White	842	88%	
Δ (Black − White)		−16%	2.39
3. All associates	N	%	t
Black	11	64%	
Non-black	401	88%	
Δ (Black − Non-black)		−24%	2.46
4. All partners	N	%	t
Black	13	85%	
Non-black	449	89%	0.45
Δ (Black − Non-black)		−4%	

any other racial category (72% versus 88%; $p < 0.05$). Comparison 2 reveals that black lawyers who regain employment are similarly less likely to regain employment with a former coworker than are white lawyers. Comparisons 3 and 4 reveal that the key mobility difference is limited to the most junior lawyers because it is only black associates and not partners that are less likely to move with a former coworker ($p < 0.05$ for associates and not significant for partners).

DISCUSSION

This study investigated race-based differences in interorganizational mobility for US lawyers. Treating the unexpected dissolutions of six large law firms as a mobility shock, we analyzed over 1,400 lawyers' post-dissolution labor market outcomes. Three key results of our empirical analyses are consistent with a race-based mobility advantage in legal careers. First, following the dissolution of their employer, black lawyers were less likely to regain employment than white lawyers or lawyers who are neither white nor black. Second, white partners were most likely to regain employment and black associates were least likely to regain employment. Third, white lawyers were more likely to regain employment in the largest, highest-grossing, and most prestigious US law firms than lawyers of other races.

Our exploratory analyses suggest that co-mobility opportunities (i.e., moving with former coworkers) may be constrained for black lawyers – especially associates – by the intra-organizational structure of work relationships. To the extent that co-mobility is indicative of a strong working relationship, black lawyers and especially associates seem less likely to possess the strong coworker relationships that are so central to the generation of career opportunities (e.g., Podolny and Baron 1997; Sterling 2015). Caution is, of course, warranted in interpreting this result because our data do not include direct measures of coworker relationships and our sample size is small. These results, though, demonstrate the importance of studying how coworker relationships typically form in law firms (e.g., Sterling and Rider 2015).

The legal services industry is notably lacking in diversity, especially in higher ranks (NALP Bulletin 2015). Legal career trajectories now resemble those in many other industries in the sense that lawyers' careers are increasingly interorganizational (Bidwell and Briscoe 2010; Rider and Tan 2015). Consequently, both individuals' career prospects and law firm diversity are influenced by lateral hiring patterns. If, as the results of this study suggest, black lawyers find it more challenging to change employers than lawyers of other races, the trend toward lateral hiring and interorganizational careers is likely to reduce diversity in legal services organizations. The higher the rate of turnover and the greater the difference in mobility rates between black and white lawyers, the greater the likelihood that law firms become more racially homogenous employers in the future.

Our study speaks to both the rhetoric and reality of diversity in the legal services industry. In recent decades, law firms have backed up their diversity rhetoric by increasing the representation of racial and ethnic minorities in the legal profession (e.g., Gorman and Kay 2010; Payne-Pikus et al. 2010). The reality is that the legal profession has indeed become more diverse. Yet, persistent inequalities are also a reality. Our study implies that despite widespread firm recruiting efforts to increase diversity through hiring, black lawyers may face an internal obstacle to career progress: establishing strong working relationships with coworkers. Payne-Pikus, Nelson, and Hagan (2013) document that African-American female lawyers tend to be especially dissatisfied with their jobs and largely due to feeling socially isolated within their firms.

Others have called for increased attention to how junior lawyers are assigned to mentoring and working relationships with partners

375

(e.g., Payne-Pikus et al. 2010; Briscoe and Kellogg 2011). Such calls cannot be dismissed as mere rhetoric, as our work suggests that continued neglect of such issues likely contributes to persistent inequality within the profession. In a separate study that analyzes the same data as this study, Rider (2014) finds that displaced lawyers tended to regain employment by moving with former coworkers. This study demonstrates that black lawyers – and especially associates – are less likely to move with coworkers than are other lawyers.

Firms interested in increasing legal diversity might want to invest in developing strong work relationships for black associates. Prior research suggests that both formal and informal mentoring contribute substantially to legal careers (Kay, Hagan, and Parker 2009), yet little is known about effective mentoring for underrepresented minorities. For example, one study finds that firm-level diversity at the partner level is unassociated with formal practices, cultural values, or mentoring programs (Kay and Gorman 2010). The issue of how firms can facilitate the formation of strong working relationships for underrepresented minorities seems fertile ground for future collaborations between practitioners and academics interested in moving on from diversity rhetoric to a more diverse industry reality.

REFERENCES

American Lawyer. 2000–10. *Lateral Partner Moves Database*. New York: ALM Legal Intelligence.

Astley, W. G. and C. J. Fombrun. 1983. "Collective Strategy: Social Ecology of Organizational Environments." *Academy of Management Review*, 8:576–587.

Bidwell, M. and F. Briscoe. 2010. "The Dynamics of Interorganizational Careers." *Organization Science*, 21(5):1034–1053.

Blau, P. M.1977. "A Macrosociological Theory of Social Structure." *American Journal of Sociology*, 83(1):26–54.

Blau, P. M. and O. D. Duncan. 1967. *The American Occupational Structure*. New York, Wiley.

Briscoe, F. and K. C. Kellogg. 2011. "The Initial Assignment Effect: Local Employer Practices and Positive Career Outcomes for Work-Family Program Users." *American Sociological Review*, 762:291–319.

Coates, John C., Michele M. DeStefano, Ashish Nanda, and David B. Wilkins. 2011. "Hiring Teams, Firms, and Lawyers: Evidence of the Evolving Relationships in the Corporate Legal Market." *Law & Social Inquiry*, 36:999–1031.

Dinovitzer, Ronit. 2006. "Social Capital and Constraints on Legal Careers." *Law and Society Review*, 40 (2):445–479.

Dinovitzer, Ronit, Robert L. Nelson, Gabriele Plickert, Rebecca Sandefur, and Joyce S. Sterling. 2009. *After the JD II: Second Results from a National Study of Legal Careers*. The American Bar Foundation and the NALP Foundation for Law Career Research and Education.

Espeland, Wendy N. and Michael Sauder. 2007. "Rankings and Reactivity: How Public Measures Recreate Social Worlds." *American Journal of Sociology*, 113:1–40.

Equal Employment Opportunity Commission (U.S.). 2003. "Diversity in Law Firms." www.eeoc.gov/eeoc/statistics/reports/diversitylaw/lawfirms.pdf

Fernandez, Roberto M. and Isabel Fernandez-Mateo. 2006. "Networks, Race, and Hiring." *American Sociological Review*, 71:42–71.

Fernandez, Roberto M. and Nancy Weinberg. 1997. "Sifting and Sorting: Personal Contacts and Hiring in a Retail Bank." *American Sociological Review*, 62:883–902.

Galanter, M. and T. Palay. 1991. *Tournament of Lawyers: The Transformation of the Big Law Firms*. Chicago: University of Chicago Press.

Gorman, Elizabeth H. 2005. "Gender Stereotypes, Same-Gender Preferences, and Organizational Variation in the Hiring of Women: Evidence from Law Firms." *American Sociological Review*, 70:702–728.

Gorman, Elizabeth H. and Fiona M. Kay. 2010. "Racial and Ethnic Minority Representation in Large U.S. Law Firms." *Special Issue: Law Firms, Legal Culture, and Legal Practice, Studies in Law Politics, and Society*, 52:211–238.

Gorman, Elizabeth H. and Julie A. Kmec. 2009. "Hierarchical Rank and Women's Organizational Mobility: Glass Ceilings in Corporate Law Firms." *American Journal of Sociology*, 114:1428–1474.

Granovetter, Mark S. 1973. "The Strength of Weak Ties." *American Journal of Sociology*, 78:1360–1380.

(1974[1995]). *Getting a Job: A Study of Contacts and Careers*, 2nd edn. Chicago, IL: University of Chicago Press.

Heinz, John P. 2009. "When Law Firms Fail." *Suffolk University Law Review*, 43:67–78.

Heinz, John P., Robert L. Nelson, and Edward O. Laumann. 2001. "The Scale of Justice: Observations on the Transformation of Urban Law Practice." *Annual Review of Sociology*, 27:377–362.

Heinz, John P., Robert L. Nelson, Rebecca L. Sandefur, and Edward O. Laumann. 2005. *Urban Lawyers: The New Social Structure of the Bar*. Chicago, IL: University of Chicago Press.

Henderson, William D. and Bierman, Leonard. 2009. "An Empirical Analysis of Lateral Lawyer Trends from 2000 to 2007: The Emerging Equilibrium for Corporate Law Firms." *Georgetown Journal of Legal Ethics*, 22:1395–1430.

Hillman, R. W. 2002. "The Hidden Costs of Lawyer Mobility: Of Law Firms, Law Schools, and the Education of Lawyers." *Kentucky Law Journal*, 91:299–310.

Ibarra, H. 1993. "Personal Networks of Women and Minorities in Management: A Conceptual Framework." *The Academy of Management Review*, 18:56–87.

Kalev, A. 2009. "Cracking the Glass Cages? Restructuring and Ascriptive Inequality at Work." *American Journal of Sociology*, 114:1591–1643.

Kay, F., J. Hagan, and P. Parker. 2009. "Principals in Practice: The Importance of Mentorship in the Early Stages of Career Development." *Law & Policy*, 31:69–110.

Kay, Fiona M. and Elizabeth H. Gorman. 2012. "Developmental Practices, Organizational Culture, and Minority Representation in Organizational Leadership: The Case of Partners in Large U.S. Law Firms." *The ANNALS of the American Academy of Political and Social Science*, 639:91–113.

Lempert, R. O., D. L. Chambers, and T. K. Adams. 2000. "Michigan's Minority Graduates in Practice: The River Runs Through Law School." *Law & Social Inquiry*, 25(2):395–505.

Lin, Nan. 1999. "Social Networks and Status Attainment." *Annual Review of Sociology*, 25:467–87.

Lin, Nan. 2000. "Inequality in social capital." *Contemporary Sociology* 29 (6):785–795.

Lin, Nan, Walter M. Ensel, and John C. Vaughn. 1981. "Social Resources and the Strength of Ties: Structural Factors in Occupational Status Attainment." *American Sociological Review*, 46:393–405.

Lincoln, James R. and Jon Miller. 1979. "Work and Friendship Ties in Organizations: A Comparative Analysis of Relational Networks." *Administrative Science Quarterly*, 24:181–199.

McEvily, B., J. Jaffe, M. Tortoriello. 2012. "Not All Bridging Ties Are Equal: Network Imprinting and Firm Growth in the Nashville Legal Industry, 1933–1978." *Organization Science*, 23(2):547–563.

McPherson, J. M. and L. Smith-Lovin. 1987. "Homophily in Voluntary Organizations: Status Distance and the Composition of Face-to-Face Groups." *American Sociological Review*, 52:370–379.

McPherson, M., L. Smith-Lovin, and J. Cook. 2001. "Birds of a Feather: Homophily in Social Networks." *Annual Review of Sociology*, 27(1):415.

Moore, Gwen. 1990. "Structural Determinants of Men's and Women's Personal Networks." *American Sociological Review*, 55:726–735.

NALP Bulletin. 2015. "Despite Small Gains in the Representation of Women and Minorities Among Equity Partners, Broad Disparities Remain." June. http://www.nalp.org/0615research. Last accessed September 10, 2015.

Payne-Pikus, Monique R., John Hagan, and Robert L. Nelson. 2010. "Experiencing Discrimination: Race and Retention in America's Largest Law Firms." *Law & Society Review*, 44:553–584.

Payne-Pikus, Monique R., Robert L. Nelson, and John Hagan. 2013. "The Intersectionality of Race, Gender, and Social Isolation in the Retention of American Lawyers in Private Law Firms." Paper Prepared for the 2nd Annual Conference of the Research Group on Legal Diversity.

Phillips, Damon J. 2002. "A Genealogical Approach to Organizational Life Chances: The Parent-Progeny Transfer among Silicon Valley Law Firms, 1946–1996." *Administrative Science Quarterly*, 47(3):474–506.

Podolny, Joel M. and James N. Baron. 1997. "Resources and Relationships: Social Networks and Mobility in the Workplace." *American Sociological Review*, 62:673–693.

Reagans, Ray E. 2011. "Close Encounters: Analyzing How Social Similarity and Propinquity Contribute to Strong Network Connections." *Organization Science*, 22(4):835–849.

Rider, Christopher I. 2012. "How Employees' Prior Affiliations Constrain Organizational Network Change: A Study of U.S. Venture Capital and Private Equity." *Administrative Science Quarterly*, 57(3):453–483.

———. 2014. *Educational Credentials, Hiring, and Intra-occupational Inequality: Evidence from Law Firm Dissolutions*. Working Paper. Georgetown University.

Rider, Christopher I. and David Tan. 2015. "Labor Market Advantages of Organizational Status: A Study of Lateral Partner Hiring by Large U.S. Law Firms." *Organization Science*, 26(5):1502–1519.

Sandefur, R. L. 2001. "Work and Honor in the Law: Prestige and the Division of Lawyers' Labor." *American Sociological Review*, 66(3):382–403.

Sauder, Michael, and Wendy N. Espeland. 2009. "The Discipline of Rankings: Tight Coupling and Organizational Change." *American Sociological Review*, 74:63–82.

Sorensen, J. B. 2004. "The Racial Demography of Racial Employment Segregation." *American Journal of Sociology*, 110:626–671.

Sparrowe, R. T. and R. C. Liden. 2005. "Two Routes to Influence: Integrating Leader-Member Exchange and Social Network Perspectives." *Administrative Science Quarterly*, 50:505–535.

Sterling, Adina D. 2015. "Pre-entry Contacts and the Generation of Nascent Networks in Organizations." Organization Science, 26(3):650–667.

Sterling, Adina D. and Christopher I. Rider. 2015. *Educational Affiliations and Intra-Organizational Allocations of Labor*. Working Paper, Stanford University.

Useem, M. and J. Karabel1986. "Pathways to Top Corporate Management." *American Sociological Review*, 51:184–200.

Wilkins, David B. 2004. "Doing Well by Doing Good? The Role of Public Service in the Careers of Corporate Lawyers." *Houston Law Review*, 41 (1):1–91.

APPENDIX 1: SIX FIRM DISSOLUTIONS

1. Heller Ehrman LLP ("Heller") was headquartered in San Francisco and also operated large offices in Los Angeles, London, New York, San Diego, Seattle, Silicon Valley, and Washington. Heller was widely viewed as one of the most prominent law firms in the San Francisco Bay Area and regularly received high ratings from legal industry publications for diversity, pro bono work, and employee satisfaction. The firm was ranked 62nd in the 2008 Vault 100 ranking of prestigious law firms and 56th in the 2008 American Lawyer 200 rankings of US law firms by gross revenues. According to the *National Law Journal (NLJ)*, Heller was the 65th largest firm in the United States in 2007, employing approximately 600 lawyers.

Heller attorneys represented major corporate clients like Apple, GE, Levi Strauss, McDonald's, Microsoft, Northrup Grunman, and Yahoo!. In 2008, their client list included Lehman Brothers and Washington Mutual, as well as two large corporations that failed in 2008, and left Heller with large uncollectable receivables. Like many law firm dissolutions (Phillips 2002; Heinz, 2009), Heller's collapse was accelerated by the departure of fifteen intellectual property attorneys for competitor Covington & Burling LLP. This departure triggered a default clause in the firm's loan agreements and Heller was unable to satisfy its creditors' capital requirements. Shortly thereafter, reported merger talks with Mayer Brown ceased. Heller announced its dissolution on September 26, 2008, officially dissolved in late November of 2008, and filed for bankruptcy in December of 2008. In mid-October of 2008, we extracted 352 website biographies for lawyers employed in Heller's US offices at the time of dissolution (see Table 12.1 for details).

2. Thelen LLP ("Thelen") was a bicoastal law firm formed by two mergers, one in 1998 and one in 2006, between a California-based law firm and two New York-based firms. Thelen had offices in Hartford, Los Angeles, New York, San Francisco, Silicon Valley, and Washington, DC. The firm was ranked 75th in the 2008 Vault 100 ranking of prestigious law firms and 76th in the 2008 American Lawyer 200 rankings of US law firms by gross revenues. According to the *NLJ*, Thelen was the 78th largest firm in the United States in 2008, employing approximately 550 lawyers.

Thelen's construction practice was widely regarded as one of the best in the country and the firm's clients included Cisco, Ford, Merrill Lynch, News Corporation, and several major public utilities. Thelen had difficulty integrating attorneys acquired in the merger with Brown Raysman in 2006 and experienced numerous partner departures in 2007 and 2008. After merger talks with Nixon Peabody failed, Thelen announced its dissolution in October of 2008, closed its doors in December of 2008, and entered bankruptcy in September of 2009. In October of 2008, we extracted 392 website biographies for those lawyers employed in Thelen's offices (see Table 12.1 for details).

3. Thacher Proffitt Wood LLP ("Thacher") was headquartered in New York City and also operated offices in Washington, DC and New Jersey. The firm was ranked 90th in the 2008 Vault 100 ranking of prestigious law firms and 131st in the 2008 American Lawyer 200 rankings of US law firms by gross revenues. According to the *NLJ*, Thacher was the 156th largest firm in the United States in 2008, employing almost 300 lawyers.

Thacher was so strongly associated with sub-prime mortgages that mortgage traders commonly referred to purchase agreements for mortgage-backed securities as "Thacher docs." Thacher clients included Citibank and UBS and the firm's biggest client was Bear Stearns. In late December of 2008, merger talks with King & Spalding ceased and approximately 100 lawyers announced that they would leave Thacher for a competitor, Sonnenschein, Nath & Rosenthal, LLP. Thacher partners voted to dissolve the firm shortly after the announcement. In December of 2008, we extracted 175 website biographies for those lawyers employed in Thacher's offices (see Table 12.1 for details).

4. WolfBlock LLP ("WolfBlock") was based in Philadelphia and also operated offices in New York, New Jersey, Harrisburg, and Wilmington, Delaware. Although WolfBlock was not ranked in the published list of Vault 100 law firms in 2008, data obtained directly from Vault indicates that WolfBlock was the 138th-ranked most prestigious US law firm in 2008. WolfBlock was ranked 135th in the 2008 American Lawyer 200 rankings of US law firms by gross revenues and, according to the *NLJ*, WolfBlock was the 149th largest firm in the United States, employing approximately 300 lawyers in 2008.

The firm's core practice was its real estate group so WolfBlock's business was hurt badly by the 2008 economic downturn. Corporate clients included Comcast and Rite Aid and a government lobbying practice operated in Harrisburg, PA and Washington, DC. WolfBlock attempted to merge with Philadelphia's Cozen O'Connor in 2007 and with Florida's Akerman Senterfitt in 2008, but both attempts failed. As partners departed WolfBlock throughout 2008, the firm's largest creditor, Wachovia, restricted the firm's access to credit and the partners voted to dissolve in March of 2009. In March of 2009, we extracted

318 website biographies for lawyers employed in WolfBlock's offices (see Table 12.1 for details).

5. Dreier LLP ("Dreier LLP") was based in New York. The firm also maintained a small office in Stamford, Connecticut and several lawyers worked in Los Angeles. The firm's corporate clients included General Dynamics, PepsiCo, and the New York Life Insurance Company. The firm was not ranked in the 2008 Vault 100, American Lawyer 200, or the National Law Journal 250 (NLJ 250).

Marc Dreier, the firm's namesake founder and sole equity partner, was arrested in early December of 2008 and charged with securities fraud following his impersonation of a Canadian pension fund official. The ensuing investigation revealed that Dreier operated a ponzi scheme that defrauded clients and investors of more than $400 million. Dreier's arrest shocked lawyers employed by his firm and resulted in quick public disavowals by firm partners (all non-equity). Wachovia, a firm creditor, also sued Dreier for defaulting on more than $9 million in loans. Drier entered Chapter 11 bankruptcy on December 16, 2008. In mid-December of 2008, we extracted 120 website biographies for all of Dreier's lawyers listed on the firm website (see Table 12.1 for details). Marc Dreier pled guilty to charges of money laundering, conspiracy, securities fraud, and wire fraud in May of 2009. He was sentenced to 20 years in prison in July of 2009.

6. Morgan & Finnegan LLP ("Morgan & Finnegan") was an intellectual property boutique firm based in New York but with several lawyers located in Washington and California. Morgan & Finnegan's clients included Canon, DuPont, Nokia, and Research in Motion. The firm was not ranked in the 2008 Vault 100, American Lawyer 200, or the NLJ 250. The firm's revenues fell sharply in 2008 and many partners departed. A former partner also sued Morgan & Finnegan for altering the firm's partnership agreement to create financial disincentives for leaving the firm. A large group of partners left the firm for Locke Lord Bissell & Liddell in February of 2009 and Morgan & Finnegan filed for Chapter 7 bankruptcy in March of 2009. In 2009, we extracted 72 website biographies from the Internet Archive for all of Morgan & Finnegan lawyers listed on the firm website in January of 2008, the last date available (see Table 12.1 for details).[1]

---

[1] Results are largely insensitive to the inclusion of Morgan & Finnegan lawyers in the sample.

IMMIGRANT OFFSPRING IN THE LEGAL PROFESSION

Exploring the effects of immigrant status on earnings among American lawyers

MEGHAN DAWE AND RONIT DINOVITZER

Immigrants played an instrumental part in the growth of the American legal profession at the turn of the twentieth century, spurring the implementation of entry barriers to the profession (Auerbach 1976). As a result, for the past generation of lawyers, admission to the legal profession – and to its most elite positions in particular – had been disproportionately limited to individuals from families of professionals and other advantaged socioeconomic classes, with financial and educational obstacles functioning in a regressive manner against recent immigrants (Nelson 1994). While immigrants played an important role in the opening up of the American legal profession, they had to struggle against several formal entry barriers – including law school training, bar examinations, and restrictions based on residency, citizenship, and "character" (Abel 1989; Auerbach 1976; Larson 1977; Sutton 2001).

The history of exclusionary practices in the legal profession very clearly highlights the efforts to stem the entry of immigrants into the profession (Abel 1989; Auerbach 1976). As early as 1909 the ABA proposed a requirement that lawyers must be US citizens, and by 1946 all states had adopted this requirement. As the professional project of law matured in the mid- to late-nineteenth century, legal education became a formal entry requirement. While the requirement of formal legal education was meant to elevate the status of the profession, the market for legal education exploded, with paradoxical effects (Stevens 2001). New immigrants and outsiders – who were not able to obtain apprenticeships because employers restricted their hiring to WASPs and who could not gain entry to the establishment universities – nonetheless persisted in their desire to pursue law as a career. Law schools opened up to meet this demand, many providing part-time and evening programs. Law schools such as Brooklyn and Suffolk, which were located in urban areas, along with the YMCA schools, catered to the immigrant population, and their enrollments swelled to the thousands (Stevens 2001; Sterling, Dinovitzer, and Garth 2007).

The professional project was not to be abandoned as bar leaders continued to express concern about the entry of foreigners into the profession and lobbied for further restrictions. As Stevens (2001: 100) noted, "[p]rejudice against foreigners throughout the country seemed to guarantee the immediate need to block their path." The ABA's Section on Legal Education made efforts to close these programs, and was explicit in its mandate. At the ABA's annual meeting in 1915, University of Wisconsin's Dean Harry S. Richards stated:

> [N]ight schools enroll[] a very large proportion of foreign names ... emigrants [sic] covet the title [of attorney] as a badge of distinction. The result is a host of shrewd young men, imperfectly educated ... all deeply impressed with the philosophy of getting on, but viewing the Code of Ethics with uncomprehending eyes
>
> (Boyd 1993).

Yet, despite the ABA's move in 1921 to require that law students graduate from an accredited law school, and eventually that they require a college education as a prerequisite, the urban law schools persisted, providing entry to the legal profession to traditional outsiders, albeit in smaller numbers.

For those outsiders who succeeded, entry into the profession – especially by way of urban law schools – was practically synonymous with entry into what Heinz and Laumann (1982) have described as the "personal plight" segment of the profession. In their first study of Chicago lawyers, graduating from an urban law school was associated not only with outsider status but also with the likelihood that one worked in small or solo practice, practicing criminal or family law, and only serving individuals. Positions in the country's elite corporate firms remained restricted to those who graduated with an elite pedigree and who had the right social capital. Studies of lawyers in the 1960s from Detroit (Ladinsky 1963) and New York (Carlin 1962) confirm this pattern. It is worth noting that for the few immigrants who attended elite law schools, discriminatory practices remained, especially among the country's elite white shoe law firms, which were the domain of the gentleman lawyers (Dezalay 1995; Yale Law School 1964). As one Ivy League law school dean noted, "in almost every case it is not being Jewish that throws a man back but lack of polish that accompanies anyone who is half a generation away from another country" (Smigel 1964: 65).

While the mid-1970s witnessed the fall of many explicit exclusionary practices (such as citizenship requirements), the elitism that under-girded these policies remained staunchly in place, and ensured that despite the tremendous growth in the legal profession through the 1980s and 1990s, the legal profession remained inherently stratified (Dixon and Seron 1995). Heinz and Laumann's research in Chicago in the 1990s revealed a profession that remained marked by ethno-religious differentiation, though it had diminished over time, a finding supported by research on lawyers in Toronto (Dinovitzer 2006; Hagan et al. 1988). More recent research based on a national sample of lawyers demonstrates that the career outcomes of lawyers are contingent on their social class (Dinovitzer 2011) and that urban law graduates remain disadvantaged in the labor market compared to elite law school graduates (Sterling, Dinovitzer, and Garth 2007; Wilkins, Dinovitzer, and Batra 2007).

While contemporary research has remained attuned to issues of inequality, the early attention to immigrant status has yielded to a focus on issues of race and ethnicity. For example, Sutton (2001) compares today's visible minorities to the 1920s immigrant cohort, arguing, "[i]f the 1920s immigrant cohort entered the legal profession through a (briefly) open window, for people of color today, the process is more like a narrowing funnel. Like the earlier generation of immi-grants, minorities who are accepted to the bar tend to occupy the less-prestigious niches of the profession" (246). In short, while scholars once acknowledged the importance of *immigrants* in the legal profes-sion, research on the outcomes of today's immigrant lawyers is virtually nonexistent, having been eclipsed by discussions of race.

The goal of this chapter is to bring the discussion of immigrant status back to the forefront. Today, immigrants represent approximately 6% to 11% of American lawyers (Decennial Census 5% PUMS; 2000 American Community Survey PUMS 2008–2010), while a rep-resentative sample of new lawyers in the United States found that 15% of lawyers have foreign-born parents (Dinovitzer et al. 2009). This chapter reinstates immigrant status in research on the legal profession, addressing two primary research questions: (1) How does immigrant status affect the earnings of lawyers? (2) What determines the differences in earnings between immigrant offspring and third-plus generation lawyers?

Drawing on data from a representative sample of new lawyers in the United States, this chapter measures the effect of immigrant status on the earnings of lawyers, and complicates past findings on the economic outcomes of racial/ethnic minorities in the legal profession. Research has revealed persistent disadvantage for racial/ethnic minority lawyers. As we find, immigrant status, as well as race/ethnicity, matter for the earnings of lawyers, but the story has changed. Analyses reveal that in the contemporary American legal profession, immigrant status does not have a uniform effect on earnings, but rather it operates differently for each racial/ethnic group. We find that regardless of their immigrant status, Asian lawyers are the highest paid lawyers in the profession. We posit that this "model minority" finding might be explained by Asians' ethnic capital.

THE EARNINGS OF IMMIGRANT OFFSPRING LAWYERS

Skilled immigrants are an important but under-researched population (Espenshade, Usdansky, and Chung 2001), as most American research has focused on less-skilled or unskilled immigrants (Smith and Edmonston 1997). Aside from research on first-generation immigrants, we know little about the earnings of professionals with foreign-born parents. While research on immigrants themselves often measures outcomes by economic attainment and income, research on their children tends to focus on educational attainment as a measure of outcomes (Alba and Nee 1997; Boyd 2009; Zhou 1997).

Stratification literature asserts that occupational attainments are determined in part by social background, including parental background. Immigrant offspring's[1] achievement might be partially due to

---

[1] A well-established term in the immigration literature, "immigrant offspring" consist of two groups of children of foreign-born parents. The second generation includes offspring who were born in the host society to one or more foreign-born parents. The 1.5 generation includes offspring who are themselves foreign born but who immigrated as children. The definition of arriving as children ranges from before age 7 to before age 15, depending on the study and the availability of data. The second and

a lack of familial capital, while higher rates of achievement might be due to having highly educated parents who work in well-paying and high-status occupations (Boyd 2009). However, the effect of social background on the occupational and educational attainments of adult immigrant offspring remains under-examined despite the saliency of social origins in stratification literature on offspring's socioeconomic outcomes (Anderson and Bruce 2004; Blau and Duncan 1967; Boyd et al. 1985; Charles, Roscigno, and Torres 2007; Sakamoto and Powers 2006; Warren and Hauser 1997). This neglect is largely due to a lack of data on social background in broad surveys, such as labor force surveys and censuses, which collect a large amount of data on respondents' labor market outcomes (Boyd 2009; Zhou 1997). By studying the economic attainments of immigrant offspring lawyers, and by measuring the role of social background, this article will contribute to sociological literature on stratification in the legal profession.

LITERATURE REVIEW

To date, little research has explored the economic outcomes of immigrant professionals, and no research has been conducted on lawyers with foreign-born parents. Given this, we draw on literature from two relevant areas to inform our hypotheses about how immigrant status might affect the earnings of lawyers: (1) literature on foreign-born and immigrant professionals and (2) literature on immigrant offspring more broadly. We also incorporate the literature on the legal profession and theories of social capital to create a more nuanced understanding of how immigrant status operates in this context.

Foreign-born and immigrant professionals

The limited research on the topic of the economic outcomes of highly skilled immigrants in the United States has reported favorable findings. Contrary to popular belief, immigrants in the United States generally are not relegated to low-end jobs. Data indicate significant upward mobility for immigrants, with movement primarily from lower to midrange jobs, but also to higher range jobs (Bean, Leach, and Lowell

---

1.5 generations (or immigrant offspring) are accepted as being distinctively situated between first generation immigrants and the third-plus generation, which refers to children born in the host society to parents who were also born in the host society (Boyd 2009).

2004), with research finding that the foreign-born are disproportionately employed in lucrative professions (Hagan 2004; Smith and Edmonston 1997). Skilled immigrant workers' potential for mobility is similar to those of their US-born peers, and their earnings and work conditions are comparable to those of native-born workers at similar levels (Portes 1981). Immigrant professionals tend to have higher levels of education than their native peers, and are nearly twice as likely as their US-born counterparts to hold a professional or doctorate degree (Batalova and Lowell 2007). An important finding from this area of scholarship is that while immigration tends to entail a downgrading of employment in the short-term, occupational status and earnings often rise faster for immigrants than for the US-born, which leads to substantial convergence over time (Chiswick, Lee, and Miller 2005; Wilkinson, Peter, and Chaturvedi 2006).

Immigrant offspring

While research on the economic outcomes of immigrant offspring is limited, studies have indicated persistent significant intergenerational economic mobility among second-generation immigrants (Borjas 2006; Carliner 1980; Chiswick 1977; Deutsch, Epstein and Lecker 2006). As yet no research has explored the impact of having foreign-born parents on the earnings of lawyers, but research does suggest that in contrast to the early history of immigrant lawyers, today there are more students with foreign-born parents in elite law schools than in urban law schools (Sterling, Dinovitzer, and Garth 2007). This suggests positive implications for immigrant offspring lawyers' incomes as elite law school graduates are more likely to be working in prestigious and higher paying areas of legal practice.

In general, research has revealed favorable findings for the earnings of immigrant offspring. In light of these findings, we expect that:

H1:   Immigrant offspring will have higher earnings than third-plus generation lawyers.

Race and ethnicity

In *Unequal Justice*, Auerbach's (1976) landmark work identified stratification in the legal profession by gender, race, and immigrant status. While subsequent legal scholarship has ignored the effect of immigrant status on the economic attainments of lawyers, recent research has continually identified an enduring opportunity structure in which gender and race are related to differential attainment in the legal profession (e.g., Daniels 1993; Heinz et al. 2001; Heinz et al. 2005). Research on the legal profession has consistently revealed a gender wage-gap that favors men (Brockman 1994; Curran 1986; Dinovitzer, Reichman, and Sterling 2009; Epstein [1981] 1993; Gorman 2006; Hagan and Kay 1995; Hull and Nelson 2000; Kay 1997; Kay and Hagan 1998; Kornhauser and Revesz 1995; Leiper 2006; Noonan, Corcoran and Courant 2005; Robinson and Wallace 2001; Seron 1996; Sterling and Reichman 2004). Similar indications of disadvantage have been found for some racial/ethnic minority groups. Like women, black lawyers are less likely to be partners in law firms (Wilkins 1999) and are more likely to take a first job that is outside the private sector (Chambliss 2000; Kornhauser and Revesz 1995). For black lawyers in particular, research shows that when they become partners in law firms, the firms tend to be smaller, the partnership positions tend to be less powerful (Lempert et al. 2000; Wilkins 1999; 2000), and they are more likely to exit the partnership (Wilkins 1999). Thus, some racial/ethnic minority lawyers seem to be relegated to the less lucrative positions within the legal profession.

The intersection between race/ethnicity and immigrant status

Instead of trying to analytically isolate immigrant status and race, scholars have argued that we ought to examine the various ways in which immigration and race interact to advance our understanding of how race operates in the context of immigration (Bannerji 1995; Gordon and Lenhardt 2007; McCall, Leslie, 2005). While workers are often exploited based on their racial or ethnic backgrounds, immigrants might be particularly vulnerable, as employers use nationality or citizenship status as a rationale for offering immigrant workers less compensation than their native-born counterparts (Brown and Misra 2005).

Race/ethnicity is an important determinant of income for second-generation Americans (Borjas 1994). Children of North American immigrants tend to compare favorably with the third-plus generation in terms of education, though there are significant differences by national origin, ethnicity, and race (Boyd 2008a; 2008b; 2009; Fry 2007; Grayson 2009; Hirschman 2001; Kao and Thompson 2003; Keller and Tillman 2008; Portes and Rumbaut 2001; Zhou and Xiong 2005). Research on the educational attainments and labor market outcomes of second-generation immigrants in the United States has shown very positive findings for Asians, somewhat less positive outcomes for blacks, and negative findings for Mexicans and several other Latin American groups (Farley and Alba 2002; Haller, Portes, and Lynch 2011; Kasinitz, Mollenkopf, and Waters 2002; Portes 1996; Portes and Rumbaut 2001; Reitz and Zhang 2004; Rumbaut and Portes 2001). Based on these findings on the intersection between race/ethnicity and immigrant status, we expect that:

H2:   Race/ethnicity will moderate the effect of immigrant status on lawyers' incomes, making the positive effects of immigrant status on income more salient for blacks than for whites, and even more so for Asians, but not for Hispanics.

Explaining attainments

We draw on two literatures to identify the mechanisms that underlie immigrant offspring's earnings: human capital and social capital.

Human capital theory is one approach used to explain income inequity in the legal profession (Kay and Hagan 1999). This theory asserts that divergent job rewards (including earnings) are caused by differences in the economic and educational attainments that cause increased productivity by workers (Becker 1985; Polachek 1975). Applied to lawyers, human capital theory attributes the divergent earnings of different individuals to law school performance and prestige of law school (Dixon and Seron 1995: 384).

Human capital has also been shown to play an important role in determining immigrants' earnings. For example, one study showed that foreign-born scientists and engineers earned higher wages than US-born counterparts, but controlling for human capital factors such as years of schooling and place of work, they in fact earned up to 9% less (Espenshade, Usdansky, and Chung 2001). Similarly, Lowell and Gerova (2004) investigated the effect of place of education among health-care workers and found that immigrant Registered Nurses (RNs) earn more than native-born RNs. They speculate this might be due to immigrant RNs being better educated than native RNs because of the obstacles they must overcome to immigrate, and that this better education translates into higher salaries.

Based on findings regarding the role of human capital in predicting the earnings of both immigrants and lawyers, we hypothesize that:

H3:   Human capital in the form of legal education will have a positive effect on lawyers' incomes in general, and will help explain the higher incomes of immigrant offspring lawyers.

Substantial challenges to human capital theory have emerged in studies of the legal profession (Kay and Hagan 1999). For instance, research continually demonstrates that women receive lower returns from their investments in human capital and employment characteristics than men (Buchele 1981; England 1982; England and Farkas 1988; Langton and Pfeffer 1994; O'Neil 1984; Treiman and Hartmann 1981).

Given the challenges posed to human capital theory, we turn, as well, to the large body of work that has explored the role of social capital in explaining differential outcomes in the legal profession (Dixon and Seron 1995; Hagan and Kay 1995). Coleman's (1988) work on social capital is particularly well suited to studying the determinants of income for immigrant offspring lawyers because he theorizes the intergenerational transmission of human capital.[2] In fact, he argues that if parents' human capital is not accompanied by social capital through parent-child relations, it is inconsequential to children's educational outcomes.

Defining and operationalizing social capital has posed many challenges. While Coleman argues that social capital itself is intangible, other studies have conceptualized it as father's education and father's occupation (Kay and Hagan 1999; Lena et al. 1993; Mitchell 1994; Parcel and Menaghan 1994a; Parcel and Menaghan 1994b; Portes 1998). In their analysis of the attainment of partnership among Canadian lawyers, Kay and Hagan (1999) identify four separate types of social capital, including Coleman's inherited (parental) capital, which is defined as father's occupational status and whether fathers are Canadian born. They find inherited (parental) social capital might influence the early stages of lawyers' careers in terms of access to legal education, articling positions, and promising first jobs. The importance of social origins (defined as parental occupation and education, family structure, number of siblings, and size of community when age 15) in the attainment of immigrant offspring groups has also been

---

[2] According to Coleman, social capital forms a particular type of resource available to an actor. Social capital enables actors to perform certain actions within social structures. Like the other kinds of capital, social capital is productive, facilitating the achievement of interests that would not be possible in its absence. However, unlike other kinds of capital, it does not exist in physical instruments of production or within the actors themselves; social capital is intangible, inhering in the structure of relations among actors and between actors. Social capital is both the potential and actual resources that individuals can mobilize via membership in social networks of family, colleagues, and clientele.

corroborated in general population studies (Boyd 2009). This suggests that, instead of the often-accepted intergenerational mobility assumed to occur as people become increasingly removed from the immigration experience, the outcomes of immigrant offspring compared to the third-plus generation might actually be the result of social background (365).

Based on this research, we hypothesize that:

H4a: **Social capital (as measured by social background) will have a positive effect on lawyers' incomes and will help explain the higher earnings of immigrant offspring.**

Other conceptualizations of social capital point to resources amassed through group membership or the use of social networks. According to Bourdieu (1986), capital is the accumulation of labor (which exists in materialized and embodied forms). "Social capital is the sum of resources, actual or virtual, that accrue to an individual or group by virtue of possessing a durable network of more or less institutionalised relations of mutual acquaintance and recognition" (Bourdieu and Wacquant 1992: 119).

Research indicates that social capital constitutes a specific resource allowing actors to realize benefits through group membership (Portes 1998). Belonging to valuable social networks plays a key role in successful employment outcomes as it has been demonstrated that income over the life course is affected by the quality of people's networks (Burt 1992, 1997; Lin 1999, 2001). As such, we hypothesize that:

H4b: **Social capital (in the form of social networks) will have a positive effect on lawyers' incomes and will help explain the higher incomes of immigrant offspring.**

DATA

This project draws on quantitative survey data from the first wave of the After the JD (AJD) study. AJD is a national longitudinal survey of law graduates that follows a sample of lawyers who graduated from law schools between June 1998 and July 2000 and were admitted to the bar in 2000 (Dinovitzer et al. 2004). The study follows a sample of lawyers that is roughly representative of the national population of lawyers in the United States. The first wave collected data about current professional employment; professional employment history; current employment and career transitions; training, education, and debt; social, political, and community participation; and other background information.

The sampling design of the AJD study consisted of two stages. In the first stage, the country was divided into 18 strata by the number of new lawyers and by region. One primary sampling unit (PSU) was chosen within each of the strata. The 18 PSUs were composed of the four "major" markets (Chicago, Los Angeles, New York, and Washington, DC), which have over 2,000 new lawyers; five of the nine "large" markets, which have 750 to 2,000 new lawyers (Atlanta, Boston, Houston, Minneapolis, and San Francisco), and nine of the remaining smaller markets (Connecticut, Florida remainder, Indiana, New Jersey remainder, Oklahoma, Oregon, St. Louis, Tennessee, and Utah). In the second stage, lawyers were sampled from each of the PSUs at rates that, when combined, could be generalized to the national population. Additionally, the study oversampled 1,465 new lawyers from minority groups (Asian American, black, and Hispanic). For our project, we examine the entire sample (both the nationally representative sample of lawyers and the oversample of minority lawyers). The final sample was composed of 9,192 lawyers in the 18 PSUs. Data were collected primarily via mail questionnaire. The questionnaire was originally fielded in May 2002, and nonrespondents were followed up via mail and an abridged telephone survey.

Approximately 20% of the sample could not be located, and about 20% of the individuals who were located had not entered a bar for the first time, or had moved from one state bar to another. Of the individuals from the original sample who were located and satisfied all criteria for inclusion in the study, 71% responded to either the mail questionnaire or the telephone interview, resulting in a total of 4,538 valid responses.

Comparisons with outside data show that the AJD sample is representative of the general population from which the sample was taken (Dinovitzer et al. 2004). However, these data are unweighted and, therefore, do not represent the national population of lawyers. The oversampled variable (race/ethnicity) is controlled for in the following models.

The survey did not ask respondents whether they were born in the United States, but only about parental place of birth. As a result, we defined respondents who reported at least one foreign-born parent as "immigrant offspring."[3] It is important to note that questions about parents' birthplace were not asked of respondents who participated in

---

[3] The 2000 census did not collect data on the birthplace of parents, so it is unknown whether the sample is representative of immigrant offspring. Furthermore, while the data used for this paper do not specify whether the respondents themselves were born

the telephone survey. As such, these respondents are not included in our analyses. Additionally, since our dependent variable is income, only respondents with full- or part-time employment were included in our analyses (N = 2215), while unemployed respondents were excluded (n = 97).

VARIABLES

Independent variables

Our main independent variable is immigrant status. As we note earlier, respondents with one or both parents born outside the United States were classified as being immigrant offspring (n = 365) and the reference category is respondents with both parents born in the United States, who are classified as third-plus generation (n = 1850).[4] Race/ethnicity is measured by a series of dummy variables representing black, Hispanic, Asian, and other respondents, with white respondents as the reference group. Native respondents were collapsed into "other," as there were too few native respondents in the sample (n = 25).[5]

Dependent variable

Following standard practice for research on professions (Morgan and Arthur 2005), income is measured as respondents' annual salaries, including bonuses. Lawyers earning more than $250,000 per year were excluded from the sample as outliers (n = 11).[6]

---

in the United States, only three lawyers in the sample received their law degrees from outside the United States.

[4] Having one foreign-born parent and two foreign-born parents were not included as two distinct categories because there were too few respondents in each category.

[5] The survey allowed respondents to select more than one racial/ethnic category. All persons giving "Asian" as one of their races were coded as "Asian"; all persons giving "American Indian" as one of their races were coded as "American Indian"; all persons giving "Hispanic" as one of their races were coded as "Hispanic"; all persons giving "white" as one of their races were coded as "white"; everyone else was coded as "other."

[6] There were no patterns among these participants indicating that their exclusion would result in a loss of important information about the sample. For example, they represented each racial/ethnic group, they did not attend the most elite law schools, and they did not have high law school GPAs.

Control variables

Demographic Characteristics – Gender is a key predictor of income for lawyers and other professionals (Dinovitzer, Reichman, and Sterling 2009; Dixon and Seron 1995; Hagan 1990; Hull and Nelson 2000; Kay and Hagan 1995; Kay and Hagan 1998; Noonan and Corcoran 2001; Robinson and Wallace 2001). Gender is measured by a dummy variable representing female respondents, with male respondents as the reference group.

Work Profiles – Four work profile measures – employment status, practice setting, geographic location, and hours worked – are used as controls, and all have been shown to be important for understanding the distribution of income among lawyers (Dixon and Seron 1995; Hagan 1990; Hagan and Kay 1995; Hull and Nelson 2000; Kay and Hagan 1995). Employment status is measured by a dummy variable representing part-time employment, with full-time employment as the reference category.

Practice setting is based on total firm size, as salaries largely depend on firms' national scale. This variable includes the categories "solo," "private firm 2–20," "private firm 21–100," "private firm 101–250," "private firm 250+," "government," "nongovernmental public," and "business." Dummy variables represent each category, with firm 2–20 as the reference category. Finally, hours worked is assessed using a continuous measure of reported weekly hours.

Geographic location is used as a control, as research consistently finds that income varies by geographic locale (Dinovitzer and Hagan 2014 Dinovitzer, Reichman and Sterling 2009; Huffman and Cohen 2004; National Law Journal 2006). This variable represents two types of labor markets: "major metropolitan area" (which includes the four "major" legal markets, Chicago, Los Angeles, New York City, and Washington, DC) and "other" (all remaining labor markets), the reference category.

Mediating variables

Human Capital – Our measures of human capital are based on law school ranking and law school grade point average (Dinovitzer, Reichman, and Sterling 2009; Dixon and Seron 1995; Hagan 1990; Heinz and Laumann 1982). Based on the 2003 US News and World Report law school rankings (After the JD 2006; Dinovitzer 2011), we measure law school rank by a series of dummy variables representing top 10, top 11–20, top 21–100, and tier 3 law schools, with tier 4 law schools as the reference category.[7] Grade point average is assessed using a continuous variable measuring self-reported law school GPA.

Social Capital – The second mediating variable is social capital, which is measured by social background and social networks. These measures were chosen because they affect occupational status (Anderson and Bruce 2004; Blau and Duncan 1967; Boyd et al. 1985; Charles, Roscigno, and Torres 2007; Dinovitzer, Reichman and Sterling 2009; Lena, Roach and Warkov 1993; Nakhaie 2007; Sakamoto and Powers 2006; Warren and Hauser 1997), particularly for immigrant offspring (Boyd 2009).

Social background is measured with two variables: father's education and having relatives who are or were lawyers. Father's education is measured with two dummy variables representing an undergraduate degree and a graduate or professional degree, with no university degree as the reference category.

In the AJD study, participants were asked if they are related to lawyers. Being related to lawyers is measured by a series of dummy variables representing mother is/was a lawyer, father is/was a lawyer, sibling is/was a lawyer, grandparent(s) is/was a lawyer, and other relative(s) is/was a lawyer, with not being related to lawyers as the reference category.

Social networks are measured with four variables: joining partners for lunch or breakfast; support from an informal mentor; and being offered their current job due to personal connections, or recommendations from law school faculty. These networking variables have been demonstrated to be key mechanisms for income and satisfaction in early lawyer careers (Dinovitzer and Garth 2007; Dinovitzer, Sterling, and Reichman 2009; Payne-Pikus, Hagan, and Nelson 2010).

DATA ANALYSIS

Descriptive statistics
Table 13.1 provides the descriptive statistics for the lawyers in our sample, and compares the distribution of immigrant offspring compared to those who are third-plus generation. We highlight here only the data for which the two groups differ significantly.

---

[7] Respondents with degrees from outside the United States or from unaccredited schools were excluded as there are not enough respondents in these categories ($n = 3$ and $n = 51$, respectively).

TABLE 13.1   Means, Standard Deviations, and T-values of Difference, by Immigrant Status, Full Sample

	Third-plus Generation		Immigrant Offspring		
	Mean	Std. Deviation	Mean	Std. Deviation	T-value of Difference
Income	$77,839	$39,244	$88,324	$43,460	−4.580***
Female	0.50	0.50	0.58	0.49	−2.578**
Part-time	0.02	0.15	0.01	0.12	1.036
Solo	0.03	0.16	0.04	0.21	−1.659
Private firm 21–100	0.11	0.32	0.12	0.33	−.325
Private firm 101–250	0.07	0.26	0.08	0.28	−.765
Private firm 250+	0.18	0.38	0.22	0.41	−1.887
Government	0.19	0.39	0.16	0.37	1.525
Nongovernmental public	0.07	0.26	0.08	0.28	−.793
Business	0.09	0.29	0.10	0.30	−.338
Major metropolitan area	0.31	0.46	0.54	0.50	−8.583***
Hours worked	45.52	8.98	46.80	9.40	−2.228*
Black	0.08	0.27	0.09	0.29	−.921***
Hispanic	0.05	0.22	0.23	0.42	−11.944***
Asian	0.02	0.13	0.42	0.49	−30.628***
Other	0.03	0.17	0.08	0.27	−4.489***
Immigrant offspring * Black	0.00	0.00	0.09	0.29	−13.554***
Immigrant offspring * Hispanic	0.00	0.00	0.23	0.42	−23.506***
Immigrant offspring * Asian	0.00	0.00	0.42	0.49	−36.936***
Immigrant offspring * Other	0.00	0.00	0.08	0.27	−12.392***
Grade point average (GPA)	3.26	0.35	3.20	0.33	2.731**
Top 10	0.08	0.28	0.15	0.35	−3.605***
Top 11–20	0.12	0.33	0.17	0.37	−2.308*

TABLE 13.1 (cont.)

	Third-plus Generation		Immigrant Offspring		
	Mean	Std. Deviation	Mean	Std. Deviation	T-value of Difference
Top 21–100	0.47	0.50	0.49	0.50	-.722
Tier 3	0.18	0.38	0.12	0.32	2.897**
Undergraduate degree	0.20	0.40	0.16	0.37	1.593
Graduate or professional degree	0.44	0.50	0.36	0.48	3.018**
Mother is/was a lawyer	0.02	0.13	0.01	0.09	1.212
Father is/was a lawyer	0.11	0.32	0.02	0.16	5.184***
Sibling(s) is/was a lawyer	0.06	0.23	0.06	0.24	-.141
Grandparent(s) is/was a lawyer	0.06	0.23	0.04	0.19	1.389
Other relative(s) is/was a lawyer	0.25	0.43	0.21	0.41	1.360
Recruitment committee	0.19	0.39	0.19	0.39	-.145
Join partners for lunch or breakfast	0.46	0.50	0.39	0.49	2.139*
Recreation with partners	0.26	0.44	0.25	0.44	.058
Editor of general law review	0.12	0.32	0.08	0.28	1.895
Informal mentor index	1.40	1.67	1.23	1.64	1.764
Personal connections	0.41	0.49	0.42	0.49	-.084
Recommendation of law school faculty	0.43	0.50	0.38	0.49	1.651

*** $p \leq .001$,
** $p \leq .01$,
* $p \leq .05$

TABLE 13.2 Means, Standard Deviations, and T-values of Difference, by Immigrant Status, Restricted Sample

	Third-plus Generation		Immigrant Offspring		
	Mean	Std. Deviation	Mean	Std. Deviation	T-value of Difference
Income	$89,812	$40,660	$102,700	$43,369	-4.365
Female	0.46	0.50	0.54	0.50	-2.436
Solo	0.04	0.20	0.06	0.24	-1.181
Private firm 21–100	0.19	0.39	0.18	0.39	.065
Private firm 101–250	0.11	0.32	0.13	0.34	-.641
Private firm 250+	0.28	0.45	0.34	0.47	-1.667
Major metropolitan area	0.31	0.46	0.56	0.50	-7.536
Hours worked	47.61	9.32	49.29	9.17	-2.336
Black	0.06	0.24	0.07	0.26	-.633
Hispanic	0.05	0.22	0.22	0.42	-8.943
Asian	0.02	0.14	0.41	0.49	-22.786
Other	0.03	0.17	0.08	0.27	-3.822
Immigrant offspring * Black	0.00	0.00	0.07	0.26	-9.431
Immigrant offspring * Hispanic	0.00	0.00	0.22	0.42	-18.011
Immigrant offspring * Asian	0.00	0.00	0.41	0.49	-28.103
Immigrant offspring * Other	0.00	0.00	0.08	0.27	-10.017
Grade point average (GPA)	3.31	0.35	3.25	0.33	1.985
Top 10	0.10	0.31	0.17	0.37	-2.757
Top 11–20	0.14	0.35	0.18	0.38	-1.449
Top 21–100	0.45	0.50	0.47	0.50	-.553
Tier 3	0.17	0.38	0.10	0.30	2.795
Undergraduate degree	0.20	0.40	0.17	0.38	.778
Graduate or professional Degree	0.45	0.50	0.37	0.48	2.325

TABLE 13.2 (cont.)

	Third-plus Generation		Immigrant Offspring		T-value of Difference
	Mean	Std. Deviation	Mean	Std. Deviation	
Mother is/was a lawyer	0.02	0.12	0.01	0.11	.341
Father is/was a lawyer	0.12	0.32	0.02	0.13	4.646
Sibling(s) is/was a lawyer	0.06	0.24	0.05	0.22	.555
Grandparent(s) is/was a lawyer	0.06	0.23	0.04	0.19	1.106
Other relative(s) is/was a lawyer	0.23	0.42	0.20	0.40	1.241
Recruitment committee	0.21	0.41	0.21	0.41	-.009
Join partners for lunch or breakfast	0.50	0.50	0.41	0.49	2.433
Recreation with partners	0.26	0.44	0.26	0.44	.130
Editor of general law review	0.14	0.35	0.11	0.31	1.479
Informal mentor index	1.57	1.72	1.38	1.72	1.600
Personal connections	0.46	0.50	0.42	0.49	1.250
Recommendation of law school faculty	0.47	0.50	0.40	0.49	1.925
General practice	0.01	0.09	0.01	0.11	-.748
Antitrust	0.00	0.06	0.00	0.00	.904
Bankruptcy	0.02	0.12	0.00	0.07	1.296
Civil litigation	0.00	0.05	0.00	0.00	.783
Civil rights/liberties	0.00	0.07	0.01	0.11	-1.555
Commercial law	0.01	0.10	0.01	0.11	-.318
Criminal law	0.00	0.06	0.00	0.07	-.183
Employment law union	0.00	0.05	0.00	0.07	-.430
Employment law management	0.01	0.08	0.01	0.09	-.424
Environmental law	0.01	0.08	0.00	0.00	1.198

Family law	0.01	0.09	0.02	0.15	−1.884
General corporate	0.01	0.10	0.00	0.07	.798
Immigration law	0.00	0.03	0.00	0.00	.451
Intellectual property	0.01	0.09	0.00	0.00	1.433
Municipal law	0.00	0.04	0.00	0.00	.639
Personal injury plaintiff	0.01	0.09	0.01	0.09	−.110
Personal injury defense	0.00	0.07	0.00	0.00	1.011
Probate	0.01	0.10	0.00	0.07	.798
Public utilities	0.00	0.05	0.00	0.07	−.430
Real estate – Commercial	0.01	0.10	0.01	0.09	.266
Real Estate – Personal	0.01	0.12	0.01	0.11	.134
securities	0.00	0.04	0.01	0.11	−2.576
Tax	0.00	0.07	0.00	0.07	.018
Other specialization	0.00	0.04	0.00	0.00	.639

*** $p \leq .001$,
** $p \leq .01$,
* $p \leq .05$

TABLE 13.3 Regression Coefficients, Full Sample, $N = 1,573$

Variables	Model 1	Model 2	Model 3
Income	$52,909***	$52,250***	$13,666
Main Independent Variable			
Immigrant offspring	–$381	$7,843*	$6,446
Control Variables			
Female	–$7,244***	–$7,179***	–$6,840***
Part-time	–$24,579***	–$24,210***	–$25,594***
Solo	–$16,867***	–$18,088***	–$16,002***
Private firm 21–100	$22,736***	$22,890***	$20,033***
Private firm 101–250	$49,191**	$49,190***	$43,142***
Private firm 250+	$63,487***	$63,227***	$54,865***
Government	–$11,479***	–$11,232***	–$11,080***
Nongovernmental public	–$17,457***	–$17,445***	–$18,973***
Business	$25,682***	$25,959***	$25,539***
Major metropolitan area	$17,410***	$17,445***	$15,839***
Hours worked	$170*	$177*	$175*
Race			
Black	$55	$1,348	$3,333
Hispanic	–$778	–$66	$399
Asian	$11,078***	$21,301***	$19,162***
Other	–$319	$133	–$164
Interaction Term			
Immigrant offspring * Black		–$13,289*	–$9,574
Immigrant offspring * Hispanic		–$9,089	–$7,831
Immigrant offspring * Asian		–$20,163**	–$17,671**
Immigrant offspring * Other		–$8,516	–$4,137

Human Capital			
Grade point average (GPA)			$11,098***
Top 10			$16,822***
Top 11–20			$7,309**
Top 21–100			$3,077
Tier 3			−$837
Social Capital			
Social background			
Undergraduate degree			−$1,808
Graduate or professional degree			−$2,295
Mother is/was a lawyer			−$5,298
Father is/was a lawyer			−$1,370
Sibling(s) is/was a lawyer			−$501
Grandparent(s) is/was a lawyer			$417
Other relative(s) is/was a lawyer			$321
Social networks			
Join partners for lunch or breakfast			$3,411**
Recommendation of law school faculty			$1,757
Support from informal mentor			$260
Personal connections			$1,157
R^2	0.661	0.663	0.684

*** $p \leq .001$,
** $p \leq .01$,
* $p \leq .05$

TABLE 13.4 Regression Coefficients, Restricted Sample, $N = 1,058$

Variables	Model 1	Model 2	Model 3	Model 4
Income	$55,373***	$54,663***	$4,012	$5,905
Focal Independent Variable				
Immigrant offspring	$1,837	$10,990*	$9,400*	$9,389*
Control Variables				
Female	-$7,079***	-$6,882***	-$6,301***	-$6,258***
Solo	-$15,409***	-$16,577***	-$13,990***	-$13,256***
Private firm 21–100	$23,807***	$23,979***	$20,668***	$20,834***
Private firm 101–250	$49,788***	$49,753***	$42,472***	$43,152***
Private Firm 250+	$63,894***	$63,558***	$53,293***	$54,165***
Major metropolitan area	$21,756***	$21,857***	$20,248***	$20,326***
Hours worked	$70	$76	$103	$77
Race				
Black	$1,000	$2,875	$5,378	$5,804
Hispanic	-$3,203	-$947	-$381	-$193
Asian	$10,096**	$19,656***	$16,503**	$16,913**
Other	-$1,975	-$1,414	-$2,616	-$2,696
Interaction Term				
Immigrant offspring * Black		-$16,450	-$13,715	-$14,181
Immigrant offspring * Hispanic		-$13,303	-$11,754	-$12,122
Immigrant offspring * Asian		-$20,531**	-$15,901*	-$15,305*
Immigrant offspring * Other		-$9,297	-$2,609	-$5,845
Human Capital				
Grade point average (GPA)			$14,121***	$13,560***
Top 10			$19,793***	$20,491***
Top 11–20			$8,114**	$8,092**

Top 21–100	$4,566	$3,743
Tier 3	$2,740	$882
Social Capital		
Social background		
Undergraduate degree	−$3,530	−$3,266
Graduate or professional degree	−$2,564	−$2,377
Mother is/was a lawyer	−$9,289	−$10,040
Father is/was a lawyer	−$2,732	−$2,184
Sibling(s) is/was a lawyer	$4,234	$4,209
Grandparent(s) is/was a lawyer	−$264	−$402
Other relative(s) is/was a lawyer	$1,570	$1,878
Social networks		
Join partners for lunch or breakfast	$3,913*	$3,645*
Recommendation of law school faculty	$778	$1,366
Support from informal mentor	$294	$236
Personal connections	$1,778	$1,787
Area of Specialization		
General practice	−$17,487	
Antitrust	$30,061*	
Bankruptcy	$641	
Civil litigation	$5,837	
Civil rights/liberties	$27,361*	
Commercial law	−$2,057	
Criminal law	−$23,312	
Employment law – Union	$57,643***	
Employment law – Management	$21,954	
Environmental law	$1,104	
Family law	$2,345	

TABLE 13.4 (cont.)

Variables	Model 1	Model 2	Model 3	Model 4
General corporate				$1,929
Immigration law				–$4,702
Intellectual property				–$2,107
Municipal law				–$910
Personal injury plaintiff				–$15,346
Personal injury defense				–$2,300
Probate				$7,085
Public utilities				$3,747
Real estate – Commercial				$5,006
Real estate – Personal				–$4,097
Securities				–$16,524
Tax				$10,954
Other specialization				–$11,656
R^2	0.633	0.636	0.665	0.681

*** $p \leq .001$,
** $p \leq .01$,
* $p \leq .05$

The most highly represented race/ethnicity among immigrant off-spring is Asian (42.5%) followed by Hispanic (23%). Most third-plus generation lawyers are white (82.8%). There is a significant relationship between immigrant status and race/ethnicity (χ^2 = 926.2, p < .001),[8] as well as by gender, with women overrepresented among immigrant offspring (57.5% vs. 50.2% χ^2 = 6.6, p = .010).

In contrast to the immigrants in the early legal profession, we find that immigrant offspring earn significantly higher incomes than third-plus generation lawyers (p < .001), with immigrant offspring earning a mean of $88,000, and third-plus generation lawyers earning $78,000. The income difference is also supported by a difference in hours worked, with immigrant offspring lawyers working more hours per week than third-plus generation lawyers (46.9 h per week, vs. 45.4 h, p = .026). One reason for the higher income may be geographic location, with immigrant offspring more likely to be working in major metropolitan areas (54.0%) compared to third-plus generation lawyers (31%) (χ^2 = 71.4, p < .001). We also find that immigrant offspring are more likely to have attended top 10 law schools than third-plus generation lawyers (14.5% vs. 8.5%) (χ^2 = 32.6, p < .001), but GPA is significantly lower for this group (3.20 vs. for immigrant offspring vs. 3.26 for third-plus generation, p = .006). While this latter difference appears small substantively, it may be enough to put one above or below one's law school grading curve.

The higher incomes we find are despite the fact that immigrant offspring are more likely to have had a father with *no* university degree (48.3%), while 44.4% of fathers of third-plus generation lawyers have graduate or professional degrees (χ^2 = 19.0, p < .001). Immigrant offspring are also less likely to have had a father who was a lawyer (2.5% immigrant offspring vs. 11.2% third-generation; χ^2 = 26.6, p < .001).

Complementing work on minority lawyers (Payne-Pikus, Hagan, and Nelson 2010), we find that only 39.3% of immigrant offspring join partners for lunch or breakfast, compared to 45.7% of third-plus generation lawyers (χ^2 = 4.6, p = .033). There is no significant relationship between immigrant status and any of the other social networks variables.

---

[8] Eighty-one percent of black lawyers, 52.5% of Hispanic lawyers, 95.9% of white lawyers, and 65.4% of other race lawyers are third-plus generation, and 83.3% of Asian lawyers are immigrant offspring.

Regression 1 – full sample

The following analyses are based on a nested series of OLS regression models predicting income using our full sample. The first model shows the main effects of immigrant status and race on income, controlling for gender and work profiles. Contrary to our first hypothesis, immigrant status does not have a significant effect on income. On the other hand, we find that Asians have greater incomes, earning $11,078 more than whites ($p < .001$). In line with prior research, we find that women lawyers earn $7,244 less than men, and that practice settings matter (income increases with firm size, lawyers working in government, business, or nongovernmental public settings, earn less than those working in small private firms). Lawyers who work in major metropolitan areas earn $17,410 more than those who do not ($p < .001$).

The second model includes the interaction between immigrant status and race/ethnicity. In this model we find that the direct effect of immigrant status increases earnings, but in line with H2, immigrant status moderates the earnings for some racial/ethnic groups. The results indicate that for blacks and Asians, immigrant status results in a lower return to income than it does for whites ($p < .05$ and $p = <.01$, respectively).

The third model adds the effect of human capital and social capital. As expected, the addition of human capital variables lowers the income premium of immigrant offspring and income increases in a linear fashion with law school GPA and law school ranking (H3), with lawyers who attended top 10 and top 11-20 law schools earning $16,822 and $7,309 more than lawyers who attended tier 4 law schools (respectively). We find that each one point increase in GPA increases income by $11,098.

The addition of social capital marginally reduces the effect of immigrant status on income (H4a and H4b). Again confirming prior work, the most important form of social capital appears to be joining partners for lunch or breakfast (H4b). Those who dine with partners earn $3,411 more than those who do not. The addition of human and social capital variables renders the interaction between immigrant status and being black insignificant, and while it reduces the effect of the interaction between immigrant status and being Asian, it remains highly significant ($p = .008$).

Regression 2 – restricted sample

Two of the most salient predictors of income in the legal profession are practice setting and firm size (Hagan, Huxter, and Parker 1988; Heinz et al. 2005). Since lawyers' earnings vary greatly by sector (public vs. private) (Dixon and Seron 1995; Kay and Hagan 1995), and with most new lawyers working full time in private practice (Dinovitzer et al. 2004), we restrict the sample to lawyers working full time in private firms (N = 1,371). It is notable that Asian lawyers in this sample are overrepresented among large (>250) law firm lawyers (25.2% of Asians work in large firms, compared to the average of 20.5%), with an above-average rate of full-time employment among lawyers working in law firms (98.1%). Thus, restricting the sample may also shed light on the interaction between immigrant status and being Asian in our earlier models.

The first three models of this regression are identical to those in the original models described earlier; however, in this regression we have added a fourth model introducing controls for specialization, as area of practice may lead to differential earnings for lawyers in private firms. As Heinz and Laumann (1982, 1995) note, the differentiation of the profession into two hemispheres is not merely by client type, but by specialization as well. Specialization has increased over recent decades, and fields of practice are important distinctions amongst lawyers. Thus, it is important to control not only for social background, legal education, and practice setting but also for area of specialization. Asians are overrepresented in certain areas of practice, which might help explain the interaction between immigrant status and being Asian. For example, compared to their 8.6% share of this subsample, Asians represent 20.0% of lawyers in tax and one-third of lawyers in securities, which are two of the most elite practice areas in the profession (Heinz and Laumann 1982). As such, we predict that:

H4:   Controlling for area of specialization will reduce the effect of immigrant status* Asian on income.

As in the first regression, the first model shows the main effects of immigrant status and race/ethnicity on income, controlling for gender and work profiles. Again, immigrant status is not a significant predictor of income, and race/ethnicity has a significant positive effect on income only for Asians (H2), though the effect is smaller for the restricted sample than for the full sample (p = .004). On average, women lawyers earn $7,079 less than men, and income continues to increase with firm size. Full-time lawyers working in private law firms earn a $21,756 premium if they work in major metropolitan areas.

The second model includes the interaction between immigrant status and race/ethnicity. As in the first regression, immigrant status moderates the effect of race/ethnicity on income (H2). However, for the restricted sample, this is only true for Asians, for whom the effect of immigrant status continues to result in a lower return to income than it does for whites (p = .010).

The third model adds the effect of human capital and social capital. As in the first regression, income increases in a linear fashion with law school GPA and law school ranking, with lawyers who attended top 10 and top 11-20 law schools earning $19,793 and $8,114 more than lawyers who attended tier 4 law schools, respectively, and each one point increase in GPA resulting in an increase in income of $13,560 (H3). Once again, joining partners for lunch or breakfast significantly increases lawyers' income, with those who dine with partners earning $3,913 more than those who do not (H4b). For full-time lawyers working in private firms, the addition of human and social capital variables greatly reduces the effect of the interaction between immigrant status and being Asian, but it remains significant (p = .041).

The fourth model controls for area of specialization within the profession. Working in antitrust, civil rights/liberties, and employment law (union) increases income for full-time lawyers working in private firms (by $30,061, $27,361, and $57,643, respectively). As hypothesized, controlling for specialization explains most (but not all) of the remaining effect of the interaction between immigrant status and being Asian (H5) (the p value decreases to p = .047).

Confirming prior research on immigrant offspring more generally, among full-time lawyers working in private law firms, immigrant offspring have higher earnings than their third-plus generation counterparts. While literature on the legal profession tends to suggest that racial/ethnic minorities have worse occupational outcomes than white lawyers, we do not find evidence of this. Instead, we find that Asian lawyers tend to have higher earnings than whites, with no racial/ethnic group reporting significantly lower incomes than whites. The main contribution of our work, however, is in our investigation of the intersection of race/ethnicity and immigrant status. In contrast to the positive association between being Asian and income, here we find that immigrant status depresses the earnings of Asian lawyers. Thus while we sought to find a connection between immigrant status and income for lawyers, what we found instead is a story about the

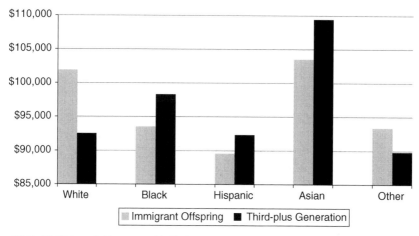

Figure 13.1: Fitted Income by Immigrant Status* Race/Ethnicity, Restricted Sample.

intersection between immigration and race/ethnicity, a story that has been largely (if not entirely) overlooked in the legal professions literature to date.

On the surface, the results for immigrant Asians seem to suggest a stratified profession operating in a regressive manner against the economic outcomes of Asians. However, analysis of fitted incomes for the various racial/ethnic and immigrant groups yields a more favorable interpretation for this group (Figure 13.1). Holding constant human capital, social capital, and a host of other variables found to be important determinants of lawyers' income in prior research, we find that Asian lawyers – irrespective of immigrant status – out-earn all other respondents. Thus, while being the child of an immigrant depresses the income of Asian lawyers, they still remain the highest earners of all ethnic groups, with the lowest income Asians (immigrant offspring) earning more than the highest income whites (third-plus generation). Furthermore, we find that immigrant status has diverging effects depending on one's ethnic group. For blacks, Hispanics, and Asians, having foreign-born parents results in a net penalty, while for whites and others it does not.

Our final model also shows that social background does not have a significant effect on earnings. This conforms with Boyd's (2009) conclusion in the Canadian context that "above average family background and other social origin characteristics are factors underlying the higher educational attainments of [immigrant offspring] in Canada compared with the third-plus generation" (359). Social background does not attain significance in our models because its effects have already been reflected in the measures for human capital.

We again find an important effect for joining partners for lunch or breakfast. Partner contact and mentorship are crucial processes and sources of dissatisfaction and exiting law firms (Dinovitzer and Garth 2007), and research indicates that racial/ethnic minorities are less likely to be mentored than whites (Davila 1987; Nicolson 2006; Payne-Pikus, Hagan and Nelson 2010; Simpson 1996; Thomas 2001; Wilkins and Gulati 1996). Payne-Pikus, Hagan, and Nelson's (2010) analysis of AJD data found that variations in contact and mentoring, aside from variations in performance and merit, explain differences in retention and promotion. Partner contact and mentorship are key avenues for diffusing knowledge and displaying firms' long-term appreciation and investment in their employees (Thomas, Philips, and Brown 1998). Additionally, partners afford visibility and sponsorship and thus might boost mentees' chances for promotion (Thomas 2001). Partner mentorship can also facilitate lawyers' involvement in challenging projects that can showcase mentees' abilities and afford opportunities for professional development (Chanen 2006). Partner mentors might help individuals should they receive unfair treatment, lend emotional support during stressful periods, and create senses of support, acceptance, and friendship (Payne-Pikus, Hagan, and Nelson 2010; Wilkins and Gulati 1996). Thus, contact with partners may have a unique ability to impact the careers and, by extension, the earnings of lawyers. Yet even though the addition of human and social capital variables explains much of the interaction effect for immigrant offspring Asians, and even controlling for area of specialization, the interaction remains significant.

DISCUSSION

Heath and McMahon coined the term "ethnic penalty," which refers to "all the sources of disadvantage that might lead to an ethnic group to fare less well in the labor market than do similarly qualified whites" (1995: 1), including a range of variables from cultural to workplace discrimination. Their concept has been used to elucidate findings that all individuals of minority ethnic status are disadvantaged in employ-ment compared to whites in similar circumstances (Heath and Cheung 2006). However, such findings are not fully supported by our research, which shows only some but not all racial/ethnic groups suffer a penalty. While whites still do better than blacks, Hispanics, and other racial/ethnic groups, Asians remain the highest paid lawyers across the board, even when controlling for other factors that are highly predictive of income.

While our ability to explain the interaction effect is constrained by our data, research on the academic and occupational outcomes of racial minorities and immigrant offspring offers several plausible explanations for this finding. For example, existing research on second-generation immigrants in multiple countries has revealed similar indications of success for Asians. This "model minority" find-ing is based on a wide range of studies and has revealed high achieve-ment by second-generation Asians in the United States, Canada, and Australia (Boyd 2002; Corak 2008; Farley and Alba 2002; Fernandez-Kelly and Portes 2008; Inglis and Model 2007; Pendakur and Pendakur 2002; Portes and Rumbaut 2001). Asian immigrant offspring have been found to have high levels of postsecondary education, and as a result, despite certain barriers to the labor market, their earnings are relatively high (Reitz, Zhang, and Hawkins 2011). Asians are overrepresented in jobs requiring high levels of education, including professional positions as physicians, nurses, engineers, and educators (U.S. Bureau of the Census 2003; Hagan 2004). Reitz, Zhang, and Hawkins (2011) argue, "[t]he relative success of the Asian second generation undoubtedly can be traced at least in part to the more highly skilled and successful Asian immigrant generation" (1055). They also find that second generation Asians earn more than third-plus generation whites. Like Boyd (2009), they argue that the generally high academic achievement of Asians likely explains why intergenerational inheritance of social class position is not as import-ant for this group as it is for others, as highly educated parents might transfer a high value on education to their offspring, and devote energy to ensuring their success – in part, perhaps, to make up for their own employment struggles (1075). However, it is worth noting that, in our data, the earnings of Asian lawyers far exceed those of whites and other racial/ethnic minorities even when controlling for law school GPA and law school rank.

Borjas (1992; 2006) argues that individuals' ethnic background might affect their social mobility. Specifically, Borjas theorizes that ethnicity operates as an "externality" in the process of human capital accumulation, such that the skills of subsequent generations are determined not only by what their parents do but also on the features or quality of the ethnic environment in which the children are raised, which he refers to as "ethnic capital" (1992: 124). For example, a highly successful ethnic environment (i.e., where most parents have high levels of education and labor force participation, prestigious occupations, and high earnings) lends beneficial traits to those raised within that enclave, which in turn has the effect of increasing their socioeconomic attainment in adulthood.

Borjas (1996) finds that ethnic capital generally has a significant effect on the intergenerational mobility of both second- and third-generation US immigrants, and argues, "[t]his human capital externality, similar to those that motivate much of the new economic growth literature and also similar to the concept of 'social capital' in the sociology literature, indicates that differences in skills and labor market outcomes among ethnic groups may persist across generations, and need never converge" (148). The ethnic capital hypothesis predicts that ongoing exposure to a specific kind of ethnic capital causes the children to regress toward the mean of that ethnic group. Put differently, ethnic capital operates like a magnetic force pulling children toward the socioeconomic attainments realized by the average person in their ethnic group, while the ethnic environment works like glue in the process of intergenerational social mobility, keeping the mean attainments of a given ethnic group relatively constant from one generation to the next (Borjas 2006).

Jennifer Lee and Min Zhou's (Lee 2012) ongoing research on the academic achievements of second-generation immigrants similarly suggests that Asian immigrant offspring attain exceptional academic outcomes, regardless of parental education, occupation, and income. Lee explores this paradox, drawing on the cultural concept of frames to examine the ways in which immigrant offspring and their parents frame success, how "success frames" vary by ethnicity, and how ethnic resources support these frames. Similar to Borjas (1992; 2006), Lee argues that ethnic resources allow Chinese and Vietnamese immigrant offspring from lower class backgrounds to overcome their parents' limited human capital. "Stereotype promise" – the mechanism by which one is promised to be associated with a positive stereotype and led to perform in a manner that reinforces the positive stereotype – disproportionately benefits Asian American students, improving their academic outcomes as a result and giving them an edge over their non-Asian peers. This might explain why the earnings of Asian lawyers remain consistently high across immigrant generations. Future research should endeavor to pursue these hypotheses.

There are of course some limitations to our study. First, the effect of immigrant status on the earnings of Asians remains unexplained, even when controlling for lawyers' gender, work profiles, human capital, and social capital. Second, our analysis engages with the early careers of lawyers and, thus, does not assess how the effect of immigrant status on earnings might change over the course of lawyers' careers. We do not know whether the effect of immigrant status will grow over time, or dissipate as careers progress, as lawyers are able to draw on other sources of capital to overcome their demographic background.

CONCLUSION

The early growth of the legal profession was based in large part on the influx of immigrants into the profession. The career paths of these lawyers were constrained by overt discrimination, entry barriers, and an elitism that limited many of these lawyers to working in small or solo practice in the personal plight segment of the bar. The dramatic growth and transformation of the profession in the following decades opened up the opportunity structure for many traditional outsiders. And while research on lawyers has documented outcomes for women and minorities, the fate of immigrant lawyers in the modern legal profession remains largely unexamined.

Our analysis of the effects of immigrant status among a sample of lawyers in their early careers tells a new story. For immigrants in the modern legal profession, career paths and outcomes are more varied, and indeed, the effect of immigrant status is contingent on one's ethnic group. Furthermore, while being the child of an immigrant depresses the income of Asian lawyers, they remain the highest earners of all ethnic groups, with the lowest income Asians (immigrant offspring) earning more than the highest income whites (third-plus generation). These findings suggest that despite the opening up of the profession, immigrant status continues to mark individual professionals in lasting ways. Uncovering the mechanisms whereby this occurs is a necessary next step.

REFERENCES

Abel, Richard L. (1989) *American Lawyers*. New York: Oxford University Press.

After the JD: A Longitudinal Study of Careers in Transition (2006) *Documentation for the Restricted Data Release: Wave I*. Edition 3.0.

Alba, Richard, & Victor Nee (1997) "Rethinking Assimilation Theory for a New Era of Immigration," 31(4) *International Migration Review* 826–874.

Anderson, Carmen A., & Christopher J. Bruce (2004) "Using Family Background to Predict Educational Attainment in Canada," 9(3) *Economica Ltd. The Expert Witness Newsletter*. www.economica.ca/ew09_3p1.htm.

Auerbach, Jerold S. (1976) *Unequal Justice*. New York: Oxford University Press.

Bannerji, Himani (1995) *Thinking Through: Essays on Feminism, Marxism and Anti-Racism*. Toronto: Women's Press.

Batalova, Jeanne, & B. Lindsay Lowell (2007) "Immigrant Professionals in the United States," 44(2) *Society* 26–31.

Bean, Frank D., Leach, Mark, & B. Lindsay Lowell (2004) "Immigrant Job Quality and Mobility in the United States," 31(4) *Work and Occupations* 499–518.

Becker, Gary S. (1976) "Human Capital, Effort, and the Sexual Division of Labor," 3 (Suppl.) *J. of Labor Economics* S33–S58.

Blau, F., Ferber, M., & Winkler, A.E. (1998) *The Economics of Women, Men, and Work*, 3rd edn. Upper Saddle River, NJ: Prentice Hall.

Borjas, George J. (1992) "Ethnic Capital and Intergenerational Mobility," 107 (1) *The Quarterly Journal of Economics* 123–150.

(1994) "The Economics of Immigration," 32(4) *Journal of Economic Literature* 1667–1717.

(2006) "Making It in America: Social Mobility in the Immigrant Population," in *NBER Working Paper 12088*.

Bourdieu, Pierre (1986) "The Forms of Capital," in J.G. Richardson, ed., *Handbook of Theory and Research for the Sociology of Education*. New York: Greenwood.

Bourdieu, Pierre., & Wacquant, Loic. (1992) *An Invitation to Reflexive Sociology*. Chicago: Chicago University Press.

Bouvier, Leon F., & David Simcox (1995) "Foreign-Born Professionals in the United States," 16(5) *Population and Environment* 429–444.

Boyd, Monica (2002) "Educational Attainments of Immigrant Offspring: Success or Segmented Assimilation," 36(4) *International Migration Review* 1037–1061.

(2008a) "Variations in Socio-economic Outcomes of Second Generation Young Adults," 6(2) *Canadian Diversity* 20–24.

(2008b) "The Educational and Economic Integration of Canada's Immigrant Offspring," Keynote Address, Presented at the Research Data

Centre Conference *Comings and Goings: Migration, Policy and Society.* Ottawa, Ontario. October 17–18.

(2009) "Social Origins and the Educational and Occupational Achievements of the 1.5 and Second Generations," 46 *Canadian Review of Sociology* 339–369.

Boyd, Susan S. (1993) The ABA's First Section: Assuring a Qualified Bar. American Bar Association.

Brockman, Joan (1994) "Leaving the Practice of Law: The Wherefores and Whys," 32 *Alberta Law Review* 116–180.

Browne, Irene, & Misra, Joya (2005) "Labor-market Inequality: Intersections of Gender, Race, and Class," in Mary Romero, & Eric Margolis, eds., *The Blackwell Companion to Social Inequalities.* Malden, MA: Blackwell Publishing Ltd.

Buchele, Robert (1981) "Sex Discrimination and Labour Market Segmentation". pp. 211–27 in F. Wilkinson (ed.). *The Dynamics of Labour Market Segmentation.* London: Academic Press.

Burt, Ronald S. (1992) *Structural Holes: The Social Structure of Competition.* Cambridge, MA: Harvard University Press.

(1997) "The Contingent Value of Social Capital," 42 *Administrative Science Quarterly* 339–365.

Carlin, Jerome. 1962. *Lawyers on Their Own.* New Brunswick, NJ: Rutgers University Press.

Carliner, Geoffrey (1980) "Wages, Earnings and Hours of First, Second and Third Generation American Males," 18(1) *Economic Inquiry* 87–102.

Chambliss, Elizabeth (2000) *Miles to Go 2000: Progress of Minorities in the Legal Profession.* Chicago: ABA.

Chanen, Jill Schachner (2006) "Early Exits," 92 *American Bar Association Journal* 32–39.

Chiswick, Barry R. (1997) "Sons of Immigrants: Are They at an Earnings Disadvantage?" 67(1) *The American Economic Review* 376–380.

Chiswick, Barry R., Lee, Yew L., & Paul W. Miller (2005) "Immigrant Earnings: A Longitudinal Analysis," 51(4) *Review of Income and Wealth, International Association for Research on Income and Wealth* 485–503.

Cohen, Philip N., & Matt L. Huffman (2003) "Individuals, Jobs, and Labor Markets: The Devaluation of Women's Work," 68(3) *American Sociological Review* 443–463.

Coleman, James S. (1988) "Social Capital in the Creation of Human Capital," 94 *The American Journal of Sociology* S95–S120.

Corak, M. (2008) "Immigration in the Long Run: The Education and Earnings Mobility of Second Generation Canadians," *IRPP Choices* 14:13 (October) 4–30.

Corley, Elizabeth A., & Meghna Sabharwal (2007) "Foreign-born Academic Scientists and Engineers: Producing More and Getting Less Than Their U.S.-born Peers." 48(8) *Research in Higher Education* 909–940.

Curran, B.A. (1986). "The Legal Profession in the 1980s: A Profession in Transition." 20 *Law & Society Review* 19–52.

Daniels, Ronald J. (1993) "Growing Pains: The Why and How of Canadian Law Firm Expansion," 43(2) *The University of Toronto Law Journal* 147–206.

Davila, Linda E. (1987) "The Underrepresentation of Hispanic Attorneys in Corporate Law Firms," 39 *Stanford Law Review* 1403–1452.

Deutsch, Joseph, Epstein, Gil S., & Tikva Lecker (2006) "Multi-Generation Model of Immigrant Earnings: Theory and Application," 24 *Research in Labor Economics* 217–234.

Dezalay, Yves (1995) *Between the State, Law, and the Market: The Social and Professional Stakes in the Construction and Definition of a Regulatory Arena.* Toronto: Faculty of Law, University of Toronto.

Dinovitzer, Ronit (2011) "The Financial Rewards of Elite Status in the Legal Profession," 36(4) *Law & Social Inquiry* 971–998.

(2006) "Social Capital and Constraints on Legal Careers," 40(2) *Law & Society Review* 445–480.

Dinovitzer, Ronit, & Bryant G. Garth (2007) "Lawyer Satisfaction in the Process of Structuring Legal Careers," 41 *Law & Society Review* 1–50.

Dinovitzer, Ronit, Garth, Bryant G., Sander, Richard, Sterling, Joyce, & Gita Z Wilder (2004) "After the JD: First Results of a National Study of Legal Careers," American Bar Foundation and NALP. www.americanbarfoundation.org/uploads/cms/documents/ajd.pdf

Dinovitzer, Ronit and John Hagan. 2014. "Hierarchical Structure and Gender Dissimilarity in American Legal Labor Markets." 92(3) *Social Forces* 929–955.

Dinovitzer, Ronit, Nelson, Robert L., Plickert, Gabriele, Sandefur, Rebecca, & Joyce S. Sterling (2009) *After the JD II: Second Results from a National Study of Legal Careers.* Chicago: American Bar Foundation.

Dinovitzer, Ronit, Reichman, Nancy, & Joyce Sterling (2009) "The Differential Valuation of Women's Work: A New Look at the Gender Gap in Lawyer's Incomes," 88(2) *Social Forces* 819–864.

Dixon, Jo, & Carroll Seron (1995) "Stratification in the Legal Profession: Sex, Sector, and Salary," 29(3) *Law & Society Review* 381–412.

England, Paula (1982) "The Failure of Human Capital Theory to Explain Occupational Sex Segregation," 17(3) *The Journal of Human Resources* 358–70.

Epstein, Cynthia F. [1981] (1993) *Women in Law.* Urbana, IL: University of Illinois Press.

Espenshade, Thomas J., Margaret L. Usdansky, & Chang Y. Chung (2001) "Employment and Earnings of Foreign-born Scientists and Engineers," 20 *Population Research and Policy Review* 81–205.

Farley, Reynolds, & Richard Alba (2002) "The New Second Generation in the United States," 36 *International Migration Review* 669–701.

Fernandez-Kelly, P., & Alejandro Portes (eds.) (2008) "Exceptional Outcomes: Achievement in Education and Employment among Children of Immigrants," *The Annals of the American Academy of Political and Social Science* 620 (December).

Fry, Richard (2007) "Are Immigrant Youth Faring Better in U.S. Schools?" 41(3) *International Migration Review* 579–601.

Glick, Jennifer E., & Bryndl Hohmann-Marriott (2007) "Academic Performance of Young Children in Immigrant Families: The Significance of Race, Ethnicity, and National Origins," 41 *International Migration Review* 371–402.

Gordon, Jennifer, & R.A. Lenhardt (2007) "Citizenship Talk: Bridging the Gap Between Immigration and Race Perspectives," 75(5) *Fordham Law Review* 2493–2519.

Gorman, Elizabeth (2006) "Work Uncertainty and the Promotion of Professional Women: The Case of Law Firm Partnership," 85 *Social Forces* 865–890.

Grayson, J. Paul (2009) "Language Background, Ethno-Racial Origin, and Academic Achievement of Students at a Canadian University," 47(2) *International Migration* 33–67.

Hagan, Jacqueline M. (2004) "Contextualizing Immigrant Labor Market Incorporation," 31(4) *Work and Occupations* 407–423.

Hagan, John (1990) "The Gender Stratification of Income Inequality among Lawyers," 68(3) *Social Forces* 835–855.

Hagan, John, & Fiona M. Kay (1995) *Gender in Practice: A Study of Lawyers' Lives.* New York: Oxford University Press.

Hagan, John, Huxter, Marie, & Patricia Parker (1988) "Class Structure and Legal Practice: Inequality and Mobility among Toronto Lawyers," 22 *Law and Society Review* 9–55.

Haller, William, Alejandro Portes, & Scott M. Lynch. (2011) "Dreams Fulfilled, Dreams Shattered: Determinants of Segmented Assimilation in the Second Generation." 89(3) *Social Forces* 733–762

Heath, A., & McMahon, D. (1995) *Education and Occupational Attainments: The Impact of Ethnic Origins.* Paper 34, Centre for Research into Elections and Social Trends, February.

Heath, Anthony, & Sin Yi Cheung (2006), *Ethnic Penalties in the Labour Market: Employers and Discrimination.* Department for Work and Pensions Research Report No. 341, Crown Copyright.

Heinz, John P., & Edward O. Laumann (1982) *Chicago Lawyers: Social Structure of the Bar.* New York: Russell Sage Foundation and American Bar Foundation.

Heinz, John P., Nelson, Robert L., & Edward O. Laumann (2001) "The Scale of Justice: Observations on the Transformation of Urban Law Practice," 27 *Annual Review of Sociology* 337–362.

Heinz, John P., Nelson, Robert L., Sandefur, Rebecca L., & Edward O. Laumann (2005) *Urban Lawyers: The New Social Structure of the Bar.* Chicago: University of Chicago Press.

Hirschman, Charles (2001) "The Educational Enrollment of Immigrant Youth: A Test of the Segmented-Assimilation Hypothesis," 38 *Demography* 317–336.

Hodson, Randy (1985) "Some Considerations Concerning the Functional Form of Earnings," 14(4) *Social Science Research* 374–394.

Huffman, Matt L., & Philip N. Cohen (2004) "Occupational Segregation and the Gender Gap in Workplace Authority: National versus Local Labor Markets," 19(1) *Sociological Forum* 121–147.

Hull, Kathleen E., & Robert L. Nelson (2000) "Assimilation, Choice, or Constraint? Testing Theories of Gender Differences in the Careers of Lawyers," 79 *Social Forces* 229–264.

Inglis, C., & S. Model (2007) "Diversity and Mobility in Australia," In A.F. Heath, S.I. Cheung, & S.N. Smith, eds., *Unequal Chances: Ethnic Minorities in Western Labor Markets.* Oxford: Oxford University Press.

Kao, Grace & Jennifer S. Thompson (2003) "Racial and Ethnic Stratification," 29 Annual Review of Sociology 417–442.

Kasinitz, Philip, Mollenkopf, John & Mary Waters (2002) "Becoming Americans/Becoming New Yorkers: Immigrant Incorporation in a Majority Minority City," 36(4) *International Migration Review* 1020–1036.

Kay, Fiona M. (1997) "Flight from Law," 31 *Law & Society Review* 301–335.

Kay, Fiona M., & John Hagan (1995) "The Persistent Glass Ceiling: Gendered Inequalities in the Earnings of Lawyers," 46(2) *British Journal of Sociology* 279–310.

(1998) "Raising the Bar: The Gender Stratification of Law-Firm Capital," 63(5) *American Sociological Review* 728–743.

(1999) "Cultivating Clients in the Competition for Partnership: Gender and the Organizational Restructuring of Law Firm in the 1990s," 33 *Law and Society Review* 517–556.

Keller, Ursula & Kathryn Harker Tillman (2008) "Post-Secondary Educational Attainment of Immigrant Native Youth," 87(1) *Social Forces* 121–152.

Kornhauser, Lewis A., & Richard L. Revesz (1995) "Legal Education and Entry into the Legal Profession: The Role of Race, Gender and Educational Debt," 70 *New York University Law Review* 829–964.

Ladinsky, Jack. 1963. Careers of Lawyers, Law Practice, and Legal Institutions. 28 *American Sociological Review* 47–54.

Langton, Nancy, & Jeffrey Pfeffer (1994) "Paying the Professor: Sources of Salary Variation in Academic Labour Markets," 59(2) American Sociological Review 236–256.

Larson, Magali Sarfatti (1977) *The Rise of Professionalism: A Sociological Analysis*. Berkeley: University of California Press.

Lee, Jennifer (2012) "Tiger Kids and the Success Frame." The Society Pages, April 18, 2012. Retrieved June 7, 2013 (http://thesocietypages.org/papers/tiger-kids-and-the-success-frame/).

Leiper, Jean M. (2006) *Bar Codes: Women in the Legal Profession*. Vancouver: UBC Press.

Lempert, Richard O., Chambers, David L., & Terry K. Adams (2000) "Michigan's Minority Graduates in Practice: The River Runs through Law School," 25 *Law and Social Inquiry* 395–506.

Lena, Hugh F., Roach, Sharyn L., & Seymour Warkov (1993) "Professional Status at Mid-Career: The Influence of Social and Academic Origins on Lawyers' Achievement," 8 *Sociological Forum* 365–382.

Lin, N. (1999) "Social Networks and Status Attainment," 25 *Annual Review of Sociology* 467–487.

(2001) *Social Capital: A Theory of Social Structure and Action*. New York: Cambridge University Press.

Lowell, B. Lindsay, & Stefka Georgieva Gerova (2004) "Immigrants and the Healthcare Workforce," 31(4) *Work and Occupations* 474–498.

McCall, Leslie. 2005. "The Complexity of Intersectionality." *Signs* 30(3): 1771–1800.

Mitchell, Barbara A. (1994) "Family Structure and Leaving the Nest: A Social Resource Perspective," 37 *Sociological Perspectives* 651–671.

Morgan, Laurie, & Michelle Arthur (2002) "Methodological Considerations in Estimating the Gender Pay Gap for Employed Professionals," 33(3) *Sociological Methods Research* 383–403.

Nakhaie, M. Reza (2007) "Ethnoracial Origins, Social Capital, and Earnings," 8 *Journal of International Migration and Integration* 307–325.

National Law Journal (2006) "The NLJ 250," Accessed at: www.law.com/jsp/article.jsp?id=1163066718029.

Nelson, Robert L. (1994) "The Futures of American Lawyers: A Demographic Profile of a Changing Profession in a Changing Society," 44 Case Western Reserve Law Review 345–406.

Nicolson, Donald (2006) "Affirmative Action in the Legal Profession," 33 *Journal of Law and Society* 109–125.

Noonan, Mary C., Corcoran, Mary E., & Paul N. Courant (2005) "Pay Differences Among the Highly Trained: Cohort Difference in the Male-Female Earnings Gap in Lawyers' Salaries," 84 *Social Forces* 853–872.

Parcel, T.L., & E.G. Menaghan (1994a) *Parents' Jobs and Children's Lives*. New York: Aldine de Gruyter.

(1994b) "Early Parental Work, Family Social Capital, and Early Childhood Outcomes," 99 *American Journal of Sociology* 972–1009.

Payne-Pikus, Monique R., Hagan, John, & Robert L. Nelson (2010) "Experiencing Discrimination: Race and Retention in America's Largest Law Firms," 44(3) *Law & Society Review* 553–584.

Pendakur, K., & R. Pendakur (2002) "Colour Our World: Have Earnings Gaps for Canadian-Born Ethnic Minorities Changed Over Time?" 28(4) *Canadian Public Policy* 489–512.

Polacheck, Solomon (1975) "Discontinuous Labor Force Participation and Its Effects on Women's Market Earnings," in C. Lloyd, ed., *Sex, Discrimination, and the Division of Labor*. New York: Columbia University Press.

Portes, Alejandro (1981) "Modes of Structural Incorporation and Present Theories of Labor Immigration," in M.M. Kritz, C.B. Keely, & S.M. Tomasi, eds., *Global Trends in Migration: Theories and Research on International Population Movements*. New York: Center for Migration Studies.

(1996) *The New Second Generation*. New York: Russell Sage Foundation.

(1998) "Social Capital: Its Origins and Applications in Modern Sociology," 24 *Annual Review of Sociology* 1–24.

Portes, Alejandro, & Min Zhou (1993) "The New Second Generation: Segmented Assimilation and Its Variants," 53 *Annals of the American Academy of Political and Social Science* 74–96.

Portes, Alejandro, & Rubén G. Rumbaut (2001) *Legacies: The Story of the Immigrant Second Generation*. Berkeley: University of California Press.

Reitz, Jeffrey G., & Y. Zhang (2004) "National and Urban Contexts for Integration of the Immigrant Second Generation in the United States and Canada," Paper Presented at a Conference on *The Next Generation: Immigrant Youth and Families in Comparative Perspective*, Harvard University, Radcliffe Institute for Advanced Study, October 29–30.

Reitz, Jeffrey G., Zhang, Heather, & Hawkins, Naoko (2011) "Comparisons of the Success of Racial Minority Immigrant Offspring in the United States, Canada and Australia," 40(4) *Social Science Research* 1051–1066.

Robinson, K., & J. E. Wallace (2001) "Gendered Inequalities in Earnings: A Study of Canadian Lawyers," 38 *Canadian Review of Sociology and Anthropology* 75–95.

Rumbaut, Rubén G., & Alejandro Portes (2001) *Ethnicities: Children in International Investment and Labor Flow*. Cambridge: Cambridge University Press.

Seron, Carroll (1996) *The Business of Practicing Law*. Philadelphia: Temple University Press.

Simpson, Gwyned (1996) "The Plexiglas Ceiling: The Careers of Black Women Lawyers," 45 *The Career Development Quarterly* 173–188.

Smigel, Erwin O. (1964) *The Wall Street Lawyer, Professional Organization Man?* New York: Free Press of Glencoe.

Smith, J., & Edmonston, B. (eds.). (1997) *The New Americans: Economic, Demographic, and Fiscal Effects of Immigration*. Washington, DC: National Acadeour Press.

Sterling, Joyce, & Nancy Reichman (2004) "Sticky Floors, Broken Steps, and Concrete Ceilings in Legal Careers," 14 *Texas Journal of Women and the Law* 27–76.

Sterling, Joyce, Dinovitzer, Ronit, & Bryant Garth (2007) "The Changing Role of Urban Law School Graduates," 36 *Southwestern Law Review* 389–432.

Stevens, Robert (2001) *Law Schools: Legal Education in America from the 1850s to the 1980s*. Clark, New Jersey: The Lawbook Exchange, Ltd..

Sutton, John (2001) *Law/Society: Origins, Interactions and Change*. Thousand Oaks, CA: Pine Forge Press.

Thomas, David A. (2001) "The Truth About Mentoring Minorities: Race Matters," April *Harvard Business Review* 98–107.

Thomas, Kecia M., Phillips, Laylwe D., & Stephanie Brown (1998) "Redefining Race in the Workplace: Insights from Ethnic Identity Theory," 54 *Journal of Black Psychology* 76–92.

Treiman, Donald J., & Heidi I. Hartmann (1981) Women, Work, and Wages: Equal Pay for Jobs of Equal Value (Vol. 2101). Washington, DC: National Academy Press.

U.S. Bureau of the Census. (2003) *Foreign-born population of the United States current population survey—March 2000, revised detailed tables—weighted to census 2000* (PPL-160). www.census.gov/population/www/socdemo/foreign/ppl-160.html.

Waldinger, Roger, Bozorgmehr, Mehdi, Lim, Nelson, & Lucila Finkel (1998) "In Search of the Glass Ceiling: The Career Trajectories of Immigrant and Native-born Engineers," Working Paper Series, *The Ralph and Goldy Lewis Center for Regional Policy Studies, UCLA School of Public Affairs*, University of California: Los Angeles.

Wilkins, David B. (1999) "Legal Ethics: Partners without Power?" 2 *Journal of Institute for Study of Legal Ethics* 15–48.

(2000) "Rollin' on the River: Race, Elite Schools, and the Equality Paradox," 25 *Law and Social Inquiry* 527–556.

Wilkins, David B., & G. Mitu Gulati (1996) "Why Are There So Few Black Lawyers in Corporate Law Firms? An Institutional Analysis," 84 *California Law Review* 496–625.

Wilkins, David B., Dinovitzer, Ronit, & Rishi Batra (2007) "Urban Law School Graduates in Large Law Firms," 36 *Southwestern University Law Review* 433–507.

Wilkinson, Lori, Peter, Tracey, & Renuka Chaturvedwe (2006) "The Short-, Medium-, and Long-Term Labour Market Adjustment of Immigrant Women: Canada and the United States Compared," 7(2) *Journal of International Migration and Integration* 195–217.

Yale Law Journal (1964) "The Jewish Law Student and New York Jobs—Discriminatory Effects in Law Firm Hiring Practice," 73 *Yale Law Journal* 625–660.

423

Zhou, Min (1997) "Growing up American: The Challenge Confronting Immigrant Children and Children of Immigrants," 23 *Annual Review of Sociology* 63–95.

Zhou, Min & Yang Sao Xiong (2005) "The Multifaceted American Experiences of the Children of Asian Immigrants: Lessons for Segmented Assimilation," 28(6) *Ethnic and Racial Studies* 1119–1152.

INDEX

enrollment rates for, in law schools, 84
family devotion schema for, 147, 153–154
job satisfaction for, 305
as law professors, 13
in law school, data findings for,
148–151
meaningfulness of work for, 307–308
motherhood for, professional perceptions of,
153–154
in professional careers, historical entry of,
144–145
time demands for, 9
typecast socialization of, 143–144, 152–160
work devotion schema for, 147
women lawyers
commitment to diversity by, 59–63
in elite firms, movement stagnation for,
11–12
firm partnerships for, 84
gender discrimination against, 303
gender disparities for, 8–10
homophily effects on, 336–337, 348–349
income disparity for, 8–9, 328
inheritance strategy for, 335–337
in large firms, movement stagnation for,
11–12
mentoring programs for, 303
rainmaking strategy for, 335–337
tangible disadvantages for, 304–305
women of color, in legal practices
angry image for, 154–156

anticipatory perceptions of, 146–148,
152–153
attrition rates for, 141–142
confidence issues for, 147
data findings on, 148–151
dynamic classroom strategies for, 168
family devotion schema for, 147, 153–154
institutional support for, 167
law school experiences of, 148–149
mentorship of, 145–146
methodological research on, 148–151
motherhood for, anticipatory perception of,
153–154
othering of, 148
overview of, 160–164
parental expectations for, 143
racially palatable individuals and, 145
real world experience for, 164–167
retention rates for, 147–148
schema of devotions for, 147
social capital for, 145–146
social isolation of, 190
socioeconomic class as factor for, 182
stereotyping effects on, 141–142, 154–156
student organizations for, 167–168
tokenism for, 144–145, 152
treatment by law professors, 158–159
typecast socialization for, 143–144,
152–160, 164–166
work devotion schema, 147
workplace culture, gender disparities and, 8–10

Made in the USA
Middletown, DE
16 March 2018